In My Own Key

Liona Boyd

In My Own Key

My Life In Love and Music

Stoddart

Published in 1998 by Stoddart Publishing Co. Limited
34 Lesmill Road, Toronto, Canada M3B 2T6
180 Varick Street, 9th Floor, New York, New York 10014

Distributed in Canada by:
General Distribution Services Ltd.
325 Humber College Blvd., Toronto, Ontario M9W 7C3
Tel. (416) 213-1919   Fax (416) 213-1917
Email customer.service@ccmailgw.genpub.com

Distributed in the United States by:
General Distribution Services Inc.
85 River Rock Drive, Suite 202, Buffalo, New York 14207
Toll-free Tel. 1-800-805-1083   Toll-free Fax 1-800-481-6207
Email gdsinc@genpub.com

02   01   00   99   98   2   3   4   5

Canadian Cataloguing in Publication Data

Liona Boyd
In my own key: my life in love and music

ISBN 0-7737-3121-0

1. Boyd, Liona.   2. Guitarists – Canada – Biography.
I. Title.

ML419.B689A3 1998   787.87'092   C98-931474-X

Cover Photograph: Keith Williamson
Jacket Design: Angel Guerra
Text Design: Tannice Goddard

Printed and bound in Canada

We gratefully acknowledge the Canada Council for the Arts and the Ontario Arts Council for their support of our publishing program.

To my mother,
who is always there for me,
with love

So it has ever been. Our Land of Heart's Desire is woven of our own thoughts and longings and emotions, and no two weave alike. And it is well if returning thence we bring with us gifts worthy of acceptance. For many to whom the Weaver gives the Flax of Dream weave hurriedly and the web is spoilt. It needs time to gather the joy and sorrow, love and suffering, the wisdom that go to make the perfect design, and through all the weft of it must run the thread of self-sacrifice like a scarlet flame, touching it to inconceivable beauty.

— J. QUIDDINGTON WEST,
The Incalculable Hour

Contents

Preface

Eight years ago I had the urge to write about my life as a classical guitarist. The concept had been percolating within me for some time, and when I finally put pen to paper I found that I derived pleasure from sculpting into words the feelings, energies, and passions that have shaped my life. Why try to write when music has been my artistic medium? Perhaps creativity manifests itself in different ways, seeking new channels and bursting out in new forms. My attraction to words has always been there since my childhood diaries and poems. Perhaps it has been the desire to invite my audience, you who have given me so much love and support and at times bared your souls to me in letters, to share something more of myself than my guitar. Perhaps some of you may take encouragement and inspiration from my struggles and successes. Perhaps, for me, it has been a salutary process, in the words of Theador Reik my "compulsion to confess" — a need to replace coy answers and evasive comments with a more straightforward approach reflective of the times in which we live.

Perhaps I simply wanted to write a story.

Liona Boyd

Prelude

Today the Santa Anas are blowing — hot desert winds that make the air taste of sun-baked eucalyptus and oleander. Crickets and cicadas sing under a cerulean blue sky, while lizards sun themselves on the cracked stone paths that meander through straggling undergrowth. Los Angeles appears pristine from this vantage point high above the city. It is here that I come in the late afternoon to reflect and write, here in the rambling, unkempt grounds of Greystone Park. Just up the hill from my front gate, it has become my own private retreat. Constructed in the twenties, Greystone now lies in splendid disrepair, and the granite balustrades of the once-elegant mansion provide refuge for wood doves and squirrels. Below me the city spreads out — a vast crystalline mirage of tangled freeways, overpasses, and high-rises, yet on the horizon, beckoning like a vague promise, the sun's rays glint off a luminous blue strip of Pacific Ocean.

Buried deep beneath us lie the faults — insidious fissures that at any moment could send our homes and offices tumbling down upon each other like poorly stacked games of Lego. Lives here teeter precariously on the whims of temperamental Mother Earth. With frequent tremors she undermines our sense of security, taunts our nerves, and dares us to gamble. A thousand faults have snaked their way under our city and lie in wait with infinite patience. This is the

"Golden State," blessed and cursed by geology — yet all of us here choose to remain and play the odds.

At the top of the gardens I recline in the refreshing shade of a giant eucalyptus while contemplating my love affair with this city of paradoxes: this fulcrum of opulence, creativity, reckless ambition, absurd fantasy, and violent crime.

A waft of parched pine and I am back in the redolent woody campsites of my childhood, or cushioned by a carpet of virgin forest in my beloved Northern Ontario, where roots run deep and loons sing across translucent lakes. Myriad memories float like perfume on warm winds.

Retracing my steps down Greystone's ragged hillside, I pass through the Peach House's electronic gates of wrought iron and walk upstairs to my music room, where books, guitars, and easel await attention. Dervin, the housekeeper, brings me hot, honeyed tea from his native Sri Lanka, and no sooner have I kicked off my walking shoes and sunk into the couch's pillowy softness than a ball of grey-and-white fur leaps into my lap and looks up at me with soulful eyes. Ours is a special language of blissful neck rubs and appreciative purring sounds. Thus preoccupied, we gaze towards the framed photos that comprise my self-styled "vanity wall" — Liona Boyd being greeted by President Ronald Reagan, hugged by Prime Minister Pierre Trudeau, wedged in between the King and Queen of Spain while posing grimly like Grant Wood's *American Gothic*, laughing over dinner with Prince Philip, hamming it up with Bob Hope, flirting with Julio Iglesias and Placido Domingo, bowing on stage with Peter Ustinov, and grinning like a Cheshire cat beside Liberace.

Was it really me in all those glossy images of showbiz and celebrity? What further escapades lie in wait for me and my classical guitar, so exquisitely delicate in sound but uncompromisingly demanding to play? Below the framed letters from the White House, telegrams from Buckingham Palace, and gold and platinum records are stacked three monolithic black guitar cases plastered with colourful, peeling stickers from around the globe — Bangkok Hilton;

Istanbul Music Festival; Hotel Nacional de Cuba; Kathmandu Sheraton; Lisbon Ritz; Quebec Festival; NHK Television, Tokyo; Rio de Janeiro Intercontinental; Petaling Jaya, Kuala Lumpur; Hotel Raphael, Paris. Every sticker has a story and triggers within me countless memories from a life of contrasts. Here is an old sticker from the Gordon Lightfoot tours; here a souvenir of my concerts in Nepal; there a tatty remnant from the *Persona* recording sessions in London. . . .

1

The

Prediction

$One summer about ten years ago, I flew into London to record my *Persona* album. After a long limousine ride from Heathrow airport, I was dropped off in front of a Regency house in Kensington where my producer, Michael Kamen, and his wife were accommodating me for the night. As I looked around, the cockney driver remarked, "'Ave you been 'ere before, luv?" I laughed, telling him that I had once lived a stone's throw from where we were standing, and had spent the first year of my life being pushed in a pram up and down the sidewalks of this same street. The iron balconies, cream-painted walls, and mottled plane trees could have been lifted straight out of my parents' first photo album. By coincidence, I had returned to the very street where my life had begun. My mother often told the story of how, when I was only a few months old, she was wheeling me along Kensington Park Road when an eccentric, white-haired lady peered through the veil of her hat into my pram to see the "dear little baby." She stepped back with a startled expression on her face.

"Dear Lord above, this child is going to be famous and travel all over
the world!" she exclaimed. Years later, my mother, a sceptic in matters of clairvoyance, admitted, "You know, Liona, that old psychic
was absolutely right."

Eileen Hancock, my mother, had been raised in Stoke-on-Trent in
the Midlands, but had been drawn to London once she had acquired
her teacher's qualifications in 1945. The long-haired brunette enjoyed
the intellectual atmosphere that flourished among her circle of
acquaintances from all corners of the world — political-science
students from India, artists from Africa, and writers from America —
who drifted through her emerging consciousness. But it was a blond,
blue-eyed youth from northern Spain who stole her heart, wooing
her with romantic dreams of travel and family. John Boyd and my
mother had both been students in the north of England — he at the
University of Durham, she at Whitelands College, which was evacu-
ated to Durham during the Second World War. They did not meet,
however, until gravitating to the same student club in London: my
mother by then an art teacher, my father waiting to pursue further
studies after his stint as a Royal Air Force pilot trainee in Oklahoma.

John had been born into an English family that had resided in
Spain for several generations and assimilated into the Spanish culture.
William and Anita, his parents, were members of the English community centred around the mining industry. To their dismay, their
handsome son gave up university studies in geology; weekends spent
at the child psychologist A. S. Neill's progressive boarding-school,
Summerhill, had stimulated his bohemian spirit and his interest in
childhood creativity and emotional development. Postwar London was
experiencing a resurgence in the arts, and he and my mother attended
concerts, lectures, and galleries, hungrily devouring the delights of life
in the cosmopolitan capital. Only one year into their twenties and after
a few months of courtship, they were married and settled in a flat on
Stanley Crescent, in that same elegant corner of Kensington.

Impatient, even at life's earliest stages, I was born one month
ahead of the anticipated date, on July 11, 1949. As at first my parents

could not decide on a name, they called me Popsy. Many years later, it was amusing to read the headline of a music review of my *Persona* album, "Boyd Becomes Very Popsy!" Eventually, John and Eileen settled on the name Leona, but my paternal grandmother was horrified, as in Spanish it means "lioness" — a name not at all befitting a delicate baby. My mother obligingly changed the spelling to Liona, and a Spanish middle name, Maria, was added to please my grandparents. As she set off to the registry office with my newly invented name, she stepped over a cleaning lady polishing the wooden stairs of the flat and exchanged a few words. "Oh, luvvy, you must call her Carolynne. It's so pretty for your baby," the woman insisted. In this rather haphazard way, my name evolved into Liona Maria Carolynne Boyd, leaving my parents happily confident that they had given their first-born plenty of choices.

I spent my first eighteen months teething on dried bananas and scampering barefoot on the grassy lawns of Holland Park and Kensington Gardens. After my sister, Vivien, announced her presence one and a half years later, we moved to Welling, near the outskirts of London, in the county of Kent. The house had billowing bushes of pink roses in the back garden and a cement wading pool where I splashed naked during the hot summer and prattled away to an imaginary playmate called Oku Poku. My parents, indulging my desire for a kitten, brought home Mimi, a tabby who lived with us until my mother's allergies and his nightly forays with the neighbourhood cats drove them to distraction. To my dismay, he was given away.

Christmases were spent with my grandparents, James and Millie Hancock, in Stoke-on-Trent. The hissing steam engines of Euston Station in Central London petrified me almost as much as the black-bear rug on my grandma's bedroom floor; both recurred with regularity in my childhood nightmares. I remember frosty mornings before the coal fires were lit: steaming bowls of salty porridge, tantalizing cornflake and Golden Syrup pies, jam tarts, and treats of Turkish delight covered in powdered sugar from my grandpa's secret store in the drawing-room bureau, where Vivien and I hung around like eager puppy dogs waiting for tidbits.

Each summer, our small family headed off to the empty, flat beaches of Norfolk, on the east coast facing the North Sea, to erect canvas tents among pine-treed sand dunes. My father knocked together rough tables and chairs out of gnarled logs after first filling his rucksack with pine needles to make a long cushion on which we sat and watched in admiration. I amused myself for hours catching sea-crabs or gathering the prettiest shells from the beach. Once, my little sister and I, blissfully occupied constructing a sandcastle, failed to notice that as the afternoon tide edged around us we were on an ever-diminishing sandbank. To my horror, Vivien's beach shoes began to float away along the channel! My father, who had been sunbathing a short distance away, came rushing to carry his two panic-stricken daughters to safety. The sea barely rose above our ankles, but that image of eddying waters has remained with me ever since. Whenever I am particularly tense, the night before an important trip or a critical performance, I dream of ominous dark waves creeping up the beach. There is no way to ever outrun those insidious tides of my nightmares.

One Christmas, at age four, I awoke to find a lovely honey-coloured teddy bear sitting beside my bed in a pale blue stroller. My new friend, who was almost as big as I, was named Moses. He still reclines regally in my bedroom today, a little thin on top, because when Vivien had her hair cut, I gave "Mosey" a quick trim, believing his hair would grow back just as my sister's did. Tonka, the leopard, came several Christmases later and together they travelled with me from continent to continent. Years later my record company, Moston Music, was named in honour of these long-time companions.

After two years in Welling, my parents became disenchanted with the blandness of suburbia. While bicycling to Bethlem annex of the Maudsley Psychiatric Hospital, where he was working with emotionally disturbed adolescents, my father noticed a straggle of caravans encamped in a nearby field. Eureka! He could buy a trailer and take us to live with the gypsies. The next weekend, my mother, sister, and I trudged over clumpy grass to meet this motley gathering. I looked in awe at the olive-skinned Romany women trailing velvet shawls, and at their swarthy menfolk who emerged from brightly decorated caravans. "The Raggle-Taggle Gypsies" sang in my head as I inhaled the unfamiliar aroma of damp grassy earth, smoking fires, and snorting horses. Bright eyes peeped from behind lace-curtained windows as I tried to pet the mongrel dogs who sniffed at us suspiciously. Living here would be even more fun than playing in the secret forts Vivien and I had constructed beneath the gooseberry bushes — something akin to joining the circus! My father's fantasies might have been fulfilled had not alternative accommodation suddenly materialized, much to my mother's relief. We abandoned "the road less travelled" and rented the upper portion of a sprawling Victorian house on Perry Vale, in South London's residential borough of Forest Hill. I was six and my sister four; my little brother, Damien, was born in the house a year and a half later. "Oh, Mummy, he's just like a big frog," I cried, watching the midwife give him his first bath.

Perry Vale had an enclosed back garden canopied by the branches of a pear tree from which my father hung a wooden swing. The hours of uninterrupted solitude, the natural beauty of our wildflower weedy garden, and the airy sensations of swinging inspired me to compose poems and songs, which I secretly hummed to myself. There was something magical that occurred when I combined my own little melodies and words. The desire to create music and songs was born thanks to my pear-tree swing.

Every night before my mother tucked me into bed, she explained the meaning of two new words. Intended to improve my vocabulary and spelling, these "morning words" were written and left on my night-table, along with a slice of pear or apple, to be memorized on awakening — *boycott, announcement, co-operate* — I can still recall the feeling of munching on a piece of fruit while trying to assimilate those difficult words. In spite of a less acute memory these days, new words never fail to fascinate me. So many aspects of personality seem to be rooted in childhood experience.

Adamsrill Junior School initiated me into the world of chalky British teachers and puddly playgrounds. At school, one of my childish essays won first prize, a treasured book from my Grade One teacher. Accused of "growling" in my attempt to imitate the boy next to me, I was removed from the chorus, which was to sing for a visiting dignitary, and in compensation I was singled out to present a bouquet of flowers onstage. Although my vocal efforts were unappreciated, when my mother began to teach me the treble recorder I discovered that blowing the correct pitches and deciphering the treble clef presented a fascinating challenge. Instrumental music was a delight.

My parents were wonderfully devoted and spent hours reading books and encyclopedias to us. Nothing could be more riveting than *Grimm's Fairy Tales, Birds of Great Britain,* and the adventures of Noddy and Rupert Bear. How our parents adjusted from their days of concerts, lectures, and university life to domestic duties and child-rearing, I cannot imagine, but Damien, Vivien, and I never suffered from lack of attention.

My parents, noticing that one of my eyes turned inward when I was tired, consulted an oculist, who stuck an adhesive patch over my good eye to rest it while strengthening the lazy one. Although I hated this indignity, which endured for several weeks, I reluctantly complied, struggling to read and write with blurred vision. Piercing wails of protest deafened my mother when she removed the bandage, which had become firmly attached to my eyelid and lashes. The experience proved almost as traumatic as my first dental extraction, performed by an appropriately named Dickensian dentist called Doctor Payne! As the right-eye squint persisted, I was carted off to another oculist, who recommended balancing exercises — standing on cement-filled tin cans while rolling my eyes from side to side. Needless to say, my weak eye did not improve after this unorthodox treatment. Finally, glasses were issued by the National Health Service — horrid little round spectacles that constantly misplaced themselves. Throughout my childhood and teenage years, I suffered wearing glasses to school until, at the age of seventeen, I unceremoniously deposited the offending pair in the garbage. At age nineteen, I miraculously scored perfect 20/20 vision; fortunately, I have never required glasses since then.

On weekends my parents used to take us on trips to the country: blackberry-picking in the autumn for my mother's home-made jams; outings to gather the wild bluebells and daffodils of Surrey in the springtime; expeditions to catch tadpoles in the weedy ponds of Kent; and fossil-hunting in the chalk hills of the South Downs. Staying with friends in the Ashdown Forest, we tunnelled mazes through the bosky hillsides of tall, musky ferns and crept into farmers' fields at dusk to pilfer succulent loganberries. My father scraped together his savings to acquire a moribund black 1936 Austin whose sputtering engine needed to be cranked by hand. Whenever it rained, we had to rearrange our seating to avoid drops from the leaking roof, but at the end of a long day's trip — probably no more than fifty miles — we children always kissed our faithful motorcar to thank it for getting us safely back to London.

Crossing the choppy English Channel by ferry and taking tunnel-crammed continental train rides filled me with excitement when we visited my father's family. In "grandma-in-Spain's" house, Vivien and I entertained ourselves feeding the chickens or begging the maid, Ascensión, for pieces of almond *turon* or quince *membrillo*. The house was always busy with the hustle and bustle of food preparation for picnics at the beach, where we sat under umbrellas eating sandy Spanish omelettes and sweet figs. Surely in Spain the first strains of guitar music must have reached my ears. At my mother's urging, my father bought a cheap souvenir guitar, which he carried to England slung over his back in a canvas case.

Vivien was usually my very best friend, but as with most sisters, on occasion my worst enemy. As the eldest, it was my prerogative to be "in charge," reporting to my mother if Vivien misbehaved. Peevishly I pilfered "sweeties" from her secret supply when she was not looking and invented scary stories guaranteed to keep her awake at night. To retaliate she chanted, "Liona the moaner." How infuriating! Not to be outdone, but unable to find a word to rhyme with her name, I neologized "quivien" — a nasty thief who stole from children — and sashayed round the house singing "Vivien the quivien" at the top of my lungs. To my great glee, she would run away, crying. Years later, Vivien was amazed to discover there was no such word.

Two mischievous neighbourhood girlfriends used to invite us into their secret playground, which was accessible only over their garden wall. The fenced-in area contained a high-tension transformer and displayed a sign marked DANGER NO ADMITTANCE. There we competed to see who could do the longest "wee-wee" on the concrete pavings, and danced around naked, like little savages, with rubber hoses, pretending to be boys. They convinced my credulous sister and me that people could fly. After hundreds of abortive "flights" off the back steps, we opted for ballet lessons; watching ballerinas on television, we agreed that their motions looked pretty close to flying. My compliant mother enrolled us in Saturday-morning classes, where Chopin's piano music helped us glide around on tiptoes imitating wood-fairies and nymphs. I loved wearing the pale grey tunic, pink headband, and ballet slippers, but was disappointed when the ballet mistress told me that flying was not on the curriculum.

A corpulent great-aunt from the Midlands, who smelled of lavender and rose-water, came to visit. Her explanation that perfume was made from flowers set me on a quest to duplicate the magical smell of her scented handkerchiefs. Tirelessly I squeezed the petals from garden rosebushes and added drops of rubbing alcohol, but my attempts at perfume creation were a failure. Sun-drying and curing banana skins with various oils, to make a "leather" belt for Mosey, proved equally futile. But with what perfect passion I pursued the improbable dreams of childhood.

Scanning *The Times* of London, my parents, anxious to expand their horizons, became interested in applying for teaching jobs in some far-away corner of the world. Since my father spoke Spanish, he was keen to answer the ads from British Columbia and Bolivia, both of which he presumed were in South America. The former replied, and to his surprise he discovered it was in Canada! However, he accepted a position, not in British Columbia, but in Toronto, Ontario, as principal of Thistletown Hospital School, the first school in the province for emotionally disturbed adolescents. My parents were excited by the prospect of a new life in Canada, although my mother was saddened by the thought of relocating so far from her own family in the Midlands.

Organizing a sale in the front garden, Vivien and I sold off old toys and my father's hand-made wooden "climbing frame," from which we had enjoyed hanging upside down like bats on a rafter in the warm summer months. I was eight years old, my sister six, and my new brother just nine months when we boarded the ship that was to take us to a new life across the ocean. My parents were still in their twenties; I often marvel at how courageous they were to blithely head off towards a foreign land with three young children in tow and no more than a few spare pounds of savings in their pockets. Our years of travelling had begun.

2

Setting Sail

𝄞

The Boyds set sail from Liverpool in September 1957. The Greek-owned SS *Columbia* was about to cross the Atlantic for her final voyage after decades of good seafaring service. Because the Suez Canal had heightened world tensions and resuscitated wartime memories, there was a general rush on immigration to Canada, and this aging ship, not recommended by the travel agency, was the only one available. As we pulled out of the harbour, receding into the mist to the poignant strains of "Auld Lang Syne" and the ship's plaintive foghorn, I watched my grandmother standing forlornly on the rainy dock. How could I know what emotions were being unleashed? I was just a child heading out for an adventure.

We explored our cabin, anxiously watching the water smack against the portholes, then assembled on deck for a lifeboat drill. "Is there any chance of this ship sinking?" I asked tentatively. "Of course not, darling," my mother reassured me. "So why are we practising?" I questioned, unconvinced, as I peered suspiciously at the icy green waters. Later a cabin boy sauntered along the corridors playing a hand xylophone summoning us to the dining room. This short melody would later become the very first tune I taught myself to pluck on the strings of a classical guitar.

The old Greek who waited on our table fussed over Vivien and me, bringing us extra "poofed reese" for breakfast and treating us to pink ice cream at dinner. These desserts were delectable, but after ten days of gluttony the mere thought of strawberry ice cream became repulsive; to this day, I cannot bear it! Every day in the cigar-smokey lounge, I patiently crayoned pictures of the Canada that I imagined awaited us: a city skirting an enormous lake, ranches of wild horses, and majestic snow-covered mountains inhabited by grizzly bears. One afternoon while drawing, I overheard two ladies mention that in the evening there was to be an amateur talent show. I ran on deck to find Vivien, who was busy playing hopscotch, and convinced her that if we practised a duet on our recorders, we could enter the competition. Mission accomplished, I scurried back, ingratiating myself with the ladies, who registered Liona and Vivien Boyd. My mother was astounded to hear us rehearsing on our bunk beds, but promised we could stay up late enough to compete. Suffering the effects of the ship's rolling motions, she was spending most of the trip in bed, nibbling dry crackers.

That night I made my debut on the concert stage. My six-year-old sister and I confidently stood in front of an audience of fellow passengers, played "The Blue Bells of Scotland" on our recorders, then curtsied at the applause. How grown up and important we felt as the ship's purser bought us fizzy orange drinks. There was no doubt that we would walk away with first prize, I assured Vivien, but it was too late for us to wait for the results. The next morning I was dumbfounded to learn that a stout tenor had claimed "our" prize. I consoled my little sister by explaining that the judge had been unable to give us the award because we were only children.

Life on the SS *Columbia* was replete with interesting activities: swimming with my father in the indoor pool, where salty waters sloshed from side to side like an old washing machine, or standing in awe as swarthy Greek sailors tossed leftover food and garbage from the side of the ship to the seagulls or whatever hungry creatures lurked beneath the waves. On the fifth day of the voyage, a violent storm caused our ship to pitch and sway, her aged timbers creaking ominously. All night the sea tossed us around in our bunks; even we children felt nauseated. Two days later, rumour circulated that we had survived one of the worst hurricanes in years and were lucky to be alive. A boat full of German naval cadets had radioed an SOS to the *Columbia* during the height of the storm, but our captain held his course, aware that he had hundreds of young children in a ship long past her prime. The shipload of cadets sank with no survivors.

For the first few weeks after we arrived in Toronto, we stayed in the roomy house of the psychiatrist Dr. John Rich, who had invited my father to be the principal of Thistletown. My mother took us for daily walks in the drifted autumn leaves of Mount Pleasant Cemetery, where we tried tirelessly to tame the black squirrels and innocently helped ourselves to the pretty funeral ribbons for our dolls' wardrobes. My parents were having difficulty finding a place to rent; I heard them anxiously phoning around after perusing the Toronto papers. Then one day we were bundled off to a cramped house in the heart of the Italian section off St. Clair Avenue and informed that this was to be our new home. Sadly, there was no secluded garden with a swing or a pear tree, but we were soon busy exploring the immigrant neighbourhood.

We had no pets, although our hearts were set on two golden hamsters promised to us by my mother for Christmas. Never at a loss for ideas, we decided to make do with a couple of crippled flies, which we persuaded my father to catch for us in the window of an enormous food store we loved to visit called Loblaws. Rag and Tag were fed on strawberry jam and released to crawl around the bathtub each evening for their daily walk. Knowing that Westmount Avenue was only a temporary home, my parents chose not to enrol us at the local school. Each morning after my father set off for work, my mother placed Damien in his playpen and taught us English, history, natural science, and mathematics around the kitchen table. It was here that I began to write out poems and essays, which I copied meticulously into a notebook entitled "My Poems by Liona Boyd." Every evening my parents took turns reading us bedtime stories — *Pippi Longstocking*, *Gulliver's Travels*, *Robinson Crusoe* — trying to continue our lives as normally as possible.

Finally, two days before Christmas, my father succeeded in relocating us to a house on Queen's Drive in Weston, in the west end of Toronto. Bundled up in scarves and snowsuits, we were introduced to the trappings of Canadian winters: toboggans, sleds, flying saucers, and ice skates. What fun to speed over compacted snow or twirl around Daddy's ice rink, created overnight with the garden hose. Even chapped lips, icy toes, and frozen mittens could not diminish our infatuation with these novel recreations. To enlarge their dwindling savings, my parents decided, in the pioneering spirit, to try their hand selling oil paintings. After all, they had both studied and taught art, and perhaps there might be an opportunity within Toronto's burgeoning population. Late into the night they sat at their easels, surrounded by tubes of paint and jars of turpentine; we watched, fascinated, as my father's canvases evolved into seascapes and bullfighters, while ballet dancers and flowers emerged from my mother's. After a few weeks of industrious painting, my father set off with the finished masterpieces to the affluent apartments on Bathurst Street. For two disappointing nights he came home unsuccessful, but on the third returned triumphant after selling a couple of seascapes. Fired by success, my parents painted many oils, which hung around the house in various stages of wetness before being exhibited at art shows in the parks and in local shopping plazas.

In the spring we were delighted when our garden bloomed unexpectedly with thousands of purple periwinkles; the Queen's Drive house began to feel like home. The hot summer months brought visits to the banks of the Humber River, where my father ran a day camp for learning-disabled children while Vivien and I built dams in the shallow reaches of the river or biked along the banks to collect frogs, insects, and wildflowers. One afternoon I persuaded her to "play dead" and lie with me on the highway's hot gravelly soft-shoulders with ketchup smeared over our arms and faces. When, to our glee, a concerned motorist pulled over, we scurried down the embankment to hide in the bushes; the minds of youngsters can invent some macabre games. Besides the constant flow of stray cats to whom we gave temporary shelter, our menagerie expanded to include golden hamsters and rabbits housed in cages constructed by my resourceful father. In the late afternoons we foraged in the garbage bins of grocery stores, riding home on bicycles laden with leafy contraband for our pets.

Dolls and bears, including one compassionately retrieved from a neighbour's garbage bin, were assembled every evening in a semi-circle to play "school." Each wore a brown cotton "uniform" that I had sewn, with yellow initials embroidered on the front. With this class of eager students, I explored creative ideas; one day I had them each write an essay on their origins, the next I painstakingly filled glasses and jars to various levels to design for them a water instrument on which I tapped out tunes spanning two octaves. Often I seemed to prefer the passive company of my precious bears and dolls to that of humans!

One summer we spent two weeks on a private island near Parry Sound, which introduced us to the pristine scenery of the Muskoka region, a cottage and resort area three hours north of Toronto. Lying on a raft of silver-birch logs, I spent blissful sunlit afternoons afloat composing poems, while Vivien tender-heartedly rescued flies and moths that had fallen into the lake and little Damien splashed around catching minnows and crayfish in the warm translucent waters. With pine-scented picnics and campfire nights, we passed the ephemeral summer days of childhood.

Once again we were forced to move, as our home was sold, and after a temporary stay on Glenvalley Drive, we moved to a house on Burnhamthorpe Road in Etobicoke, another suburb of Toronto. We were becoming accustomed to the itinerant way of life: packing, unpacking, and changing schools.

During the fifth grade, I began to read voraciously, staying up late at night to immerse myself in the exciting worlds of *Treasure Island*, *The Yearling*, and *Paddle to the Sea*, which told the story of a figure in a canoe carved by a Native boy living in Canada's Lake Nipigon country. "Paddle" sets out on an adventure-filled journey of rivers, rapids, and lakes until he finally reaches the Atlantic Ocean. Inspired, I wrote about a girl who carved a Popsicle-stick figure and dropped it through the grating of a Toronto storm sewer. It floated on to have interesting encounters — meeting water rats, narrowly missing a sewage plant, and finally reaching Lake Ontario. Almost thirty years later, *Paddle to the Sea* was to become my sixteenth album and first children's recording.

Although Canada was good to us, my parents missed England. I would often hear my homesick mother choking back tears at night; Toronto had not yet become home to Eileen and John, whose roots were tugging them back across the sea. One day we were told that passages had been booked on the SS *Ryndam*, sailing from Montreal. My father had been offered the principalship of a school in a year hence, so he was returning without immediate prospects but felt something would turn up. Out came the old wooden chests into which we crammed our belongings, one trunk containing nothing but teddy bears and dolls! My parents decided to leave behind with a friend the cheap Spanish guitar that had adorned our walls, conceding that it was too cumbersome to carry back to England.

We shared the comforting feeling of going home to the country where our accents did not obtrude, and where our friends and family would welcome us back. Canada had provided an interesting three-year interlude in my childhood, but I promised my bears that soon we would be playing amongst the daisies in a new garden across the ocean. I was certain that my mother and father were going to be happy again. At ten years of age, I had not enough life experience to know or understand the Chinese saying that cautions,

"You can never dip into the same river twice." Time is the great destroyer — you change; things change; life is a shifting kaleidoscope of places and events in which nothing and no one remain the same.

3

Grammar School Girl

Saint David's Mansions, a four-storey apartment block in Sydenham, southeast London, became our new home. Grandiose in name only, it backed onto a large grassy wasteland where debris from demolished buildings was scattered. Through a child's eyes, this was an enchanting place abounding in splintered planks, wrecked furniture, and smashed staircases. On this hill, it is said, the queen of the ancient Britons, Queen Boadicea, made her last valiant stand against the Romans, around A.D. 60. The Dump provided a fantastic playground where Vivien and I spent hours racing up and down the slopes on imaginary horses, or finding secret hiding-places under stones to conceal coded messages. In the springtime, the rugged terrain bloomed with clumps of daisies, straggling wild roses, and cornflowers. I used to lie in the long grass and watch the scudding clouds sweep over London while memorizing my favourite poems, or play out scenarios from my fertile imagination: one day I was Cathy of *Wuthering Heights*, the next a captive Indian princess from a cowboy western.

Vivien and I collected an assortment of large garden snails and wrote numbers on their backs with coloured markers. These decorated creatures were released into the garden, where we amused ourselves keeping log books to track their meanderings through the privet bushes. To this day I harbour a maudlin concern for garden snails, picking them off the sidewalks and depositing them in the grass. Occasionally we staged snail races on the low concrete roof of an abandoned air-raid shelter. What patience we must have possessed! Damien pestered his big sisters until we gave him his own pet snail, which he painted red, named Poke, and housed in a marmalade jar beside his bed. How easily we children were entertained as we immersed ourselves in our new surroundings, scarcely looking back at the life we had abruptly abandoned in Canada.

The carefree summer came to an end in September, when I was taken to the imposing ivy-covered Sydenham County Girls School. Because of our time in Canada, I had missed the critical entrance exam to grammar school; however, the headmistress improvised a test consisting of a few arithmetic problems and an essay on the theme "I Was a Stowaway," which, having had firsthand experience aboard two ocean liners, jump-started my imagination; I wrote non-stop for an hour. The headmistress must have been sufficiently impressed by my creative ramblings, as I was summoned to her office for an interview. Confidently, I rattled off stories about our stay in Toronto. She cut me short, looked at me severely, and instructed me in impeccable Queen's English to simply answer "Yes, mistress" or "No, mistress." My "undisciplined" years in Canada had left me with some deplorable habits! At one point I made the mistake of replying "Okay, mistress" to her questions. "My dear, a young lady must never use that dreadful American word," she reprimanded, frowning over her horn-rimmed spectacles.

I was trundled off to buy the compulsory school uniform: tunic, blouse, navy blue bloomers, gabardine coat, and a hat with an embroidered crest. The school motto was "Aim High," a dictum I proudly sported on my blazer. All this uniform business made me feel I already belonged to that privileged mob of English grammar-school girls.

To my parents' satisfaction, the headmistress placed me in class 1A, with the brightest kids. Swinging my new leather satchel, I tried to blend in to the pony-tailed throng. Once classes began, I was grateful for my mother's years of extra coaching in mathematics and English. The sheer size of the school of two thousand girls made me apprehensive for the first few days. My new classmates thought my "American accent" most peculiar — that same accent that Canadians had found so "English" — but they did their best to make me feel at home, clapping enthusiastically after my presentation on Canada in geography class. The elderly English mistress used to invite me to walk with her during the morning recess so that she could talk about poetry — Wordsworth, Browning, and Tennyson. This exposure to the magic of words and rhyme inspired many poems, including a parody of Longfellow's *Song of Hiawatha*, which recounted the story of Hiawatha's visit to Sydenham County Girls School and to my delight was selected for the annual yearbook. For the first time in my life, I loved going to school in spite of having come from the relaxed educational system of Canada. Within the more rigid discipline of the British system, however, even my innocent cartwheels on the school lawn got me into trouble for showing my knickers. Luckily, I excelled in most subjects, receiving weekly "gold distinctions" in the headmistress's office. "Thank you, mistress," I piped up proudly in my best schoolgirl English.

Each morning, dressed in a blue uniform and felt hat, I jumped on the red double-decker bus and clambered to the top for the half-hour ride to school. At lunch-time, the plump cockney cooks allowed me to venture into their steamy kitchen for my ration of cheese as, thanks to my parents, I had been brought up without eating meat. The "sweets" of pink blancmange and spotted dick seemed a scrumptious change from my mother's healthy dinners of brown rice and vegetables. On Fridays we were marched single file to the local swimming baths and forced into the frigid chlorinated water, which stung our eyes and turned us into shivering lumps of gooseflesh. Class 1A used to return with stringy dripping-wet hair and chattering teeth in the chilly days of the London winter. Apart from swimming, the other class I was not too fond of was music. Scales and music theory seemed a bore, but in the school assemblies I happily belted out such rousing hymns as "Onward, Christian Soldiers."

Creating things with my hands gave me great satisfaction. After mounting some pressed wildflowers from the Dump on strips of cardboard covered with cellophane, I glued on pink ribbons and persuaded Vivien to accompany me door to door to offer my bookmarks to the people on our street. As pleased as Punch, we sold the handicrafts for a shilling each. Next I struck upon the idea of doing odd jobs on Saturday afternoons. As a child I never had reservations about knocking on the doors of total strangers; it never occurred to me that it could be dangerous for an eleven-year-old girl and her nine-year-old sister to walk unescorted into unfamiliar homes. The Londoners seemed so hospitable and friendly. The world and her people were all to be trusted. We shopped at the greengrocers for one elderly lady, swept a man's stone yard, returned an empty gas tank for a granny in a wheelchair, and received a few shillings for our labours. Each Saturday we skipped off to perform odd jobs, telling our parents that we were meeting school friends.

Having a secret from our parents felt naughtily delicious. Our hard-earned pennies were spent on treats from the local sweet shop, where jars of tantalizing confectionary made our mouths water: powdered-sherbert cones with licorice-stick suckers, milk drops, jelly babies, dolly mixture, and blackjacks.

My father slipped and broke his leg while playing football with his students, a bunch of rough, tough emotionally disturbed adolescent boys, and was hospitalized for six weeks. Each day my devoted mother bused across London to visit him, leaving us to our own devices. They began to realize that England offered few options for my father's career, and that many friends seemed trapped in economic ruts. In contrast, they remembered the open-ended challenges and opportunities in Canada. A position of art teacher in the Etobicoke school system was available, so after only one year they decided to board ship once again and return to their adopted land. I am sure it was with many regrets and considerable emotional turmoil that they waved sad goodbyes to their relatives and friends for the second time.

For Vivien and me, the move was simply another episode in our wandering lifestyle. We accepted their decision without question. Although it meant leaving our favourite schools, we sensed their disillusionment with life in the "old country" and were prepared once again to sail the Atlantic. For the third time, my parents stuffed our wooden trunks with dolls, teddy bears, books, and canvases, and boarded another Greek liner, the SS *Arcadia*, to carry us three thousand miles to a country that now felt familiar.

4

A Guitar
for Christmas

𝄞

After a week's sea voyage, we were once again back in Toronto, where my father rented a house in the west-end suburbs. The Boyd tribe moved into 14 Paragon Road, presuming it would be for only a year or two, as experience had accustomed us to frequent changes; however, it was to serve as home for fifteen years. Vivien and I were enrolled in the seventh and eighth grades at Dixon Grove School. Although we had been away for only a year, Canadian school required readjustments on our part. Ahead lay the challenges of those critical years of adolescence, when identity has to be forged among peers.

Canadian girls seemed so much more sophisticated in attitude and dress than their English counterparts. Rather than navy blue school uniforms and knee-socks, our classmates decked themselves out with fashionable outfits, nylon stockings, and handbags. Instead of simple pony-tails and braids, these girls backcombed and sprayed their hair. Vivien and I were teased about our "weird way of talking" and interrogated on our church affiliation. On discovering that I did not attend Sunday school, one sanctimonious girl determined to expose my true religion. Leading her on, I invented a couple of Native Indian deities, inspired by my grammar-school poem "Hiawatha." "Our family worships the wind god, Mudjekeewis, and the fire goddess, Wawataysee," I stated mischievously, with an exaggerated English accent, defiantly flinging back my two pigtails. "Ah, so you really are pagans!" she retorted. The news of my strange religion spread throughout the eighth grade, giving the students a reason to look on their English classmate with added suspicion. Knowing I was already different from the other kids, I took perverse delight in this ridiculous deception.

To satisfy a budding interest in biology, I posted notices at the local mall: "SOS. Nature lovers desperately in need of an aquarium." Miraculously, my sister and I received four calls from generous Torontonians and we convinced my father to pick up our booty in his old black Pontiac. One became a soil-filled ant colony, another a salamander vivarium furnished with damp moss, the third a weedy fish tank, and the last home for Phred, the pet toad. As Damien was also fascinated by anything that crept, crawled, or flew, my poor mother had to tolerate the boxes of cecropia moths, daddy-long-legs, and garter snakes that he housed in his bedroom. Having read Gerald Durrell's childhood autobiography, *My Family and Other Animals*, I enjoyed the humorous parallels between our outlandish families.

A sudden interest in breeding tropical fish stimulated the entrepreneurial spirit that had surfaced during my odd-job escapades in London. As angel-fish, filters, and thermostats required more than my weekend allowance, I decided to salvage empty pop bottles from local building sites, returning them for two-cent refunds. Setting off by bicycle to explore houses pungent with drying paint provided the thrill of a private expedition. Each time, I returned triumphant, with sandy Coke and beer bottles to rinse with the garden hose; long before the days of recycling, I was inadvertently doing my part for ecology! Now, in addition to fish-purchasing power, I had my first savings account at the Royal Bank of Canada. How proud I felt when it reached one hundred dollars.

Construction-site scavenges gave rise to another scheme during the dog days of August. The thirsty Italian workmen paid twenty-five cents for soft drinks from the catering vans. I persuaded Vivien to join me in selling Kool-Aid at fifteen cents a glass and put Mother in charge of production. Dragging a box of ice cubes, we trudged off to the construction sites, where shirtless bricklayers and carpenters gulped down the chemical brew, happily dispensing sweaty dimes and Sicilian smiles. Had I been given hand-outs by wealthy parents, I never would have experienced such pride and delight in watching my black mollies, swordtails, and angel-fish swim around their second-hand aquarium.

When fall came, I was placed in Kipling Collegiate's Grade Nine enrichment class. Students were given a choice of art or music and home economics, but taking both art and music was disallowed. My obdurate parents marched up to the school arguing that the arts would play a larger role in their daughter's life than home economics ever would. How right they were; I still loathe housework and am a hopeless cook!

After a frustrating week of broken oboe reeds, I settled on the clarinet. Kipling was fortunate to have an exceptional music teacher in Barry Gosse, who inspired the students and produced an acclaimed annual show. It was his classes that introduced me to the works of Beethoven, Gershwin, and Aaron Copland. What a fascinating world of rich orchestration and harmony! I had never enjoyed the theoretical aspects of music, but loved studying the lives and works of great composers. At my mother's suggestion, I memorized Rimsky-Korsakov's "Song of India" on the clarinet. However, that instrument was not intended to feature in my future; I gave it up after one year. Nevertheless, the wind family must have held some appeal, as I taught myself to play the melodica, a small keyboard instrument that is held in the hand and blown into.

When Christmas time approached, I coerced Vivien and my girl-friend Sandra to join me in a carol-singing experiment. We plodded hesitantly up the snow-covered driveways. While Vivien and I began our recorder duet, Sandra broke forth with the words to "The First Noel," but nervously wet her pants in the first chorus, causing us to flee down the street. After I dried her off over the heat vent at Paragon Road, we ventured forth again with our Yuletide serenades. People were welcoming, as door-to-door carol singing was a novelty. Occasionally we were invited inside for a slice of Christmas cake or cup of hot chocolate, but usually, to our delight, we were handed some silver or the odd dollar bill.

Although I was a reticent and self-conscious teenager, some inexplicable force seemed to drive me during those early musical performances. I loved the feeling of making music and sensing people's appreciation of it. After a couple of nights my accomplices quit, complaining of frozen feet; undaunted, I set off alone, playing recorder or melodica, returning only when my fingers became too stiff from the cold. Half the proceeds were donated to the Toronto Humane Society, as I had always cared about animals. My self-motivated carolling had provided immense pleasure, satisfying the combined needs of performing and supporting a good cause.

Although English literature and science were my favourite subjects, I excelled in art, thanks to my parental role models, and one of my autumn landscapes hung for years in the principal's office. Vivien and I still had pronounced English accents, but with the British pop invasion we suddenly became acceptable to our classmates; rather than making fun of our hair, they rebelliously started to grow theirs.

My parents discouraged us from watching too much television, for which I remain forever grateful. I am happy to have been granted a childhood in those more innocent days. Reading books, writing poems, ballet practice, painting, and drawing met with approval; we were permitted to watch "The Wonderful World of Disney" and an occasional "Ed Sullivan Show" on Sunday evenings while my mother treated us to ice cream and chocolate cake. Disney's dramas on the lives of Beethoven and Strauss were inspirational, and I sat glued to the set watching the Beatles make their American TV debut. The world of showbiz, however, struck no chords of interest in me at all other than as an observer. The other two programs that my parents allowed were the BBC's Shakespearean productions and a serialized version of *The Scarlet Pimpernel*. Those daring exploits of a handsome English nobleman rescuing beautiful ladies from the guillotine so fired my imagination that, swept up in the early stages of adolescent romanticism, I constructed an imaginary white charger out of our basement trunks in order to relive and embellish his adventurous missions.

My youthful intellectual parents attended lectures, art galleries, and concerts, kept company with radical friends in Rochdale College, and immersed themselves in interesting books on philosophy or art. Our family still seemed different from those of my school chums, due in part to our feeling more English than Canadian. Neighbourhood kids teased Damien that his father was a "hippy" for sporting longish hair and a beard — a rarity in those days. I think this awareness of being different drew our family closer together, giving my sister and me a sense of identity and self-confidence.

High school was the time of the swinging sixties, which brought us pantihose and miniskirts. Our poor legs turned shades of blue and purple as we struggled to walk to school during the cruel winter months. In a moment of bravado, I supported a fellow classmate's presidential campaign by go-go dancing to the Rolling Stones' "Paint It Black" before the school assembly. It was obvious, however, that I was not cut out for acting when my girlfriend and I were given the roles of mad professors in a school play, *The Mish-Mosh Bird*. Two characters with long black beards collapsed in uncontrollable fits of giggles, Sir Laurence Olivier style, during their serious speeches.

At age thirteen, my casual choice for a Christmas present was to change my life. "Why don't you give me that old guitar hanging on the wall and some lessons?" I suggested offhandedly. It was the instrument my parents had bought in Spain when I was six years old. Given to friends when we left for England, it was handed back on our return. Apart from giving voice to the few simple melodies that my mother had taught herself to pluck, it had served merely as a wall decoration symbolizing our links to Spain. Come Christmas morning, the slightly warped guitar in its rough canvas cover was waiting for me beneath the tree. I bent my fingers around the neck, inhaling its woody aroma, and tried to play the slack, untuned strings. This was obviously going to require a good deal of patience.

Every Wednesday evening I visited John Perrone, a local classical guitar teacher. Crammed into a tiny studio, we laboured through simple exercises in Aaron Shearer's *Method Book One*. My mother insisted on half an hour's practice each day, which I performed compliantly but without notable enthusiasm. I was no child prodigy. Besides, ballet had become my overriding passion.

After a few months, the renowned English guitarist Julian Bream came to play in Toronto. Remembering his playing from the BBC, my mother suggested we attend so I might experience classical guitar at its best. Apart from one Toronto Symphony Orchestra performance, I had not been exposed to live classical concerts. With great anticipation, we found our seats in the Eaton's department store auditorium, where pianist Glenn Gould recorded many of his albums. One solitary chair and a tiny footstool were all the bare stage displayed. How could a single guitar player fill the hall with sound? Scanning the program, I was thrilled to recognize a work by Fernando Sor, who had written some of the studies I had been learning. As the audience located their seats, I felt a secret advantage: I also played the classical guitar!

Bream's London accent in his introductory remarks came as a surprise. Spellbound, I watched while he arranged the tails of his jacket and adjusted his footstool. The fragile lute that he cradled in his arms had a crisp treble tone, thinner than the guitar's but most pleasing in its delicacy. My eyes fixed on each small movement of his hands while my ears feasted on the crystalline beauty of the notes. The music of John Dowland, Robert de Visée, and J. S. Bach danced and sang under Bream's nimble fingertips.

After the intermission, he returned to centre stage with guitar in hand to play the Spanish music of Francisco Tárrega and Isaac Albéniz. Now I was completely captivated. Never could I have imagined a more exquisite sound than that which was emerging from this lone musician and his simple wooden instrument. The richness of tone, coloration of phrases, and subtle shadings of sound were an aesthetic revelation. This was the epiphany — the moment when I fell in love with the classical guitar. I determined to learn to play it, so that one day I too would be able to draw such beauty from six strings.

My new enthusiasm convinced my mother that I needed the top classical guitar instructor available. She located a Viennese teacher considered the best in Toronto. Visions of a tall, imposing figure who taught music in the strict European tradition formed in my mind. No doubt he would chastise me for insufficient practice and rap my knuckles with his tuning fork. Eli Kassner had no time for more students, but at my mother's insistence, he agreed to hear me play.

My father drove me to Kassner's house in suburban Willowdale. There, upon pulling into the driveway, I saw a scruffily clad gardener tugging weeds out of the rockery. As he approached our car to greet us, I realized, to my surprise, that the blue-jeaned gardener was Eli Kassner himself! Far from towering above me, Eli looked up at me from his stocky, five-foot frame and smiled warmly. "Velcome, come into ze haus." After listening to a few short pieces, instead of rapping my knuckles, he accepted me as his student. My new teacher inspired me from the start with his obvious love for the guitar; from then on, my mother never had to remind me to practise, as all my spare time was devoted to this new interest.

Eli scheduled my lessons late in the evening in order to offer extra time, gratis. He first selected "El Noy de la Mare," a simple Catalan folk melody, which I memorized in a week. After a couple of months, he gave me Andrés Segovia's transcription of "Asturias" by Isaac Albéniz. This seemed an advanced piece, but I diligently persevered, trying to imitate Bream's recorded version. In a few weeks I had it mastered; Eli was most impressed. However, a career in music was the furthest thing from my thoughts.

The world of ballet had always resonated with my dreams of romance and make-believe. Since my early dance classes in England, I had loved the bodily sensations of graceful choreographed movement. After five months of lessons at the local school, I made my ignominious debut as a ballerina. My parents sat proudly waiting to see their daughter glide onto the stage with three other nymphs to dance a Mozart minuet. Seconds before my entry, I realized to my chagrin that in the excitement, I had forgotten to remove the heavy warm-up socks used to cover our ballet slippers and it was then too late! Four sylphs pirouetted daintily from the wings in pink-satin tunics, but one had ugly white knee-socks and a red face! My parents must have sunk through the floor in embarrassment.

My love of dance persisted nevertheless, and I studied the Cecchetti method with Gladys Forrester and her assistant, Brian Foley. Additional lessons were provided by a Danish teacher, Teenie Gollop, whose name, evoking the image of sugar-plum fairies, seemed perfect for a ballerina. Each evening I practised *barrés* and *pliés* to scratchy recordings of *Coppélia* and Tchaikovsky's *Swan Lake*. Vivien and I watched our reflections in the darkened living room windows as we leaped around the room in frilly white petticoats. Many years later, neighbours across the street told us that they were often entertained by our evening dancing displays. It had never occurred to us that we had an audience observing our arabesques through the undraped windows!

The highlight of my short-lived stint as a ballerina was a performance of *La Boutique Fantasque*, in which I danced the role of Queen of Hearts. I loved the music, the rehearsals, and the excitement of performing with advanced dancers. Through movement and music, we created a world of fantasy in which toys came to life.

After watching a spectacular Royal Ballet performance at the O'Keefe Centre, while prowling backstage for autographs, I came

face to face with Rudolf Nureyev. I was instantly smitten. The Russian
with the high leaps, high cheek bones, and wild hair was to feature
regularly in my teenage daydreams, and his photos adorned my bedroom wall along with those of Julian Bream and Segovia. When
Vivien bestowed nightly kisses on her horse pictures, I did likewise
with the posters of my idols. Our chosen destinies had begun to take
shape.

Eli Kassner prepared me for the Royal Conservatory guitar examinations, which I successfully passed using my new Goya guitar, and
my mother helped me study for the required harmony and music-
theory tests. Aware of the importance of competitions in polishing a
student's performance skills, Eli entered me in the annual Kiwanis
music festivals. Some years, in addition to performing solo, I played
duets with his other students, enjoying a great sense of accomplishment on receiving several first and second prizes playing works by
Manuel de Falla and J. S. Bach. The world of guitar composers was
rapidly opening up, thanks to a good teacher's guidance.

My schoolteacher father had long summer holidays during which
we piled into his VW bus to tour around the continent. In the sixties,
provincial and state parks were not congested; consequently, our
destinations were unplanned. These were wonderful days: camping
on empty beaches of the Oregon coast; browsing through rock shops
in Utah; exploring the Grand, Bryce, and Zion canyons in Arizona;
pitching tents in Alabama campsites that were dripping with Spanish
moss; and enjoying hot roadside picnics in Nebraska and Iowa. A
generous Texan farmer invited us to stay at his watermelon ranch; a
truckload of Alberta Hutterites rescued us in the torrential rains of a
furious midnight thunderstorm. Inspired by the natural beauty of our
vast continent, which drew us to the Rockies, the Smoky Mountains,
and Yellowstone, I kept a log of each holiday, gluing in maps,
photos, and poems composed along the way. Eight-year-old Damien
sang Beatle songs to entertain his sisters; Vivien ran off in search of
horses at every stop; I played guitar, avoiding dishwashing duty,
insisting it was bad for my nails. From a piece of wood pilfered from

my pop-bottle building sites, I constructed a peculiar wooden finger-board with strings attached and black lines delineating the frets. Using this compact device, I was able to practise left-hand stretches, *legatos*, and finger patterns while our VW bus rumbled along miles of freeways and dusty back roads. This ingenious contraption was certainly more practical than trying to play on a real guitar. Eli Kassner showed me how to practise right-hand finger combinations using a candy package whose cardboard edges approximated the distance between two guitar strings. Trying to keep cool in the unbearable Texas heat, we wrapped soaking wet towels around our bodies, frolicked in the water-sprinklers of parks, or opened the windows of our un-air-conditioned vehicle to catch the breeze. How much richer and more creative those unplanned family holidays seemed than the summer-camp routines of our classmates. They bonded our family together, as we shared common discomforts, challenges, and discoveries.

In 1965 we drove west to Calgary to visit my parents' English friends. Jan Truss, my mother's school friend, was a writer of children's books. Her children, Martin and Sally, we knew from our childhood seaside camping holidays in England. Martin now sang folk-songs, played the guitar, drove a car, rode his horses bareback, and made my heart beat faster. He wrote out the chords to "Where Have All the Flowers Gone?" and taught me to jive at my sixteenth-birthday party. My hazel-eyed childhood pal, whom I remembered chasing along the beach and building castles in the sand, had become a handsome western cowboy who galloped me on horseback across the grassy ranch lands and played hide-and-seek with me in the hay loft. With hesitant kisses, we explored the exquisite new sensations of first love. Passionate letters flowed back and forth during the next year, but by the summer of '66, my teenage cowboy had faded into memory, as I was in the throes of a brief but intense romance with another guitar-playing folk-singer.

Hans and I first met in 1962 at the home of the Schroer family in Beaver Valley, a ski area one and a half hours north of Toronto. We walked the craggy hillsides unaware of what futures were hidden in the cards. Liona Boyd, Hans Grunsky, and Oliver Schroer were all destined to make their mark in the world of music. How could I not be impressed by the handsome, dark-haired nineteen-year-old who wrote his own songs and strummed the guitar? His husky tenor voice charmed me with "Puff the Magic Dragon" until my heart was filled with adoration. But I was only a pony-tailed kid to him; a few years had to pass before we would meet again. After forming a folk group, Jack's Angels, in Europe, he returned to Toronto. He was twenty-one, and I was a blossoming seventeen-year-old with straight blonde hair, minidresses, and fast fingers on the guitar. We took long walks, collected bouquets of forget-me-nots from the banks of the Humber River, and played our guitars in the secluded sandy beaches of the Toronto Islands. Now it was Hans whose dark eyes became misty as he held me in his arms and whispered the lyrics to his songs. Together we listened to the folk-singers at the Riverboat coffee house, owned by Bernie Fiedler, in Toronto's Yorkville district. Then, hand in hand, we strolled along Hazelton Avenue, the mecca of Toronto's hippy scene, where Indian skirts and bell-bottom trousers trailed along the sidewalks to the strains of wind-chimes and guitar strumming. For the first time, my mother allowed me to borrow her make-up and pink lipstick; how grown up I felt!

But all too soon the summer idyll came to an end, as Hans had a plane ticket back to Vienna. On our last evening, after a stroll through James Gardens, he tried to slide his hand under my blouse, but I prudishly squirmed away, explaining that I was too young. Fortunately, he understood my adolescent shyness; we spent our last hours hugging, laughing, crying, and kissing until our faces were so blotched that I had to make a beeline for the privacy of my bedroom. I moped around for weeks while we exchanged long, poetic letters. On the back cover of one of his record albums, Hans used a photo of us sitting side by side in the garden of Paragon Road. After a few months, however, his treasured missives dwindled to a halt; Cupid's arrow had landed elsewhere. In the eighties, Hans and his new family returned to Toronto, where under the name Jack Grunsky he developed a successful career in children's music, winning a Juno Award for one of his albums. Oliver Schroer, my brother's Beaver Valley playmate, came on the music scene later and was nominated for a Juno Award for his 1993 album of ethno-fusion fiddle music.

The boys in Kipling Collegiate held minimal attraction for me. I could never understand how my girlfriends could fall to pieces over some pimple-faced sixteen-year-old on the football team. I developed a mad crush on an older Czechoslovakian student with whom I shared some of my poetic efforts and courageously invited to our Sadie Hawkins dance. Swaying to the music of the Righteous Brothers' "Ebb Tide" in our darkened school gymnasium was a sensual experience like no other.

The CBC had produced Dostoyevsky's *Crime and Punishment*, starring Geneviève Bujold and Paul Koslo. To my great surprise, I was introduced to Paul Koslo at a guitar party, and after a few exchanges he asked me out on a dinner date. At twenty-three, with the brooding intensity and charismatic persona of an early Peter O'Toole, Paul seemed to belong to another generation. Imagine my delight on discovering that the young actor also sang and played the guitar! Paul led a rather bohemian life, typical of the times. I became his "Lady Guinevere," with quixotic promises of elopement, castles, and ten children unfolding in his daydreams. There were never any attempts to get under my blouse; ours was a courtly love! After a few months, however, the different lifestyles of the Grade Twelve schoolgirl and the struggling young actor dabbling in psychedelic drugs caused inevitable problems; even my liberal parents, who took us to mingle with the flower-bedecked, beaded, and bearded "long-hairs" in Toronto's Queen's Park "Love-In," started to disapprove when they realized he was often stoned. In pursuit of his career, Paul decided to relocate to L.A., where he wrote ardently for two years, but time and distance diluted our romance. Many years later, when I saw him on the screen playing one of the leads in *Voyage of the Damned* with all his hair shaved off, I hardly recognized my young sweetheart, who had serenaded me with Donovan songs and braided purple morning-glory flowers into my hair.

The Toronto Guitar Society, an organization of students, players, and aficionados, was founded by Eli Kassner. His parties and the society's after-concert receptions often brought together a potpourri of Toronto's artistic community: composers, film producers, dancers, actors, and visiting guitarists. For me, these were memorable events, and my parents made sure to introduce their daughter to all the interesting characters who congregated there, even though I was always the youngest. Music, food, and wine ensured that the festivities lasted well into the early hours. The composer Harry Somers waxed poetic, Malka and Joso sang folk-songs, and David Phillips and Paula Moreno made the walls quiver with fiery flamenco music and dance. At one of these gatherings, Julian Bream, my musical idol, momentarily fell from grace. Intoxicated on Eli's spiked punch, he lunged after me until I pushed him off; then, teetering precariously over the wooden bannister, he proclaimed in his strong cockney voice that all these guitar-society parties were "nothing but a f—— bloody bore." Even the top classical guitarist in the world had to let off a little steam from time to time. Although he had insulted his hosts and offended the guests, we forgave; his down-to-earth humanity somehow endeared him to us all the more.

A year or so later, Bream conducted a ten-day master-class in Stratford, Ontario, for which I was selected from an audition tape. About thirty people were allowed to audit the classes, in which fifteen performers sat in a semicircle around the maestro. I judiciously positioned myself near to what appeared to be the end of the line, but to my consternation, he started with the students on my side. The first boy excused himself, complaining of a broken nail, and the next one muttered that he would prefer to play later, having just changed his strings. Then Bream's eyes alighted on me, leaving me no option but to play first in front of all the intimidating onlookers! Shy in those days, I would find butterflies fluttering in my stomach even while playing for friends. To make matters worse, a film crew was taping the master-classes; two cameras zoomed in close as my weak legs propelled me towards the empty seat next to Bream. But as soon as the Chaconne by J. S. Bach started to flow from my fingers, I forgot about everything else. It was then one of the most difficult pieces in the guitar repertoire, having been written originally for violin. Fortunately, Bream seemed favourably impressed. We tackled it section by section, as he expounded on stylistic issues and improved some of my fingerings while relating amusing anecdotes about his own career. Two of the greatest qualities in Bream are his passion for music and his British sense of humour. After the shock of having to play first, I relaxed, enjoying the opportunity to soak up some of the vast musical knowledge emanating from the master sitting before us.

One afternoon, after Bream had trooped us down to the banks of the Avon River to conduct his class alfresco, the famous sitarist Ravi Shankar joined us on the grass. Seeing me struggling with a bar chord, Bream examined the dint on my left index finger. "You're going to have one hell of a time with bar chords, Liona," he observed. In contrast to most players, whose first fingers are flat and can depress all six strings, I had to adjust fingering in order to compensate for the uneven physiology of my finger. But if the guitar great Django Reinhardt could make magic with only three fingers, who was I to complain?

A public recital at Stratford's Festival Theatre was arranged for Bream's top students. Selected along with four other pupils, I decided to play the Prelude from Bach's Cello Suite No.1 and Etude No. 7 by Heitor Villa-Lobos. It was a noon-hour concert, but I rose before dawn to practise warm-up scales in preparation for the ordeal ahead. At the theatre, on whose intimidating stage I had admired the performances of William Hutt and Martha Henry, we chosen ones were pretty nervous, as this was our first real concert and a music critic from the Toronto *Globe and Mail* was coming to review our playing.

Assiduously, I polished and tuned my guitar, then ran through the two pieces a few more times for luck. Liona Boyd was to be the third student to play. The concert had already started when some ragged string lengths at the tuning pegs caught my attention. Thinking the guitar looked a little unkempt for the cameras, I borrowed a pair of nail-clippers to tidy it up. My nerves must have already been jumping like yo-yos as, to my absolute horror, a loud snap signalled that I had just clipped off the upper portion of the second string. I now had a five-string guitar and only a few minutes left. Frantically running around backstage like a chicken with its head cut off, I looked for Bream and breathlessly told him of the disaster. There were no spare strings in my guitar case as being inexperienced at performing in public, I never imagined the need for them. After a few panic-stricken moments, I seized upon a tangled ball of old trebles in a classmate's guitar case and, with trembling fingers, filched out a second string to wind onto my instrument. Miraculously, it held its pitch. A new one would have kept stretching out of tune, as it takes hours for a string to settle in. With thumping heart, I performed my two selections perfectly.

In the documentary, my calm stage presence completely belies the self-inflicted backstage drama. To quote the old axiom, "Mistakes are made to learn from"; only through each unpleasant experience can one know how to prevent them in the future. To this day, I always make sure to carry a supply of extra worn-in strings and am meticulous when trimming the ends! A Cuban, Mario Abril, who ripped through Isaac Albéniz's flashy piece "Asturias," received raves from the music critic, while I was dismissed as having little promise. Not one of those students succeeded in building a performing career, and mine certainly came close to a calamitous takeoff!

5

Mexican Adventure

In June 1967, the Boyd family embarked on a grand adventure. We were going to live in Mexico, as my father had been granted a year's sabbatical to study art at the Instituto Allende, an international school of fine arts. In our atlas, San Miguel de Allende was only a grey dot lost in the central plateau of Mexico. At first, it seemed unthinkable that we were actually planning to move there for an entire year, upsetting our normal schedules, abandoning our schools and friends, and leaving behind the familiarity that held our days together. My parents started to play *mariachi* records during the dinner hour, poring over highway maps and tossing out Spanish phrases to each other. Vivien and I looked forward to the exotic change of scenery, but we were unable to imagine how we could survive without the usual props that supported our daily routines. One of my greatest concerns was that we would be deprived of "our" music; after all, we were children of the sixties and the innovative pop and folk-songs of the era were being indelibly etched into our teenage psyches.

During the week prior to leaving, I painstakingly taped all my favourite records: the Rolling Stones, the Beatles, Gordon Lightfoot, Donovan, and of course, the master song craftsman of the decade, Bob Dylan. Beethoven, Mozart, Segovia, and Julian Bream took their places beside Mick Jagger's "Going Home" and "Lady Jane."

When we reached the date on the calendar with the huge red circle, my family piled into the blue VW bus that was to carry us fifteen hundred miles south into the unknown, towards that remote dot in the atlas. In true sixties style, we had painted colourful flowers on the van's interior and designed an ornate sign that read "Toronto to Mexico" for the back window, to share the adventure with fellow motorists. Our lumpy luggage, which was roped to the roof, included essentials for a year's survival: blankets, canvases, paints, books, clothes, a Spanish dictionary, and a home-made butterfly net.

Damien, who had developed a keen interest in entomology, had been busily studying all the beetles, spiders, and butterflies he hoped to collect in the "land of the plumed serpent." Every time we set up camp, he erected a white sheet and an ultraviolet spotlight to lure any nocturnal creepy crawly in the vicinity. Vivien and I grimaced at the gigantic bugs he plucked off the sheet, but I felt sorry for the fragile moths and butterflies that he "put to sleep" within his chloroform jar. They flapped helplessly inside my brother's glass prison, as he rattled off their Latin names and made a dated entry in his log while assuring us they felt no pain. It was the beginning of an enormous collection he still treasures to this day.

We continued southward along endless, tidy highways through the undulating countryside of Missouri and Tennessee to the flat terrain of Texas, where the sky expanded to meet the horizon, until, after San Antonio, one solitary empty highway dissecting the parched desert led onward to the Rio Grande. We made camp under the stars to the deafening chorus of the night creatures: tree frogs and cicadas. As the fireflies danced around us, my father added a sense of drama, broadcasting his beloved tape of Carl Orff's *Carmina Burana*. I felt adrift, adventure beckoning and destination unknown. My old world was beginning to crumble; the familiar was giving way to the new.

After several days of journeying, the skyline of Laredo appeared out of the dusty plain. Excitedly, we motored up to the customs area, where Mexicans waited patiently with bulging bundles and silent children. Order gave way to apparent disorder as officious immigration authorities with curling black moustaches dispensed visas with exaggerated authority. Then, with passports stamped, we were ready to enter another world.

Our trusty VW rumbled us across a hundred miles of scrubland, through the twisting mountain passes to Matehuala, where human-like forms of the great Joshua trees beckoned us along empty desert roads to the state of Guanajuato. Approaching San Miguel after five days of travel, I became aware of a worried expression on my mother's face. She had noticed the small homes of crumbling adobe. "How am I ever going to live in one of these dilapidated places for a year with John and the children?" I could almost hear her muttering to herself. We drove up and down bumpy cobblestone roads observing *reboso*-wrapped women and sombreroed menfolk leading burros laden with chopped wood. How quaint and charming — most certainly different from Toronto — but where could we ever find a place to live? We motored into the central town square, or El Jardín, where people strolled or sat enjoying the afternoon sunshine. Vivien and I jumped out dressed in our miniskirts, which immediately elicited a fusillade of wolf-whistles. Damien scurried around the flowerbeds of the Jardín looking for stray scorpions, while my parents searched for a one-legged man whom they had been told was the rental expert. Receiving inquisitive looks from the locals, my father resuscitated his Castilian Spanish and my mother tested her University of Toronto version.

Our initial impressions of the housing situation had been entirely wrong. Disintegrating adobe walls and cracked paint often hid exquisite homes with ornamental fountains, marble staircases, and tiled patios where pots of vermilion geraniums, exotic succulents, and magenta bougainvillea vines cascaded in riotous profusion. At the Instituto, a young American welcomed Vivien and me, pinning yellow sunflowers in our hair. We already sensed we were in for an exciting year.

Investigating the local market, we picked our way through piles of ripe bananas, papayas, avocados, mangos, and tomatoes. "*A peso la pila!*" the young vendors shouted, waving a sample of the produce and smiling effusively at my sister and me while women with tiny, silent babies squatted on straw mats amid the despined cactus leaves and maize tortillas. At the interior stalls, one could sit on wooden benches to eat hot stew ladled from copper cauldrons. "Señora," a portly cook called to my mother as he scooped up a skinned sheep's head complete with its grinning teeth from his boiling brew. "*No gracias, señor,*" she volunteered, thankful she had brought us up as vegetarians!

Strung across the road flapped a canvas banner advertising a classical guitar concert to be held that night. What incredible luck! Vivien and Damien opted out, but my parents and I arrived promptly at the Bellas Artes concert hall for an eight o'clock performance. We were the first comers; by nine o'clock, however, the little hall was filled to capacity. Now I appreciated the expression "Mexican time"! The Bellas Artes, an imposing colonial building dating from the previous century, housed a fine-arts school. Two-tiered arched stone cloisters enclosed a rectangular courtyard at whose centre obtruded a stone fountain shaded by the scented foliage of lime and orange trees — the perfect setting for a concert.

After the program, by one of Mexico's top classical guitarists, Manuel López Ramos, we were invited by some American residents to a reception in a magnificent home on the hillside with a breathtaking view of the town. Parched, I gulped a drink, unsure of its alcohol content. Suddenly, the room slid out of focus as if viewed through the wrong prescription lenses. Too late I realized I had just swallowed a strong rum and Coke. With the high altitude intensifying the effect of the alcohol, and being an "impossible drinker," I was doubly afflicted. My mother walked me around in the flood-lit garden, encouraging me to take deep breaths, and ordered a cup of black coffee. Luckily, when the maestro wished to hear me play, my fingers found their frets for Sor's Etude No. 11 and Torroba's "Suite Castillana," although my head was still swimming in the stratosphere. *Borracha* or not, I seemed to have made a favourable impression on López Ramos, who invited me to study with him.

A month later, after we had established residence in San Miguel, my mother and I took the three-hour bus trip to Mexico City, where Ramos proved a disappointment. "Which method did you study, my dear?" he asked. "Sor, Aguado, Carulli?" I replied that my teacher, Eli Kassner, used various method books from which he chose suitable pieces. "Nonsense, you need to learn a specific method so that you can pass it on to others. You students all imagine you are going to be performers, but you all end up as teachers — especially you girls. I shall prepare you to become a teacher." Already playing an advanced repertoire, I definitely intended to perform rather than instruct, so after watching Ramos pencil three pages of simple exercises from one of his "method" books, I paid my three hundred pesos, vowing I could make better progress under my own tutelage.

Out of curiosity, I tracked down a local guitar teacher in San Miguel. He looked like a fairy-story troll; hunch-backed with limping gait aided by a walking stick, he had almond Asiatic eyes that smiled from a broad face generously sprinkled with moles and a fuzzy beard. The maestro, who had once studied with a student of Segovia, was the town's only classical guitarist. With my parents, I visited his home, a subterranean "troll" house under a bridge, which he shared with many fertile felines. Hoping to impress, he played a rather uneven Bach gavotte as we sat in his musty room with its one small open window. Our polite applause led him to launch into an impassioned Bach prelude, but at regular intervals he cleared his throat and, aiming straight through the window, spat past my mother and me. We exchanged glances, her eyes threatening me not to giggle. Finally, it was my turn to play a couple of numbers, but he continued these distracting displays of marksmanship. The maestro was a sincere and kindly fellow, but he was not destined to be my teacher.

My father had rented a Mexican-style house with a small enclosed patio and rooftop terrace that looked out over the town towards the distant purple mountains. Only a five-minute walk to the main town square, up a steep cobbled road, Calle de Umarán 58 became our new home. Twice a week, Porfiria came to sweep and swish buckets of water over our tiled floor, disturbing, to Damien's delight, stray insects that hid in dark corners. Within a few days, he had co-opted various gardeners at the Instituto to save him the most ferocious-looking specimens, which he proudly presented to us in jars at the dinner table. He persuaded my parents to buy a loquacious parrot, Loro, who rode around perched on his shoulders squawking at the local blackbirds.

No industry was permitted in San Miguel de Allende, which pre-served its sixteenth-century Spanish colonial style. The Mexicans treasured the town as a national monument — the birthplace of the 1810 revolution. The Jardín was dominated by an impressive European-style church, La Parroquia, built of pink sandstone whose rich hues changed with the sun's rising and decline. In front of this baroque monument, the Jardín bustled with activity: shoeshine boys, urchins selling Chiclets, tortilla vendors, and country folk peddling their wares. I spent many an hour on the wrought-iron benches imbibing the clean mountain air under a daily blessing of blue skies. We discovered a quiet, treed area, El Chorro, where underground mountain streams provided the town's water supply and chattering women gathered to wash clothes, laying them on the stone walls to dry. Across from El Chorro, in the French Park, tall white lilies grew beside a redolent stream, boys played soccer in the dust, and young couples sat with their arms intertwined behind the gnarled trunks of eucalyptus trees. The night skies, adazzle because of the high altitude and pure air, flaunted millions of diamonds that twinkled down on us during nocturnal family walks through the winding, darkened streets. Never had the Milky Way appeared so brilliant! We were falling in love with this quaint hillside town, which was beginning to feel like home to the Boyd family.

In San Miguel, two thousand of the fifteen thousand inhabitants were non-Mexicans, who, like our artist friend Leonard Brooks, enriched the colourful local culture with such activities as string-quartet recitals. It was with Leonard's ensemble that I first sight-read a Haydn quartet. The town boasted an English library, which enabled me to discover the writings of Jean-Paul Sartre, James Joyce, Ayn Rand, and E. M. Forster. Many afternoons found me eagerly devouring Lawrence Durrell's *Alexandria Quartet* in the cool, shaded corners of El Chorro. The jovial doorman at the Bellas Artes, in return for the odd bottle of tequila, allowed me to stay on during the siesta time. The entire quiescent former convent was mine alone for two hours each afternoon. I played my guitar, listening to the rich reverberations from the old stone walls, to the accompaniment of the courtyard fountain, which splashed rainbows into a tiled pool. A delicate scent of citrus blossoms hung in the still, warm air as I learned "Recuerdos de la Alhambra," Tárrega's haunting tribute to another timeless palace.

Mischievously, I smuggled Bernardino, a piano-playing friend, into my secret retreat during siesta hour. After he had entranced me with a soulful Chopin nocturne, we clambered onto the roof through an old trapdoor I had accidentally discovered. Inching our way along the red slate tiles, we were able to peek down unseen into the adjacent gardens where Carmelite nuns spent their cloistered lives. Silently, we watched the girls pinning up sheets to dry and wondered how they could live severed from the rest of the world in this nunnery unchanged over the centuries. Discovering that our white pants were covered with rusty-red stains from sliding along the rooftop tiles, Bernardino and I tried in vain to disguise the incriminating evidence by rubbing in white chalk, which only turned them bright pink! After siesta, when the heavy wooden doors creaked open and people began to wander around, I sidled past the old doorman, hoping he did not notice how my pants had miraculously changed colour.

One sunny winter morning, while strolling to the Los Dragones restaurant for our habitual cup of *café con leche*, my family and I were approached by an animated Mexican prattling away in a mixture of English and Spanish. He beckoned us to follow him through the shadows of a narrow doorway.

"My name is Miguelito Malo," he announced, an intense stare projecting from his Pekinese-like face. Suddenly we were standing in the most amazing archaeological museum, where ceramic bowls, pipes, and figures were displayed in rows of glass cases. What an unlikely place for such a cache of pre-Columbian art. Our eager host explained how this was the result of his years of archaeological excavation. We listened in fascination as he told us how his passion for archaeology had been born when, as a youngster, he had unearthed a clay artifact, which his Catholic mother had seized from him and flung far into the cacti. "Those things are the work of the devil and should never be touched by God's children," she scolded. Thus began his obsession with the ancient and mysterious gods from an earlier civilization.

As he grew older, Señor Malo secretly excavated these strange treasures that lay concealed beneath the desert's dusty face, until he eventually possessed one of the most important collections in the country. A few years later, we learned the terrible fate that befell Miguelito Malo. Mexico City authorities demanded that he hand over the priceless collection to the National Museum of Anthropology and threatened to confiscate it all. Miguelito, who had devoted himself to the care of the relics of his Indian antecedents, in his frustration and despair took a hammer to his cherished artifacts, returning them to the dust from which they came. After destroying everything, he shot himself there among his broken dreams. It was one of the tragedies of the town.

We became acquainted with a family whose undernourished burro provided their sole source of survival. Every day they walked miles over arid scrubland carrying bundles of firewood on the back of their beast of burden. The husband used to take his few pesos profit and head off to drown his sorrows in the *cantinas*, while his patient, diminutive wife waited on the sidewalk, with baby in arms and ragged children clutching her long skirts. My parents bought them medicine and donated clothes gathered from our closets. It was our small effort to assist one family with the poverty that Mexico's country-folk endure. The sickly baby at her mother's breast grew over the years into a slight doe-eyed girl; on successive visits, we saw her selling tortillas on the market floor. She had survived her impoverished childhood, but at fifteen died giving birth. The wizened little grandmother was now having to nurse yet another baby — her daughter's. Such tragedy and suffering were woven into the fabric of the peasants' daily lot; I could only marvel at their resilience and fortitude as their smiling faces accepted the harsh life doled out to them.

Our town was home to an amazing number of weird and wonderful characters: garrulous Larry from the cement jungles of the Bronx, living in a state of euphoria among San Miguel's natural vegetation; the svelte southern gentleman who furnished his living room with coffins; the paraplegic rock guitarist pushed around in a wheelchair by his devoted mother; the epileptic newspaperman bellowing animal sounds; the sometimes psychotic painter staring with vacant smiles at the Parroquia. Sharing the sun with us, they enriched my "people repertoire" with the great varieties of humankind. Our town had become a haven for artists and writers: a crucible of interesting ideas and lifestyles. It was here we met Neal Cassady — Kerouac's model for his "beat" hero, Moriarty, in his book *On the Road.* A few weeks later, his body was discovered beside the railway lines. Death in San Miguel from exposure and too much liquor somehow befitted his legendary nomadic lifestyle.

The renegade Canadian writer Scott Symons turned up in town. We spent Christmas Day in his home, a rented chapel, sipping pulque with an odd assortment of friends. Scared by an outbreak of hepatitis and a reluctance to visit the local doctor, they lined up the next day for gamma globulin injections administered by my mother and sister, who were adept at giving allergy shots. But after a few weeks Scott and his young lover were fleeing south, with the Mexican police hot on their tail trying to catch and deport them. The two men vanished for months to the safety of the wild southern hills of Oaxaca, their only "crime" an unacceptable love affair. Symons's boyfriend came from an influential Canadian family who intended to rescue him from the clutches of this "latter-day Oscar Wilde." Months later, by cover of night, they turned up at our door, furtively heading for the border to return to Canada, where Symons's new novel, *Place d'Armes*, had been awarded the Beta Sigma Phi First Novel Award. My father helped repair their old car's headlights and sent the fugitives on their way, Scott having entrusted his precious new manuscript to us in case of capture by the *Federales*. There was never a dull moment in San Miguel; the days were filled with intriguing events — a far cry from the equanimity of my Toronto high-school life.

Into my world drifted a continuous stream of bizarre characters worthy of the pen of Guy de Maupassant. An English poet with aristocratic connections and a tendency to stutter took a fancy to me, and invited himself to our house. "Good gracious, no dinner!" he exclaimed in plummy Oxford English, to the consternation of my mother, who endeavoured to throw something together for him to eat while Vivien and I giggled in the kitchen and my father plied him with literary conversation and tequilas. We attended one of his poetry readings, but the combination of alcohol and nerves ensnared him in his own words, such that the aristocratic bard was unable to complete his masterpiece and slunk off through a side door with a beet-red face. An invitation to model for a local charity fashion show flattered me, but decked out in an oversize sailor suit and clutching a large pink paper flower, I self-consciously dashed between tables to the wolf-whistles of dark-suited businessmen, zigzagging along the circuit like a panicky jackrabbit in the high-beams of an oncoming car. The embarrassing experience left me vowing never again to participate in such an ordeal. So much for my debut as a model.

Liberal with reading matter and movies, my parents were strict in matters of dating; Vivien and I had 10:00 p.m. curfews that extended to 11:00 p.m. for fiestas. Mexican girls were chaperoned, as marriages were customarily arranged between families, so we *gringas* were much sought after by San Miguel's teenaged boys. My first unintentional "conquest" was the dashing occupant of a green Mustang that flashed around the Jardín. There was a certain feeling of security in the company of Jaime Fernández, the bright and attractive son of the ex-governor of the state, but that relationship was soon nipped in the bud. His experience at Hot Springs High School in Arkansas had evidently given him certain expectations of North American girls, and at seventeen I had no intention of losing my virginity in the back seat of anyone's green sports car!

Eventually we met two friends, Raphael and Emilio, who escorted us around town, helped improve our Spanish, and danced away many evenings with us at La Escondida while our heads pounded with the music. Often our parents joined us on the dance floor, while little Damien sat riveted by the local rock group, Los Finks. One night, after a gun-slinging shoot-out, we beat a hasty backdoor retreat. Another day, buckets of water and bricks were dropped on us from the overhanging rooftops, narrowly missing Vivien; Raphael's enraged betrothed had discovered he was dating my sister. Life in Mexico had its own particular hazards.

Whenever a birthday or Saint's day rolled around, we were awakened in the early-morning hours by *mariachi* music floating up through our open windows. My father always crept downstairs and balanced his hidden microphone next to the window in order to preserve the performances for posterity. At times the local police who patrolled the night streets arrived to demand a serenade permit, but after a few swigs from the communal bottle of tequila, the officers invariably overlooked this formality, contributing their voices to the off-key strains of "Adoro" or "Cuando Calienta el Sol." Serenades from our Mexican admirers were a romantic experience of which we never tired.

There was a nip in the air as my mother, Vivien, and I wound our way through the chiaroscuro of wet-washed streets to the opalescent dawn of open desert on the edge of town. The massive church of San Antonio stood solitary among scattered maguey cacti, and travel-weary pilgrims flagellated themselves with straw whips and crawled on bloodied knees towards the stone steps. The dusty plain soon filled with a milling throng of devout peasants, curious onlookers, tortilla vendors with smoky braziers, and sellers of garish-coloured drinks which competed for brilliance with towers of dancing balloons. Suddenly, shrieks rent the air. An enraged bull destined for the *corrida* had broken its tethers and was charging straight towards us! A fear-inspired burst of energy enabled the three of us to leap into a cattle-truck standing at least six feet high! We looked at each other in disbelief at our amazing acrobatics while the crowd observed in silent amusement.

Our Mexican boyfriends took us horseback riding at the local ranches, biking to villages where women scrubbed clothes in the river, and, secretly, exploring in the damp catacombs deep beneath the Parroquia. On most evenings we joined in the communal stroll, or *paseo*, circling the Jardín: girls walked in one direction holding hands, while boys walked in the opposite, each group surveying the other. On fiesta nights, highly decorative, highly dangerous fireworks often injured the macho youths who dared each other to pick up exploding fragments of *castillos*. Relishing San Miguel's tapestry of novelties, my family fully immersed itself in this strange, rich culture.

One day my brother came home with a box concealing a tiny field mouse given to him by a friendly gardener at the Instituto. "Should I tell Mummy or keep it a secret?" he asked. As I predicted, our indulgent mother allowed him to keep little Federico in his room. In the evenings, after racing around the house, he returned, tempted by his treat of Chihuahua cheese. One night, while we sat in the fire-lit living room, my mother and I knitting sweaters, Vivien reading her horse book, my father glancing at "El News," and Damien spreading his butterflies to the Mexican music playing on the radio, we saw little Federico scurry in front of the fireplace. The next moment he was on the couch, and no sooner had he put in an appearance there than we spotted him running along the window-sill. Suddenly we realized there were many Federicos sharing our address. My father, using the lettuce shaker, devised a humane trap from which each day a whiskered captive was released at a distance from the house. The Mexicans laughed as they saw him walking down the hill with his home-made contraption, trying to appease the compassionate concerns of his children!

Vivien rode daily on a horse entrusted to her by an absentee owner. Clinging to her waist, I sometimes joined her to plod over stony, cactus-sprinkled desert and mountain-goat trails. Once she was set upon by wild dogs, forcing her against a prickly pear cactus. Valiantly, she limped home with bloody legs after spending hours extracting the thorns from her horse's flank. Damien and I watched in horror as my father tugged with his steel pliers at the barbed spines deep in her legs.

In 1967 everyone in the art world, on whose periphery we lived, seemed to be dabbling with mind-altering drugs. My liberal parents reluctantly decided to allow Vivien and me to quell our curiosity by smoking marijuana once, "just for the experience." Seeing the burned-out, stoned faces of many American kids who came to Mexico looking for cheap "grass" and "magic mushrooms," they thought they should confront the San Miguel drug scene rather than run the risk that we might be tempted to experiment on our own. One evening, after Damien had been put to bed, we turned on our favourite Simon and Garfunkel tape and rolled a couple of joints from a small packet of "Acapulco gold" my father had been given by a fellow artist; neither he nor my mother had ever tried grass before. Amid giggles, we puffed and choked on the acrid smoke, trying to convince ourselves the music sounded different, but eventually we had to admit our efforts were futile and slunk off to bed with sore throats. The Boyds' valiant attempt at psychedelia had been a bust; my parents thankfully threw away the dry leaves and never touched the weed again. Years later, while at university, I sampled hashish with equally dismal results. As a last resort, at my brother's urging, I fried an entire home-grown marijuana plant, which I ate with honey. My mother never could understand why her frying pan smelled so odd! As nothing seemed to work on my impervious brain, I lost interest in the whole experiment. Since then I have never felt tempted to experiment with any kind of hallucinogenic drug.

Our family was frequently invited to attend exhibitions and art-gallery openings. San Miguel's natural charms, perfect climate, reasonable cost of living, and stimulating community had seduced painters and sculptors from around the globe to pursue their creative muses in the tranquil hillside colony. That year I gazed at thousands of paintings: some were disturbing or incomprehensible to my young eyes, some were bland and meaningless, yet others spoke to me of the artist's spiritual quest for beauty and truth. I watched Lothar Kestenbaum perfecting his figurative bronze sculptures; saw Dan Brennan, a modern-day Gauguin, struggling to capture shapes and colours in his passionate canvases; observed with fascination the talented hands of Jesus Cuellar, the Gómez brothers, Louis Reiback, James Pinto, York Wilson, and Leonard Brooks. Absorbing the massive earth-tone murals of the Bellas Artes, I sensed the influence of Mexico's master muralist, Diego Rivera; in awe, I gazed at the huge wall painting by Siqueiros that dominated one of the rooms. In our town, art made its presence felt everywhere.

My father devoted his time to palette knife and paint brushes on his rooftop eyrie, while my mother made charcoal drawings sitting on the stone steps of the market-place. In the evenings, while fingering the Castelnuovo-Tedesco guitar pieces sent by Eli Kassner, I could hear them printmaking together on the kitchen table. Their art and the art of San Miguel was opening up a new awareness in my psyche, engraving a profound and lasting imprint on my life. It was to be many years, however, before I was tempted to develop my own artistic talents.

Nineteen sixty-eight was the year Mexico hosted the Olympic Games, and government orders had been issued to "clean up the country" in time for its deluge of international visitors. This decree was reinterpreted by our local authorities to mean "Rid the town of all the hippies." The San Miguel police were a sinister-looking breed of Lilliputians in dark blue uniforms who, armed with rifles, patrolled their headquarters in the Jardín. Nobody trusted them in those days; both Mexicans and *gringos* were fearful of an encounter. Since the police were paid so poorly, they supplemented their incomes with bribes and false arrests. This was to be their field day! Gerard, and Peyote Pete and Crazy Carl, were implicated in drug-possession charges, rounded up, and paddy-wagoned back across the border, but our neighbour, furious that his maid had taken it into her own hands to throw his precious marijuana away with the trash to protect him, set off to the local garbage dump in a vain effort to retrieve it. The police were having a marvellous time. They decided that anyone with long hair or beards, including many of our own friends, must be tidied up, so they were seized one by one to have their heads shaved in public. My brother and father had to lie low for a few days while the sacrificial blood-letting ran its course. After the son of a New York psychiatrist was dragged in by police for an unexpected haircut, making headlines in *The New York Times*, things gradually settled down again. All this unpleasant activity had given us an uncomfortable week, making us realize that our Shangri-La had its dark side too.

After six months, complying with the law, we motored up to the Reynosa border to renew our tourist visas, but when we returned, we were told no hippies were being allowed into Mexico and were given a curt refusal of re-entry. We were hardly hippies, but the VW bus with painted flowers did nothing to help our image! After trimming a few inches off our menfolk's hair, we drove on to the next crossing. "*Buenas noches*, we were expecting you," the officious Mexican gloated behind his curling moustache, and forbade us entry. Off came another inch of the male Boyds' hair; we bundled back into the bus and headed off determinedly to the next checkpoint a hundred miles farther along the border. A Texan in front of us was forced to hand over a fistful of greenbacks to the corrupt guards, who let us sail through without a hitch in the afterglow of their windfall.

In May, our VW bus spluttered us south to the steamy tropical port of Veracruz, where soothing marimba music filled the streets. Crossing the isthmus to the Pacific coast, we camped on the beach at La Ventosa, wandered in awe through the Oaxaca pyramids of Mitla and Monte Albán, were bitten mercilessly by sandflies in San Blas, and spent a glorious week camping in Pie de la Cuesta in Acapulco. Vivien and I befriended two flirtatious Jamaican boys from Montego Bay, with whom we shared fresh coconut and stolen kisses on the wave-washed sandbanks. Our next stop, Parracho, specialized in building guitars and guitar cases, causing the air to reek of drying fish-glue. Nearer to our San Miguel "home," we picked teeth off the floor of Guanajuato's claustrophobic tombs, where hundreds of skulls were piled high, and mummies with horrific facial expressions had been preserved by the volcanic soil. In the silver-mining ghost town of Pozos, we explored the ornate façades of old colonial mansions, the remains of churches open to the sky, and the deep echoing wells of abandoned mine shafts. Only the persistent desert wind rattled the town's old stones, and impudent cacti protruded through the crumbling walls.

Everywhere we travelled I religiously practised my guitar, learning new pieces by Alexandre Tansman, Sylvius Leopold Weiss, and Manuel Ponce, which Eli sent by mail. Everywhere in Mexico there was music to be heard: it spilled out from jukeboxes in the open *cantinas* and lightened the work of the women as they swept the sidewalks. Boys sat in doorways picking out popular songs on cheap guitars, while the harmonies of trios floated over the walls from garden parties. Market-places and cafés were alive with *ranchero* songs pulsating from tiny transistor radios and as night fell *mariachi* players strolled through the Jardín. Frequent parades with legions of uniformed schoolchildren marched around the square to the repetitive notes of off-key brass bands spurred on by strident drums. Through the open doors of churches, the wailing chants of female voices could be heard; their music had an eerie, pagan quality, compelling in its intensity. At one nightspot, where they supplied indigenous musical instruments, we often participated until late into the night, learning the lyrics to traditional ballads while enjoying the sonorous voices and plaintive guitars. Winding our way home through the narrow streets, we sometimes turned a corner and encountered young fellows dressed in the gaily coloured ribbons and dark cloaks of medieval troubadours: an *estudiantina* group singing and playing in the traditional manner at the window of a sweetheart. Mexico had developed within me a lasting affection for the poetry of the Spanish language and the expressive rhythms of Latin music.

Thinking back to the days in San Miguel, I am haunted by the sounds — plangent bells from the pink Parroquia echoing over the rooftops of the town and floating up the hillsides telling the hours; corn tortillas crackling and spattering in roadside stalls; braying burros struggling up and down the cobblestones; street vendors calling out in their sing-song lilt; black clouds of querulous birds settling into the trees at dusk; and the happy strains of *mariachi* and *ranchero* music drifting from behind those colourful crumbling walls of adobe that I had grown to love.

6

The
Commitment

♭

In July 1968, we realized that our exciting year in San Miguel had suddenly come to an end. Dolefully, my parents packed up the contents of Umarán 58. My father rolled up the hundred canvases painted during his sabbatical leave, crated the metal sculptures, and proudly showed us his Master of Fine Arts degree from the University of Guanajuato, which was affiliated with the Instituto de Allende. Damien prepared cases of butterflies, cockroaches, scorpions, and two live tarantulas for his friends at the Royal Ontario Museum's department of entomology. As we danced to the sentimental strains of "Bésame Mucho" and "Adoro," Vivien and I choked tearful good-byes to our Mexican sweethearts. Were we really about to leave this magical place that now felt like home? Without our realizing it, our heartstrings had become attached to this quaint little town and the endearing eccentricities of her inhabitants. How would we be able to return to Canadian suburbia, where there would be no soulful *mariachis*, purple mountains, or crooked cobbled streets?

The VW bus was crammed to capacity, every square inch put to use in my father's scrupulous packing. To our chagrin, when we reached the Laredo border, the customs officials dismantled all the rooftop·packages and zealously seized a jar of seeds, to discover on further examination that their "drug" trophy was nothing more provocative than parrot food. My ten-year-old brother sat motionless with blanched face and saucer-like eyes. This time he was lucky; our feathered contraband, drunk on tequila, and ensconced beneath the butterfly net, made it all the way to Canada. It took all of us several weeks to readjust to Toronto. We missed the noise and smells of *el mercado* when shopping at the sterile supermarket, longed for the good friends we had left behind, and nostalgically replayed *mariachi* tapes from our exhilarating year south of the border.

Leaving San Miguel signified the end of my carefree adolescence and left me facing a dilemma. English literature had always attracted me, but classical guitar had become an intrinsic part of my life. Eli encouraged me to audition for the Faculty of Music at the University of Toronto, and after a prerequisite recital, I was accepted in the Bachelor of Music in Performance course. On the first day, we were required to harmonize "O Canada." I desperately tried to extract from my comatose brain anything concerning triads, parallel fifths, or major and minor intervals learned from my Royal Conservatory theory courses, and burst into tears before Dean John Beckwith. He reassured me that I would be placed with the other beginners.

On discovering that we were required to play keyboards, I rushed off to an old warehouse on Queen Street West to purchase a second-hand piano. As guitar-plucking nails are too long for piano playing, I always had a poor wrist position and resented the time this new instrument took away from my precious guitar practice. With determination, I studied music history, theory, composition, and analysis, but always felt disadvantaged in keyboard harmony, being the only student without previous piano experience. How I disliked all those complex rules of music theory — rules I follow instinctively when composing today. Of greater interest was sight-reading Schubert and

Haydn quartets in chamber-music ensembles, accompanying my fellow students Theodore Gentry, a counter-tenor, and Mary Lou Fallis, a soprano, in songs by Dowland and Villa-Lobos, and performing dissonant twelve-tone compositions and avant-garde creations following the trends in contemporary classical music.

In need of extra tutoring in harmony, I arranged for private lessons, which entailed early-morning streetcar rides to an eccentric teacher who taught me how to hum intervals and recognize various chordal patterns in Beethoven's symphonies, while grazing from glass dishes overflowing with candies and carrying on what sounded suspiciously like drug deals over the telephone.

Kathy Bogyo, a blonde-haired violinist of Hungarian extraction whose cellist sister married the renowned pianist Anton Kuerti, became my friend. Dashing off to recording sessions, she never had time to study music history, but was a natural at music harmony. During dictation exams, we draped our long tresses over the manuscripts; when the invigilating professor ducked behind his piano to play the next chord, I quickly glanced at her paper and copied the notes. In return, Kathy availed herself of my help with history essays and we both passed our classes with flying colours. This rare peccadillo of my youth proved advantageous, but to this day I remain hopeless at musical dictation. Kathy went on to play with the Saarbrüken Radio Orchestra in Germany, and her cellist sister, Kristine, and her husband run the Mooredale Concerts in Toronto.

Like paired species in the ark, most of the students in my class married one another during the four-year course. Those studious boys held no appeal for me, so I gatecrashed wine-and-cheese parties at the Graduate Students' Union and attended dances at the International Student Centre. Looking back, it was obvious even then that I was destined for a different lifestyle from most of my colleagues at the music faculty. All the major names in the classical guitar world came to Toronto for recitals, which I attended with religious zeal. The playing of Segovia, Yepes, and Bream inspired me, as did classes with Oscar Ghiglia and Alice Artzt. How exciting to be able to study with people who had given concerts around the world! Works by Manuel Ponce, Mario Castelnuovo-Tedesco, Alexandre Tansman, and Reginald Smith Brindle were added to my repertoire as my interpretive and technical abilities improved.

The faculty often arranged recitals where I played to small audiences at universities around Ontario, but my first major concert was presented by the Ottawa Guitar Society in 1970. Needing moral support, I persuaded my mother to accompany me to Canada's capital, about three hundred miles east. Fraught with pre-concert nerves, I feared a complete collapse before curtain time, but once I was onstage the music relaxed me and all went splendidly. The program, including Bach's "Chaconne" and Lennox Berkeley's "Sonatina," received a favourable writeup in the *Ottawa Journal.* En route to the airport our host insisted that we take in the city sights, including the residence of Prime Minister Pierre Trudeau, where we dutifully snapped a photo. Not even in my wildest imaginings could I have believed that within a few years I would be a frequent guest there.

When the first Communist Chinese delegation visited Canada, I was honoured to be invited to perform at a private dinner party for them in Toronto. Dr. Michael Kasha, president of the Molecular Institute of Biophysics in Florida, had developed a revolutionary guitar design and flew me to Colorado, Washington, and Florida to demonstrate his impressive new instruments. We were the guests of honour at several receptions after these American concerts, where I felt thrilled to be so doted on — all because I had plucked a few strings attached to a curved wooden box! What a fantastic way to make a living, I marvelled, as I was rowed through the Tallahassee mangrove swamps by Dr. Kasha's son and treated to a fine southern meal by his wife, Lilly. The seeds were being sown for my nomadic life as a performer.

Besides studying music, I took classes at the university in English literature, Spanish culture, Italian, and psychology, but never a day passed without two or three hours' practice on the guitar. For a Mexican friend, I laboured to compose a romantic theme for his short film *El Llanto del Gaviota* and recorded it using the excellent acoustics of our family bathroom! During warm summer evenings, I serenaded the neighbourhood kids while perched on our front-porch steps. The guitar had become so much a part of my daily routine that I never dreamed of leaving it behind, even on family outings.

Each summer we returned to San Miguel to continue our love affair with the quaint hillside town. Many of our golden *gringo* friends had moved on, yet the adobe walls and familiar cobblestones echoed with the comforting feeling of home. Like seasoned residents, we proudly showed the newcomers around the town. Escorted by Tony Ponce, a boy from the neighbouring town of Celaya, and Fernando, Vivien's bullfighter friend, my sister and I were often driven to the nearby sulphur springs of Taboada, where we floated around flirtatiously in the steaming water while the strains of *ranchero* music drifted through the jacaranda trees. On Sundays, *mariachi* groups added to my appreciation of the experience as I watched the guitar players finger their way through my favourite Mexican songs. The summers drifted by in a haze of art-gallery openings and fiestas.

Before we set off for Mexico each summer, my sister, who was studying dentistry, found temporary jobs: collecting dew worms on the golf course at night, or photographing kids on ponies. Not to be outdone in the workforce, I decided it was time to find a source of income. On the supermarket bulletin board, an advertisement of my skills as a classical guitar teacher soon netted a man and his daughter, who came for Saturday lessons, but ten dollars a week was not exactly impressive; I needed a "real job." A notice in the window of the restaurant in Westway Plaza advertising for a waitress caught my eye. I was offered the position and told to report for work the next morning. All evening I agonized over my decision, realizing that eight hours a day waitressing left precious little time and energy for guitar.

As the early-morning sun hit our little corner of suburbia, I made up my mind. I could not visualize myself balancing dinner plates and smiling for tips. Instead, I would experiment with a scheme dreamed up overnight. With guitar in hand, I set off by bus to the Kingsway, an affluent area just south of our neighbourhood. Walking bravely up the imposing driveways, I offered whoever answered the door a ten-minute recital, explaining that I was a music student earning next term's tuition fees. The curious homemakers invited me to play; one kind granny ironed away happily as I serenaded her with Tárrega's "Adelita." The carol-singing escapades of my youth had been good training; I made more money in four hours than I would have all week as a waitress! Sometimes I wonder if any of those women who listened so attentively later recognized me when they read about "Canada's First Lady of the Guitar." Eventually, for two evenings a week after my university classes, I taught at Eli Kassner's Guitar Academy, where I was assigned students of all ages. I enjoyed the challenge of inspiring my pupils and helping them learn the pieces and exercises that I had once struggled with. Looking back, I cannot imagine how I found time to teach, attend classes, prepare essays and recitals, practise piano and guitar, and still squeeze in concerts, dances, and parties. The days must have been longer then!

It was becoming obvious that I needed a better guitar, so one summer Eli suggested I travel to Madrid to hand-pick an instrument by the master luthier José Ramírez. The chance to visit my grandmother in Spain was an added bonus, as the years had been passing between us. I flew to Bilbao to spend a week in the company of my father's mother, sister, nieces, and an odd assortment of elderly Spanish relatives. Interminable dinners that lingered well past midnight, day trips to Santander, and excursions to my father's birthplace in Portugalete rekindled fond childhood memories of Spain's Basque province. My grandmother, Anita Boyd, spoke English with a Spanish accent as she recounted stories of her youth in Linares — the birthplace of Andrés Segovia — and of her only son, who had chosen to live in distant Canada. My grandfather, whose family tree could be traced back to Mary, Queen of Scots, had been spared in the trenches of the First World War when a bullet was deflected from his heart by a can of sardines in his knapsack. How fragile are our human destinies. But for a few sardines, I would never have existed!

On the train to Madrid, I shared a compartment with two elderly Spanish ladies. Fascinated by my playing, they invited me to stay at their house, thus eliminating my need for a *pensión*. A few guitar tunes for the hospitable *señoras* and their neighbours yielded free lodgings for four days!

Consulting a tourist map, I negotiated my way to Concepción Jerónima, where the famous guitars used by Andrés Segovia were sold. After introducing myself, I was led by an aristocratic Señor Ramírez to the auditing room. Five instruments were laid out for my evaluation. All sounded exquisite; it was going to be a tough decision. Each one had its particular appeal, timbre, tone quality, and balance. Ramírez repeatedly returned to listen in the doorway, congratulating me on my playing. "*Señor,*" I said apologetically, "this is very difficult, but I have narrowed it down to three. These two have wonderful trebles, but this one has a fantastic resonance in the bass notes." Then I asked, "Whose is that guitar in the glass cabinet?" "I keep her for a special performer, somebody who will make her sing beautifully on the concert stage. Would you like to try her, Liona?" he offered. I cradled the lovely guitar and began to play Eduardo Sainz de la Maza's "Campanas del Alba." Ramírez sat transfixed and breathed a sigh of appreciation as the last note died. "My dear young lady, it is obvious that you are destined to become a performer. If you want to buy her, she will be yours." I was over the moon! This was the guitar with the richest tone of all, and while playing I had been envying the future owner. With profuse thanks, I counted out my thousand dollars' worth of crumpled traveller's cheques, which I had earned from teaching, and promised that he would not regret having chosen me for his special guitar.

In their tiled patio, my Spanish ladies were treated to an inaugural concert on my new instrument. The next day, while exploring the winding streets, museums, and markets of Madrid, I was offered a guided tour by a bearded Harvard history professor, who also invited me to eat *paella* in an outdoor restaurant redolent with musty wine cellars and Spanish cigars. The following evening, José Ramírez and his family took me to a flamenco tableau, where in the small hours of the morning I was handed one of the brittle gypsy guitars. Perching precariously on a stool, I played Albéniz while the flamenco troupe cheered with Spanish *"Olés!"*

Guitar mission accomplished, I travelled by bus to Paris for a few days of sightseeing in the city I vaguely remembered visiting as a child en route to Spain. A raucous Galician bagpipe player ensured that no one on the bus slept more than forty winks. Our arrival on Bastille Day found the city in a festive frenzy. A Toronto friend had arranged for me to stay in the Montmartre apartment of a film-director friend of his who was away. Claiming the keys from the concierge, I dragged my guitar and suitcase to the third floor. Exhausted by the long trip, I slid between the satiny sheets of a double bed. Something cold and hard touched my foot; I reached down to see what could be concealed beneath the covers. In my hand lay a gun whose shiny metal surface glinted in the moonlight. In whose bed was I about to entrust my body and why the need for such protection? My heart quickened as I gingerly placed the pistol on the night table, bolted the windows, and checked the doors.

With four days to explore the City of Light, I set about learning the *métro* routes that took me to the Impressionists in the Jeu de Paume, the Old Masters of the Louvre, and the dusty guitar editions in Left Bank music shops. While strolling along the banks of the Seine, I was approached by a dark-eyed man who engaged me in conversation, intimating that he was a count with a château outside Paris. Never for a moment doubting his sincerity, I chatted away in high-school French over a croque-Monsieur lunch. I should have known better than to let myself be charmed by a dubious stranger picked up on the streets of Paris. But trusting only in the best of human nature, I naïvely let him walk me around until, as dusk began to fall, I realized I had no idea where we were. After mentioning I needed a phone to confirm my flight to England, I was ushered into a deserted office off a darkened courtyard. Before I knew it my "Count" had bolted the tall wooden door and was now looking upon me with the eyes of a predator who had just cornered his quarry. He lurched against me, pressing his mouth against mine, grabbing my breasts. My heart pounded with surges of adrenalin. What an idiot I had been not to have foreseen his real intentions! As he dragged me to the ground, I realized there was only one way to prevent being raped. Feigning passion, I panted, "Wait, I have a fantastic apartment, the best French wine, and sexy silk sheets. Let's go there to *faire l'amour.*" I prayed he would believe my heart was pounding with desire rather than pure terror.

Arm in arm, we started out along the winding back streets until we hit a boulevard filled with jostling students. I scanned the sidewalks, desperately searching for a *gendarme* to whom I could plead for protection. To my relief, a blue uniformed saviour eventually came into view and, grabbing on to him, I let forth a torrent of Kipling Collegiate French. Admonished by the law, the potential rapist fled the scene. Greatly relieved, I wound my way through the convoluted streets of Montmartre, but not without the paranoia of imagined footsteps, which kept my heart racing until the apartment doors were double-locked. From then on, I resolved to be more cautious when alone in strange cities. Perhaps the gun in the bed had been an omen.

Next stop was London. Under Eli's guidance, I had been learning "English Suite" by the guitar scholar and composer John Duarte, with whom I had arranged a meeting in England. Carefully guiding my precious Ramírez through the maze of the London underground, I travelled to his flat above a grocery store. Duarte chewed on his pipe as I played. "Mmm, not bad, my dear," he mumbled. "Don't tell me you're planning to be the next Segovia? Unless you started at age six and can run through all the repertoire by age fourteen, you haven't the foggiest chance of giving concerts! It's too bloody competitive, and girls seldom stick with it. Face the facts and become a teacher."

López Ramos's chauvinism was echoed by this dour Englishman, who spent the next two hours disparaging my guitar idols, Lagoya, Bream, and Williams. In disbelief, I listened to his negative assessment of the guitar world, depressed by his prediction that I would never play concerts. Perhaps it had all been a Pollyanna pipedream and Eli was too encouraging; after all, Toronto was a provincial backwater compared with London. Later, back at the home of my parents' friends with the prized Ramírez close to the bed, I felt weary and disillusioned. Had all my dreams of performing been nothing more than a misguided chimera? Duarte's words haunted me as I continued my courses at the University of Toronto.

Once my career took off, I crossed paths with him again. He wrote critical record reviews for the British press, dismissing my repertoire as pretty picture postcards. "Your programs should include more substantial contemporary works," he advised. To that end, he composed for me "Danserie Number Two" — so trite and musically unsatisfying that after learning it, I decided my audience would be better served without his contribution. Duarte is a gifted arranger and is often included on international guitar juries. We even maintained an intermittent correspondence, but I have to wonder to what extent his acidulous critiques have crushed the spirits of other budding performers. How easily my own faith might have been sabotaged had I taken to heart the barbs aimed at me over the years. One has to develop a thick skin to survive in this business of music, I was learning.

Each time the great Andrés Segovia came to play, I was enchanted by the delicately romantic interpretations of the elderly maestro. It was Segovia who had initiated a renaissance of the classical guitar in this century, inspiring a new generation of concert guitarists: John Williams, Narciso Yepes, Alirio Díaz, Oscar Ghiglia, and Christopher Parkening. Many of the well-known pieces of the guitar repertoire were dedicated to the great man by Rodrigo, Torroba, Castelnuovo-Tedesco, and Ponce. For years, people flocked to his recitals convinced it would be their last chance to hear the master, but amazingly, he always returned the following year, until his death in 1987, at the age of ninety-four. Segovia's concerts and albums inspired me profoundly, but because of his renowned rigidity in teaching, I was reluctant to participate in his classes. On several occasions, however, I had the chance to play for him.

Once, in 1970, Eli Kassner decided to attend a post-concert reception in Segovia's honour and take two of his prize students to show off before the maestro. Sometimes the last thing a concert artist wants to hear after performing is a student nervously plowing through guitar pieces. Segovia, however, graciously consented to listen to Eli's pupils. As Lynne Gangbar presented her pieces, I sensed that our maestro was tiring; perhaps he would rather pay some attention to his buffet plate than to another student. After I played "Madroños," which he applauded, I plunged into Castelnuovo-Tedesco's "Sonatina," on Eli's urging and against my better judgment. Segovia became redder and redder in the face, stomped his silver-tipped cane, and bellowed, "She is playing at twice the correct speed and has changed all my fingerings!" Then the enraged maestro stormed out and did not emerge from the bathroom for twenty minutes. Perhaps his famous temper had been inflamed by a bursting bladder. When a becalmed Segovia returned to "the scene of the crime," all seemed to have been forgiven as he congratulated Eli and me. In future, I promised I would slow down my fingers. This man's life was too precious for such shocks to his nervous system!

Segovia heard me play several times after that traumatic initiation; he was always most courteous and complimentary, never again uttering a harsh word. In New York, the day after my concert at Town Hall, after I had become a professional, he suggested I join him for coffee in his suite at the Westbury Hotel. "My dear, I do regret that I was not able to attend your concert last night," he said in that soft, old-world Spanish voice. "I was obliged to attend a dinner held in my honour." How immensely grateful I was for that dinner, as my nerves might have snapped had the great maestro honoured me with his presence at the concert. After coffee he invited me to play on his lovely Fleta guitar; what a privilege to feel his well-worn finger-board and strings beneath my fingers. "You play beautifully and with much expression, my dear. You will have a magnificent career," he said.

Then he wrote on a little card, "Through your beauty and talent you will conquer the public," adding as an afterthought, "philharmonic or not." How prophetic were those last three words. Segovia must have already sensed that my career would not be directed exclusively towards the symphony orchestra set. The old maestro had great intuition!

I, and the entire guitar world, was saddened at Segovia's death, yet I marvelled at what a fantastic life he had experienced. How fulfilling and rich his career had been, giving concerts that touched, and even changed, people's lives the world over. Segovia had struggled for recognition at the beginning of his career, withstanding years of prejudice and criticisms that the guitar was not a serious instrument. I admired his perseverance and dedication. If he was rigidly against classical guitarists delving into pop music, as did his student John Williams, or flamenco, as did his other protégé, Christopher Parkening, one has to keep in mind that after a lifetime fighting for the classical guitar to be accepted as a concert instrument, he resented its "debasement" in other styles. Even though he played in huge concert halls, he remained adamantly against amplification, insisting on natural sound. Most guitarists today have sacrilegiously embraced amplification, but Segovia was of another time, another generation. Whenever I feel jet-lagged from long concert tours, I wonder how a corpulent Segovia in his eighties and nineties used to survive a schedule that spanned the continents. How privileged I was to have shared even a few brief occasions with such a musical giant.

Fantasizing about a new guitar duo and hoping that a romantic chord might be struck between the American Christopher Parkening and me, Eli Kassner encouraged me to stay overnight and cook breakfast for his Californian house guest, who was just a year my senior. Parkening was Segovia's favoured prodigy and a rising star in the guitar world. That breakfast was one of my all-time culinary disasters. Sadly peering through toast smoke at his amorphous grey glob of rubberized eggs, he commented, "Geez, Liona, it sure is good you play the guitar." After going to see a movie together, we savoured a few friendly kisses on a park bench, but we were both too involved with other romances to pursue a relationship. Much as I adore Chris's playing and find him to be a rare and exceptionally generous human being, we would not have been the best match, as my horse-riding, bible studies, and fly-fishing skills are severely deficient.

For most of my university days I lived at home. During the day, guitar in hand, I hitchhiked to the subway, as the '70s were kinder and safer times. In my third year, deciding to reduce the time spent commuting, I rented a small lopsided room near the campus with a household of vociferous Hungarians. Living alone for the first time, I felt proudly independent and pleased with my decision to move away from the shelter of my family. On the very first morning in my new quarters, I was abruptly awakened by the unmistakable sound of a close gunshot. A drunken tenant had killed his landlord in the adjoining house, which was soon swarming with police officers. I wondered if I had perhaps made a mistake in exchanging the quiet of suburbia for this turbulent neighbourhood, but after this dramatic welcome, things quieted down. I played guitar in the morning hours before classes, and late into the evenings after cooking dinner on a grimy iron stove in the cellar. Realizing the entire house was a fire-trap, I secured a long piece of rope to a radiator beside the window, in case a creative exit from my rickety third-storey room became necessary.

It was easier, living downtown, to attend the opera, ballet, or symphony whenever my frugal budget allowed. An ensemble of singers, flute players, and a harpist from the University of Chile in Santiago came to give a concert on the campus, and I sat in the first row soaking up as much of their inspiring music as I could. In some sense, their music touched me more profoundly than much of the contemporary classical music I was studying, yet none of my professors or fellow students from the music faculty had deemed this performance worthy of their attention. Afterwards, the group whisked me away to a Latin night spot, where I faked my way through rumbas and tangos! There should be more to a music student's education than dissecting harmonic structure in Schoenberg's symphonic string quartets.

The muse aroused Peter Anson, an intense young poet, who wooed me with candlelit readings of Yevtushenko and harpsichord performances of Bach's *Goldberg Variations*. We lay in each other's arms as he recited the abstruse poems he dedicated to me, which were later published. However, *la donna è mobile*, and a few months later, it was Claude Emanuelli, an international-law student, who lulled me with his gentle Côte d'Azur voice reading *Le Petit Prince*. During my fourth year at the university, 1971–72, I entered the Canadian National Music Competition, where I won the first round of auditions and was chosen to travel to Trois-Rivières, Quebec, for the finals. Having never returned to *la belle province* since docking there as a child, I enjoyed the bus ride along the scenic banks of the St. Lawrence River: those very banks I had sketched as a ten-year-old to win both first and second prize in the SS *Ryndam* art contest. I was the only competitor opting to stay in a local seminary, and was ushered by the priests into an austere little room with a cross hanging above the narrow bed. How much more atmospheric it felt than a hotel. The alarm was set for six, but before it even had a chance to ring, the young novices roused me from sleep with their Gregorian chants, which floated sublimely through the stone cloisters. Luxuriating in this unexpected offering of sacred music, I crunched on some crackers I had brought along for breakfast. Perhaps their auspicious pre-dawn chorus inspired me. That day, I walked off with first prize.

One of the organizers, Eleanor Sniderman, wife of Sam Sniderman, owner of the Sam the Record Man stores, approached me after the awards ceremony in Toronto. "Would you like to make a record?" she inquired. I was speechless. "Thank you, but I am not at all ready for that and plan to continue studying," I replied. "Please call me in a few years." After rushing home to share the amazing news with my family, I phoned Eli. My teacher had said that one day I would make a record, but I had dismissed such flights of fancy. Although this tempting proposal had just been dangled before me, I wisely resisted, realizing it was premature. Ahead of me lay thousands of hours of scales to practise, technique to polish, and repertoire to conquer.

7

Paris à la
Bohême

𝄞

$\mathscr{A}$lexandre Lagoya came to play a concert in Toronto in 1965. The renowned French classical guitarist, born in Egypt of Greek and Italian parentage, had formed a guitar duo in 1955 with his French wife, Ida Presti; together they toured the world to international acclaim. After their concert, Eli Kassner held a reception at which I was given an opportunity to play for the charming French duo, never suspecting what a major role the maestro would play in my yet-unformulated career.

In 1967, a tragedy befell the guitar world when Ida Presti died suddenly of an aneurism in Rochester, New York. After several years had passed, Lagoya bravely resumed a solo career, which in October 1971 brought him back to Toronto. He remembered the girl with the long blonde hair who had performed a Bach bourrée for him and his wife six years earlier. Lagoya agreed to hear me play again and offered a private lesson at the Park Plaza Hotel. I stayed up late the night before, polishing pieces to present to my guitar idol. During the lesson we conversed in Spanish, since Lagoya's English was limited, as was my French at that time. With refined Parisian mannerisms, the forty-three-year-old maestro welcomed me to his suite, which was permeated with the smell of French cologne. Offering tips on phrasing and fingerings, he complimented me on my interpretations of a Torroba suite, and a Bach allegro that I had transcribed. Lagoya had developed a right-hand technique radically different from Segovia's regarding wrist position and the angle at which the nails strike the strings. He carefully adjusted my wrist to the right and showed me how the tones produced by that side of the nail were stronger and more even than those of left-side pluckers like Segovia and Bream. It would take time to apply such a drastic technical change to my advanced pieces. Was I starting to imagine things? Weren't Lagoya's hands lingering a touch too long on mine in demonstrating the wrist position? Didn't he lean over my shoulder a little too frequently? It gradually dawned on me that Lagoya was impressed by more than my prowess on the guitar. I cheerfully chatted on about nail shapes and string brands, trying to sound very matter-of-fact while my heart quickened. Before I left, he kissed me twice on the cheeks, as is the traditional French custom, and suggested I study with him at Mount Orford in Quebec the following summer. Thrilled that such an eminent guitarist had praised my playing, I resolved to practise harder than ever and apply his ideas to my pieces.

Two days later, my mother came breathlessly to tell me that Lagoya was calling "long-distance from Montreal!" He had just played concerts in Quebec and had two free days before continuing on to New York. Would I join him for dinner if he was to fly back to Toronto? He had photocopied some unpublished Bach transcriptions and would give me as many lessons as I could take in a day. What student could refuse such a tantalizing proposal? I felt flattered, intrigued, and a little nervous. To have the great Lagoya offering to teach me seemed a triumph. I was not so ingenuous as to think music was all the maestro had on his mind, but somehow even his romantic advances struck me as excitingly novel. He was infinitely more intriguing than the boys in my music classes, and at the back of my mind was the memory of his late wife, Ida, and their fantastic success as a duo. Could Lagoya be looking for another partner with whom to conquer the world? The irresistible fantasy flitted around my head like a skittish butterfly.

My sister and I had recently been lamenting the fact that, although now in our twenties, we were both still virgins! Surely by the age of twenty-two it was high time for some sexual adventures. In spite of all my teenage romances, physical contact had never progressed beyond necking sessions and passionate goodnight kisses in darkened doorways. Several boyfriends had "dropped" me after their amorous advances had been thwarted. Vivien and I agreed to set aside our self-imposed puritanism to find out what we were missing. After all, were we not children of the liberal sixties? In sisterly conspiracy, we promised each other this would be the year to relinquish our chaste condition. But to whom? Lagoya had definitely arrived at the right moment.

The maestro offered a long lesson on Bach followed by a candle-light dinner the first evening. The second I spent at the Park Plaza Hotel with him. Sheepishly, I had asked my mother whether she would mind my not returning until the next morning. To my surprise, she was supportive and even agreed not to tell my father. At last I would "become a woman" and enter the mysterious world of adulthood. The long-anticipated experience, although exciting and pleasurable, seemed somewhat of a let-down emotionally. I remember walking along Bloor Street, thinking, Is that all there is to it? How could anyone have ever equalled my imaginary passionate encounters with Rudolf Nureyev or Doctor Zhivago? Lagoya, thrilled that I had allowed him to be my first lover, promised many more musical and romantic lessons if I would come to study with him in Quebec and Nice. Only later did I discover that he was one of the world's indefatigable charmers, with countless conquests around the globe. Lagoya swore he had fallen madly in love with me, but having observed him over the years, I have to laugh at how naïve I was.

Vivien, most impressed by my sudden "loss of innocence" and not to be outdone by her sister, followed suit with a fellow student a week later!

In 1972, after the university examinations had been passed and my Bachelor of Music degree completed with honours, I packed my bags for the train ride to the Jeunesses Musicales du Canada summer school at Mount Orford, Quebec. My high-school French was proven pitifully inadequate when I found myself among a crowd of students speaking fast Québécois French. Wooded hills of maple and pine, warm shallow lakes, and the buzz of relentless mosquitoes defined those hot summer days at the camp, where classes were conducted in small wooden huts scattered around the rustic grounds. From the fifty guitar students, ten of us were selected for Lagoya's group, where he taught each student individually, working on interpretation and style, tossing out interesting historical comments about the composer and the time period, and impressing on us the superiority of his right-hand wrist position. I was assimilating so much information, making notes on pieces I enjoyed hearing other students play, and listening diligently to Lagoya's musical expostulations. What a great teacher he was!

During the afternoon siesta hour or after dinner, I was often summoned for a "private lesson." Lagoya would help me with particularly difficult fingerings and phrasings while perched on his narrow camp-bed, intermittently interrupting his instruction with declarations of *amour*. He amused me with stories from his days on the road with his late wife: their chaotic tours in Mexico, fights with dishonest impresarios, and meetings with famous composers. To me, Lagoya represented a wondrous world I thought I would never be part of. He confided secret thoughts about touring and recording, the agony of pre-concert nerves, and the ecstacy of a great performance. Lessons in music and lessons in love were combined by my skilled *maître de musique*.

A month later, I followed Lagoya to l'Académie Internationale d'Été de Nice in France, to spend two weeks in intense musical saturation. Students were housed in a circular building with small pie-shaped rooms. Young people from all over the world had come to study music, but the majority were guitarists wanting to work with Lagoya or flutists who had come to learn from Jean-Pierre Rampal. Occasionally I was invited to lunch with Lagoya and Rampal at their hotel, Le Petit Palais. The stories of Rampal's escapades made Lagoya's seem mild by comparison. The king of the flute had at his beck and call hundreds of sweet young things with stars in their eyes, to whom he taught more than music, according to my flute-playing room-mate. Never let it be said that classical musicians lead dull, celibate lives!

By then, I had met Monelle, Lagoya's attractive Parisian live-in girlfriend, with whom I was often taken to dine in the enchanting restaurants in Nice or St-Paul-de-Vence, the quaint hillside town once inhabited by Picasso and Chagall. My maestro had to behave himself with the lovely Monelle in tow; besides, I was developing a fondness for his tall, tanned, and bearded young assistant, Yves Châtelain. Lagoya talked to both of us about forming a guitar ensemble, but with the passing of time, our lives and careers flowed in such different directions that it became impossible.

As lessons were conducted in French, my ability with the language improved daily. Every morning I used to get up at six o'clock, before the other students were awake, and scurry down into the rose gardens to play for a couple of hours. If the gardeners chased me away, I tucked a paper tissue under my strings, ensuring that nobody's sleep would be disturbed. At eight, we scoffed crusty baguettes, unsalted butter, and blackcurrant jam, washed down with steaming bowls of *café au lait*. After breakfast, when the students rushed back to their rooms to practise, an ear-splitting cacophony of sound bombarded us from the windows of the residences — French horns, flutes, voice, and trumpets — each playing parts of different pieces or warm-up scales in various keys. At nine-thirty, we began the long climb towards the Franciscan monastery, Saint Cimiez, where Lagoya conducted his master-classes. Why did I not think to buy a lighter case, rather than haul my leaden airline travelling-case for forty-five minutes each way? No doubt it was purely a matter of economy as I was trying to save every franc. In those days, I had never heard of lower-back pain, chiropractors, or strained shoulders, and I resigned myself to the arduous daily task, envying the flute-players.

Lagoya sometimes singled me out to demonstrate his wrist position to the other students, and even asked me to contribute Albéniz's "Zambra Granadina" to an outdoor music festival in the picturesque hillside town of Gillette: my first performance using his technique. The new angle was beginning to feel comfortable, but for delicate tones the left side of the nail still sounded sweeter. When one is playing classical guitar, it is amazing how the tiniest difference in nail-length and shape alters the sound, and in contrast to the piano, where only one key corresponds to each pitch, many notes on the guitar can be found on three or four different positions, as well as several harmonic points. Before the right-hand fingers can pluck the note, the left-hand fingers have to determine the correct position on the fret-board; should they be a millimetre out of place the string will "buzz." Although a guitar is one of the easiest instruments on which to learn to strum a few chords, it is one of the most difficult on which to perform classical music.

My teacher was scheduled to begin an American tour, but insisted I come to live in Paris to continue our lessons. Yves Châtelain, talented guitarist and madcap driver, offered to take me in his old beat-up Citroën "Deux Chevaux." The French Alps provided a spectacular backdrop to the roadside stalls where we stopped to buy lavender-honey and imbibe flower-fragrant air. On a whim, after a week in Paris, we decided to travel to London astride his powerful new motorbike. We whizzed along highways and country lanes, I in a leather jacket, clinging to his waist for dear life. Surprising my parents, who were vacationing in England, we zoomed into London after crossing the Channel by ferry. What a novel experience to have suddenly become a "biker"! On returning to Paris, Yves asked if

I would like to live in an old château thirty miles outside the city. Friends of his parents knew the famous Dubonnet family, whose Château de Montgermont was vacant. An impecunious Canadian guitar student was welcome to stay there until more convenient lodgings could be found.

Through the verdant rolling hills of the French countryside, Yves drove me to a sight I could hardly believe. There, on top of a hill, circumscribed by wrought-iron gates, sat a magnificent château with copper turrets and curved stone stairways. On either side of this fantasy castle loomed mysterious woods, while in front spread undulating lawns with a daisy-fringed lily-pond. Was this splendid structure about to be mine? My spirit soared in a long glissando.

We crunched up the white gravel driveway and sounded the heavy iron knocker, which sent echoes from another age resonating from the interior. Tongue-tied with excitement, I followed the friendly Hungarian caretaker to my room. There was a velvet-canopied bed, a kitchen area, and a large bay window that looked into a courtyard where chickens were strutting around. I threw my arms around Yves and whispered that I would feel like Rapunzel living in this lovely dream château straight out of my childhood story-books.

Yves made weekly visits to replenish my food supplies and speed me into Paris for concerts or dinner. Apart from his visitations, which had become increasingly intimate, I spent two idyllic months in bucolic isolation. In the afternoons, I spread a blanket beside the lily-pond and serenaded the bullfrogs; late into the candlelit nights, I played my guitar to the hooting of owls in the shadowy pine forests. Camembert cheese, French bread, and farm vegetables bought at the local village provided sustenance, sometimes supplemented with succulent wild berries I picked from the bushes and marinated in sweet red wine. The old concierge must have wondered why this strange Canadian seemed content to live alone and play guitar for hours on end. One day I asked him if I could try to ride one of the horses I had befriended in a nearby field. He retorted that they were not for riding, but were there to be eaten! To my horror, my poor friends were destined for the *chevaline* stores, to be served up later with *petits pois* and *pommes frites*!

An unpleasant undercurrent seeped into those days of pastoral paradise. Having missed my period, I started to panic; Yves might have made me pregnant. Sure enough, my waist was expanding, but I never allowed myself to suspect that all that delicious French bread and cheese could be the cause. During sleepless nights, I cursed my carelessness. How could I have been so stupid? After another month, I wrote an embarrassed note to my mother asking if I should return home. "Darling, don't worry. It's probably just the change in environment," she replied, sounding a lot more confident than Yves, who commiserated over my plight. His friend knew a doctor who would perform an abortion if I wished, but knowing it was illegal, I had nightmares of some back-alley butcher hacking my insides to pieces. Preoccupied with this concern, I decided to visit a clinic in Paris for tests. The Tunisian doctor seemed more interested in conniving to get a date than solving my dilemma; in desperation, I sought out another clinic, where they X-rayed my lungs! These experiences diminished forever my faith in French doctors. I promised Yves, who shared my distress, that if the blessed "curse" ever arrived, I would take him out for a fantastic meal in a fine Paris restaurant. A week later, to my immense joy and relief, the problem resolved itself. I rushed off to find Yves, who was auditing a Conservatoire class given by Lagoya, who had just returned from his tour. I crept into the hushed classroom, where a student was struggling through a Villa-Lobos étude, and whispered to Yves that he would be treated to a gourmet dinner that night. Seeing the Cheshire-cat grins on our faces, Lagoya must have wondered what could be making his two prize students so happy on that cold November morning. How regrettable that my second month in the beautiful château of my dreams had been overshadowed by this unfounded fear. I later found out that the penicillin I had taken for a sore throat was probably to blame, but from that time on I felt great empathy for any woman in a comparable situation.

As Lagoya had returned to Paris, I bade *adieu* to my story-book setting and moved to a small room up ten flights of stairs on rue Gay Lussac in the Latin Quarter. Later I was offered a *chambre de bonne* (maid's room), up eight flights of circular backstairs in an elegant mansion located in the eighth *arrondissement* on avenue Velasquez and overlooking Parc Monceau, in return for giving an eleven-year-old, Marie-Odile, English, Spanish, and piano lessons. The room itself was as tiny as a closet, but as I was supporting myself on meagre student savings without any assistance from my parents, I was delighted to live rent-free. I do not know how I managed to haul the heavy guitar case up and down those countless winding stairs or endure the sagging mattress, whose sharp springs poked through its cloth covering, but I was young and full of the spirit of adventure. A small gas stove, one tiny reading-light with a frayed yellow lampshade, and a *toilette à la turque* down the hallway comprised my accommodation, *à la bohème*.

Adjacent to my hole in the wall lived a Guadeloupian woman from whose window drifted exotic unfamiliar spices and perfumes, while the apartment at the end of the corridor housed a noisy family of Spaniards who often invited me to strum a few chords in their garlicky kitchen. The room at the top of the staircase housed a young draftsman with long, red hair and bloodshot eyes who gave me generous bowls of hair-washing water because my tap ran icy cold. I persuaded Camille to take me by *métro* to the famous Parisian market, Les Halles, where at five in the morning we sipped steaming onion soup in the company of butchers and fishmongers in their traditional blue overalls. The market scene from *Irma la Douce* had come alive. Although Camille received occasional visits from a Moroccan girlfriend, he seemed a loner; much later it occurred to me that he was probably a drug addict. After losing his job, he sorrowfully predicted that he would end up joining those dishevelled souls sleeping in the *métro* or huddled around the outdoor heating vents. When Camille did not emerge from his room for several days, I tapped, then pounded, on the door until his unshaven, emaciated face blinked at me with vapid eyes and a voice that seemed to come from some far-away place whispered, "I am dying." I wrapped a blanket around his shaking shoulders and ran for help. The *police secours* lifted his ravaged body onto a stretcher while our concierge with her grey hair bun and sour expression looked on with utter disdain. Twice I visited the hospital, where a heavily sedated Camille lay in a tangle of intravenous tubes, but one day, I learned he had checked out, leaving no forwarding address.

Every other week, I hauled my guitar case through the madness of the Paris Métro to catch the train to Soisy Sud Montmorency, where Lagoya and Monelle shared a country-style home. After my monastic meals of bread and cheese, dinner *chez* Lagoya was a feast. Refusing his steak *tartare chevaline*, raw horse meat with onions, I stuffed myself with his spaghetti *flambé* and Monelle's home-made chocolate mousse, knowing two weeks would pass before the next gastronomic opportunity. He taught me in the living room, where his trophy from Canada, a huge polar-bear pelt, lay on the floor. My lectures against hunting endangered species fell on deaf ears.

With assiduous determination to master the instrument, I thought nothing of practising seven or eight hours every day. Several times, the great Spanish guitarist Narciso Yepes and the Venezuelan, Alirio Díaz, came to perform in Paris. After their concerts, since they knew me from the Toronto Guitar Society, they offered me some impromptu coaching. Once, Yepes had to come puffing up my eight flights of stairs in order to tell me that a lesson he had promised had to be postponed. Studies by Aguado, Sor, and Carulli helped me focus on tone production, while the Rodrigo concertos, works by Maurice Ohana, several sonatas by Scarlatti, and "Guajira" by Emilio Pujol expanded my repertoire. Films playing on the Champs-Elysées occasionally seduced me away from my guitar, as did a poetry reading by the exiled Chilean poet Pablo Neruda. We conversed in Spanish while he signed my program, then he drew me a small flower — perhaps one of the yellow flowers of his poems — now a treasure in my library.

The maestro was a patient teacher who always gave generously of his time. Our romance had faded months before, and he had assumed an avuncular attitude towards his private student from Canada. Monelle, laden with food, struggled breathlessly up my stairway, when I was bedridden with the flu, and sometimes handed me the keys to her apartment so I could luxuriate in a rose-oil-scented bath. With her Parisian perfumes and *haute couture*, she represented sartorial splendour and sophistication far beyond my aspirations. Content in my student outfits, I was more excited about a new fingering or guitar technique. How uncomplicated yet strangely focused my life was then.

There were plenty of lonely times when I longed for the company of a friend with whom to share this sensual city, but no romances interrupted my eighteen months at avenue Velasquez. On cold, draughty evenings, the only thing that buoyed my spirits was the sheer joy of playing guitar and mastering new music. Where, I wondered, could all these hours of sedentary, solitary study lead me? But is not "alone" an anagram for the usual spelling of my name? The creative process necessitates periods of aloneness. I am forever grateful to my parents that they never resorted to the common practice of over-organizing their children's leisure time. Rather than trying to "socialize" me as a youngster, they had taught me to enjoy my own company. Those solitary times of concentration, and even frustration, are essential in the development of creativity.

Some of my most poignant memories are of early-morning walks around the city. As the pale winter sun began to light the mosaic of grey-slate roofs beneath my window, cooing pigeons pecked the dried bread I left for them on the eavestroughs. With tatty map and a few francs in the pocket of my green woolly coat, I set off to explore the streets once trod by Dumas, de Maupassant, and Piaf, experiencing that wondrous light that streaked the streets in contrasting sun and shadow, illuminating the rooftops, washing the monuments, and in days past, inspiring the paintbrushes of the Impressionists. I watched the aproned merchants sweeping their little sections of the pavement or opening up their striped canvas awnings. I savoured the tantalizing baking smells wafting from the *pâtisseries* and the aroma of freshly brewed espressos drifting from neighbourhood bistros. On foot I explored the Latin Quarter, the Ile de la Cité, the flower market, and the Jardin du Luxembourg as the paintings of Seurat and Monet came to life before my eyes. In the cemetery of Montmartre, I laid a small bouquet of flowers on the grave of the composer Fernando Sor. Meandering around the Marché aux Puces flea market, I was jostled by multicoloured crowds of students, North African street vendors, charlatans, and pickpockets. I was trying to survive on a pittance, and even the modest *métro* ticket became an extravagance, so I learned to pick up used tickets, cover the tell-tale hole with my thumb, and thrust it forward for repunching by the unsuspecting guard.

In late November, I was invited to share a concert tour of England with a young British guitarist, John Mills, for whom I had prepared duets by Manuel de Falla, Enrique Granados, Dowland, and Bach. At John's parents' cold, damp home in Long Ditton, near the Thames River, I resorted to morning, afternoon, and evening baths in an effort to keep warm, and bought a hot-water bottle to thaw my fingers. We played together for several guitar societies around the country, and I gave a solo concert in Durham, where my parents had been students. One of their friends, Dr. Malcolm Brown, head of the university's geology department, showed me the moon rocks he had been analysing in his laboratory. Looking at the strange, dull rocks plundered from the heavens, I shared his awe. After trudging over the foggy moors, we nibbled scones and strawberry jam in a quaint little tea house as childhood memories surged through my mind.

The concerts were well received, but the hours before curtain time were pure agony. John worked himself into an uncontrollable nervous sweat, pacing up and down backstage, cursing the day that he had started to play guitar, with references to wrist-slashing and suicide. Each time he swore would be his last. His histrionics kept me on edge, wondering if I might have to pull off the entire show alone. Eventually, I came to recognize this as his normal routine. As soon as we struck the first chords, all his stage fright disappeared and he played exquisitely. After the concert, my partner was always so complacent about his exemplary performance, glowing and blushing like a bride as he accepted compliments, but I was ready to strangle him!

Taking chilly walks beneath cloudy skies past rows of identical houses, mangy alley cats, and the smell of coke fires, I knew I did not want to live in England, much as I appreciated the friendliness of her people compared with those defensive Parisians. By then, I must have become a Canadian.

In 1973, during a second summer course at the Académie Internationale d'Été de Nice, Lagoya asked me to perform Henri Tomasi's "Le Muletier des Andes" and a Bach fugue. One afternoon, commiserating about dwindling finances with Nadine, a Belgian guitarist, I suggested we try our hand at busking. Hastily we rehearsed some duets — "Spanish Romance," two Scarlatti sonatas, and "La Paloma" — then positioned ourselves on a bench close to one of the outdoor cafés to begin our serenade. To our delight, people responded warmly, and as I plucked away, Nadine walked around with my floppy pink sun-hat collecting francs and centimes. How easy it was! Our new-found confidence kept us moving from café to café, hauling in more cash than we could have imagined. Nadine, a beautiful dark-haired girl, had fallen prey to Lagoya's charms, as had most of the other attractive female students. We giggled and wickedly compared notes on our dear maestro.

While glancing at a map in the academy office, I noticed that Venice was not far from Nice, so with the guitar classes behind us and our newly found riches in hand, we jumped on the overnight train to arrive just as an orange sun suffused with streaks of gold was rising over the shimmering city. My first glimpse of Venice was breathtaking. The passionate music of Mahler's Fifth Symphony, used by Visconti in his movie *Death in Venice*, was playing its heart-wrenching harmonic progressions in my head as we heaved our

Eileen and John Boyd, my parents, as newlyweds in 1948.

Five weeks old, with
my mother, Eileen.

Two years old,
with teddy
bear "Moses"
in England.

In the
garden at
Welling with
Vivien.

A brotherly hug from Damien, 1959.

The Boyd family camping in 1955: Vivien, John, Liona, Eileen.

Summer memories: at seventeen with my heart-throb, Hans (Jack) Grunsky.

With my maître de musique, Alexandre Lagoya, at Jeunesses Musicales in Quebec.

With Gordon
Lightfoot.
(*ARTHUR
USHERSON*)

Classical music meets country legend Chet Atkins in Nashville.

Giggling backstage in Tokyo with Bernie Fiedler, 1984.

Backstage with pan-flute virtuoso Georges Zamfir (left) and my "manager without portfolio" Seymour Heller. (JAMES LOEWEN)

Roger Moore gets a guitar lesson on the set of *Moonraker*. (PATRICK MORIN)

Me and Julio (Iglesias, that is).

Rehearsing for a performance with the Tokyo Philharmonic in Japan, 1980.

guitars onto the *vaporetto* and began a magical early-morning ride down the Grand Canal to Piazza San Marco. This was "such stuff as dreams are made on." Every change of vista revealed elegant *palazzos*, courtyards, and ornate bridges, giving the illusion of travelling through one of the paintings of Canaletto.

Strong Italian cappuccinos cleared our heads from the night's jostly train ride as we searched for a *pensióne* to fit our budget. We walked streets remembered from Hemingway's novel *Across the River and into the Trees*, peeked into museums and galleries, and persuaded two flirtatious gondoliers to take us to the Lido, where we strolled on the beach of the Grand Hôtel des Bains. Nadine and I said goodbye after five days in Venice; she boarded a bus for Belgium, while I, ever the romantic, chose a train whose peeling painted letters spelled out "Orient Express." After practising guitar scales in the disinfectant-laden air of the ladies' *toilette*, I wrote a bumpy letter home to my parents as the Italian countryside gave way to the mountainous terrain of the French Alps. Since it cost no more, I decided to get off for a day in Lausanne, Switzerland. It was 4:00 a.m. when the train pulled into the station, and I dragged my bags into the empty waiting-room; the coffee shop was closed and the whole place appeared deserted. Perched on one of the wooden benches, I began to run through Lagoya's studies. When people eventually started drifting in and out of the station, someone threw what appeared to be an old gum-wrapper on the floor beside me. Absorbed in my music, I paid no attention until, after ten minutes, my eyes alighted on a crumpled-up bill of twenty Swiss francs lying on the ground. Some kind-hearted Swiss worker had thought I was playing to earn a little money. What a shame that I never had the chance to acknowledge my benefactor's early-morning donation. The windfall would tide me over the entire day.

At 6:00 a.m., when the cafeteria opened, I devoured a bowl of hot chocolate and a bread roll, checked my bag and guitar into a locker, and set out to explore the town. My feet started to complain by midmorning, so I accepted an invitation from a young art student to a boat ride on Lake Lausanne. Later, I climbed to the tower of a cathedral with a bearded man who furtively showed me the blood-stained rag he carried in his satchel — evidence gathered from a man he was seeking who had stabbed his mother to death — or so he said! Then he generously loaded me up with three bars of Swiss white chocolate from his aunt's store. Through my travels, I was learning just how bizarre the world's inhabitants can be. After sipping frothy beer with two German boys hiking around Europe, I hoisted my case and guitar aboard the train, leaping on just as it started to shunt out of the station. By the next morning, it had deposited me in Paris, where I resumed my monastic life of six hours' practice a day, frugal meals, long walks, and lessons with Lagoya.

In July, the month of my twenty-fourth birthday, I decided to fly to Mexico to vacation with my parents, who were spending the summer there. How wonderful to see them again and revisit old haunts in our beloved San Miguel de Allende. Tony Ponce, the boyfriend I had met in 1968, had been writing to me and even flew once to Nice, attempting to see me on his way to Egypt. He was thrilled to renew our acquaintance and promptly presented me with an enormous diamond ring. I accepted this dazzling gift, not fully aware of its significance, as we danced the evenings away at local *discotecas.* When his parents invited my family to a formal dinner, we began to realize that Tony intended to make me his wife! His solicitous mother had decorated one wing of their Celaya home in Louis XIV style for my arrival. It was pure Versailles. As fond as I was of Tony and his delightful family, I had never imagined him as my husband; all his jewels and riches could not persuade me. I was in pursuit of art, not wealth. I returned the ring and advised him to focus his efforts on one of the local *señoritas* rather than hanker after a classical guitarist with her heart set on a concert career.

Many years later, Seymour Heller, who became my U.S. manager, told me how he had met a wealthy Mexican couple holidaying in Las Vegas. It was only when Seymour opened his briefcase, inadvertently revealing one of my concert brochures, that Tony recognized his long-lost girlfriend and, much to Seymour's amazement, explained how he had wanted to marry me! What a small world we inhabit.

That July I soaked up the curative Mexican sunshine, taking long walks around San Miguel, climbing up to the three crosses on the mountain top, and reacquainting myself with the familiar cobblestone streets. My parents, pleased that I had been savouring Paris, were impressed by the progress in my guitar playing. In August I flew back to France to resume the Spartan student life and pursue my musical mission — studies with the maestro.

A few months later, a fellow guitar student arranged a short concert tour in Belgium and Holland, where an irate train conductor fined me ten francs for putting my guitar on an empty seat! I felt terribly apprehensive before playing the recitals in Haarlem, Maastricht, and Ijmuiden, but was pleased by my improving performance skills and the enthusiasm of those small, hushed audiences. I remember long bike rides along the canals, freezing cold recital halls, an outing to Amsterdam's famous red-light district, and a few days in Antwerp, where I stayed at the home of Nadine, my busking partner from Nice. Her mother owned a Belgian truffle shop and invited me to fill a large box with as many chocolates as I wanted. A few days later, my satiated stomach could not bear the sight of another crème praline, fondant, or white-chocolate bonbon; the entire box had passed my lips during the return train trip to Paris. Self-restraint was never my forte when it came to chocolate.

Aware that I needed more performing experience, I agreed to play for Musicroissants, a Sunday-morning recital series at the Canadian Cultural Centre. After receiving compliments from the two dozen people comprising the audience, I gobbled up my remuneration — two plates of buttery croissants. On a couple of occasions, the director of the American Cathedral in Paris let me play while people were filing into pews prior to the service. Some inner spirit was guiding me to perform.

People sitting in my line of vision to the left often distracted my concentration, so I cut out random heads from magazines and glued them on my wall as if to simulate an audience. With this motley crew peering at me from the plaster, I trained myself to ignore their stares; over time they became my familiar room-mates, assuming characters of their own.

During one of my lessons in November 1973, Lagoya casually mentioned that in exchange for recitals, certain cruise lines offered free passage. Given a chance to peer through another crack in the surface of the world, I was bitten at once by the travel bug. After unsuccessful phone calls from the local post office to the cruise line Croisières Pacquet, I presented myself in person at their head office. Patient determination kept me and my trusty Ramírez glued to the reception area for two hours until Monsieur le Président, emerging from his smoke-filled office, agreed to see me. Fluent now in French, I brazenly explained my desire to play on one of his ships. The corpulent executive eased himself into an armchair, an amused expression flickering across his face. Offhandedly motioning for me to play, he lit a pungent Gitane. Grabbing the guitar from its case, I ripped through some flashy Albéniz piece. "*Formidable — vraiment incroyable. Ma chérie*, pick any cruise, it's yours," he declared magnanimously, loading me down with pamphlets on his ships and their exotic destinations. I spent the evening salivating over alabastrine Greek islands, Tunisian beaches, and Moorish castles. A two-week cruise to Málaga, Casablanca, the Canary Islands, and Senegal seemed an absolute smorgasbord of delights.

A month later, I set off from Gare St-Lazare to Marseilles. Fantasies of moonlit deck encounters and ballroom romances with handsome European gentlemen floated through my head as I practised scales in the corridor of the crowded train that was clattering me south to adventure. There, anchored in the harbour, floated a gleaming white vessel with "Massalia" painted on her prow. The first set-back was having to room with a chain-smoking bridge teacher, Brigitte — so much for the promised private cabin! Although I kept a sharp eye out for romantic prospects, there seemed a predominance of overweight Germans with stocky wives in tow — workers from a Frankfurt factory whose management had generously sent their employees on this North African junket — quite the antithesis of the cruise clientele I had expected.

Leaden skies let loose their driving rain, and winds whipped soggy deck streamers as a veiled Marseilles faded into the distance. Groaning and pitching, we crossed the Golfe du Lion towards Casablanca, whose legendary name kept me bubbling with excitement and anticipation. The next morning, the *Massalia* heaved into port in the midst of a pelting hailstorm; once the gangway was lowered we were herded into groups, and I brandished our ship's flagpole like a standard bearer heading into the fray. Huddled under plastic umbrellas, our sodden group listened to the tour guide's undecipherable French. After a bus ride into town to visit the mosques and souks, I looked around expectantly for blue men and shady Arabs — my idea of Morocco — but not even one camel came into view as we sloshed through deep puddles, hearing the crunch of hailstones beneath our sandals. Where were Rick's Café and Casablanca's characters of international intrigue? The Canary Islands excursions were even more depressing, as torrential downpours dogged us for several days, causing some disgruntled passengers to fly home.

During my Christmas Eve concert in the ballroom, while I was serenading a few valiant souls with Antonio Lauro waltzes, a huge swell tilted the stage to starboard, causing the orchestral equipment to slide and topple behind me. Music stands capsized in a cadenza of crashes; curtains cascaded to the side in screeching cadences; trumpet cases keeled over and an electric organ slithered threateningly towards me — only great feats of balance prevented my chair and footstool from following suit. The queasy audience sat pinned to their seats as I detected the dreaded *mal de mer* fermenting in my stomach. Bracing my back against the chair, I tore into "El Abejoro," hastily thanked my audience, who from the bright side of the stage lights I imagined to be a "whiter shade of pale," and with guitar in hand, staggered along the swaying corridors towards my cabin. Dramamine tablets saved the night. But it was too late for Brigitte, who kept me awake till dawn as her six-course meal returned intermittently, with chilling sound effects.

On December 25, as we rounded the cape of Mauritania, the storm became so intense we dared not venture from our room let alone face the thought of Christmas dinner. Even our poor cabin-boys did not appear. Reports of the violent weather, which had caused a ship to go down, were spotted in the Toronto papers by my parents. Petrified by the ferocity of the raging seas, I cursed the day I had ever heard of "luxury cruises." After its Christmas lashing, *Massalia* sailed smoothly into quiescent waters, anchoring in the harbour of Dakar. By dugout canoe we snaked along steamy rivers to native villages, where I bargained for bright serapes, leather ottomans, and a turtle-shell stringed instrument for Eli Kassner. Back on board, I played a final concert accompanied by a Dominican priest reading medieval French poetry, then spent my last evening in Málaga dancing the night away with two Air France pilots. A decade would have to pass, however, before I was tempted to accept another cruise.

Back in Paris, Lagoya's coaching continued for another month, but the time had come to draw the curtains on my student life. Finally, I felt ready to embark on a career in music. The day before leaving, I realized I had never visited the famous Eiffel Tower, the first check-point for most tourists. After one and a half years of residency, how embarrassing to admit I had not ascended the monument on which I had gazed daily from my window. Sitting in the dizzy heights of the tower's restaurant, I treated myself to a penurious last supper — a greasy plate of *frites* covered with ketchup, that plebeian North American delicacy. In the evening I packed up the little room, stuffing my few belongings into a suitcase, and bid fond *adieus* to Marie-Odile and her parents, in whose maid's quarters I had been holed up like a chirping cricket. Yves Châtelain, whom I had not seen in months, drove me to Orly airport the next morning. Warmly, we hugged farewell, "all passion spent." My life in France had come to a close and I sensed a challenging new chapter about to begin, as Air Canada sped me home across the wintry, grey Atlantic.

8

Have Guitar, Will Travel

My life has been blessed with doors that open at appropriate moments. Just when I am wondering where to go next, a new direction is shown to me, either by a chance meeting or a serendipitous opportunity. After intense study with Lagoya, I knew the time was right for my first recording. While in Paris I had received correspondence from Eleanor Sniderman, who was awaiting my return to Canada, as she had accepted the position of artist and repertoire consultant for Boot Records, a small label owned by Stompin' Tom Connors. Tom was the country singer/songwriter from Prince Edward Island who, after enjoying success in the music business, had decided to create his own independent label. With no knowledge about record companies, I was easily persuaded that signing with Boot would be a wise step towards a professional career. Tom was no aficionado of the classics, but possessed a strong sense of national pride. After learning that no Canadian classical label existed, he made the meritorious gesture of recording some home-grown talent. With his

Boot Master Concert Series, Tom helped launch not only my recording career but also that of the Canadian Brass.

In 1974, Eleanor was still married to Sam Sniderman. This was a
decade before the acrimonious divorce during which Eleanor "came
out of the closet." How fortunate to have these two well-connected
people helping me launch a musical career. Eleanor introduced me
to the man who ran Boot Records for Tom Connors, Jury Krytiuk, a
cheery three-hundred-pound Ukrainian-Canadian. The label took its
name from the stomping boot Tom used to thump up and down on
a wooden board to his down-home Maritime music. It was difficult
to get excited about the name of my new record company, and
the ungainly stomping boot logo on the album jacket, but I hoped
this detail would be overlooked by my classical followers, who
would never comprehend what a stomping boot had to do with
classical guitar.

Jury Krytiuk drew up a five-record, five-year contract whereby
I would receive an 8 per cent royalty on all sales once expenses had
been paid. Neither my parents nor I understood the complexities of
record contracts, but a judicious inner voice cautioned me to change
the five-year term to two. Eleanor volunteered to produce my debut
recording and, with her mind set on simplicity, decided to name it
The Guitar. She secured a top engineer, David Green, who booked
the best studio in downtown Toronto, Manta Sound. Never having set
foot in a recording studio, I was completely ignorant about sound
variables and microphones, so I left every decision to David. My task
was to play through each piece three or four times until Eleanor
assured me that we had a "perfect take." Selecting from works I had
carefully polished under Lagoya's tutelage, I chose a prelude, a
presto, and two gavottes by Bach, Albéniz's "Zambra Granadina" and
"Rumores de la Caleta," Tomasi's "Le Muletier des Andes," two
sonatas by Domenico Scarlatti, João Guimarães's "Sounds of Bells,"
and Debussy's "La Fille aux Cheveux de Lin." She praised my
interpretations and enthused about the fine "product" we would
soon have. Repeatedly predicting I would become a major star on the

classical-music scene, she assured me that I would be selling out concerts from coast to coast and riding around in limousines. Never having been in a limousine, nor having harboured the slightest desire to ride around in one, I thought all this sounded ridiculously excessive; years afterwards, every time I stepped into one of those huge black or white monsters after a sold-out show, I could not help remembering Eleanor's wild prophecies.

Together the three of us edited the record; David Green introduced me to the magic of the studio, demonstrating how he could splice a good part of one take onto a better part of the next take, thereby cutting out the imperfect or less-musical sections. He could even vary the overall tone by adding different degrees of treble, bass, and reverb. Before this initiation, I had never understood how Julian Bream's guitar sustained notes so much longer than mine ever could. Ah, the wonder of reverb!

Each day I shared the pleasures of recording with my parents. We could not imagine the tremendous effect an album would have on my fledgling career and chuckled at my producer's wild imaginings. Eleanor's persistence in trying to obtain a perfect test-pressing, one of the final steps in the manufacturing of a vinyl record, caused her to reject ten before one met with her approval. How could I not be impressed by the attention she was lavishing on this project of ours?

We hired David Falconer, who had casually photographed my father exhibiting his oil paintings in the park. In retrospect, I am amazed how my debut record portrait was contrived so haphazardly. He photographed me in Toronto's Edwards Gardens wearing my mother's home-made skirt of purple panne velvet and a cotton blouse purchased from a street vendor in Amsterdam. In contrast to the perfectionism of the recorded sound, we did seem rather casual with the album's packaging. The "liner notes" for the back of the jacket were written by my mother and me, in collaboration with Joseph Pastore, a bright young man who had approached me to play in New York. Pastore decided to fly to Toronto to meet me, arriving in a flashy Great Gatsby–style white suit. A guitar fanatic with a vast knowledge of the music world, he talked non-stop. Never before had I met anyone so driven and energetic.

Both Pastore and Eleanor Sniderman wanted to manage me, but being a novice in the music scene, I was wary of commitment. I worried that Eleanor's forty-page contract would have tied me up for life, that every decision in my musical career would have to be approved or vetoed by her. I didn't even think of consulting a legal expert. Pastore was insistent that without the right New York connections and plenty of money behind me, there could never be any hope of my succeeding as a concert artist. He explained the depravities of the music business: Mafia involvement, payola, crooked record-company deals, dishonest agents, "free goods," kickbacks, pirated records, and the fierce competition. I simply wanted to enjoy playing my guitar for appreciative audiences. Was this another pipedream? After Pastore's ominous warnings and Eleanor's contract, I began to have second thoughts about "the music business," and sat glumly at the dinner table asking my parents if I was making a mistake to pursue such a career.

Most of my recitals I booked on my own or with the help of my mother, who used her maiden name when writing letters to the concert promoters, gathered from a list obtained from the Canada Council or the guitar-society network. Printing up a little brochure, I used a quote from Christopher Parkening, who had inscribed the back of one of his albums for me: "One of the most excellent guitarists I have heard." I added a quote from Alirio Díaz, who had written, "I predict that she will become one of the most distinguished artists of the classical guitar." One day, I called the library in Mississauga, a suburb of Toronto, which ran a Sunday-afternoon concert series.

"Hello, I am a classical guitarist and I'm interested in playing for you," I said, talking with as much confidence as I could muster.

"What is your fee?" the library director inquired.

"Normally, my fee is four hundred dollars," I bluffed, "but as your library is only a short distance from my house, I'll take three hundred."

"Oh, that is out of the question, my dear," he replied, "we cannot afford that much."

"Well, as it's a local engagement, what would you say to two hundred?" I countered bravely.

"No, I'm sorry, miss, we can't pay so much," he insisted.

"Oh well, I understand that the Union minimum is one hundred and twenty five, so let's settle for that," I pleaded.

"No, I'm afraid that's still too high," he continued. "Look, one hundred is my very last offer and well below my normal fee, but as a special favour to the library, I'll accept that," I stated with finality. There was an unbearable silence, then an embarrassed cough on the other end of the phone.

"I'm afraid, Miss Boyd, that fifty dollars is the very most this library could afford for an unknown musician," he said apologetically.

"I'm sorry, sir, but that is simply too low; I couldn't do an entire concert for that small fee."

I thanked him and hung up disappointed, as I realized how much I needed to start performing. On that Sunday, however, I would only be sitting at home playing for myself; perhaps fifty dollars should not be sneezed at so quickly. Some people had to work several hours to earn that, and it was more than the eleven dollars I had been receiving for playing at the Unitarian churches. I hastily called back to tell the librarian he had a deal. I would play for fifty dollars, and if I sold out the place, I hoped he would invite me to return next year. Two months later, the Mississauga library was jammed and the librarian completely amazed. Slipping fifty dollars into my pocket, he vigorously shook my hand, asking if I would like to play again. The next season, he booked me for three hundred and fifty dollars, but by then my name was becoming known and someone more skilled than I negotiated the fee.

I began to play small recitals for the network of guitar societies scattered around North America, which were run on a shoestring by devoted enthusiasts. A hundred people attended my Haddonfield, New Jersey, performance, and I received accolades from a college crowd in Cleveland. The Vancouver, Halifax, Washington, Portland, and Seattle guitar societies invited me to give recitals; I accepted any offer that came my way, while eagerly awaiting the release of *The Guitar.*

Now it was time to find an agent to handle concert bookings, as we could do only so much, and it did not look very professional for my mother and I to be negotiating the fees. Ed Oscapella, a fellow music student who had decided to become a concert agent, began to book small concerts in churches and high schools. Sometimes the fees were guesswork, sometimes the scheduling bad; he, like I, was at the very beginning of his career, feeling his way into the music business.

A Northern Ontario library tour sent my mother and me driving to small but welcoming audiences in places we could barely find on the map. In these remote locations, we bedded down in inexpensive motels, concocted sandwiches in the car, and shared frequent giggles about some of the characters we encountered. Staying in people's homes for concerts in Nanaimo (British Columbia), Corvallis (Oregon), and Dallas (Texas) gave me glimpses into a variety of different life-styles. On the tour I rattled off amusing anecdotes over my hosts' home-cooked dinners, autographed their children's guitars, and played the obligatory piece to impress the neighbours. In Dryden I was assigned a musty sleeping bag in a kids' room crammed with toys and friendly cats; Milwaukee billeted me at the beautiful country estate belonging to the Brumder family; in Washington, D.C., I was presented by the National Guitar Society and I met composer Sophocles Papas; in Victoria my hosts offered their living-room couch, but I was kept awake by their crying baby; in Regina I was the guest of two priests who cooked me pancakes for breakfast. In some towns my concerts were combined with master-classes, where I dispensed technical and musical advice to groups of eager young players. Experiencing North America from a new perspective, I took great enjoyment in the opportunity for travel; living out of a suitcase became second nature.

There were always latent pre-concert nerves to contend with, but onstage, absorbed in the musical interpretations, a new confidence and stage presence began to blossom inside me. The once-shy adolescent was becoming accustomed to meeting new people at every turn, and I easily interacted with the strangers seated beside me in planes or buses — friendly exchanges took place with lumberjacks, farmers, housewives, and travelling salesmen as our lives overlapped for fleeting moments of time. All the interesting travel and appreciation of my talent convinced me that I had found the perfect career.

While on a plane from Seattle to Vancouver, I struck up a conversation with a man in his mid-thirties who had been part of the music business in New York, but had recently exchanged the hectic pace of the Big Apple for a quieter, more reflective life in San Francisco. As we sat together sipping our Northwest Orient coffee, Cal explained he was a songwriter and "ideas person" who had worked with Burt Bacharach and Andy Williams. He seemed intrigued by my tales of guitar societies and the Boot Record deal. "Please call me collect anytime you like," he insisted, as he helped carry my guitar case off the plane and scribbled his phone number on the back of my boarding card. His distinctive style of writing, natural sense of humour, and the lively twinkle in his eyes kindled my interest. Not having shared any romantic relationship for more than a year, I decided that Cal was at least worth a phone call. Our first half-hour conversation evolved into daily calls from San Francisco, during which Cal pleaded that I come and visit him "on the coast."

He was a prolific writer, and a deluge of letters and poetry penned in his strong calligraphy started to flow into my life. After a month of this fervour, I capitulated to his demands, agreeing to join him in San Francisco for a few days. Obviously I was destined to meet up with this crazy character who had fallen head over heels in love. My mother insisted I must be quite mad!

A return Air Canada ticket arrived by courier, and Cal was on the phone, ecstatic that I had finally consented to spend time in his company. He collected me and my guitar at the airport, and we drove south towards Big Sur. A tape of Neil Diamond's music for *Jonathan Livingston Seagull* provided the soundtrack as he swept me along the Pacific Coast Highway. The vistas were overwhelming: white surf pounded the jagged, rocky coast and miles of unspoiled beaches played host to seagulls soaring through the air. Cal was thrilled that he could introduce his Canadian import to his beloved Northern California.

Determined to do the right thing, he had rented two separate rooms at the Big Sur Inn, where we were given redwood logs to burn in the fireplaces each evening. For me everything was novel, exciting, and charged with romance; I do not think that my room was ever used except to store the guitar! Thus began one of my most turbulent love affairs, which endured for three years and involved more break-ups, make-ups, fights, tears, and promises than I care to remember.

Cal was separated from his wife and awaiting a divorce. He rented a delightful little house in Stinson Beach where, in between my growing number of concert commitments, I stayed with him and his Husky dog, who raced us up and down the beach each morning. He taught me about his Jewish upbringing and religion, and gave me insights into the popular side of the music business. Together we attended classical concerts, sipped hot cider in Carmel, and shopped for fresh crab at Fisherman's Wharf. The telephone seemed to run Cal's life, as he was producing music and drama packages for television. Most of the time, Cal treated me like a princess, but suddenly he would become violently jealous of my dedication to the guitar, furiously accusing me of loving my music more than him. These erratic, unpredictable mood swings began to concern me. Between trips with me to New York, Lake Tahoe, and Bermuda, he acquired a house hidden in Mill Valley, where the air smelled of redwoods, eucalyptus, and pine. A mother deer with her fawn visited our over-grown garden each morning to nip tender shoots from the rambling, flowering bushes. I was sure I had landed in paradise; however, my musical aspirations were drawing me on. "The woods are lovely, dark, and deep, / But I have promises to keep, / And miles to go before I sleep," I repeated to myself from some half-remembered poem. Although I loved the rustic house, I never really "moved in," despite Cal's demands that I make a more serious commitment. The symbols of home, my bears Mosey and Tonka, remained in Canada.

My inchoate concert career was beginning to take shape. *The Guitar* had been released to critical acclaim, my photo graced the cover of *Sound* magazine, and overnight my music was played on radio stations, from CBC's classical programs to CHUM-FM, a pop station at the opposite end of the listening spectrum. Eleanor proudly escorted me to radio interviews and arranged for a feature story in *Time* magazine. Despite my rejection of his management, Joseph Pastore presented me at Carnegie Recital Hall in March 1975. For this career milestone, Eleanor and Sam Sniderman both flew down to New York with William Littler, the music critic from *The Toronto Star.* Apprehensive about all the attention this one concert was attracting, I visited a hypnotherapist to see if he could help calm my anticipated stage fright. His relaxing suggestions must have worked, as I played well and received a good review in *The New York Times* that praised my "flair for brilliance."

An exultant Sam and Eleanor wined and dined me in an Italian restaurant after the concert. What a great feeling of relief that it was all over! A Toronto debut at the St. Lawrence Centre was followed by recitals in Atlanta, Louisville, Nashville, and Memphis, and a five-city tour of Newfoundland, where my guitar case was forced to share the taxi trunk with a crate of ripe-smelling cod. It exuded a fishy odour for weeks! Suddenly my name seemed to be attracting everyone's attention, from our local Etobicoke weekly newspaper to international music publications. My mother meticulously cut out every article and pasted them in the first of many large scrapbooks.

9

On Tour
with Lightfoot

♪

*E*leanor invited me to the annual Juno Awards, Canada's equivalent to America's Grammys. I had no appropriate evening dress, so the dark purple gown sewn by my mother for the New York concert had to suffice. Sitting humbly among the throngs of glitzy executives, agents, promoters, and artists, I wondered where, if at all, I fitted into this "music business" scene. After the show, Eleanor introduced me to one of my teenage music idols, Gordon Lightfoot, who jokingly suggested that I give him a few guitar lessons. How thrilling to actually shake hands with the famous singer whose voice Vivien and I had taken with us to San Miguel, and how exciting to hear that he had enjoyed listening to *The Guitar*.

In March 1975 Gordon Lightfoot played his annual concert series at Toronto's Massey Hall; I was invited by his sister Bev. After the performance (I had taken my brother, Damien — also a great Lightfoot admirer), I was invited to a private party at Gordon's Rosedale mansion, which was filled with his buddies from the music industry:

his band, friends, hangers-on, press agents, and a good sprinkling of adoring female fans. He approached me with his old classical guitar, thrusting it into my arms as he motioned to his friends to gather round. "Liona Boyd is one hell of a classic-guitar player. She'll play for you if you'll all keep quiet!" he yelled. At this point, I realized how totally unprepared I was, as my velvet blouse had terribly tight sleeves. Quickly managing to tune the old strings, I launched into "Una Lágrima," a haunting tremolo piece by Gaspar Sagreras. Halfway through the selection, I felt my right arm start to tingle; the sleeve was cutting off my circulation at the elbow. Only prayers and a fierce determination helped my fingers keep moving to the end. My luck held until Gordon's friends started applauding. Somehow I pulled off a couple more selections, with my arm feeling as if it were in the grip of a blood-pressure cuff. The curly-haired singer seemed immensely pleased by my impromptu performance. "One day, Liona, I'm gonna take you on the road," he said, smiling. Surely it was a courteous compliment rather than a real promise; my simple guitar playing could never be compatible with his folk-pop band.

Several months later, while I was in San Francisco, the phone rang. Gordon was on the line, asking if I could fly to Minneapolis in a couple of days' time; his opening act had just cancelled. Desperate for a quick replacement, he explained that there would be two sold-out shows of five thousand people and absolutely nothing to worry about. Nothing to worry about! I had not even played for an audience of one thousand, never mind ten thousand in the same evening! But I knew this could be the break all aspiring performers dream about. At a loss as to what to say, I breathlessly told him I needed time to think.

In a terrible dilemma I ran to find Cal, beseeching him to help me decide what to do about this fantastic offer, which required a decision within the hour. Surely Gordon's audience would boo me right off the stage, as they would not be expecting a classical guitar performance. Could I be running the risk of ruining my classical reputation by playing for a pop crowd? I agonized over the imagined

ramifications of accepting such an offer, but after much vacillation
realized that I would never know the consequences without actually
playing the shows. Two days later I arrived, with much trepidation,
in Minneapolis.

Gordon was wonderfully kind, striding on stage to introduce me
to the audience. "Here's a girl from my home town of Toronto,
Canada, who plays beautiful classical guitar and looks like an angel,"
he spoke into the microphone, as five thousand people listened
in silence. His petrified "angel" was frantically trying to warm her
trembling hands on a hot-water bottle, attempting to calm her pounding heart, and wishing she were anywhere else in the world but in
the wings of Northrop Auditorium at that moment. The next minute,
Gordon was beckoning me onstage. I tried to force a smile as the
deafening thunder from ten thousand hands welcomed me. Playing
"La Fille aux Cheveux de Lin," "Campanas del Alba," "Rumores de la
Caleta," and "Sounds of Bells," I realized that my fears had been
unfounded when the crowd gave me a tumultuous ovation.

For the second show I felt more relaxed, and Gordon brought me
out to take additional bows at the end of his set. The great reviews
in next day's papers reassured me that it had been a wise decision
to accept. "There'll be more concerts for you soon," Gordon promised.
I flew back to California bursting to tell Cal of my triumph before a
"pop" audience.

In May 1975 I was contracted to play with the Calgary Philharmonic
Orchestra and quickly learned the piece they requested, *Fantasía
para un Gentilhombre* by the great Spanish composer Joaquín
Rodrigo. Unfortunately, there was not enough time to study the
concerto thoroughly; never having played with an orchestra before,
I was not even sure how to interact with a conductor. CBC Radio was
taping the performance — my first CBC broadcast! I was terrified
at the prospect. We had two brief rehearsals, which only made me
furious with myself for not being more prepared. In contrast to opera
singers, ballet dancers, and even concert pianists, guitarists are
solitary creatures who never indulge in music coaches. Once our

studies are finished, we are on our own. Although Pavarotti would not dream of tackling a new opera without the assistance of a coach, we guitarists would not think of asking for help. In a sold-out hall, intimidated by the CBC's array of microphones, I ploughed through the concerto, only just grabbing some of the notes and missing certain chords and runs altogether. Backstage, I wanted to melt into the carpet on my dressing-room floor. A jovial representative from the Calgary Guitar Society bearing a large bouquet of red roses made me feel even worse! I phoned Cal from my hotel room and sobbed that I intended to quit giving concerts; this would be my last ever orchestral performance. I prayed I would never run into the poor conductor and decided I would succumb to amnesia.

Since that first embarrassing performance, I have often played the Rodrigo concerto and realize just how unprepared I had been for that ill-fated première. It is wonderfully exhilarating to feel the power of an entire symphony backing you up, but for many years, given a choice between solo or orchestral performances, I would opt for the former. During solo concerts, I become more completely immersed in my musical interpretations; with a symphony, one has to think about the balance between the guitar and the other instruments, making sure to follow the conductor's movements out of the corner of one's eye. As a soloist, I am responsible for the entire concert and can shape the mood and quality of the performance, whereas in an orchestral setting, the total statement is beyond my control.

A six-week classical tour of northern British Columbia and the Yukon was arranged, starting in late November 1975. The program included solos as well as ensembles with flutist Robert Aitken and David Grimes, a performer on the synthesizer, a novel instrument in those days. Our trio gave about fifty concerts and numerous work-shops, often playing to three audiences each day after driving hundreds of miles between the towns. We performed in high schools, churches, and hotel dining rooms, presenting classical music to the folks in Kitimat, Terrace, Williams Lake, 100 Mile House, Prince Rupert, and Whitehorse, to name a few. Cal called from San Francisco every morning and evening. "What the hell are you doing in December freezing your ass off in places with names like 'Kitty mat' when you could be in the redwood forests with me?" he shouted into the phone.

On our free days, I occupied myself learning new repertoire, editing, and fingering Milton Barnes's "Fantasy for Guitar," based on the theme "Land of the Silver Birch," which I performed a few months later on a CBC half-hour TV show called "Music to See." In the Yukon Territory, the mercury plummeted to -60°F, causing a small split in the back of my Ramírez guitar due to the sudden fluctuation in temperature and lack of humidity. Our audiences never failed to demonstrate their appreciation, but there were times when the travel was unbearable. We often rose at 6:00 a.m. to hit the road by seven for a school concert at nine in the next town. Afternoons required musical workshops, where we taught students on our individual instruments; evening concerts for the community were invariably followed by late receptions. I ruefully concluded that these tours were easier on male flute or synthesizer players than on female guitarists, as every night I had no choice but to stay up restringing the guitar, ironing a concert gown, and washing my hair while my fellow musicians were free to turn in. Tradition has it that folk and pop artists pay their dues playing to rough crowds in smoky bars; I was paying mine in all the remote, snowbound communities of northwest Canada.

An arduous Saskatchewan Arts Council tour the next season took me through the waving wheat fields to such enthusiastic rural communities as Rosetown, Yorkton, Weyburn, and Estevan, playing in high-school gyms and cafeterias where various volunteers, including the mother of television host Pamela Wallin, shuttled me along prairie roads. Through the guitar-society network, it was arranged for me to perform a concert in Nashville, Tennessee, where Chet Atkins, the legendary country guitarist, found a seat in the audience. Chet was a lanky man in a casual, blue-jean suit who insisted on calling me LI-ona, to differentiate my name from that of his wife, Leona. Every bit the fine southern gentleman, he projected a friendly manner with his slow Tennessee drawl.

Chet invited me to call by his office at RCA the next day to take a look at his collection of classical guitar music and vintage instruments. A reporter from *The Canadian* magazine, a national weekly that was stuffed into Saturday newspapers across the country, was writing "Scarlatti in Nashville," a story on my trip, and tagged along to cover my meeting with Atkins. Chet listened attentively to a few of my pieces, offered compliments, then asked if I could teach him how to get his tremolo to sound more even. The legendary country picker, who could also get his fingers around a number of classical pieces, seemed pleased to share guitar tips and exchange stories about classical players we both knew. It was the beginning of an enduring friendship based on respect for each other's artistry, even though our styles and repertoire were different. *The Canadian* magazine put my photo on their cover and dubbed me "The First Lady of the Guitar," a title that has accompanied me ever since. My star had begun to ascend.

Television appearances on everything from talk shows hosted by Juliette, Elwood Glover, Laurier LaPierre, and Bob McLean, to "Celebrity Cooks" and "Good Morning, Seattle" helped expand my audiences. But Chet Atkins was responsible for my first major U.S. television exposure by recommending me to the "Today" show, where I was interviewed on my career by Gene Shalit. Just as I was about to step in front of the lights, one of the friendly camera operators whispered, "Play well, Liona, twenty million people are watching you." I could have hit him with my fret-board for his poor sense of timing! The CBC gave me a prime-time TV special, on which I played St. Preux's "Concerto pour une Voix" and duets with Hagood Hardy and Chet Atkins, and bantered with the Canadian Brass and David Clayton-Thomas. Television had become a great way for my classical guitar to reach a wider public than even Segovia could have imagined.

Ed Oscapella, having been offered a position with the Canada Council, disbanded his office. I decided to sign on with Haber Artists, an ambitious new agency formed by the former manager of the

National Ballet of Canada. David Haber, who entertained hopes of becoming Canada's answer to Sol Hurok, made the mistake of taking on too many artists, leaving himself insufficient time to dedicate to our individual careers. He booked Canadian and American dates for me, plus a few international appearances, although most foreign offers came through contacts I had established on my own. Constantly writing letters, especially on planes, I spent hours corresponding with colleagues, agents, and music impresarios or penning articles for music magazines. There was so much more to a career, I was discovering, than just playing the guitar.

Eleanor Sniderman had had a falling out with Boot Records, so they suggested I produce a new album myself: *The Artistry of Liona Boyd*. I chose the music of Lauro, Pescetti, Cimarosa, Besard, and Mussorgsky — twelve previously unrecorded works for guitar, including my own "Cantarell" and three pieces written for me by a young Transylvanian composer, Robert Feuerstein. Through a contact established after a concert in Washington, D.C., I mailed President Jimmy Carter one of my albums. To my surprise, he responded, and over the next few years, I received three personal letters from the White House. He wrote, "I really enjoyed hearing you play, and thank you for affording me the privilege. . . . Rosalynn and I appreciate your kindness and send you our best wishes. . . . I particularly appreciate your thoughtful gesture of including 'Recuerdos de la Alhambra.' It's great! Sincerely, Jimmy."

Gordon Lightfoot decided he would present a concert at Maple Leaf Gardens to benefit our Canadian Olympic athletes in June 1976; he invited Sylvia Tyson, Murray McLauchlan, and his opening act from Minneapolis to share his stage and the national television broadcast. At first, I felt intimidated at the thought of playing my classical guitar in the middle of such a vast hockey arena, but Gordon assured me that I would have no trouble being heard. My music boomed out of speakers stacked like skyscrapers on either side of the stage. With millions of viewers, what a great way to expand my audience! Never before had I seen such lavish backstage provisions:

huge bowls of fruit salads, vegetable and deli plates, sandwiches, and champagne — a veritable feast compared with the humble cup of tea I always requested prior to my guitar-society recitals!

Shortly thereafter, Gordon offered me the chance to participate in his U.S. summer tour. As my experiences in Minneapolis and at Maple Leaf Gardens had been so positive, I was eager for more. Meeting up with the balladeer and his band at Innotech Aviation, a Toronto private-aircraft terminal, I clambered into the Lear jet for the flight to our first "gig" in Colorado. Gordon had neglected to warn me that there was only one small toilet, which had been stuffed full of guitars and baggage, rendering it inaccessible during the flight. After four long hours, we arrived in Denver, where it started to pour with rain, which certainly did not help my predicament. Our plane was kept sitting on the tarmac for half an hour while obnoxious immigration officials fired questions at us about U.S. work permits. Gordon became more and more impatient, as we were already late for our sound check, and I was increasingly desperate to release the three or four soft drinks I had blithely consumed on the trip down.

Finally, we were ordered to get off the plane and unload all our equipment for inspection, but I made a beeline for the ladies' room. After the immigration formalities were over, we sloshed through puddles into waiting limousines. Remembering Eleanor's predictions, I smiled to myself. "Your concert at the Red Rocks Amphitheater has been washed out and relocated to the Denver Coliseum," an anxious-looking promoter informed us. "Don't worry. We have provided buses to transport the crowd over to the new venue. The Lippizaner stallions were there last night, but everything has been cleared up for your show." We were ushered into the cavernous stadium, which retained a distinctly horsey aroma, dumped our baggage in the locker rooms, and hurried onto the huge, hastily erected wooden stage. It already was six-thirty and the show was due to start at eight, so time was in short supply. Just as we began to test our microphones, the stadium doors gave way and thousands of screaming kids flooded into the arena, determined to lay claim to the front seats. Gordon had to beat a hasty retreat from the stage without doing a proper check or he risked being mobbed by excited fans. The promoter assured us that the sound men could set the mike levels themselves. Back in the change room, I zipped up my lacy cream dress, trying to control my agitations over our aborted sound check.

I will never forget the agonizing feeling of having to walk onstage to play for twelve thousand restless kids who had been rained out and were not anticipating an opening act. To my horror, as my fingers struck up the first chords of "Asturias," no sound came through the speakers. I leaned into the voice mike to say, "Good evening, everyone," hoping to explain that the sound system needed to be adjusted, but nothing could be heard except my own tiny unamplified voice, which in a stadium built for thousands hardly made it to the first row. "Just keep on playing, honey!" the engineer yelled. I could see Lightfoot running around the speakers shouting at the technicians. Valiantly, I played on with a sinking heart as the audience shuffled uneasily and a few whistles could be heard. Why, instead of "If You Could Read My Mind," were they being subjected to an inaudible classical guitarist? How thankful I was that no one could read my mind at that moment!

After an excruciating eternity, the massive speakers boomed forth with my chords and the audience relaxed. Once the set was over, I groped my way off-stage, blinded by the super-trouper lights. What a total catastrophe! Gordon was already striding onstage to the loud cheering of fans as I hid in the locker room ready to burst into tears, convinced I had just ruined my career. Even Gordon's words of comfort later that evening did nothing to console me. Fortunately, this mortifying scenario was never repeated. The many concerts Gordon and I shared were well received, with very few technical hitches. After that Denver disaster, however, I always raced onstage first to make sure that my microphones were working.

We played so many different cities on both sides of the border, including Philadelphia, Traverse City, Peterborough, Hamilton, Montreal, and Boston, that tours dissolved into a blur of Lear jets, limo rides, hotel check-ins, press interviews, and jammed concert venues. I studied my sheet music while sitting beside Gordon on the plane, and he used to glance over at the jumble of notes and numbers, amazed that I could hear the sounds of music from the written page. "Why don't you write your own stuff instead of playing all these tunes by composers who died hundreds of years ago?" he asked. "Classical guitarists don't write their own music, they play the works of the great guitar composers or else transcribe pieces by famous masters like Bach, Scarlatti, and Albéniz," I smugly replied. It was however, Gordon Lightfoot, with that casual remark, who first made me think about trying to write my own music. The seed had been planted.

Gordon and I became good friends, but avoided any romantic entanglements. He was routinely approached by beautiful women with stars in their eyes — from eighteen-year-old groupies and poetry-loving college students to older married women. Our curly-haired Canadian troubadour impressed the ladies with his romantic ballads and blue-jeaned, rugged good looks. Sometimes one of his female conquests would accompany us in the plane, but Gordon did not enjoy being away from home for long stretches of time, and the band appreciated shorter tours, as they had wives and children in Toronto. Pee Wee Charles played steel guitar, Terry Clements acoustic and electric guitars, Barry Keane drums, and Rick Haynes bass: a good-natured group who amused themselves with practical jokes to make life on the road more tolerable. We usually played Thursday, Friday, and twice on Saturday and Sunday, rarely staying away for more than a week. Backstage, Gordon made a habit of popping his head into my dressing room to wish me good luck before the show. That quick hand-squeeze or pat on the shoulder as I waited in the wings to make my entrance meant a great deal. Probably he never realized how appreciated those small gestures of support were. Gordon always invited me to join him in press interviews, and he insisted that my name be up on the marquee with his. "You just can't get Liona off the bottle!" he used to joke as

I warmed my hands on a hot-water bottle, one of my standard pre-concert routines.

But Gordon was a temperamental man. I witnessed frequent altercations between him and various road managers, light and sound technicians, and promoters. Even his band members occasionally came under fire. I was sure that my turn would come; it was only a matter of time. Amazingly, however, during the two years we toured together, Gordon never uttered a harsh word in my direction, always treating me with utmost consideration. One night, as we wearily flew home in the Air Canada first-class section on the "red-eye" from Edmonton, after playing for the Klondike Days festival at the Coliseum, Gordon saw me trying to sleep curled up in two adjoining seats and came over to tuck me in with a couple of extra pillows and a warm blanket. It was those small thoughtful gestures I will never forget. Lightfoot found himself under considerable pressure in 1977, signing, then unsigning, with superstar manager Jerry Weintraub and disputing with Warner Records. Here was a taste of the tough side of the music business that Pastore had warned me about.

We were booked in all the major summer festivals and outdoor venues from Tanglewood and the Merriweather Post Pavilion to Pine Knob, Michigan, and the Garden State Arts Center. Playing before these massive audiences gradually became routine, until I felt quite at home in front of the ten thousand to twenty thousand people that Gordon drew each night. The most difficult concerts to endure had been those early student recitals with friends, family, and teachers sitting in the front row; twenty thousand people dissolve into a massive sea of blackness from which I could detach and concentrate solely on the music. After some Spanish selections, I used to announce, tongue-in-cheek, "Now for something completely different. I'd like to play for you two pieces from the top ten in Europe — in 1780." The crowd invariably laughed before I launched into Bach's "Prelude and Gavotte." It was astonishing how receptive and attentive Gordon's audiences were to my rather specialized music. The people who came to hear "Sundown" or "In the Early

Morning Rain" listened with fascination to the contrasting sounds of Villa-Lobos and Granados.

One evening I was coerced by Gordon to join a few fans and the band for a drink in the hotel bar in Fort Worth, where we had performed to a sell-out crowd at the Tarrant County Convention Center. As we sipped our margaritas, a power failure forced us to resort to candles. Tiring of the noisy, smoke-filled lounge, I decided to head up to my room carrying a candle. "No candles allowed in the rooms, ma'am," the waitress admonished in her Texan drawl. Knowing that without a candle or flashlight my room would be totally dark, I tried a second time to abscond with an unlit candle in my handbag, but she intercepted me and I had to hand it back. Feeling angry and desperately tired, I groped my way up the outdoor staircase and stumbled into a pitch-black room, hoping I would not trip over my guitar case. Striking a match from a package I had been given by a sympathetic Pee Wee Charles, I proceeded to carefully light a corner of what felt like the standard Hertz Rent-a-Car sign on top of the television set. This provided enough light for me to find my way into the bathroom, where I could wash my face and brush my teeth. My next target was a green American Express Card folder, which burned brilliantly in the tub, followed by the room-service menu, dry-cleaning slips, and the Do Not Disturb sign. It was the only way to light the room and was certainly much more dangerous than a candle. I hoped that no other late-arrival guests were busy creating bonfires in their bathtubs!

After falling asleep at around one-thirty, I was startled by the sound of someone knocking on the door of my room. The alarm clock glowed two-thirty. Blearily feeling my way to the door in the dark, I heard Gordon asking to be let in. "My God," I thought, "has Gordon finally decided that his groupie scene has become boring in comparison with a blackout romance with his opening act?" He had never before come to my room, so I was caught off guard by the unexpected visit. Gordon explained that he was concerned I would be afraid to be alone in the dark. Standing at the doorway in my nightgown, with my hair in curlers and cream on my face, I was very thankful for that Texas blackout. To my disbelief, Gordon entered the room, and I heard him taking off his socks and shoes. Before I knew it, he had climbed into the far side of my king-sized bed, mumbling, "Goodnight, sweetheart, I'll be gone by the morning. Weird smell of smoke in this room, eh?" I tried to fall asleep, slightly uneasy knowing that Gordon's head was lying a few inches away from my pillow. Suddenly I felt him jump out of bed. "What next?" I thought. "Is he having to use the bathroom every few minutes after all those beers and margaritas?" "I forgot, my guitars are in my own room," he explained, zipping up his leather jacket. "I'll be back in five minutes." Sure enough, a few minutes later, there was Gordon banging open the door with his two guitars. I eventually fell asleep and woke around nine to find a pile of ashes in the bath, an empty bed, and no guitars. Had I dreamed it all?

At breakfast Gordon looked a little sheepish and inquired if I had slept well that night. The band, busy wolfing down their scrambled eggs, paid no attention to the loaded question. Later I wondered if perhaps Gordon himself had been afraid to be alone in the dark. Whatever his reasons, I thought it most chivalrous of him to have kept me company. The one night Gordon Lightfoot and I shared a bed was not quite as people might have speculated!

On my birthday, July 11, we had just arrived to play at the Saratoga Springs Performing Arts Center. While I was having lunch in a restaurant with Gordon and the band, a beautifully lit birthday cake approached us, carried on high by two smiling waiters singing "Happy Birthday." "Oh, Gordon, you shouldn't have!" I exclaimed. "No, it's nothing to do with me," he insisted, as the cake drew near. "Oh, how sweet of you guys," I said, addressing the band, who looked puzzled, until the creamy concoction headed straight past us to the very next table! Gordon must have felt badly that my birthday had not been acknowledged; he excused himself from the table for a few minutes. Later, beside my dessert plate, I found a little wrought-iron cannon about four inches high. "Where did this thing come from?" I queried amusedly, not realizing it was for me. "Well, that's the best present I could find in the gift shop," Gordon mumbled. I thanked him with a hug and kiss while the band cheered. Later that night, when our plane was boarded by Canadian customs officials on our return to Toronto, we were asked if we had anything to declare. "Oh, nothing at all," Gordon answered confidently, until Barry chirped up, "Except for Liona's cannon." "What cannon, miss?" the unsmiling official demanded, making me unpack my entire suitcase until he satisfied himself that I was not importing illegal firearms into Canada.

As often happened, Gordon drove me home from the airport, since I lived en route to his house in Rosedale. At 4:00 a.m., when we pulled up in front of my parents' Paragon Road house, he asked if he could use our toilet facilities for a moment. "By all means," I replied, "but creep into the house quietly 'cause my parents' bedroom is quite near the bathroom on the main floor." After pointing him in the right direction, I tiptoed back down the hall. Suddenly I became aware that my mother had awakened and, without a stitch on, was sleepily stumbling towards the bathroom door, thinking it was me in there. Our family has always been unselfconscious about nudity, and on summer nights we always slept *au naturel*. I reached the bathroom door just as she was about to enter. She had already turned the doorhandle, pulling it slightly ajar. In an urgent whisper, I emphasized, "Don't go in the bathroom!" My mother, seeing my panicked eyes and being in a somnambulistic state, had a vision of a monstrous bear that I had locked in the bathroom. Letting out a blood-curdling scream and pulling the door shut fast, she ran off confused to her bedroom, howling all the way! At this point, Gordon was convinced that my mother had seen him standing there taking a leak; she must be shrieking at the sight of a naked man. Gordon fled from the house, embarrassed by what he presumed my mother had seen. By now, Mother was back in bed fully awake, laughing uncontrollably about the impact she must have had on the unfortunate Mr. Lightfoot, who while peacefully relieving himself had been abruptly interrupted by a naked woman backing into the door and letting out hysterical shrieks. Never again did Gordon dare come into our house on the way home from the airport, even though I assured him that my mother would not be giving any repeat performances. He was not taking any chances.

New York's International Creative Management booked Gordon and me four concerts in Lincoln Center's Avery Fisher Hall. This was to be the Big Time in the Big Apple; both of us were excited and apprehensive about how we would be received by the New York critics. Cal decided to smuggle himself into the luxurious Pierre Hotel, where Gordon's entourage was staying. It was the first and almost the last time that I took a boyfriend on tour. Whenever I sat down to practise the guitar, I felt guilty for neglecting Cal, who would stretch out on the bed and tell me my pieces sounded so good they did not require rehearsing. "Why don't you come over here and let me give you a cuddle instead of going over and over that same old music?" he would complain. If I decided to oblige, I immediately felt guilty for neglecting the guitar, which was, after all, the reason we were in New York. Cal's amorous demands were not allowing me enough rest; these conflicts left me feeling unfocused and distracted. I resolved that, in future, I must separate my personal and professional lives.

Variety gave us a great review, saying, "Liona made the guitar sound as if it were invented for her alone." Hopefully no other guitarists read *Variety*! During a couple of meetings with London Records, who had taken over the international distribution of my albums from Boot, I tried to convince them that the Lightfoot tour was exposing me to massive audiences. Why could they not make a stronger effort at record distribution in the cities where I would be appearing? It was all rather futile, as the ultra-classical executives at London had their heads so buried in operatic negotiations and symphonic scores that they neither knew nor cared who Lightfoot was. Regrettably, they missed a unique marketing and sales opportunity for my albums because of their narrow classical outlook. As soon as my Boot contract expired I signed a five-album deal with CBS Masterworks in New York, which released *The First Lady of the Guitar* and *Spanish Fantasy*. At last I had a strong label with better international distribution.

Gordon and I flew off to Texas to woo sell-out crowds in large venues, including Fort Worth's Tarrant County Convention Center. The Texans, our most ebullient and enthusiastic audiences, loved us both. In the border town of El Paso, Mexicans whistled and shouted loud bravos after my Spanish pieces. Two fierce Dobermans had been released into Gordon's Lear jet to sniff out any drugs, but luckily no illicit substances were detected. In Cincinnati I asked one of the backstage organizers for a Coke; he returned twenty minutes later and whispered that the supply would be arriving with the promoter within the hour. I gave him a puzzled look, explaining that all I wanted was a Coca-Cola! Somehow I always felt too ingenuous for the tough world of rock and roll with its leather-jacketed promoters and macho crews.

Gordon was honoured in October 1976 by the city of Duluth, Minnesota, home to many of the sailors who had drowned on the *Edmund Fitzgerald* when it sank in Lake Superior. The ship's tragedy had been chronicled by Gordon in his epic ballad "The Wreck of the Edmund Fitzgerald," which was then number one on all the charts. In every city we played, arenas and hockey stadiums were jammed to capacity. I was becoming accustomed to large crowds and stages on centre ice. Vivien, studying dentistry in Chicago, came to see us in Kalamazoo, Michigan, incredulous that her sister was about to pluck her guitar pieces before twelve thousand people.

It was an exciting time in my career, offering me a taste of the lifestyle shared by major performing stars — backstage introductions to John Denver and Kris Kristofferson, private jets, limos, post-concert parties, and wild applause. In between my Lightfoot tours, I continued to play smaller recitals — Powell River, British Columbia; Wolfville, Nova Scotia; Cape Breton; Lennoxville, Quebec. I played *Fantasía para un Gentilhombre* with the National Arts Centre Orchestra under

Mario Bernardi at two concerts in Ottawa, relishing the contrasts between the large and small concerts, and appreciating each situation for its individual satisfactions; the variety of experiences kept everything fresh and stimulating.

In Seattle, after giving a private guitar lesson to the chief design engineer of Boeing, Murray Booth, I was invited on a fascinating tour of his plant, where he recklessly allowed me to clamber into Air Force One, the U.S. president's plane, which was being refitted in one of the hangars. As I sat in the pilot's seat and snapped a photo, a silent alarm was triggered; the next thing we knew, two Boeing officials in cars with blaring sirens raced up to the plane to reprimand him and confiscate my film.

In August 1976, Gordon accepted four dates at the Universal Amphitheater in Los Angeles. Having never been to the City of Angels, I was elated at the prospect of visiting Beverly Hills and Hollywood. We stayed at the Hyatt on Sunset Boulevard, and every evening were driven over the twists and curves of Laurel Canyon to Universal Studios. The evenings were so chilly that, wearing only a thin cotton gown, I froze on the outdoor stage during my first show. For the remaining three performances, I warmed my fingers on a hot-water bottle hidden behind my chair. On a whim, I looked up my lost love from 1966, Paul Koslo. He came to hear the concert and later partake in my feast of fruit, cheese, and wine in the private Winnebago I had been assigned on the amphitheater back lot. Following his dreams, Paul had pursued his acting career in Hollywood. Even more "spacey" and dissipated than he had been during his acid-tripping days in Toronto, my romantic teenage heartthrob had become a movie star. I preferred to remember the hippie idealist passionately strumming his guitar in my parents' living room. Memories are sometimes better left shrouded in the past.

Gordon had developed a drinking problem, which was becoming harder and harder to conceal. At the slightest provocation, he exploded at his employees. Some evenings our headliner was decidedly tipsy before the shows, causing his promoters acute consternation.

The making and breaking of management deals, combined with a series of erratic romances, was exacting its toll from the troubled troubadour from Orillia. Wisely, Gordon overcame the drinking habit in the early eighties. One day he asked what I was doing with the cheques he generously paid me every week. I explained that I was saving up to help my parents buy a larger house. Paragon Road could no longer contain all the Boyd gang, and I was embarrassed to have only a small basement room to call my own. Gordon introduced me to his accountant, who set up my corporation, Liona Boyd Productions Inc. Little did I know that, twenty years later, this relationship would cost me all the fees I had earned from Gordon, as the accountant involved me, along with many others, in poor real-estate investments. That same year, we relocated to a more spacious house in Etobicoke, on the shoreline of prehistoric Lake Iroquois, which is now part of Toronto.

While on the road with Gordon, I used to listen from the sidelines to his endless problems with lawyers, agents, and managers. I had always reasoned that everything would become easier once I "hit it big" as a recording artist, but money and success complicate life; within a few years, I was experiencing the same professional headaches.

Towards the end of my Lightfoot tours, my sporadic life with Cal had become a daily roller-coaster ride and I was increasingly afraid of his emotional ups and downs. His volatile nature was too much of a contrast to my more even temperament. On several occasions, I flew back to Toronto only to find that my disconsolate lover had put himself on the next plane and turned up on the doorstep of my parents' house begging forgiveness. Finally, I decided that his ongoing jealousy towards my career was intolerable. The situation was exacerbated by the knowledge that he had countless contacts in the music world, yet refused my requests for introductions. One night he screamed at me for wanting to play on a telethon. The next moment he was in tears, telling me I was the love of his life. The dizzying see-saw of feelings grew unbearable, and one December evening in 1976, after a dispute, he started to hit me uncontrollably. Terrified by his aberrant behaviour, I fled to a neighbour's house, where I spent the night wrapped in a blanket on the carpet after calling the police. Physical violence was something I had not anticipated. The next morning, I packed all my belongings while an officer observed, and caught a plane to Mexico, where my parents were spending Christmas.

It was a terrible trip. I cried on the plane, knowing it was finally over between Cal and me. On arrival in Mexico City, I learned that the airline could not locate my guitar; bad enough to lose my boyfriend, but losing my guitar was even worse! A girlfriend of Mexico's famous actor Cantinflas, whom I had met on the plane, tried to ameliorate my distress, inviting me to stay in her sumptuous Camino Real suite while the airlines searched for my missing guitar. I could not have been the best of company. After three days of anxious waiting, I was thrilled to see Cantinflas's chauffeur miraculously materialize with my guitar, exclaiming triumphantly, "She is found in Seattle!" I fought my way through the crowded bus station to the only available transportation — a third-class Flecha Amarilla bus crammed to the roof with peasants and bleating goats. I had to support on my knees a wizened peasant woman with a tubercular cough, who dumped a basket containing her squawking rooster at my feet. After four interminable hours of bumping along mountain roads and lurching to an uncertain halt at every dusty village, the bus deposited me in the darkened market streets of San Miguel de Allende. I struggled my way to the central Jardín, where I knew my anxious parents had been waiting for hours, expecting me to arrive on the first-class bus, La Estrella del Norte. The bells of the Parroquia started to ring as I dragged my guitar case over the familiar cobblestoned streets. It was midnight on Christmas Eve. The stresses of the preceding week left me so enervated that I spent the next week in bed, cursing the emotional maelstrom that Cal had put me through.

10

"Bond, James Bond"

During 1978, Haber Artists continued to handle my Canadian, U.S., and some international dates. Since I had played arenas and stadiums as Gordon Lightfoot's opening act the year before, Haber was able to book solo recitals in some of the more intimate concert halls. Many in the audience had been introduced to my music through Gordon's shows, which were building a new following south of the border. My gamble in Minneapolis had paid off. Next, Haber packed me off to New Zealand for seventeen concerts organized by Graham Atkinson, the former manager of the National Ballet of New Zealand. Lured by the opportunity to see another part of the world, I agreed to the six-week tour, knowingly sacrificing much of my precious Canadian summer. In August, alone in a straw-roofed hotel room in the antipodean paradise of Fiji, my first layover, I dreamed up the idea of transcribing three Domenico Cimarosa sonatas in the key of D to create a guitar concerto, which a year later I recorded with the English Chamber Orchestra in London.

A cold rain greeted me in Auckland, where in a damp little motel I reviewed the gruelling tour schedule which involved motoring hundreds of miles all over the North and South islands. On the black-and-white television, a live broadcast of the Commonwealth Games in Edmonton showed Canada's prime minister, Pierre Trudeau, smiling in his shirtsleeves as he watched the high-jump competition. How warm and summery it looked — how very far away. I brewed a cup of tea, filled a hot-water bottle to warm my chilly sheets, and prayed the six weeks would pass quickly. New Zealand was the worst tour of my career: endless cold motels; greasy, overcooked food; and a wearing schedule of press interviews, TV shows, and concerts. I shivered my way through performances in Timaru, Wanganui, and Invercargill, even using electric heaters on the stage in Christchurch, where I could see my breath in the air. For some inexplicable reason, I lost half of my hair; as I combed my normally thick tresses, strands pulled loose as though I were victim of some chemotherapy nightmare. The stresses of this tour were taking their toll.

Two rock fans, presuming I was one of their kind, bought front-row seats to the Auckland concert. The teenaged boys told me later how puzzled they had been by my lack of onstage "gear." After the initial shock, when my guitar whispered instead of wailed, far from being turned off by the acoustic and classical nature of my presentation, they converted to avid fans who enthusiastically pursued my meanderings around their country. At each concert, the long-haired "groupies" sat transfixed, radiating the wide-eyed awe of adolescent obsession. I wonder if they ever realized their dreams of becoming guitarists.

Atkinson and his obese, loud-spoken wife travelled with me. They were hardly my idea of good companionship on the road, so I started to compose the lyrics and music to songs as we wound our way across sodden sheep-dotted landscapes. The six songs, which were completed by the time the tour had ended, were eventually produced in the recording studio by Eric Robertson and made into demo tapes. For someone who hates wasting time, I had to find a creative way to pass the endless hours imprisoned in the back seat of Atkinson's station-wagon.

After putting me through six weeks of this exhausting schedule, Atkinson handed me a cheque that bounced when I returned to Toronto. The Canadian High Commission spent months trying to help me collect, but Atkinson had already absconded with the profits and could not be traced. My only compensation had been a ten-dollar sheepskin he bought me — no doubt after a pang of guilt — in the airport gift shop. When I visited Auckland a decade later, I was informed that the crooked promoter was serving time for embezzlement. I hate to think how many other innocents he had exploited. New Zealand is a beautiful country, but that dreary tour of 1978 left a bitter after-taste. My only treat was being stranded for two days on the tropical island of Tahiti when Pan Am developed engine trouble en route to Los Angeles. At that point, however, I felt so desperate to get home to North America that Papeete's beauty was all but lost on my travel-weary eyes, which were still counting sheep.

As my career expanded in the late seventies, I welcomed any offers of international exposure. Some music from Dr. Carlos Payet, a young San Salvadorian composer and professional psychiatrist, arrived in the mail. "Cabellos de Oro" and "Lejanía" were lovely melodic pieces that he had dedicated to me. After learning how much I had enjoyed his compositions, Payet arranged some performances for me in San Salvador, where I was welcomed like one of the family by the Guttfreunds, patrons of the arts. Enchanted, I sat eating home-grown canteloupes in their garden gazebo surrounded by tropical flowering trees whose perfumes scented the warm air, while sweet trilling birds strutted around displaying their plumage. On the second night of my stay, the earthquake that devastated Guatemala jolted me out of bed. Fearing another *terremoto* might play tremolo during the night, I judiciously plotted an escape route out of my room into the garden.

The symphony orchestra of San Salvador comprised seventy enthusiastic musicians who, between gigs playing Beethoven and

Brahms, moonlighted in local bands around town. As there was no dressing room in the theatre where we performed Rodrigo's *Fantasía para un Gentilhombre* and Vivaldi's "Concerto in D," I resorted to tuning my guitar between two cars in the outdoor parking lot! Later that evening, I ran into the concert-master serenading tables in a restaurant and several members of the brass section waiting to be hired on the street that was famous for *mariachis*.

The following day, while I was halfway through a solo concert, a power failure plunged the hall into darkness. As luck would have it, I had just started "Etude No. 17" by Fernando Sor, the easiest selection in the program; miraculously, my fingers made it through to the end without a slip. The audience, most impressed by my dexterity in the dark, was clapping wildly when the electricity returned, just in time for Sor's "Variations on a Theme by Mozart" — a piece that would surely have ended in disaster without lights to see the finger-board. Payet developed a severe case of infatuation that inspired him to write "Danza Norteña" and "Brisas del Lempa," which I later recorded on my album *Virtuoso*. Sadly for him, I was unwilling to reciprocate his affections; thus scorned by his Canadian muse, he became embittered and refused to write more music for me.

Carlos had introduced me to a gynecologist friend who also fell under the spell of my guitar. For years, he continued to send his ardent poems, songs, and love missives and he plastered an entire wall in his house with my pictures. A record album of his romantic songs featured my photo on the back cover and an opera he wrote was dedicated to me. What his poor wife must have thought of her husband's obsession I dared not imagine. After another enthusiastic eye-doctor started to write, I resolved to stay away from El Salvador; I might have the entire medical profession in chaos! Latin men are utterly helpless when it comes to the lethal combination of blondes and guitars!

As one of the world's leaders in nuclear technology, Canada had sold CANDU reactors to South America, and the minister of External Affairs, Don Jamieson, planned an "anti-nuclear-proliferation" tour to caution various countries to act responsibly when dealing with nuclear power and its military implications. The Canadian government invited me to travel with the delegation in January 1977 to perform at various state banquets as a goodwill cultural offering from the Far North. In addition to the after-dinner performances for Latin American heads of state, five public concerts and a few TV shows had been planned. When I scrutinized the tour schedule and read "concert at Torre Tagle Palace, Lima, Peru; private jet to the Campeche estate in Santos, Brazil; free day at the Cartagena beach, Colombia," my eyes lit up in anticipation.

I flew down to Rio de Janeiro ahead of the thirty press and diplomatic personnel comprising the Canadian delegation. A tangerine dawn was breaking as my Varig 747 banked over Sugar Loaf Mountain to the accompaniment of "The Girl from Ipanema," which was being piped over the sound system. Yes, I had finally made it to Brazil and was eagerly gazing down at a breathtaking view straight out of my Grade Twelve geography textbook. The traffic was chaotic, the humidity close to 100 per cent, but everywhere I was aware of music in the air and beautiful, smiling faces. The Brazilians embody a most aesthetically pleasing mixture of races, with toasted golden skin, slender African necks, and lithe figures. On the beaches and boardwalks, we drove past both men and women wearing *tangas*, the scantiest bikinis ever designed; when the Canadian delegation arrived, I could sense that no one was in any great hurry to return to Ottawa! Two days earlier, their private military jet had aborted a takeoff and ploughed into a snowy field at the end of the runway, causing everyone to evacuate down the chute. What a relief to have avoided that traumatic episode. There would be adrenalin enough for me in Brazil.

The Canadian embassy staff whisked me around for TV, radio, and newspaper interviews; because I spoke Spanish, everyone took it for granted that I understood Portuguese, the language of Brazil. On one musical variety show, a befeathered, scantily clad hostess approached me after I had played "Sounds of Bells" and rattled off unintelligible questions, shoving her microphone into my face for an answer. "*Si, he tocado la guitarra clásica por doce años* — yes, I have played the classical guitar for twelve years," I replied in Spanish to her torrent of Portuguese, which I was later told had dealt with Canada's cold weather! "*Es mi primera visita a Brazil*," I improvised, when she asked me what sort of guitar I played. The disjointed interview continued as I attempted to decipher her rapid-fire questions. Why did she keep talking about violins, I wondered. Finally the penny dropped — the word for guitar in Brazil must be *violáo*, and here I was a *violinista*! "*Hablo español pero absolutamente no hablo portugués* — I speak Spanish but absolutely no Portuguese," I said, emphasizing the "no" by making a zero with my thumb and index finger and directing it at the camera. The Canadian consul, John Bell, who was with me, cringed in embarrassment, and later explained that I had made what is considered *the* most obscene gesture to millions of Brazilians on their prime-time TV — a rather undiplomatic way to begin a concert tour!

The next day was my debut in Rio. As I sat tuning my guitar in the dressing room before show-time, all the lights suddenly died. "Oh, it's probably just a short blackout," I mused, recalling the frequent power failures in Mexico. After five minutes in the dark, I noticed a faint burning odour and anxiously opened the door. The corridor was filled with smoke, and orange flames shot from the direction of the hall. In panic, I grabbed my guitar and raced to the back door, where my audience was milling around making way for arriving fire trucks. In all the excitement and commotion, no one had thought to rescue the artist from her dressing room! I later learned that two television cameras had overloaded the power supply, sparking a fire that had rapidly spread to the carpets and chairs. Fortunately, the flames were soon extinguished, but it took one and a half hours before the smoke dissipated from the hall. Meanwhile, the good-natured audience waited patiently, seating themselves on the grassy slope behind the rear doors. Never have I played to such a packed hall as I did that unforgettable night in Rio. The temperature topped a hundred degrees, but people overflowed into the aisles, even seating themselves onstage, barely allowing room for my chair. Hushed during my playing, the audience broke into noisy, exuberant applause after each selection. Brazilians must be born with music coursing through their veins, so responsive are they to melody and rhythm. Such intense approbation is exhilarating for a concert artist; to this day, Brazil tops my list for audience reaction.

Occasionally during the course of a concert, I am overcome by a sensation that in some ways approximates an out-of-body experience. So intensely concentrated and involved am I in the music flowing through me that I have the illusion that I am observing the performance rather than creating it. Although my fingers are producing the music, my physical being seems to be floating somewhere up in the rafters of the theatre. Rio was one such memorable high point among my many concerts. The next day, back in Rio, John's foot was almost amputated by the propellor of a mishandled speedboat after he dived off our government yacht. At a private clinic, the international mecca of plastic surgery run by Dr. Pitanguy, I sat by his bedside with a bouquet of roses for him after they had miraculously reattached his unlucky extremity.

After accompanying me to a ridiculously disorganized television special, where the equipment seized up each time we began taping, my promoter, despairing of the congested traffic, bundled me into a police car whose blaring sirens forged a path towards the Museu de Arte de São Paulo — a novel way to arrive for a performance! Afterwards I signed autographs for the mob of beaming guitar enthusiasts, then, in the company of the attentive Canadian consul, strolled around the Hilton Hotel where I was staying. It was after midnight, but the traffic jams were worse than rush hour in New York, and colourful crowds pushed and shoved along the sidewalks. Hundreds of beautiful women with tight-fitting dresses, elaborate hairstyles, and heavy make-up leaned against the street lamps and parked cars. As they flashed dazzling smiles in our direction, I wondered what they were all waiting for. John laughed at my naïveté, explaining that this was the centre of São Paulo's transvestite quarter; all the gorgeous ladies were actually men! I was speechless with disbelief. We elbowed our way into one of the small bars spilling infectious Brazilian samba onto the side-streets. After gyrating with me to the tropical rhythms, John was approached by a cinnamon-coloured beauty inquiring which doctor and treatments I had been using. Later, I was told that the transvestites combine hormonal therapy and plastic surgery to enhance their feminine appearance. This "man" obviously thought I was a smashing success and had been eyeing me with envy.

As I was playing my final encore in Brasilia, I became aware of a gigantic cockroach with long, waving feelers making slow and steady progress towards me across the wooden floor. The concert hall was designed with a lowered stage separated from the bank of audience chairs by an orchestra pit, so everyone had ringside seats for the monster's approach. The women told me afterwards how they held their breath, expecting shrieks at any moment. A North American cockroach would never have fazed me, thanks to my lifetime of exposure to Damien's entomological enterprises, but in Brazil insects grow to Amazonian proportions! Notes tumbled over one another faster and faster as I slid my chair backwards a few inches at a time to counteract the creature's inexorable approach, but he was determined to head for the music; soon only millimetres remained between him and my skirt, which draped invitingly on the floor. I placed both feet on top of my wooden footstool, frantically praying that he would make a detour. But my guardian angel must have been off-duty that night! I felt the "thing" creep up my open sandal, his feelers tickling my ankle. Knowing that only a few bars of music remained, I willed myself to ignore the sensations, although my trembling left-hand vibrato was becoming more and more erratic. With the last chord finally struck, I leaped into the air, using my concert skirt to fling the unwelcome visitor to the floor. The audience clattered to their feet, rewarding me with a standing ovation, yelling, "Bravo, Liona. Bravo!" It seemed a fitting finale to this unpredictably exciting tour of Brazil.

The next morning's 6:00 a.m. wake-up call found me feeling like a springbok shot by a tranquilizer dart, thanks to a late-night reception in Jamieson's honour at which I had been coerced to perform. In a somnambulistic stupor, I stuffed my suitcase for the drive to the Brasilia airport, where our Canadian delegation was patiently awaiting Jamieson's limousine. With a flash of silver wings, a sleek Gulf Stream II materialized out of the cornflower-blue skies and taxied up beside our government's jet. Down her steps filed several well-groomed attendants in uniform, followed by a distinguished-looking businessman. Gary German from Noranda Inc., who had been chivalrously carrying my guitar case in the heat, asked if I would like to meet Edgar Kaiser, Jr. — someone he knew from various business dealings. To me, the name Kaiser conjured up no other association than buns ordered in a New York deli. "Sure," I replied drowsily, suddenly conscious of my straggly unwashed hair, red eyes, and rather dissipated appearance. Edgar Kaiser nevertheless greeted me with enthusiasm and extended an invitation into his air-conditioned plane, leaving poor Gary and my guitar to melt on the hot tarmac.

I was introduced to the crew and offered a revivifying drink of iced orange juice. The springbok sprang back to life. "May I have your telephone number in Toronto?" the blond-haired man in his late thirties inquired with a twinkle in his eyes before I left his plane. I had never heard of Edgar Kaiser, nor his grandfather, the legendary tycoon Henry Kaiser, but his charming manner and account of how he had played guitar and written songs years ago in Buenos Aires aroused my interest and persuaded me to scribble my phone number on his monogrammed note pad. Edgar Kaiser was not the dark Latin-lover stereotype of my fantasies, but he was bright and charming, and ran a two-billion-dollar empire.

My South American tour concluded with visits to Bogotá, Cartagena, and Caracas, where Antonio Lauro, the composer, invited me to dine with his family after an impromptu recital for his students. On my return to Toronto, Edgar started to phone me from various corners of the world where he was deal-making — Belgrade, Reykjavik, and

Paris — hoping we could meet in New York. Dinner at the 21 Club was followed by dancing at Regine's trendy disco, where the staff bent at the waist like plastic juice straws as they passed us, obsequiously whispering, "Good evening, Mr. Kaiser." How very impressive that everyone from the *maître d'* to the coat-check girl knew his name! Edgar explained how his grandfather, the Californian Henry John Kaiser, had founded a shipbuilding company that, after the First World War, was expanded into Kaiser Industries, a multinational conglomerate dealing in steel and aluminum. His grandson, Edgar, had taken over the interests of this powerful family, including the Kaiser Permanente, a health-maintenance organization. After graduating from Stanford and Harvard, he ran Kaiser Resources Ltd. in Vancouver, exporting coal to many countries around the globe. He visited these countries in the spanking new executive jet I had seen in Brasilia, which he referred to as "Silk," after the registration letters *SLK* painted on her side.

One morning, Silk picked me up after a concert I had given in Tempe, Arizona, at Arizona State University's Grady Gammage Memorial Auditorium, designed by Frank Lloyd Wright. The young fellow from the student committee who drove me to the airport to "catch my plane to New York" looked on in disbelief as he handed me my paltry cheque and watched me ascend into a multi-million-dollar jet. The seductive world of Edgar Kaiser, whose high-flying international deals were conducted with great aplomb, started to reveal itself as I became privy to his intriguing business affairs. What a contrast to my non-materialistic lifestyle — where the Tokyo Stock Exchange and the price of crude oil never intruded on my consciousness. Before I knew it, I was buying a few shares in Kaiser Resources to feel a part of his mercurial business scene.

Edgar and I began to see each other whenever our busy schedules would permit. I had just finished recording an album of short melodic pieces, *Miniatures for Guitar* and had to juggle concert and studio commitments in order to accommodate our dates. He bought a block of tickets for his Kaiser Resources executives to attend my concert at Vancouver's Orpheum Theatre and later hosted a reception. My new *amour* was serenaded with guitar music in his exquisitely furnished private apartment atop the Waldorf Towers in New York. I admired the art collection at his rambling house in Vancouver, and dined at the Fairmont Hotel in San Francisco after racing around the "City by the Bay" in his Italian sports car. It felt as though I had been hurled into the pages of a Harlequin romance novel. Edgar regaled me with stories of his eighteen months in Vietnam with the U.S. Agency for International Development, his CIA and Trilateral Commission connections, his days at Harvard, his time as a White House Fellow under President Lyndon Johnson, and his experiences with the international Young Presidents' Organization and an ultra-exclusive men's club, Bohemian Grove. It was difficult not to be impressed by the many charity boards and international business councils on which he had served. High above the strato-cumulus, I succumbed to Dionysian delights during my initiation into the "Mile High Club." At heart, my business magnate was a romantic who sang me songs while picking out the chords on my guitar. How could I possibly resist his attentions? Edgar commissioned a gold brooch inlaid with rubies and diamonds, and a hand-carved cherry-wood music stand depicting the Garden of Eden, which became one of my most treasured possessions. He was a truly fascinating young man, with a love for the arts, music, and poetry, in addition to a brilliant business mind; fate, however, did not intend our lives to continue to flow together.

In retrospect, I must have seemed utterly naïve and unsophisti-cated compared with the glamorous society women Edgar had dated. My clothes were often unstylish things picked up at the Toronto Symphony sale or home-made by my mother. Focusing on my career, I had neither the time nor the inclination to be concerned about the latest fashions, and I remember him despairing over my *basse couture* outfits and K-Mart lingerie. I shudder to think how my flyaway hair and unorthodox wardrobe must have been viewed by his friends. *Stereo Review* and *Guitar Player* magazine held more

interest for me than *Vogue*. I had never heard of Judith Lieber
evening purses, Ferragamo shoes, or Christian Dior negligées. In
contrast, Edgar was constantly calculating the style and image he
wished to project as "young tycoon." Everything, from the expensive
cuff-links and Swiss watch to the pinstripe suits, was intended to
maintain this impression. The elite world of Edgar Kaiser seemed to
exist in another dimension, but I sometimes wondered who really
had the happier life. He would be up at dawn placing urgent calls to
Europe and Japan; being responsible for manipulating millions of
dollars around the world was a stressful job. Edgar's secretary, Sue,
organized his entire life, including our "dates," but a sixth sense
made me suspect she harboured more than secretarial ambitions
towards her boss; my intuition would later prove to be correct.

In March, *People* magazine published a story on my career that
unfortunately mentioned my friendship with a certain Mr. Kaiser, age
seventy-two — Edgar's father! The magazine was forced to print
an apology in their next issue, but I felt badly about the mistake,
especially as Edgar's father was in failing health.

Kaiser Junior explained how he could be an easy target for women,
many of whom wanted to have his child in order to get financial
support. I was shocked that Edgar had to concern himself with such
chicanery, but I confess that during some idle moments, I pondered
the fantasy that he had planted in my mind. If I were to bear the son
he desperately desired, I would probably become Mrs. Kaiser, with a
life of Hawaiian mansions, private jets, and the best recording studios
money could buy! In return, I would have to learn to live with Mr.
Kaiser's complex personality, considerably large ego, and reputed
taste for glamorous women. No doubt it would spell the end of my
guitar profession, but had I not already had a wonderfully satisfying
career, and had I been in love rather than infatuated, I would have
to admit that I too might have been tempted by that clichéd strategy
of romance novels.

Edgar, I am sure, must have realized that I would make a hopeless
wife for someone with his lifestyle. Would I know how to select

cashmere suits in the fashionable boutiques of Paris, chat with the ski crowd in Saint-Moritz, or host New York dinner parties for his fellow tycoons? Would I have wanted to spend days at hairstylists and dress designers in order to fulfill the role of Mrs. Tycoon? I would have failed him miserably; luckily we both made the right decision, but in 1977 ours was indeed a sweet romance.

At the end of the summer, Edgar suddenly jetted in to Toronto; he had "something serious" to discuss. We walked hand in hand along the Humber River trail in James Gardens, where the air had that nostalgic autumn tang and the maples were streaked with orange. "It's to do with my secretary, Sue," he started. I already knew before he spoke another word; Edgar was about to be given a son.

Edgar and I still exchange occasional phone calls and send each other Christmas cards. Through our friendship, I was exposed briefly to a way of life known to only a privileged few. Even something as simple as accepting an orange juice in a Brazilian airport can influence your life and inadvertently enlarge your perception of the world!

As my concerts in Brazil had been so well received, I was invited back for return engagements in São Paulo, Belo Horizonte, and Rio, where Madame Villa-Lobos, the widow of Brazil's famous composer, came backstage to offer congratulations on my interpretations of her husband's music. For my debut recital in Salvador, a charming town in the province of Bahía, I was accommodated in the Convento do Carmo, now functioning as a hotel. On the first evening, the Canadian ambassador to Brazil, Jim Stone, and his wife cajoled me into bringing my guitar down to the central courtyard. Under a full moon, we leisurely sipped Cointreaus, enjoying the evening air perfumed with the scent of night-flowering vines blanketing the old walls. My playing attracted three other guests, who drew close to listen. The producer, director, and assistant director — Cubby Broccoli, Lewis Gilbert, and Bill Cartlidge — of the James Bond films had been scouting around South America in search of locations for *Moonraker*. The ambassador made introductions and we conversed into the night, interspersing our repartee with their requests from my repertoire.

The next evening, after my recital in a resonant church, the Bond team and I strolled around the town together exploring the "movie set" streets, which were lined with the brightly coloured wooden houses characteristic of Salvador. Lewis Gilbert was one of the most interesting and amusing men I had ever met. Born in England, he was at that time based in Paris. *Alfie* and two of the James Bond pictures were among his many successes. Cubby and Lewis, both classical music aficionados, invited me to stop by their studios to watch some of the *Moonraker* production whenever I was next in Paris.

A couple of months later, booked to perform in the French capital, I checked into the Raphael Hotel on avenue Kleber, where the Bond team was staying. What fun to be on the set of *Moonraker* as a guest of the producer and the director! Their handsome British star, Roger Moore, invited me to lunch in a rustic café near the Château de Vaux-le-Vicomte, where the shoot was under way. As we motored through rolling French countryside in his Rolls-Royce, with the haunting theme of *Concierto de Aranjuez* on the tape deck, I felt as though I had stepped into an episode of "The Saint." It was the only time in my life that I swallowed raw oysters; one does not say, "No, thank you," to James Bond! Roger showed me a few pieces he had learned to finger on the classical guitar, then impressed the director with his prowess by pretending I had just given him a quick lesson.

The filming was fascinating to watch — shouts of "action," "camera rolling," noisy helicopter flights, and daredevil stunt men. The cheerful British unit demanded their ritual tea breaks, while the serious French insisted on long gourmet lunches — much to the chagrin of the Brits. Roger, dressed in black 007 garb, scouted around the magnificent château trying to find the washrooms I had requested. As I followed his trim figure down the granite staircases, I imagined I had been drawn into the film itself; instead of toilets, we were in search of secret subterranean chambers. In *Moonraker*, when the

First meeting: an afternoon at Harrington Lake with Pierre and Margaret Trudeau (with Justin).

With Pierre Trudeau at an ACTRA Awards dinner. (*Canada Wide Feature Services*. Used with permission)

Mother and I do the Great Wall of China.

My best friend, Dale Mearns, and I at the *Paul Anka Show.*

Arthur Erickson, a great architect and travel companion.

Joel Bell and the "new-look" me at the Toronto Arts Awards.

My husband Jack and me, with actress Shirley Jones, at Beverly Hills fund-raiser.

The Boyd Gang at my wedding to Jack: Damien, Colin, Vivien, me, Mother, and Father. (*Lee Salem*)

Hamming it up in the back garden of the Peach House.

The second great love of my life, Muffin. *(LEE SALEM)*

Barefoot in California, 1994. *(KEITH WILLIAMSON)*

Posing by the pool, today. (*Tiziana Orsini*)

Château de Vaux-le-Vicomte is seen from an aerial perspective, I am on set ensconced in the back of Roger's Rolls so as not to be spotted by the cameras! During one of the breaks, when I played Carlos Payet's "Lejanía," Moore observed accurately that the melody echoed my name. "I bet Payet was in love with you when he wrote that piece," he remarked. Roger was a most astute man. I autographed one of my albums for him, and a few years later he selected it for a BBC Radio show, "Desert Island Discs," in which celebrities name ten favourite albums they would choose if stranded on a desert island. I would not have minded being stranded with Roger on that island along with my disc!

The Bond team invited me to the Billancourt studios, outside Paris, where I witnessed more filming. When stray sparks from the special-effects explosions ignited a chemically treated wooden ceiling, a panicky extra pushed open the huge set doors, creating a draft that spread the flames even faster. Never have I seen people run as fast as Lewis, Cubby, and Bill scrambling out to safety. "These French blokes are bloody pyromaniacs!" Lewis growled angrily as the stand-by firemen rushed to hose down the blaze. For the remainder of the shoot, I judiciously positioned myself beside the exit. It was fascinating to watch John Glen, the editor, painstakingly piecing together the rough cuts of Bond's extravagant adventure, or to talk to several of the actors, including "Jaws," Bond's seven-foot nemesis with teeth of steel.

One evening a group of us were sitting around a candlelit table, enjoying a dinner in one of the Latin Quarter restaurants. Bill was describing in vivid detail how the space station would be blown to smithereens, explaining in a low, serious voice the number of guards who would be killed. The precise choreography of a Bond production can be as complex as any military manoeuvre. I gradually became aware of the incredulous expressions on the faces of a couple of elderly American tourists dining at the table adjacent to ours. Evidently they believed themselves privy to the malevolent machinations of a gang of British terrorists!

My performing and recording itinerary had kept my calendar crammed to capacity. The few days at home in between tours were whirlwinds of unpacking and repacking, answering telephone messages, and sorting records to sell after concerts, all while trying to squeeze in a few social evenings with friends. Tom York had become my confidante when the trials of touring left me exhausted and road-weary. An acclaimed author, intellectual, sensual adventurer, jazz aficionado, and United Church minister, Tom York offered sanctuary and friendship, dispensing spiritual wisdom and tempering my "have guitar, will travel" *modus operandi.* I found his conversation stimulating, occasionally exasperating, but always challenging. We shared fireside chats at a Hockley Valley retreat, Abraxas, where my parents were members of a primal-therapy team, as well as snowshoe expeditions in the dead of winter, jazz albums by candlelight, and three New Year's Eves. I read his books *We, the Wilderness, Trapper, Snowman,* and *Sleep in the Woods,* affectionate poems he occasionally dedicated to me, rough drafts from his novel in progress, and transcripts of his Sunday sermons. Tom was a most extraordinary person who touched the lives of many with his non-judgmental ministry and his compassionate tolerance for humanity's weaknesses. He had survived with the Inuit in remote Arctic outposts, lived with the Natives in northern British Columbia, weathered an anchoritic winter in a remote Maritime cabin, fathered four children, and served a faithful Toronto congregation who defended his unorthodox services when they occasionally raised the eyebrows of church elders. Sadly, Tom, my beloved and loyal friend of the late seventies, died at the hands of a drunken driver on January 2, 1988. I sorely miss his calming presence in my life and hope his spiritual journey continued in the world beyond.

In the seventies, my father left the teaching profession to help run a therapeutic retreat; Vivien, after qualifying at the University of Toronto's dental school, went away to gain further experience at Michael Reese Hospital in south-side Chicago; Damien was studying for his degree in biochemistry at the University of Toronto; my

mother qualified as a massage therapist and pursued university studies in Spanish, as well as keeping busy with all aspects of my career.

In relation to the business side of my career, in between my
concert engagements, my mother and I had been having all kinds
of high-pressure meetings with lawyers and accountants. Noticing a
break in my schedule, I suggested replenishing our energies with a
week's holiday in Puerto Rico, where our Spanish could benefit from
a workout. How wonderful it would be to escape from the harried
world of concerts, guitar players, and anything connected with the
business of music!

Our packing was simple — a couple of cotton dresses, white slacks,
bikinis, and sandals. We flew via New York to San Juan, where a welcoming wall of hot, humid air hit us as we alighted from the plane.
A taxi with blaring Latin music took us to a small hotel picked at
random from a travel book. Within moments, we were sipping piña
coladas in a bougainvillea-filled terrace. What a lovely feeling to be
so far from the clutches of lawyers and accountants!

I had brought along a cheap Japanese "sun guitar" to play on the
beach and use to learn a Bach prelude for the Canadian Brass's new
record, *Unexplored Territory*. An hour's practice was enough to keep
my fingers flexible. "Let's go exploring the town," I suggested to my
mother, who was busily hanging our crumpled dresses in the closet
and sorting out traveller's cheques.

San Juan is a modern city with rows of tourist hotels, but we
headed for the central square in the older section of town. Suddenly
I heard my name called, and a group of long-haired, long-nailed
fellows I recognized from the Dallas and Seattle guitar societies
approached. "Eileen, Liona, we didn't know you were coming!" they
told us excitedly while, to my horror, Robert Vidal, the Paris Guitar
Competition mogul, padded towards me with the guitarist Oscar
Ghiglia at his side. "Why are all you guitarists here?" I started to
query, before realizing we were standing in front of a banner that
read "International Guitar Festival of Puerto Rico." "You must come
to the concert tonight," they insisted, as more guitar acquaintances

came to greet me. "So how is everything with your recordings? When are you playing in Seattle next? Where do you get your nail-polishing paper from? Do you know a good agent in Toronto who can organize concerts for the Puerto Rican players?" Questions flew from all directions — just what I had come three thousand miles to escape! Already the participants were inviting us to dinners and plotting out our next few days. "Oh, you'd love to meet Enrique! He has all your records. Liona, why don't you give a surprise master-class at the university tomorrow?" I looked at my mother in despair. We had to forfeit our planned evening's stroll around old San Juan to attend a soporific performance, followed by a reception where I was set upon by wide-eyed aficionados. "Tomorrow we're getting as far away from San Juan as possible," I resolved. I hated to appear ungrateful to people who obviously appreciated my work, but there are certain times when one needs to escape. This was definitely one of them.

I consulted a yellowing map on the wall of the hotel, and noticed a little town at the extreme opposite side of the island called Boquerón. We had been warned that it was dangerous to go "out on the island," but like an adventurer who throws a dart at an atlas and determines to go wherever it lands, I had made up my mind. We would go in search of Boquerón. As no buses or trains went there, we hired a garrulous taxi driver, who barrelled us over the twisting interior roads for three hours as we hung on for dear life.

The village was even more beautiful than we had imagined: a sleepy fishing outpost with not one tourist in sight. We were welcomed by the owner of a dilapidated hotel built on poles over the water's edge; my mother and I were his only guests. Our spacious room had large open windows and warped wooden floors. For eight dollars a night, it was perfection, in spite of a fierce-looking cockroach who was waiting to greet us in the bathroom sink! Boquerón turned out to be an idyllic spot — with quaint little streets and deserted, white sandy beaches stretching into the distance. The village fishermen, who spotted us immediately, decided to put on a show of local hospitality, bringing offerings of sweet pineapples and coconuts. Although our San Miguel Spanish was almost a different language from the local dialect, we managed to communicate. At dawn the next morning, I was gently lifted from my dreams by the mellifluous voices of the fishermen singing while preparing their boats, which were beached only a few yards from our room. As I lay in bed, feeling the warm caress of Caribbean breezes across my face and enjoying the sound of lapping waves, I knew this was the Puerto Rico I had dreamt of discovering.

We spent five perfect days in Boquerón. The handsome captain of the lobster fleet took us sailing in his boat to Rockefeller's private coral-strewn island, where we cooked a fresh red snapper on the beach. While we were on board, *el capitán* insisted on plying us with champagne, which we surreptitiously tossed into the blue Caribbean waters whenever he looked away, realizing that champagne and the boat's undulations were not compatible. Every day the appreciative "locals" were treated to guitar playing; one star-spangled evening, I gave an informal concert aboard one of their boats. With our new-found friends, we drifted through pearly seas around the indented coastline. A gentle purring of the motor was the only sound in that tropical night, as we cut through smooth warm water that shone with green phosphorescence whenever we trailed our fingers on its surface — an eerie green glow like that magical sea in the Rupert Bear stories of my childhood.

During one of our walks to the beach, we were assured by an elderly man that we had no need to worry about the gallant attentions of these friendly Latinos; they were so competitive that each one was watching like a hawk for any suggestive moves that his companions might try to make. What fun to have half a dozen coffee-eyed Puerto Ricans to flirt with! We felt comfortably safe in their charming, animated company. How many of life's rich experiences could so easily be passed by because of fear and misunderstanding. Certainly having my mother along helped, as Latin men tend to have great respect for *mamitas.* Playfully they taught us Spanish phrases in their local dialect and listened enthralled to my Agustín Barrios waltzes.

Each evening, when dusk dropped her velvet curtains, our empty hotel opened a bar at the end of a rickety wooden platform extending over the water. Here we danced with our new-found *amigos* to the juke-box music of a fellow from Spain called Julio Iglesias. How could I have guessed that several years later, I would be ensnared by that charismatic character from Madrid?

On our last day, while I was playing a Tárrega étude beside the pellucid tidal pools of a deserted, palm-strewn beach, two women appeared mirage-like on the horizon, slowly strolling along the water's edge towards us. Hearing my guitar, they had come over to greet us. To our astonishment, they turned out to be the wife and daughter-in-law of the one and only person I had been told to look up by a guitarist friend from Tennessee! They insisted we spend the evening in their villa, twenty miles inland, to discuss music and mutual acquaintances. It seemed that even the most desolate beach of a Puerto Rican fishing village could not guarantee protection from the amazingly ubiquitous world of the classical guitar!

11

Pierre

Robert Kaplan, a member of Parliament who later became Canada's solicitor-general, was an acquaintance of my parents. Hearing I had played at a private seminar for the renegade psychiatrist R. D. Laing, it occurred to him that my guitar music might please the ears of our country's leader, Prime Minister Pierre Trudeau. He suggested that if I was ever in Ottawa, he would introduce me.

In June 1975, after a concert of Boccherini with the Orford String Quartet in the National Arts Centre, I casually placed a call to Bob Kaplan, sceptical that anything would ensue. To my surprise, within minutes he had organized a visit with the prime minister and his wife at their country residence on Harrington Lake. It was one of those serene summer Sundays when Ottawa families picnicked on the parkland beside the Rideau Canal or headed off to their favourite haunts in the Gatineau Hills. During the forty-five-minute drive, perhaps sensing my apprehension, Kaplan urged me not to be intimidated by the fact that his friend was our prime minister. I took a deep breath and watched the wooded scenery speed past. On arrival at the gatehouse, we gave our names to a security Mountie, who peered curiously at me before allowing us to pass.

Pierre and Margaret Trudeau were enjoying an intimate afternoon with their two young children, Justin and Sacha. They extended a friendly welcome, inviting us to join them for a swim in the lake, which sparkled in shades of sapphire, just a stone's throw from the house. Having anticipated only Boccherini and not a bathing party, I accepted Margaret's magnanimous loan of her gold-lamé bikini. Six months pregnant, Margaret appeared radiantly healthy and happy. "I read the story about your trip to Nashville in *The Canadian* magazine," she volunteered enthusiastically. "I think Pierre glanced at it too."

The Trudeau children splashed around like playful puppies or availed themselves of their athletic father's water-piggybacks. I slipped into the cool glassy water, hoping the skimpy bikini and I would not part company, and began a leisurely breast-stroke towards the wooden raft supporting our handsome head of state. Years later, I read how Margaret had first met Pierre while swimming out to a raft at Tahiti's Club Med. Bob Kaplan and Margaret reclined in deck-chairs on shore while I dangled my legs in the lake water watching Pierre amuse his young sons, who shrieked with delight at their father's backward somersaults. His offer to teach me the technique was politely declined, as I realized that my upcoming guitar performance would be aesthetically jeopardized by stringy wet hair and streaked mascara. Already my fingertips and nails were being softened. At times, the restrictions of playing guitar can be a royal pain!

Later, when the hot summer sun had lost its bite, everyone sat in the living room sipping iced fruit drinks while I tuned up my strings. Bob and Pierre relaxed into armchairs; Sacha, Justin, and Margaret propped themselves against cushions on the floor. Thankful for the fine acoustics, and made to feel at ease by their casual attitude, I played a selection of short numbers. Before "El Colibri" by Julio Sagreras, Pierre told his attentive boys to visualize the hummingbird they often saw skimming around their garden, and encouraged them to ask questions about the guitar.

Both Pierre and Margaret rhapsodized over my music, wishing me continued success. Before leaving, I autographed a copy of the Boot record album and Bob Kaplan snapped a quick photo of us all by the front steps. How amazing that I had been able to maintain my calm in the company of our famous prime minister and his "first lady"! "See, I told you they'd love your music and appreciate the company," Bob enthused on the return drive. Back at the hotel, I immediately called my mother to relive for her my exciting hours at the lake. A few days later, to my delight, I received a personal thank-you note from Pierre Trudeau, but never did I expect to be face to face with him again.

One snowy afternoon, on February 13, 1976, in Kamloops, British Columbia, while engrossed in Rodrigo's guitar concerto, I heard a timid knock on the door of my hotel room. "Hello, I'm staying in the room adjoining yours," a well-dressed gentleman said, beaming. "I was so enjoying the music I had to find out who was responsible." I explained that he had been overhearing my rehearsal for an upcoming symphony engagement. "Malcolm Turnbull's the name, editor of the Vancouver *Province*," he continued. "I'm in town covering tonight's Liberal fund-raising dinner at which Prime Minister Trudeau will be speaking." Feeling a dishevelled mess, standing in the doorway with no make-up and hair that needed a wash, I was anxious to return to my practice and not become involved in conversation. I declined his invitation for a drink, but mentioned that he might convey my greetings to the prime minister. Four hours later, while I was fingering through the final movement of *Fantasía para un Gentilhombre*, my neighbour called in an excited voice. "Miss Boyd, could you come over to the Stockmens Hotel, where Mr. Trudeau and his staff are staying? The dinner and speeches are wrapping up now. When I gave your greetings to the prime minister, he suggested you join him, as he is in the mood for some music. Please bring your guitar."

With so little time to get ready, I flew into a panic, leaping into the bathtub to wash my hair. Why did such an important invitation have to materialize at the last minute? As if whipped by a whirlwind, my Rodrigo score lay scattered on the bed along with the remains of the last room-service meal. Only one dress in my suitcase seemed worthy of a prime-ministerial command performance: the long, burgundy concert gown sewn by my mother. After hastily zipping myself up and using the blow-dryer, I dialled the front desk for a taxi.

In the lobby of the hotel, the prime minister's aide, Bob Murdoch, grabbed my guitar case and escorted me to Trudeau's suite. Numerous RCMP officers stationed in the corridors were keeping vigil in the open-doored adjacent rooms. Was I imagining it, or were they giving me curious looks? Should they not have checked my bulky black guitar case, which in other times or places might have aroused suspicion? The prime minister appeared in good spirits after the dinner and speech to his party faithful. He carefully hung up my coat, murmured appreciatively over the burgundy dress, and poured two glasses of white wine. "Margaret and I often play your record, and the boys enjoy listening to it. Could you play for me tonight?" he requested. For half an hour, Besard's Renaissance dances, Sagreras's "Una Lagrima," and Lauro's Venezuelan waltzes elicited gestures of approval and conversation about my student days in Paris led him to recount stories of his adventurous treks through Europe and North Africa as a young man.

Pierre Trudeau was a dashing and charismatic man. His voice had a gentle resonance, with just the slightest French lilt to the phrasing; he sported his characteristic red rose in the buttonhole of his stylish, dark grey suit. I had to pinch myself to believe that here I was — fly-away, uncurled hair, in my mother's home-made gown — serenading the leader of our country in his private hotel room. As he poured a little more wine and brushed his lips across my hands that had just finished their music-making, I noticed a softer, more romantic look in his eyes than his television image had ever revealed. "Please let me know if you are coming to Ottawa soon for any reason. *Merci* for such beautiful music, Liona." Pierre pronounced my name slowly, stressing the last syllable. Helping me on with my winter coat, he lifted my hair in a touching gesture. As my hands reached for the handle of my guitar case, he said, "Just a little moment, then I'll walk you to the elevators." His arms wrapped around me, his hands stroked my hair, and he kissed me very gently. My head spun in circles like a gyroscope. Blindly, I stumbled past the RCMP officers, my heart racing in disbelief that Canada's world-renowned political giant had just put his lips against mine and briefly held me in his arms. Never had I anticipated this type of response to my playing. Back in my hotel at 1:00 a.m., I realized that it was now St. Valentine's Day. Cupid had caught me completely by surprise.

Concert bookings at Carleton University and Ottawa's Camp Fortune steered me east to Ottawa, where I kept my promise to call him. "I would be so pleased if you could join me for a nightcap after your performance," he said. "I'll send my driver over to collect you." Once again, I was peered at by the two Mounties stationed at the gatehouse. He ushered me into a spacious living room carpeted in plush beige and adorned with decorative bowls of flowers. "Tell me more about yourself, Liona," he suggested, pouring the drinks. Then he interjected, "Would you like some nuts? I think the maids keep them in the pantry." He disappeared, leaving me to survey the room. Framed photos of world leaders were arranged on the grand piano: portraits of Queen Elizabeth and Prince Philip autographed to the Trudeaus, Pierre and Margaret standing beside Giscard d'Estaing, and pictures of the two boys, Justin and Sacha. Why had Pierre invited me to his house? There had been the odd rumours of marital problems, but after all, he was still married; surely the leader of Canada could not afford to be flirtatious with a single woman, I reasoned. Perhaps he was dazzled by my music and needed some artistic stimulation that was lacking in his politically charged days.

"Here, I found some macadamias and salted almonds," Pierre said. "The staff have left, so I had trouble locating them in the kitchen." He tipped the treats into a crystal bowl and eased himself onto the couch. Munching on macadamias, I told Pierre about my parents, their initial apprehensions about settling in Canada, and our family travels, including the year we spent in Mexico. Seeming to be interested in my life, he questioned me about Vivien and Damien. Whenever he mentioned his sons, Pierre's face lit up, but I noticed that any allusion to Margaret elicited the opposite response. I had no idea then that the Trudeaus' marriage had fallen apart. Later I learned how poor Margaret, desperately unhappy with political life, had been struggling to "find herself" by becoming part of the New York jet set and its intrinsic drug scene. Canada's first lady had been placed on medication by a psychiatrist trying to balance her emotional ups and downs; cocaine, marijuana, and amphetamines were also taking their toll. The prime minister was having to assume responsibility for the children and carry on a hectic political life while his marital relationship was in a shambles.

"Would you like to see the house?" he volunteered. As we tiptoed around the dining area and sun room and along the "tunnel" that led to the pool and sauna, he pointed out the art: Inuit carvings, oil paintings, and bronze sculptures. His guided tour included the enormous kitchens, with refrigerators that we raided for ice cream and fresh blueberries. I hoped my teeth would not turn navy blue! If they did, Pierre did not seem to care; he kissed me tenderly in the darkened hallway out of sight of his driver, who had been patiently standing by to take me back to the Château Laurier Hotel. "I must see you again, *ma belle princesse*," Trudeau whispered. "Let's try to find a way." Still very much in awe of the man, I found it mind-boggling that the prime minister was interested in more than my guitar music.

Several weeks later, I received a request from the government to fly to Ottawa to perform at a banquet in honour of James Callaghan, the new British prime minister. It was pretty easy to guess who had initiated the invitation. As this would be my first time playing before a head of state at an official function, I was simultaneously excited and terrified. What if I was nervous, forgot my notes, and embarrassed the Canadian government? It was a major responsibility.

I selected a group of appealing pieces to play in Rideau Hall, the official residence of the Governor General. Seated directly ahead of my small podium, positioned a few feet away from the head table, was a smiling Pierre Elliott Trudeau, who stood up to introduce me to the distinguished crowd of Canadian and English politicians and diplomats. After my recital, there was a proud and happy look on our prime minister's face as he presented me to James Callaghan and several of the cabinet ministers. "Liona, you look so lovely tonight," he whispered in my ear before the evening was over. "I'll have my driver bring you over to the house for a glass of wine."

When Queen Elizabeth and Prince Philip visited Canada in October 1977, I was invited to perform after a dinner hosted by Trudeau at the National Arts Centre. Only a few yards from the head table, I serenaded the royals with Tárrega, Bach, and Dowland. A smiling Pierre had given me an introduction — explaining my British origins and praising my "talent and artistry." I tried to imagine that I was playing for him alone, but could not ignore the fact that a very regal and elegantly dressed head of the Commonwealth was seated at his side. Knowing what a great thrill it was for me to play before them, Pierre made a point of bringing me to the table for personal introductions. The Queen smiled approvingly. "Mm . . . lovely playing." How incredible to feel the attention and appreciation of the royal couple whose portrait had gazed down on me from classroom walls on both sides of the Atlantic.

When Pierre hosted a farewell banquet for retiring Governor General Jules Léger, I was booked to perform in the Confederation Room of the Parliament Buildings' west block, and when the president of Mexico, José López Portillo, came to Canada, I was again booked to perform at Rideau Hall. Usually, state dinners are decorous affairs with lengthy speeches and a polite, hushed atmosphere. Mexicans, however, will always be Mexicans. As I made my entrance in a white, lacy gown, the Latino delegation let out appreciative wolf-whistles and loud calls of "*guapa,*" "*rubia,*" "*que linda.*" I was instantly back at that embarrassing San Miguel fashion show! What a different crowd from the subdued James Callaghan banquet! Addressing the audience, Portillo waxed poetic. "Tonight I have heard, not the hands of a guitarist, but the wings of an angel. When I think of Canada, I will always remember the angel who played for me in Ottawa." Several Canadian politicians told me that on a subsequent visit to Mexico City, they were met by President Portillo, who was still talking about the impact of my playing. Ah, the romantic soul of Mexico! Pierre was absolutely delighted that I had scored so highly with his visitors. Back at Sussex we cuddled in front of the fireplace, chuckling about their undignified whoops and whistles.

Pierre Trudeau's marriage to Margaret was over. She was spending more time in New York with her friend Yasmin, the daughter of Rita Hayworth and Aly Khan, than she was in Ottawa. Pierre and his staff assumed responsibility for Justin, Sacha, and their new brother, Michel, with whom Margaret had been pregnant during my visit to Harrington Lake. Pierre began to call me frequently, charming my mother by asking for "Miss Liona." As I grew accustomed to our secret relationship, I started to spend time in Ottawa whenever my schedule permitted. Usually, Pierre's driver, Jack Deschambault, would meet me at the airport; if he was otherwise occupied, a couple of RCMP officers would escort me to the residence.

Because the prime minister was a swimming devotee, our dates invariably included a dip in the frigid waters of his beloved pool. Easing myself down the steps, I splashed around, trying to keep warm while he dived in like a pelican to start his forty laps. Sometimes, after playing a concert at the National Arts Centre, a midnight swim was the last thing I desired, but putting on a brave face, I feigned enthusiasm; fireside back rubs and embraces always warmed me up afterwards. Pierre would often carry me on his strong shoulders, as he did with his boys, and playfully piggyback me up and down the pool. After this workout, we would float on our backs or tread water while sharing many a giggle over the humorous incidents in our separate, and very different, careers. Like any proud parent, Pierre recounted anecdotes about his boys and their school experiences, as well as their differing personalities and their relationships with the nannies, who seemed to come and go quite frequently. In his political life, he was having to tackle such issues as inflation, separatist threats from Quebec, and the drawn-out air-traffic controllers' strike over bilingualism, which resulted in the resignation of one of his key ministers, Jean Marchand. Perhaps my friendship provided a lightness that was in contrast to his weighty marital and political imbroglios. As the leader of the country, Pierre must have been burdened by many pressures, but he always seemed in good spirits during the times we shared.

I met few of Pierre's friends. Since he was still legally married, our romance had to be kept extremely private at the beginning, even though, by early 1977, Pierre and Margaret had officially separated and he had taken custody of the boys. After concerts and official functions, however, he introduced me to his sister, Suzette, and several of his ministers and staff. Cécile Viau, his cheerful personal secretary, was usually instrumental in coordinating our meetings, arranging phone calls and plane schedules. One evening, I joined Pierre at Jim Coutts's for a dinner party, where we danced with Don Harron and his wife, the singer Catherine McKinnon. Fortunately, there were no press to reveal our friendship.

On another occasion, Pierre and I were invited to the Ottawa house of Michael Pitfield for dinner. A December blackout compelled us to use candlelight, and Michael's wife, Nancy, had to cook our dinner in the flickering flames of the fireplace, lending a perfect romantic touch to the evening. Our relationship, however, presented some difficult moments for Pierre. Margaret, for the sake of her children, decided at one point to return to Ottawa for Easter dinner. No sooner had the boys seated themselves at the table than they apparently began an animated account of my activities with them and their father at Harrington Lake during the preceding days. Easter supper at Sussex Drive must have had a few awkward silences. Another evening, when Margaret suddenly arrived back at Sussex, Pierre had to whisk me out of the house and arrange for me to stay at the Château Laurier. A society function was being held in the hotel, and the lobby was swarming with press. Fortunately, Bob Murdoch discovered the fire-escape stairs, enabling Pierre to slip in without being spotted.

We skinny-dipped in a hot tub at his friend Delano Bouilly's home in Ottawa and attended a Rosedale pool party where everyone nonchalantly disrobed. Although the prime minister had no reservations about walking around naked in front of strangers, I tried to stay covered until I was submerged in the water. At least it felt warmer than the pool at Sussex! Pierre made efforts to attend as many of my concerts as possible, even bringing his boys along to performances at the National Arts Centre. If he was in town, I stayed with him at Sussex Drive or Harrington Lake. My road manager's jaw fell open when Pierre and the RCMP once showed up to collect me backstage. After giving a fund-raising concert for abused women, I was driven by the organizers to "my friend who lives at Harrington Lake." Instead of remaining in the house, Pierre came bounding out to invite the two drivers in for a cool beer. The man was definitely a risk-taker. How easy it would have been for gossip to travel!

Pierre enjoyed listening to the country songs I had written, including one I dedicated to him called "So Many Years Apart" — "'cause age is not important in the language of the heart, / who cares that our two birthdays fell so many years apart?" He loved the melody and the lyrics about our contrasting stages of life, and could not understand why I had not found a singer to "make it a hit." Tanya Tucker heard my demo after a TV show in Las Vegas on which we both appeared, and together we rewrote one of the verses to fit her own life. Although keen to record it, she unfortunately broke up with her older boyfriend, Glen Campbell, thus rendering the song inappropriate. To this day, it remains unsung in my files of music.

Careful to maintain appearances in front of the boys, Pierre and I went to great lengths to ensure that the various maids and nannies could never be certain where I had spent the night. At Sussex Drive, my cases would be deposited in the "Peach Room," where Pierre insisted I rumple up the sheets and pillows, wet a few towels, and open the soap packages to leave the impression I had slept there overnight. But I was pretty certain that we were fooling no one, especially the head housekeeper, who had become familiar with my comings and goings. When I shared occasional meals with Pierre and his growing family, I was moved by his obvious love for them, his patience with their sometimes unruly table manners, his bedtime stories from the classics, and his efforts at bilingualism.

We were free of round-the-clock RCMP surveillance for only six months in 1979, after the Liberal government was narrowly defeated by Joe Clark's Conservatives, who formed a minority government. After eleven years at the helm, Pierre was suddenly no longer prime minister. He and the boys were obliged to move into Stornoway, the official residence for the leader of the opposition. It seemed a gloomy, confining place in comparison with Sussex Drive. No longer shadowed by RCMP officers, we were able to stroll around enjoying relative privacy, go out for dinner to a restaurant in Hull, and drive the streets of Ottawa in his Mercedes like "just plain folks." Unfortunately, the summer of '79 had been heavily booked by my New York agent and I did not have as much free time as Pierre would have liked during his hiatus from running the country. He took his boys camping, went canoeing in the Northwest Territories, and then set off for Tibet, while I played concerts across North America and made a recording in England.

Over the eight years that Pierre and I used to see each other, from 1976 to 1983, we spent many glorious days and nights at the lake during the summer and autumn months. The country residence was a perquisite for Canada's prime ministers. One July, the boys were given a Newfoundland puppy and fell in love with him at once. Together we took long hikes through the woods, but "Newfie" was a bundle of kinetic energy and even Justin and Sacha were worn out long before the rambunctious animal, whose wagging tail almost bowled over little "Misha." Pierre had to explain to his dismayed children that the dog was being sent off to school.

Pierre and I frequently canoed around the lake during the tranquil evening hours before dusk; he pointed out the beaver-dams and taught me the French names of the various birds we spotted along the shore. Sometimes I paddled with Pierre, but other times I simply lay back listening to the peaceful dipping of the wood against the water, filling my lungs with the fragrant evening lake smells. It was such a serene spot, totally private except for the small lodge where a few RCMP security officers stayed. On occasion, we took a picnic basket to a tiny island in the middle of the lake, spread a blanket over mossy rocks and ferns, and lay in each other's arms after feasting on pâtés, cheeses, and fresh fruit salad prepared by Pierre's personal chef, Yannick Vincent. A few years later, while composing "Love in the Afternoon," my memory drifted back to those hours of diurnal dalliance, when the warm summer sun and the grasshoppers were the only witnesses to our lovemaking. I can still picture the deserted cottage we paddled to on the far shore. The air around it smelled of dry peeling paint and hot dusty window-sills. The water was so pure then that we could take long, refreshing gulps as we swam.

One day, the RCMP was put on an extra security alert because of death threats to the prime minister. We were asked to stay indoors and not stray too far from their sight. In the afternoon, however, flouting their cautions, we paddled off to a distant corner of Lac Mousseau and swam around the canoe among pale water lilies, before hauling ourselves back into the boat to lie naked in the warm sunshine. Suddenly, a low-altitude plane materialized out of the blue, circling above us twice before flying away. Because we were alone on the lake, it startled us; we suddenly realized how vulnerable we were to any terrorist's assassination attempt. After all, Pierre, like any head of state, had attracted his share of enemies. We never ascertained if it was merely the RCMP officers checking up on us, because we were too embarrassed to inquire. I hoped that if they attempted more reconnaissance manoeuvres, we would at least have some clothes on!

In the evenings, we sat beside the water listening to the loons, gazed at the canopy of stars overhead, or took walks along the road leading to the main house. Once, we were severely startled by a huge black shape lumbering towards us out of the darkness. Pierre grabbed me, and together we leaped into a ditch at the side of the road; terrified, we both let out screams, convinced that an enormous bear was about to attack. The "bear" turned out to be a burly RCMP officer taking his evening run; he was as scared by our vocals as we were by him. The next time, we made sure to carry flashlights.

In the autumn evenings, we lit a fire in the living room, and I concentrated on guitar practice while my over-burdened lover ploughed through piles of documents and briefs. Pierre enjoyed hearing me learn new pieces, and became quite familiar with the guitar repertoire; my transcription of "Gymnopédie No. 1" by Eric Satie remained his favourite. Pierre disliked television and I cannot recall its ever once being on during my visits. If the children were with us, one or two nannies always assisted, but sometimes we enjoyed being completely alone in the house, with no need to tiptoe around upstairs. We shared bubble baths and champagne while listening to classical albums by candlelight. A portion of the bedroom carpet had to be replaced when, on one occasion, we were oblivious to the expanding pool of melting wax from two red candles. For romantic evenings, Pierre often wore his floor-length Moroccan robe and I a long gown of brocaded silk. These were times of escape from the pressures of two demanding careers.

While up at Harrington, we dressed casually — shorts and bathing suits in the summer, blue jeans and sweaters during the cooler months. When I was without a warm hiking jacket or boots, Pierre lent me some of Margaret's outfits, which she had abandoned in the hall closet. I was literally filling her shoes. Margaret was extremely jealous and possessive about Pierre, but it was hard to be sympathetic, as she was the one carrying on frivolous affairs with a variety of men, hobnobbing with the Rolling Stones, and partying her nights away at Studio 54 with the jet set in New York and Los Angeles. In her book

Consequences, Margaret complained that I had absolutely no taste in clothes and that on returning home unannounced, she had seen my "hideous purple coat" hanging in the downstairs closet. Pierre never once complained about my attire. Music, art, and politics ranked higher on our list of priorities than designer clothes. Of course, witnessing the preparations for a candlelight lobster dinner that Pierre and I were about to share certainly did not assuage Margaret's animosity that evening. In many ways I felt genuinely sorry for her, part of me understanding why she had felt compelled to run away from her regimented life at Sussex Drive and the role of prime minister's wife. After marrying very young, she had plunged into motherhood, wifely duties, and the public forum far too fast. I was glad to hear she eventually became more satisfied with her second marriage and two additional children. Margaret was a stunning young woman; it was easy to see how Pierre had been mesmerized by her beauty and flower-child philosophies. Once, when he ruefully implied that his marriage had been a big mistake, and that he should have proposed to me instead, I reminded him that, thanks to Margaret, he had three wonderful boys. With me, he probably would have ended up with nothing more than a collection of record albums!

Any feelings of guilt quickly diminished when I realized that I was not the cause of Pierre and Margaret's marital difficulties. In some romantic sense, I believed I was helping the leader of our country unwind from his stressful political duties, although I am not foolish enough to presume I was the only diversion during the years we dated. Such is the world of powerful men.

Once, just before Christmas, I stayed a few days at Sussex Drive, enjoying the company of Pierre's three boys and showing them a few chords on the guitar. The house was gaily decorated with ornaments, a gingerbread house, a large pine tree, and cards from all over the world. My eyes alighted on two Christmas cards — one from Queen Elizabeth and Prince Philip and the other from Prince Charles and Princess Diana. On hearing that Pierre was only going to stuff them into a government archives box, I asked if he would allow me to keep those two once the holidays were over. "Well, if you insist, Liona, I'll give you one, but not both." I chose the Queen and Prince Philip's. "Here's a Christmas present for you," he said, handing me two cans of maple syrup from a crate he had been given by a government minister, Marc Lalonde. Pierre was never generous with gifts, and I always paid for my plane tickets to and from Ottawa. Even Margaret had accused him of being "parsimonious," and I suspect it was partly this aspect of his personality that had driven her to write her candid books, since he offered her and the boys only minimal support.

One time I hinted that a little memento might be appreciated. Christmas cards of Pierre and the boys, most containing affectionate notes saying he hoped I would be able to see him more frequently, were always forthcoming, but seemed slightly inadequate for a man of his means. Pressed, he rummaged in his drawer and came up with a gold-dipped peanut on a necklace chain that was given to him by Jimmy Carter's brother, Billy, and an embossed leather box of Ceylon tea from the Sri Lankan Summit Conference — merely trinkets to him, but in my hands, treasures. I recalled Margaret's complaints that Pierre never took time to buy Christmas gifts for the boys. Instead, he selected presents from the many souvenirs he had amassed during the years of official visits. Once, in his suite in Montreal's Queen Elizabeth Hotel, my eyes alighted upon an ookpik doll thrown on a chair. "Could I please keep him?" I ventured, but was rebuked for even asking. Pierre had decided that the Inuit ookpik would come in useful for the boys next Christmas. Luckily for us, neither Margaret nor I were very materialistic, as generosity was hardly Pierre's forte.

While I sat flipping through the in-flight magazine on a plane to Ottawa, who should take the seat next to me but our former prime minister John Diefenbaker. Then in his late seventies, Diefenbaker was showing the effects of years of Parkinson's disease. When I shook his hand, his face lit up with a faint smile of recognition as he remembered my performance at one of the state dinners. We chatted on about insignificant subjects — the weather and flight-departure time. "Dief" had been leafing through the *Globe and Mail* magazine supplement when he came across an article on famous Canadians and their favourite snacks. On turning one of the pages, he discovered a photo of Pierre next to a recipe for chocolate-chip cookies. He muttered some unintelligible remark under his breath, followed by a sarcastic "dig" intended for my ears, as he pointed at Pierre's photo. I smiled innocently. They had been political rivals for years. There had been a great furore, fomented by the press, about the money Trudeau had lavished on his indoor swimming pool at the Sussex Drive residence. The Conservatives were making the most of this controversial situation, hoping to substantiate assertions that hard-earned taxpayers' money was being squandered on the profligate indulgences of our hedonistic prime minister. Pierre, however, was able to exonerate himself, proving to the press that the pool had been funded entirely by private donations. Diefenbaker grumbled that he had never understood Trudeau's need to swim at home. "Why can't the guy take himself off to the local health club once a week?" he asked me. I nodded sympathetically. What he did not realize was that the woman sitting beside him on the plane would soon be splashing around in that very pool. My telling Pierre about the magazine article and Dief's disparaging comments about his cherished pool provided one of our better chuckles that weekend. It wasn't every day that one got to rub shoulders with two prime ministers.

We still had to exercise extreme caution over the media and the public discovering our romance. Clandestine rendezvous with a classical guitarist would do nothing to improve a political image that already had suffered battering due to Margaret's indiscretions. One September morning, Pierre and I were at 24 Sussex getting ready to drive up to Harrington for a few days, when we saw that a group of reporters had clustered around the entrance awaiting comments from the prime minister on his latest political debate. To leave the grounds, we had to drive right past their cameras and microphones, as there was no rear driveway to use for escape. There was nothing for it — this time I had to be smuggled out; it would have been imprudent to let the press see us leaving together at nine in the morning. Pierre asked me to crouch down on the back floor of the car while he and the driver piled two heavy coats over me. I kept still as a statue as we pulled past the gatehouse and Pierre waved convivially at the press, tossing out a comment towards their anxious microphones. The RCMP driver gave me a sly sideways glance in the rear-view mirror as I squirmed out from beneath the hot coats once we were on the main highway. The police were probably keeping a detailed log of all my comings and goings. With that perfect guitar-player cover, I would have made a great Mata Hari! Somehow the challenge of keeping our affair secret added an extra touch of romance and intrigue to our encounters. Certainly Pierre's staff must have been aware of our relationship, as he often sent his aides to pick me up, but fortunately everyone involved remained discreet.

On a few occasions, I had to sidle past hotel vestibules full of press for us to share some private hours together. It became such a risky business that I purchased a short, brown wig that enabled me to walk past the "paparazzi," who scarcely gave me a glance. Before this handy disguise, Pierre always cautioned me to wear a scarf, as he considered my hair a dead giveaway. In retrospect, it seems surprising that some of the scandal-seeking press did not pursue us more aggressively. But in Canada this was a time of liberal thinking; Pierre himself had declared, "The government has no business in the bedrooms of the nation." Perhaps the Canadian media had agreed among themselves not to exploit the prime minister's life. In contrast, when I toured Latin America, the headlines declared, "Pierre Trudeau's Girlfriend Arrives," and even my grandmother in Bilbao had sighted similar reports in the Spanish tabloids.

On trips to Toronto, Pierre and his personal aide, Ted Johnson, sometimes stayed downtown in the penthouse of the Holiday Inn. On one occasion, in need of some fresh air, he suggested a stroll around nearby Chinatown. We felt quite daring holding hands in public, but avoided eye contact with passers-by. Pierre was in a reckless mood that night; on seeing a film crew in the process of shooting a movie, he steered me towards the crowd that had gathered around the floodlights. "Let's go over and be extras in their film," he suggested mischievously. Amazingly, nobody seemed to recognize us! We stood anonymously watching the camera crews and director until, when it all seemed rather uneventful, we started to make our way back to the hotel. As we were about to cross Dundas Street, a Greek taxi driver leapt out of his cab in a dither. "Oh, Mr. Prime Minister, amazing to see you here. Very pleased to meet you!" He pumped Pierre's hand up and down and told him how much he admired him. "I think you play beoootiful guitar, Miss Boyd," he added breathlessly, turning towards me. "My friends are never going to believe this!" I know that in a strange way, Pierre and I were rather glad that at least somebody had recognized us after all. Such are the egos of politicians and performers!

One evening, after attending a government function at one of the Toronto airport hotels, Pierre came to pick me up at my parents' house. The inconspicuous street numbers made it difficult and he confessed he had spent time stalking around our neighbours' gardens trying to peek in the windows. I could just imagine their state of disbelief if they had looked out and seen the prime minister of Canada creeping furtively through their petunias!

Pierre tried to book me for as many official functions as possible, but sometimes my schedule was already fixed; I had to forfeit the president of Portugal and the premier of Thailand. He succeeded, however, in arranging private Sussex Drive recitals for Jamaican prime minister Michael Manley and German chancellor Helmut Schmidt, who put in a special request for the music of Bach. Feeling that it was safe for us to appear at the odd entertainment and music industry event, Pierre escorted me twice to the Junos and to the ACTRA Awards, where we shared our table with Ed Asner. He even drove me home, carefree in the knowledge that there were no press following us. Next day, the Toronto papers featured a picture of me on their front pages, dabbing whipped cream off Pierre's tuxedo. During our second Juno Awards together, *People* magazine's

photographer clung to us all evening like a shadow. Having borrowed one of my friend Gloria Loring's *décolleté* gowns, I piled my
hair up with a few bobby-pins; in those days, I would never have
dreamed of going to a hairdresser. Fortunately, the prime minister
liked the natural look, and that suited my busy timetable. After
the show, Pierre decided it would be wise for us to leave separately,
so he and his aide escaped in their limo to the Royal York Hotel,
instructing me to follow by cab twenty minutes later. At that hour,
there were no taxis to be found near the Convention Centre. I trailed
around the deserted lobby in my evening dress until two members
of The Guess Who offered to flag a cab for me — how embarrassing!
After winning the Juno Award for best instrumental artist, I should
have departed in the company of my escort, with whom I had been
seated all night, or at least with somebody from my record company.
"What on earth took you so long?" an impatient Pierre complained.

A dinner was arranged to pay tribute to some outstanding young
achievers in various disciplines of the arts and sciences. It was to be
held in Ottawa's Château Laurier ballroom, and the invitees, including me, would be presented to Queen Elizabeth, the guest of honour.
Pierre suggested that I fly to Ottawa a few days earlier so that we
could spend some time up at the lake. The maple leaves had turned
brilliant orange and we took exhilarating hikes through the painted
autumn woods. He reiterated his love and great pleasure in our
relationship. "We'll have to be careful that the reporters don't get
suspicious. To divert their attention, my staff has arranged for Karen
Kain to sit with me at the head table during tomorrow's dinner, but
if it bothers you, I'll make sure you have a place there too." I felt
piqued that after our two intensely romantic days, Pierre would be
viewed by the national media with the beautiful ballet star Karen
Kain at his side. "When you arrive at the ballroom, *ma chérie*, ask for
one of the women attending to seating arrangements, and I will have
left a message to have you placed at my table," he assured me.

When I arrived at the gala black-tie event, no message had been
left, or if it had been, no one appeared to know anything about it.

I was seated in one of the remote corners of the room beside Carroll Baker, the country singer, and could see a glowing Pierre at his raised head table next to the gorgeous Miss Kain. I had tremendous admiration for Karen and her outstanding talent as a dancer, but the hurt I was feeling kept my stomach in knots all night. How could Pierre be so insensitive? Because of him, I had not arranged for another dinner date and was surrounded by strangers who puffed smoke into my eyes all evening. I felt angry and offended. At the end of the dinner, one of his aides sought me out. "The prime minister is looking for you," he said. "Fine, he can come here and find me if he wishes to," I replied unsmilingly. I saw Pierre pushing through the crowd in my direction. When he stood before me — all charm, red rose, and smiles — I could not pretend to greet him warmly. "How have you been, Liona? It's so nice to see you in Ottawa!" he said, playing to the reporters who had trailed him. "Just fine, thanks," I replied coldly, avoiding eye contact. "Is there anything the matter?" he asked, lowering his voice. "You know damn well what the matter is," I retorted, at a level inaudible to any of the journalists, and hurried away before disgracing us both with the tears that were starting to well up in my eyes.

That entire evening in Ottawa was an unmitigated disaster for me. My plans were to return to Toronto after the dinner, as I had a busy schedule the next day, but on arriving at the airport to catch the 11:00 p.m. flight, I found that it had been cancelled. In those days I never carried credit cards, and twenty dollars was all the cash in my purse. I felt stranded and abandoned, yet could not bring myself to return to Pierre's house. Perhaps Karen Kain was already teaching him some of her ballet *pliés* around the pool! My few dollars secured a taxi that deposited me at an Ottawa hotel, where I pleaded with the night manager to let me send him a cheque for the room the following day.

The next morning, the newspaper featured a dazzling picture of Pierre and Kain smiling at each other. I choked on my Air Canada coffee and Danish pastry. I had always been willing to keep our affair secretive, but his method of "diverting the attentions of the press" failed to impress me. I felt betrayed. Pierre phoned the next day to apologize. "But you know how much I love you, *ma chère* Liona. Why didn't you come up to my table and ask me to find you a seat?" He could not understand how having to ask for a place in front of the head-table guests, including his beautiful ballerina, would have done more damage to my pride than being exiled to the far reaches of the ballroom. Perhaps my sensitivity was exacerbated by feelings of exhaustion, thanks to Pierre's amorous attentions. I told him to forget about the incident, and that I was sorry to have appeared so glum at the Queen's reception. Sometime later, he asked me to attend a small Ottawa dinner party in honour of Prince Charles, but I had already been booked for a concert. An invitation to fly with him to Korea had likewise to be declined, but we did succeed in seeing each other a couple of times in New York.

In July 1981 I was engaged to perform a fifteen-minute program in the Château Montebello in Quebec. My audience would comprise all the leaders of the Western world who were attending the Twentieth Economic Summit Conference. At the Ottawa airport, I was met by a military woman who drove me the sixty kilometres to the Château. On approach, I noticed several RCMP officers standing half-hidden behind the roadside bushes and pine trees. Terrorism posed a real danger to such a gathering of world powers. Arriving at a checkpoint, I was photographed and given a badge that allowed access to the hotel, but no one bothered to search my guitar case — an obvious receptacle for smuggling weapons, as proven by those infamous Mafia violin cases. No sooner had I arrived at my spacious room and rolled my hair into curlers than the phone rang. Pierre was anxious to see me and was sending Ted Johnson to guide me past the clusters of walkie-talkie-toting secret-service men swarming around the corridors. We were stopped at every turn, but Ted's badge worked wonders. Before long, I was safely in Pierre's suite, and we tumbled onto the bed, exchanging happy embraces and laughing about the excessive security. Watching Pierre dress for dinner, I thought what a refined and elegant man he was, and how great it felt that he had wanted me to share this important summit he was hosting. After debating the OPEC oil-crisis, runaway interest rates, and Soviet Union concerns, were all these international heads of state really going to be listening to me play my party pieces in a few hours? Pierre and I, planning to meet again after the event, kissed each other good luck and promised not to giggle if everyone became too serious and our eyes met.

My concert was arranged for nine-thirty, but it was after ten when I was finally escorted into the dining room where the G7 leaders were finishing their desserts and coffee. As Pierre stood up to say a few words of introduction, I scanned the faces that were so familiar from my television screen. The energy flowed into my fingers and I launched into the music. Aware of what a unique privilege it was to have the attention of these political giants, I played confidently and expressively, smiling at them during my introductions and sensing their appreciation. When I had struck the last chord of my fifteen-minute set, a jubilant Pierre bounded up to my chair and led me to the table to meet his guests. I was presented to Ronald Reagan, Helmut Schmidt, Margaret Thatcher, François Mitterrand, Zenko Suzuki, and Giovanni Spadolini: the leaders, respectively, of the U.S., Germany, Britain, France, Japan, and Italy. Margaret Thatcher showed particular enthusiasm, asking why I did not play in London more often when Pierre explained my English origins. "Liona, stay here and listen to Diane Juster's singing," Pierre whispered to me, motioning to a large armchair at the side of the main table. "No, I just thought of a better idea," he added roguishly, and pulled a spare dining chair in between him and Reagan. Wow! I was going to be seated with all the world leaders! The protocol staff must have been raising their collective eyebrows.

Diane Juster, in the pre-Margaret days, had been a girlfriend of Pierre's, and I smiled to myself, thinking how shrewdly he had planned the entertainment. She was one of Quebec's leading *chanteuses*, and it was understandable that Pierre had been attracted to this dynamic artiste of soaring voice and passionate songs. He and I sat holding hands under the table, sipping the drink he offered to share with me. Diane's set, which was supposed to last fifteen minutes, extended past thirty; I noticed that Helmut Schmidt was nodding off to sleep and that Mitterrand kept examining his watch. Thatcher, however, exemplifying stereotypical British fortitude, sat upright, head held high and a smile on her face. Reagan, aware of the familiarity between Pierre and me, whispered compliments about my guitar playing and asked about the harpist who was accompanying Diane. "I can't understand a word. What are these French songs all about?" he asked, so I tried to give him a vague idea of their content. He told me he loved the sound of the harp and found it a perfect accompaniment to voice. "It's a beautiful instrument, don't you think?" he said under his breath; I agreed that after the classical guitar, it was definitely one of my favourites! I told Reagan I had visited Pacific Palisades, where I knew he had lived before the White House; and he confessed homesickness at the mere mention of the name. Encouraged by his friendly manner, I asked if he might allow me a photograph with him. After all, this was a rare opportunity; I was learning to seize the moment — *carpe diem* — as they come but once.

At the conclusion of Diane's long set, Pierre asked me to remain beside him as we stood to say goodnight to everyone. For a brief moment, I enjoyed the illusion of being the first lady of more than the guitar! When I saw Reagan and his entourage leaving the room, I raced up to him with Pierre's aide, Ted Johnson, and the official photographer in tow. Instantly, three bodyguards flung themselves in front of the U.S. president — a conditioned reflex to any sudden movement towards their chief. Reagan laughed, telling them to relax, and said he had promised to take a photo with me. The consummate actor graciously allowed the cameras to shoot away as we posed together.

Back in my room, I changed and waited for Ted's knock at the door. Somehow he had discovered a back staircase that avoided the crowded lobby, enabling us to reach Pierre's suite without too many embarrassing security stops. We indulged in strawberries, kiwi fruit, chocolate, and white wine, and made love to a loud Mahler symphony on the radio, lest the secret service be eavesdropping along the corridors. What an adventure to be in the arms of my amorous prime minister while most of the maximum-security officers were none the wiser! Getting back to my room with dishevelled hair at two in the morning might prove more challenging. "I think you made quite an impression on our visitors," Pierre said, proudly hugging me as he loaded me up with souvenir Summit Conference matches, fruit, and chocolate bars, which I stuffed into my bulging handbag. Pierre was always magnanimous with superfluous hotel-room goodies. He made sure the coast was clear and kissed me goodnight, whispering, "*Je t'aime.*"

In August 1982, I performed a private concert for President Chun Doo Hwan of Korea, and in October I was delighted to be awarded an Order of Canada decoration. The medal is an honour bestowed by the governor-general on citizens who have contributed to Canadian society through humanitarian deeds or scientific, literary, athletic, or artistic accomplishments. Pierrot Productions, who were shooting a documentary on my career, recorded the event on film. Governor General Ed Schreyer, placing the medal around my neck, whispered, "I remember how President Portillo of Mexico thought you were an angel when you played for him. Congratulations, Liona." Wearing a floor-length gown of dusty rose, I stood proudly among the gathering of distinguished citizens and politicians.

At the reception I was seated with a fellow recipient, film director Norman Jewison, and Pierre put in a brief appearance to greet my mother, who had accompanied me. They had never met, although over the years they had become telephone acquaintances. He invited us both to join him at Sussex "for a night cap," arranging for his driver to take us there later. My mother had already listened to my descriptions of the official residence, including the various plant pots where I had discreetly dumped portions of the cognac and sherry I had felt obliged to accept! But Pierre gave her a personally guided tour, letting her quietly peep into the sleeping boys' bedrooms and asking her advice on how to care for a vivarium of salamanders they had collected from the woods at Harrington. Having tolerated Damien's various menageries, my mother had become an expert on anything that crawled, from iguanas to tarantulas. He invited her to go swimming, but she protested that she had no bathing suit. "*Pas de problème.* You don't need one here," he said, shrugging both shoulders and subtly wobbling his head with his characteristic French mannerism. My mother declined anyway. Laughingly, she recounted how once I told her that I was "flying CP Air to Santiago" and, hearing it as "see Pierre," she had presumed that we were planning a rendezvous in Chile! That was before CP Air renamed itself Canadian Airlines International.

Like errant children, Pierre and I hurried off to the pool and sauna while my mother remained in the living room, browsing through coffee-table books on Canadian history and Native art and sipping sherry, which she chose not to share with my favourite plant pot. When she and my father had decided so many years earlier to book passage on the SS *Columbia* to Canada, how could she have ever imagined that the leader of her adopted country would one day be entertaining her in his private residence and showering kisses on her eldest daughter?

From that day on, I was allowed to wear the Order of Canada medal. My years of trekking across the continents with guitar in hand, battling intemperate climes to represent Canada in far-away places, struggling to compose and transcribe new repertoire, staying up late into the night to memorize concertos, and giving concerts or radio and television interviews in the capitals and backwaters of the world had finally brought me some official government recognition — what a feeling of gratitude and accomplishment.

Several years later, in April 1985, when I visited Jamaica to play at the international music festival, Jamfest, my mother had another opportunity to meet Pierre. He was vacationing in Ocho Rios as a guest in Lady Mary Mitchell's house, to which he invited us for lunch. We enjoyed swimming in the tepid Caribbean waters and reminisced about our times in Ottawa while sunbathing on the sandy beach. Justin, Sacha, and Michel had certainly grown up since I had last seen them, but were just as delightfully energetic as I remembered. A few years earlier, Pierre had wanted me to give them classical guitar lessons and sought advice on which instruments to buy. Michel studied from Shearer's Book 1 and Justin opted for country style, but other hobbies intervened and their guitars lay neglected in the closets of Pine Avenue. As I watched their boyish antics in the palm-dappled sunlight, I wondered how they would have reacted had we produced a little sister for them to romp around with. She would definitely have played the guitar!

On a couple of occasions, Pierre had suggested that, although he never intended to be married again, he would be happy to have us live together and share a child. For some reason, he was sure we would produce a little girl, which would please his paternal instincts after three boys in a row. "I have full-time nannies who could care for her while you're away giving concerts, so it wouldn't really interfere with your career," he had reasoned. If this proposition had resonated with my own desires, our lives would have taken a completely different turn. Although I felt honoured in a sense to be entrusted with this fantasy, some inner compass was steering me in another direction.

During all the years of our relationship, I cannot ever remember the feeling of being completely "in love" with Pierre, although I had loved him in a caring and trusting way. Perhaps we both were always holding something back because of our all-consuming careers. At first I had been flattered by his attentions and infatuated with his position and power, but even after those aspects assumed less significance, I always remained full of admiration for his remarkable mind and the calm strength with which he conducted his political and family life. Pierre was a man with very definite opinions, strong ethics, and high standards for himself and others. Those Jesuit priests who had been his teachers at Jean-de-Brébeuf College had done a fine job in honing his sharp intellect, flair for extemporaneous speeches, and powers of logical reasoning. He always tried to be fair and just, whether settling a political crisis or refereeing an argument between his sons.

Pierre had an unusually gentle and sensitive nature that seemed to set him apart from many other politicians. His passionate love for music, art, and nature revealed an aspect of his personality that almost seemed in contradiction to the forceful political spokesperson most people saw. On the other hand, his cerebral and rather off-hand approach to practical matters of state infuriated his detractors, who portrayed him as an elitist snob. Pierre never pandered to the media, and refused to conceal his obvious derision towards many of his critics. This attitude hardly scored him points in the press gallery, although many media pundits admired the way he stood up for his ideals, brilliantly defending his vision of Canada even in the face of considerable criticism.

At the start of his career as prime minister, the charismatic Pierre Trudeau was hailed around the world as a unique leader who would strengthen Canada's position in the world — so young and hip compared with his predecessors. Here was a swinging bachelor who had dated Barbra Streisand; a brown-belt judoist, a skier, and a diver — a man who slid down bannisters in Buckingham Palace and dared to wear sandals to the office. Canadians adored his eccentricities at first, but inevitably, as the years unfolded, public opinion impugned his unorthodox persona and policies. Western Canada resented his loyalties to Quebec, and many blamed Canada's economic woes on their headstrong leader. In May 1979, he was defeated by the Conservative opposition, led by Joe Clark.

In December, however, the vicissitudes of politics saw the new government fall abruptly, and the following February, after an energetic campaign, a revitalized Pierre was once again running the country. He had agonized over whether he should re-enter public life. But, fired up over René Lévesque's separatist movement and his own desire to repatriate Canada's constitution from Britain, he had decided that the country needed a leader who would fight for the fundamental issues. Only after several years of promulgating his belief in a united Canada, and presenting dozens of world leaders with his peace initiatives and polemics against nuclear arms, did he finally decide to retire from politics for good.

In 1984, watching Pierre give his farewell speech with his boys onstage beside him, I, along with millions of fellow Canadians, was overcome with emotion. We were witnessing the end of an extraordinary era in Canada's history. Although I admittedly had only a small part in the overall drama, I felt gratified by the role I had played in Pierre Trudeau's life, and he in mine.

12

"Me and Julio"

My performing schedule was always hectic during the latter part of the seventies. Two concerts were arranged in Chile in October 1978 through the Beethoven Society, Santiago's classical concert sponsor, for which I transcribed "Moonlight Sonata" and "Für Elise." The hospitable Canadian embassy held a luncheon in my honour. "Please help yourself to the salad," the hostess insisted, noticing I had bypassed the bowl of lettuce on her buffet table — a precaution learned from my San Miguel days. "It's not like Mexico. In Chile, nobody gets sick. Here, let me put some on your plate." As a result of her insistence, and my reluctance to appear impolite, I became violently ill and ran a high fever for the next six days. Although my hands went through the motions of playing concerts to full houses in the Teatro Nacional and the Teatro Municipal, the rest of me struggled in a drugged daze. I had swallowed enough penicillin, codeine, and Kaopectate to kill a horse!

The son of Arturo Alessandri, one of Chile's former presidents, became enamoured of me, attentively presenting himself at the hotel room every few hours, laden with medicines. Thinking that fresh air would do me some good, the self-appointed nursemaid insisted on driving me to one of his family homes at the base of the spectacular Andes Mountains. But I was too feverish to really appreciate the breathtaking scenery, my sole preoccupation being whether I would be able to reach the bathroom in time!

At the conclusion of my trip, the Canadian embassy held a second reception, to which many of the upper-class Beethoven Society members had been invited, as well as several guitarists, writers, and composers from the university whom I had suggested be included. There was a tangible undercurrent of tension between the two disparate factions, who were at opposite poles of the political spectrum. Each group kept to its own side of the room, while I tried to alternate between them. Two students confided in me about the hideous measures that their right-wing government had used to quell freedom of expression. Before they eventually killed him, the military had mutilated the hands of Chile's beloved singer/songwriter Victor Jara so he could not play his guitar. It was horrifying to learn of such atrocities, and I shuddered to think how evil man could become.

It is always a moral dilemma when an artist is invited to perform in countries with repressive regimes, as acceptance might be construed as approval of that government. Still, I believe that cultural contact and communication are some of the best ways of penetrating the barriers created by politics. Living behind the ideologies are human beings struggling to survive. Music has a universal appeal that reaches deep into the human psyche. Who can listen to a Mahler symphony and not be moved by sublime emotions? From darkest despair to absolute joy, music is able to convey our deepest feelings more intensely than any other art form and is integral to humanity itself. I know of no society devoid of music. Even through my simple classical guitar, I felt that I had touched some emotional chords in Chile.

What a tragedy that many Latin American symphony orchestras suffered tremendously during the years of upheavals and pernicious military rule. The vibrant music created under the regimes that once gripped Peru, Chile, and Argentina is a wonderful testament to the survival of the human spirit. Pinochet tried to silence the voices of Victor Jara and his contemporaries, but their message lived on within the hearts and minds of the people. I left the land of Pablo Neruda and Isabel Allende laden with tokens of my audience's appreciation — records, poems, a collection of classical guitar music — and a renewed appreciation for the democratic country in which I lived.

A colourful intrusion interrupted my North American touring schedule when, in November 1979, the Rotarians of Trinidad decided to present a couple of concerts as part of their fund-raising campaign. My mother, who had enjoyed her introduction to the Caribbean in Puerto Rico, offered to be my travelling companion.

The evening air was steaming hot as people crowded into tiers that were stacked up to the rafters in the school auditorium of hilly San Fernando, Trinidad's second-largest city. The typical Third-World scenario of unresponsive microphones entailed heated discussions between the stage manager and the electricians. The pandemonium ended, however, when, in the nick of time, Father Michael came careering down the hills on his motorbike, black cassock flying in the breeze, with the missing connection cord tucked into his robes. These pre-concert shenanigans are routine whenever one leaves the technical security of North American shores. As a performer, I have learned to be tolerant and not panic; everything usually falls into place by an often delayed show-time. The hall lacked air-conditioning, so, with windows flung wide, the intermittent barking of dogs and screeching of motorcycles added touches of local colour to my Scarlatti sonatas; the concert proceeded like the calm after a storm.

A large turnout in Port of Spain's Hilton ballroom, my second concert venue, delighted the Rotarians, who booked me again a year later. Afterwards, on the pool-side patio, under a blue-velvet sky adorned with millions of scintillating stars, we were treated to an impromptu concert by a group of steel-drum players. With admiration, I listened to their amazingly complex rhythms and syncopations:

a sensuous mix of African, Spanish, and Indian styles. In addition to popular repertoire, the talented band had arranged the music of Tchaikovsky, Rossini, and Chopin. Those European composers would have been amazed to hear their masterpieces interpreted by the agile brown fingers of the Caribbeans.

The governor of Trinidad, Sir Ellis Clarke, asked us to tea at his imposing residence on the Queen's Circle, and later offered a guided tour of his racehorse stables. Although I knew nothing about thoroughbreds, I tried to sound knowledgeable while bravely patting their velvety foreheads, hoping they would not chomp off one of my fingers and thus put an end to my career. The governor extended an invitation for us to join him in his royal box the following day. "This is probably the closest we will ever get to Ascot," I opined, as we dolled ourselves up in frilly dresses and flowery sun-hats. In between sips of champagne, Sir Ellis whispered the names of the horses he predicted would come in first — and invariably they did! We decided to take his tips and make cautious bets, but we later wished we had been braver. The charming governor, we discovered, owned most of the animals himself.

Jetting to Europe, I sometimes flew supersonic from New York to Paris. A most efficient way to cross the Atlantic, the Concorde soared fifty thousand feet into the skies, destroying our ozone layer at Mach II — twice the speed of sound! The meals and service were superb, despite Air France's annoying habit of handing out cigars, but I never grew accustomed to the fact that Concorde windows always felt hot to the touch!

There were so many interesting characters to meet on those flights. The producers, politicians, and tycoons who sat beside me offered their business cards and made me feel a part of an elite international club. During one trip, I chatted to Henry Kissinger and gave him a *First Lady* record. This led to his asking for my hotel name and phone number, but I did not feel quite ready to take on America's secretary of state. The producer Mike Nichols shared confidences about his marriage, and the editor of *Playgirl* sent a year's subscription in plain-brown envelopes, much to my family's amusement.

When I was returning from one of my jaunts to Europe, the Concorde lost an engine halfway across the Atlantic. Suddenly, the plane descended steeply from its normal flying altitude of fifty-two thousand feet, and in a somewhat subdued voice, the pilot announced that we were going to attempt to land in Reykjavik, Iceland. Hardly reassured, we passengers silently eyed each other, thinking our own disconcerting thoughts. A roughness to the engine's sound kept us on edge as champagne was passed around by nervous stewardesses. An hour later, the captain returned to the intercom to say that they were going to "try to land in 'alifax, Nova Scotia." What a relief that I could jump on a safe Air Canada flight! But several more hours passed before he informed us that plans had changed again: we would soon be "trying to land" in New York!

Flashing fire-engines and ambulances were standing by — we apparently lacked brake power — but a long screeching landing brought us to a final stop. The catatonic Frenchman buckled in across from me had beads of perspiration glistening on his brow, which had turned ashen white. I swore I would never travel by Concorde again, but several years later, a Royal Command Performance forced me to fly supersonic. For someone with nerves of steel, it is a wonderful way to travel.

The head of CBS Records International called from New York in 1979 to say that Julio Iglesias was looking for a guitarist to contribute a short cameo appearance to his upcoming Madison Square Garden show. "You'd be perfect, Liona. Here's the telephone number of his manager, Alfredo Fraile." Having spent hours enjoying Julio's sensuous renditions of "Abrazame" and "El Flor de Piel" after my introduction to his music in Puerto Rico, I thought this sounded a splendid suggestion. The next day I called Fraile, who encouraged me to come to Miami the following week to meet Iglesias and discuss the idea. The only problem was that the next week I would be in British Columbia playing with the Victoria Symphony Orchestra and would still be on the West Coast five days later, playing in Seattle.

But, without even considering the distance and the expensive airfare, I booked a gruelling twelve-hour flight to Miami with changes in Minneapolis and Atlanta. If Julio wanted me to play in his concerts, it would help expand my following in Latin America in the same way Gordon's tour had in North America. Quite apart from the concert business, I was also intrigued to meet the Spanish singer with the seductive voice and irresistible smile.

I practised Spanish phrases on the plane and, close to midnight, wearily dragged my bags and guitar case into the Coral Gables Holiday Inn. The meeting with Julio was to be at noon the next day. After sleeping lightly, I rose early and at eleven in the morning, called Fraile. "I am so very sorry, Señorita Boyd," he told me. "Julio left Miami this morning and I'm departing for New York in two hours. My apologies, but we completely forgot that you were coming today." I felt deflated and utterly miserable; that long trip had all been for nothing. The next day, knowing I had made a fool of myself, I took another three planes back to Seattle.

A few weeks later, Fraile called me in Toronto, apologized for his error in timing, and asked if I could come to Montreal, where Julio would be playing in two weeks. Why had he not suggested Montreal in the first place? Undaunted, I flew there and checked into the hotel where the Spanish group was staying. When I informed Fraile of my arrival, he asked if I would join them for dinner. "We'll call for you in one hour, just before leaving," he reassured me. One hour passed . . . one and a half hours . . . two hours . . . two and a half hours . . . and still no telephone call. Spaniards are often late, but this was getting ridiculous.

Eventually, the front desk informed me that Fraile and Iglesias, plus entourage, had left the hotel ninety minutes earlier. That same sinking feeling I had experienced in Miami returned as I spooned my lukewarm onion soup ordered from the room-service menu. Perhaps they would all be back around 10:00 p.m. and would call me then. By 11:30, becoming bored and sleepy, I screwed my hair up into a plastic shower cap and sank into a comforting hot bath. Just as I was scrubbing off my eye make-up the phone rang. It was Fraile, apologizing that he had forgotten to call. Julio would now like to meet me and was up in his room waiting. Ninety per cent of me felt like banging down the phone and crying, but 10 per cent remembered those possible Latin tours. Using every Spanish curse word, I skidded around the bathroom, drying off and putting myself back together as fast as possible. "Probably these mix-ups are not Julio's fault," I rationalized, trying to remain calm.

Fraile met me and ushered me into a room full of people lounging around as if sated after a hearty dinner. Julio, lying on a couch draped by two Latin beauties, gave me the distinct impression he had drunk too much wine for supper. "Hi, Liona, wanna come to bed with us?" were his opening lines. Fraile laughed and told Julio that I had brought my guitar to play for him. This was hardly the quiet meeting of two artists that I had imagined. Sitting across from Julio, I played through a few Spanish numbers, while he let out approving grunts and winked at me with his dark Latin eyes. "You play great. Come and be my special guest in tomorrow's concert. But tonight, let's make love so that we can get to know each other better," he continued, motioning to the bedroom, from which one of the half-clad, sultry Latinas had just emerged. While accepting his first offer, I declined the second as diplomatically as possible. However was he going to cope with all these various women? I was not about to find out.

Miraculously, the next day Fraile remembered to pick me up for a sound check. A sober and much nicer Julio came over to talk backstage, expressing his appreciation for my record albums, which he had been given by CBS. My hopes for the Latin American tour started to climb. How thrilling to be playing in the same concert as the handsome singer whom I had spent so much time listening to on vinyl.

The stadium, which seated fifteen thousand people, was rapidly filling up with a Spanish- and French-speaking crowd. Several of the Montreal Symphony musicians who had been hired for Julio's orchestra chatted with me, surprised that I was part of the program. Julio promised to give me a good introduction midway through the second half of the show, and asked if I would play two selections. Presumably this was to be a kind of audition to determine if his public would appreciate an interlude of guitar music. Finally, I would be able to prove to Fraile and Julio what a great addition I would be to their upcoming South American tour and Madison Square Garden concert. As I sat in the dressing-room, confidently rehearsing my pieces, Julio's voice floated down from the intercom with fragments of my favourite songs. This was going to be an evening to remember.

During the intermission, Fraile came rushing into my dressing-room. There had been a change in plan. He wanted me to open the second half of the show in five minutes' time. "Don't worry, Liona, we'll give you a wonderful introduction, and Julio will say nice things about you afterwards. But we want you to play only one piece. Now, let's go!" "This is not fair," I despaired, as Fraile ushered me towards the gigantic stage. People were still returning to their seats and Julio was nowhere to be seen. At times like that, an artist really needs a manager. It was awful. Fraile steered me onto the stage without the promised introduction. The thousands of people, expecting Julio, were no doubt confused when a classical guitarist started to play, totally unannounced. I had hardly risen from my seat when Julio launched into his first song, from the opposite side of the stage, giving me no word of thanks or recognition. Mortified, I slunk off to my dressing-room, remembering the kindly consideration that Gordon Lightfoot had always shown me on the road. They had mis-used me in a most embarrassing way, and I felt sick inside. Instead of a professional artist with a huge following of my own, I had been treated like some amateur groupie by both Julio and his manager.

Feeling dejected because of their lack of respect and sensitivity, I packed my guitar case and called a cab to take me back to the hotel, in no mood to talk to either of those selfish Spaniards. Once again, I had made a total idiot of myself. "Liona, you have only yourself to blame for this disaster," I reflected. "When are you going to come to your senses and realize that most of these pop stars only care about themselves?" The international division of CBS New York had meant well in suggesting a cameo appearance in Julio's concert, but after Montreal I knew it was patently foolish to expect anything to result from my efforts. My disappointment was exacerbated when I calculated that, between Miami and Montreal, the bill for my expenses was several thousand dollars.

A few years later, CBS invited my parents and me to one of Julio's Toronto shows, and after some hesitation, I decided to accept. Backstage, Julio apologized. "Liona, I'm so sorry for what happened at the Forum." "You have a beautiful and talented daughter, Mummy," he told my mother, giving her a hug and a kiss. Julio's music meant too much for me to hold on to any resentment. I have met Julio several times since, and whenever I hear his voice, the magic is always there. A few measures of his songs never fail to lift my spirits. Although Julio Iglesias was responsible for one of my most embarrassing concert experiences, I admire him as a fellow artist and will always be grateful for his songs, which have meant so much to me over the years. As proof of my devotion to his music, I turned down a 1982 invitation from Pierre Trudeau to be his partner at a dinner for Andreas Papandreou. With a certain Spanish singer performing that night in Toronto, even the Greek and Canadian prime ministers did not stand a chance!

In April 1980, I was invited to give a concert tour in Japan, and I asked my mother along. This was to be the first time for either of us in the Far East, so we requested a few days to visit the holy Buddhist shrines of Kyoto. There would be concerts in Tokyo, Obihiro, Kumagaya, Hakodate, Yokohama, as well as Fukuoka and a number of television shows, including an hour-long documentary for the NHK network.

On the day of our arrival, a strange and alarming phenomenon occurred. Whenever I picked up the guitar to run through repertoire, my fingers refused to function; all strength seemed to have ebbed from my hands. As I stumbled through Lennox Berkeley's "Sonatina," I looked helplessly at my anxious mother. "I've no idea what's happened, but I can't seem to play, and the tour begins in two days!"

I despaired. Collapsing into a restless jet-lagged sleep, I tossed and turned in desperation, feeling utterly incapable of performing. The next morning, I was awakened by my mother, who had dreamed in the night of the word *calcium.* "We must get you some tablets at once!" she insisted and set off, fuelled by her night's inspiration. Without knowing a word of Japanese, or where she was going, she was able to purchase some calcium pills from a druggist by writing out the chemical symbol Ca, which he recognized. After I swallowed them intermittently, the strength miraculously returned to my hands. Never doubt your mother's intuitions!

We took an immediate liking to Tokyo and spent our free time strolling around the parks and temples, glorying in the cherry blossoms that beautified the city in April. Mr. Tanaka, our host and promoter, was a model of courtesy, constantly bowing to us and making sure that our smallest concerns were met. For three weeks, his assistant, Mishi, struggled valiantly around airports and train stations with my guitar case and a bag stuffed with bulky concert programs. Taxis driven by polite, white-gloved chauffeurs whisked me from concert halls to TV stations, where I appeared on several widely viewed shows such as "Good Morning, Tokyo."

In that amazing country, with thousands of amateur classical guitarists, the two thick, glossy guitar publications featured me on their covers. Never before had I been interviewed and photographed so much as I was during that first visit to the land of the rising sun. They photographed me in the park picking cherry blossoms; they photo-graphed me in the early-morning produce market eating strawberries; they photographed me tuning my guitar during sound checks before concerts; they photographed me at a reception held by the Canadian embassy. They even insisted on photographing my mother and me as we arrived, exhausted and travel-weary, at each new hotel. It seemed the press could never get enough photographs — an obsessive compulsion in a land that seemed to be run by Sony, Fuji, Sanyo, and Canon.

CBS Sony was jubilant finally to have me in Japan. The entire

Masterworks division had been decorated with *First Lady of the Guitar* posters. My surprised mother and I, called on to give speeches to all their smiling employees, received rounds of applause for our impromptu efforts. Strolling through Tokyo one evening, we came upon an area where my concert flyers had been plastered on every lamppost. How appreciated I began to feel in this strange country where they loved the guitar. What an extraordinary fuss everybody was making. My records, including the newly released *Spanish Fantasy*, were apparently selling like hot cakes. To profit from the CBS promotion, King Records had obtained distribution rights from London Records and issued my two earliest recordings. For the Japanese market, they used poetic titles: *A Teardrop* and *The Girl with the Flaxen Hair*.

A performance with the Academica Orchestra enticed young Prince Anomiya, the grandson of Emperor Hirohito, to attend. His presence was considered such an honour that Mr. Tanaka bubbled with excitement. A private tea party had been arranged during my precious twenty-minute intermission so that the prince, an enthusiastic guitar student, could meet me. It became quite a challenge for me to keep the conversation flowing while balancing my dainty cup, swallowing the proffered sweetmeats, and smiling at the silent, reverent guests. And all the while, His Highness, a shy and nervous teenager, giggled at everything I said.

The acoustics were good, the hall full, and the responses as enthusiastic as could be expected. Haber had warned me that, in Japan, audiences would clap very softly. In North America or Europe, we are used to more expressive applause, and to an artist who has not been forewarned, it can be disconcerting. Everywhere we went, people bowed to us, and soon my mother and I were bobbing up and down like yo-yos. Actually, this is a great hand-saver for guitarists; so often my fingers have been crushed to the point of pain by forceful handshakes from enthusiastic fans.

Everywhere we went, the concert promoters and television-station managers gave us little souvenirs — usually silk-brocade purses or scarves — and we soon ran out of our Canadian maple-leaf spoons and small Inuit carvings. Fans overloaded me with gifts as well: paintings, flower baskets, and a mobile of a thousand tiny paper birds made by schoolchildren. Obihiro, on the northern island, was perfumed by the irresistible aroma of white chocolate, which the town manufactured, and several delicious bars were bestowed on us on our arrival. In Hakodate, however, the pungent odour of drying fish and various foul-smelling seaweeds assaulted our western nostrils. The prices on our room-service menus were steep by Canadian standards, and we were never quite sure what we were ordering, so my thrifty mother went out foraging in the streets, returning to the hotel laden with cakes, pears, and tangerines, which she had negotiated from the tiny grocery shops in the neighbour-hood. We were highly amused by two signs we saw: step-by-step illustrations in the trains graphically instructing how to use a western-style toilet, and a notice in our hotel that read No Swords Allowed and No Disgusting Behaviour Permitted! Things were indeed different in the land of the samurai.

After I played a concert in Yokohama, the local agent seemed in a hurry to close the hall and refused to let any autograph-seeking guitar enthusiasts backstage. He ushered me into a car at the rear of the building, and as we drove away, I caught a glimpse of many disappointed-looking teenagers clutching my concert programs and being turned away from the stage door. Knowing how much an autograph or a smile from one of my own guitar heroes had meant to me in the past, I was overcome with guilt at denying those students the same pleasure.

Towards the end of the tour, I was booked to perform with the Tokyo Philharmonic Orchestra in the cavernous Bunka Kaikan Hall. The guest conductor, Argeo Quadri, an elderly Italian from La Scala in Milan, told me during rehearsal that he would not permit the use of a microphone. So that I would not be drowned out, he began dismissing members of the orchestra, until only a handful of musicians remained on the stage and it appeared I would be accompanied by a string quartet rather than a symphony orchestra. "This is becoming ridiculous," I informed him. "I insist on using a small microphone so the guitar can be heard and all the strings won't have to play *pianissimo*."

We had a heated showdown onstage, the maestro angrily gesticulating and waving his baton threateningly in my direction. He stomped his feet on the wooden stage like some enraged Rumpelstiltskin, growling that Segovia would never have condescended to use a microphone. I felt certain that Segovia would never have agreed to play with an orchestra in this four-thousand-seat auditorium, where a guitar could barely be heard past the third row in a solo concert, never mind with the Philharmonic to drown it out. Sticking to my guns, I fought back in French, throwing in a few Italian expressions remembered from my university classes. Meanwhile, our bewildered Japanese representatives, not understanding the languages and unable to comprehend our histrionics, tried to resolve the situation by bowing apologetically to each other, exercising the Japanese propensity for maintaining harmony. The maestro's host, with a hang-dog look of pleading in his eyes, informed me euphemistically that "the kind and understanding gentleman would be so very grateful if you would please be so graciously accommodating to perform without audio amplification, as it would make him wonderfully happy." My enraged conductor had just spat out some choice Italian words and stormed off the stage! But without subtle support from electronic amplification, in spite of the orchestra's reduced numbers, my playing, with its variety of tonal shadings, would be perceived as scarcely audible scratching, so I also marched away, leaving the puzzled orchestra members patiently awaiting a decision. Mr. Tanaka and the Philharmonic manager must have eventually talked some sense into the conductor, and he finally conceded to share the stage with my offending microphone.

The concert went splendidly. Afterwards, a charming maestro dissolved into smiles and hugs, magnanimously inviting my mother and me to be his guests at La Scala. After weeks of being immersed in oriental politeness, he must have found his volatile Latin temperament craving a catharsis. I had come to Japan at the perfect time to help restore the conductor's equilibrium!

13

"Why Do You Need Royalties?"

In the late 1970s, I was becoming more and more frustrated by the comings and goings at Haber Artists, where a continuous stream of fresh-faced young assistants had to be trained from scratch. Eventually, Sandy Castonguay and Costa Pilavachi, who possessed a refreshing degree of business acumen, came on board, taking over negotiations on my behalf. Sandy, like several future agents and managers, suggested that signing autographs after concerts no longer befitted my ever-increasing stature as an international artist. "By allowing yourself to be accessible to the public, you destroy the mystique that classical artists should preserve," he insisted. I had always been willing to meet members of my audience face to face, especially young guitar enthusiasts to whom it meant so much. What a thrill it had been during my student days to acquire Julian Bream's and Segovia's autographs backstage; what a treasured moment when Narciso Yepes had allowed me a close-up view of his nails. Resisting my agent's counsel, I made a point of continuing to meet individuals from those seas of shadowy faces in the darkened theatres. I remember the shy smiles of a little girl in a wheelchair who offered me a crayoned portrait, and the nervous eyes of pimply-faced teenagers presenting, like sacred offerings, pieces they had composed for me. I have signed everything from guitar straps, T-shirts, plaster casts, and the undersides of stage chairs, to thousands of programs, record covers, and music books. It is thanks to all those enthusiastic fans that my guitar career exists, and I will never take them for granted.

One thing that disconcerts me is to be rushed before a concert. I make every possible attempt to reach the venue at least three hours before a performance to adjust speakers, microphones, stage curtains, and lights. However, due to delayed flights, flat tires, traffic jams, or nonchalant promoters, pre-concert panic is sometimes unavoidable.

In Nuuk, the capital of Greenland, my plane touched down on the icy landing strip at 8:20 p.m. for a 9:00 p.m. performance. Trying to iron my concert gown on the backstage floor while tuning uncooperative strings was not the best introduction to a new country. People expect me to glide off a plane right onto the stage, unaware that guitar strings and their players need time to adjust and acclimatize. Latin American concerts are notorious for their late starts, but there the unperturbed audiences expect recitals to begin at least half an hour later than advertised, so nobody voices concern.

Every performing guitarist can relate to a recurring nightmare I have. In my version of this dreadful dream, I am frantically preparing to set off for a concert, having forgotten to practise and feeling totally unprepared. Usually, I am dashing around a hotel room, slapping make-up on my face, and sprinkling talcum powder into my unwashed hair in a vain attempt to resuscitate it. All the gowns I pull out of the closet are either torn or dirty, and nothing seems to match. One of my guitar strings has snapped and I cannot locate a replacement set anywhere. (In other versions of the dream, my precious guitar has developed a nasty crack or my trusty footstool is broken.) To add to my frenzy, I am desperately late! Eventually, I reach the concert hall, where colleagues and critics are anxiously

awaiting my arrival, and realize to my horror that this is an important
international guitar festival. While trying to tune up, I notice that
I have neglected to file my nails. One is about to split, so with
trembling fingers, I struggle to repair it with Krazy Glue, praying it
will hold together. Finally, after a long introduction and thunderous
applause, I am propelled onstage, with thumping heart, dry throat,
and clammy hands. I cannot remember the chords to the first piece,
so I quickly jump into the next, but when that also draws a blank,
I start to improvise, inventing entire contemporary-sounding sections
to the compositions. Nobody in the audience breathes. Mental blocks
sabotage each of the pieces, which dissolve into weird improvisa-
tions with special effects — even vocals! Some in the audience are
already walking out. Mercifully, at this point, I wake up — the nightmare is too unbearable! Believe it or not, most of these individual
situations have actually happened to me, but never could so many
things go wrong at once. We guitarists all have disaster anecdotes
that we love to recount when we get together. How could anyone
who is not a player empathize with the anxiety caused by out-of-tune
or fraying strings, the pain of cracked callouses, or the anguish we
suffer on realizing we have filed our nails too short before a concert?
Such agonies can be appreciated only by fellow string-pluckers.

The Kolmar-Luth agency in New York agreed to take over my
U.S. bookings, arranging an engagement at Town Hall, my second
successful concert in Manhattan. In addition to Kolmar's dates, which
were scattered around the continent, I teamed up with Chet Atkins
for an outdoor "gig" in Chautauqua, New York; accepted the Vanier
Award; was named Artist of the Year and Honorary Mayor of the City
in San Antonio, Texas; performed in the Bermuda Music Festival;
shared the billing on an Alberta TV special with an upstart comedian
named Jim Carrey; and gave a joint concert with Anne Murray in
Wilmington, Delaware. Stickers from Phoenix, San Diego, Kansas City,
and New Orleans vied for space on my well-worn guitar cases. Hiring
my own Lear jet was the only way to deliver two performances
scheduled too closely together. Through hundreds of zigzagging

bookings, I soon became intimately familiar with the walkways, lounges, and ladies' rooms of airports from Pittsburgh to Dallas. I knew which empty nurseries could provide a retreat for an hour's private practice and which coffee shops served the best muffins or were the least smoky. Days in the air had become my way of life.

In first-class lounges or on board planes, I was frequently approached by prominent businessmen, who slipped me their cards along with invitations to dinner. Most were politely declined, but some provided interesting diversions from concert halls and recording studios. The Toronto entrepreneur Ben Webster trailed my tour of Western Canada, and Frank Stronach, the charismatic CEO of Magna International, gave me glimpses into his world of international business deals, racehorses, and antiques. I found it exciting to be in the company of successful and attentive men, knowing full well that I was merely a pretty ornament to adorn their sizeable egos.

A concert in Copenhagen was arranged, where I was warmly received by the Danish public and hailed by the press as "the new Segovia"! A few days later, to my immense satisfaction, the Liège Guitar Festival gave me equal billing to my teacher, with whom I fondly reminisced about our escapades in Paris and Nice. Alexandre Lagoya had acquired a new batch of adoring female students, and took wicked pleasure in recounting the details of his recent conquests. My dear maestro seemed to possess such an insatiable appetite for young women that I wondered how he ever found time for the guitar!

After participating in another music festival in Paris in June 1981, at which I performed Casterède's "Homage to Pink Floyd," I set up meetings with certain CBS record executives, hoping to encourage them to release my albums in France. For some reason I was not seeing French sales on my royalty statements as I was for most other foreign countries. "*Mademoiselle*, we are proud to have Lagoya on our label, but we're not interested in a girl from Canada," they told me, shrugging their shoulders over a plate of *crudités* during lunch. How different from our humble Canadian approach, where we are receptive to European talent, often believing it superior to our own. The rejection was disappointing, as the French love classical guitar and had always appreciated my performances.

The head of marketing cast scornful glances at my album covers. "You think a pretty picture will sell these records?" he scoffed. "In France, we specialize in serious artists." Were my "Zambra Granadina" and "Cimarosa Concerto" any less serious than Lagoya's "Carnival of Venice"? Music should stand on its own merits, regardless of the appearance of the artist. I deplored the attitude that equated serious music with stiff traditional images, and resented their chauvinistic response to a feminine image. All my covers were simple portraits; this was still some time before I posed on a white horse for the *Best of Liona Boyd* album. Since when had they criticized Yepes's bald head or Parkening's turtleneck sweaters? Trying to convince them that I had an interesting and unique repertoire was as impossible as explaining an American recipe to a French chef. I gave up.

Greece was another country where, other than a few imports, my albums were not distributed. The chauvinism that was rampant throughout the music business reared its head again in Athens, where I took a lengthy taxi ride to visit a recording company executive. He effusively predicted how saleable my records would be in his country. "Why don't you join me for dinner so we can discuss their release?" he suggested. I was delighted that my initiative to show up at his office was going to generate positive results. "Perhaps you'd like to call by my house to see the litter of puppies our dog has just produced," he added. "By the way, my wife is away today," he continued, lowering his voice and adopting that unmistakable look I had seen often enough before. "No, if you don't mind, I'm a little tired and would prefer to meet at the restaurant," I replied, wondering if accepting dinner was a mistake. "Fine, sweet-heart," he agreed. "I'll be at your hotel at seven forty-five." I cringed a little at his familiarity.

After taxiing in rush-hour traffic for over an hour, I made it back to my downtown hotel, where I steamed out a dress to make myself presentable. At eight o'clock, a call came through: "Sorry, sweetie. I fell asleep and don't feel like going out to dinner now — perhaps next time you come to Greece." I was starving, and furious at his weak excuse. I hoped the man's puppies would give him some good bites on my behalf. This was no way to treat one of CBS's best-selling classical artists. Wolfing down a packet of cookies for dinner (I had spent my last remaining drachmas), I felt furious at all the sleazy executives who related to me only as a single woman, and then remembered a New York lawyer taunting, "Why do you need royalties? You're a woman!" Once again, a man in the music industry was trying to take advantage of his position of power. There had been too many times when business managers, agents, and promoters dangled career offers before me while making suggestive overtures. Already I had forfeited television opportunities and concert bookings by withholding sexual favours. I had no doubt that had I stroked his puppies, or whatever else he had in mind, the executive would have assured my record distribution in Greece, but I was becoming tired of the games men play and their attempts at exploitation.

Although hardly a militant feminist, I support the women's movement's fight for equality. Because of their stand on issues such as equal pay and the right to control our own reproductive systems, laws and attitudes have gradually improved. But it seems we still have far to go in the music business. My modest contribution to women's liberation was to have succeeded in the male-dominated world of guitarists. It was satisfying to know that, by forging an independent creative career, I was serving as a role model for young women pursuing similar goals.

In 1982, the Shakespearean actor Nicholas Pennell and I staged *The Rose and the Fire*, combining poems by Federico García Lorca with the music of Manuel de Falla, Granados, Albéniz, Torroba, and Rodrigo. The evocative music, theatrical lighting, and dramatic readings provoked rave reviews in Stratford and Chicago. I composed and recorded the musical soundtrack to a short film of *The Olden Days Coat* by Margaret Laurence, then jetted to Monaco for the "Monte

Carlo Show," which beamed my playing to five continents. Television proved an easy way to reach new audiences, so I appeared without hesitation on shows hosted by René Simard, Alan Thicke, Mike Douglas, Merv Griffin, Dinah Shore, John Davidson, Toni Tennille, and Paul Anka, as well as "Entertainment Tonight," often staying in the guest-house of my friends Gloria Loring and Alan Thicke. How mind-boggling it was to know that millions of people around the world were watching my fingers on their TV screens.

In the studio green rooms, I enjoyed encounters with such fellow guests as Sir Edmund Hillary, Loretta Lynn, Neville Marriner, Helen Reddy, and Pia Zadora. Alvin Karpis, once the FBI's public enemy number one and the last surviving member of the Barker gang, told me, as we shared an "Alan Hamel Show" limousine, how he had taught Charles Manson to play guitar while living in San Francisco "in a place with a great view of the Bay" — Alcatraz! The notorious bank-robber, now seemingly an affable elderly man, sent me frequent letters from his home in Alicante. Brooke Shields and I chatted on a flight to New York, and Toller Cranston skated around me and my guitar with flamboyant choreography during *Stars on Ice*. The consummate actor and raconteur Peter Ustinov shared two concerts with me after we had been awarded Doctor of Laws degrees from the University of Lethbridge, and to my amusement Nancy White added a new character to her satirical skits: Fiona Freud, Second Lady of the Guitar. How curious that my own appellation, once private, had become communal property. Taking a holiday alone at Club Med in Guadeloupe, I began to realize that the privacy I had taken for granted all my life was no longer possible: fans announced their presence with star-struck gazes, cameras and requests for autographs. It was gratifying to be so appreciated, but I made a mental note to avoid the nude beach!

Columbia Artists Management International (CAMI), one of the most powerful New York agencies, decided to represent me in the U.S., so it was a cordial farewell to Kolmar-Luth. When CBS Master-works suggested I record an album of baroque repertoire with the

English Chamber Orchestra, conducted by Andrew Davis, I locked myself away for two weeks, industriously transcribing Cimarosa, Marcello, Albinoni, and Bach. In the summer of '79 I recorded them at CBS's London studios in England, despite my 102-degree fever, which caused the cancellation of one of the three sessions. When I listen to that album, I am amazed how well I played under such time and health pressures. Perhaps the constant doses of penicillin and cough syrup helped to relax me during this milestone recording of my career.

That same year, encouraged by the writer Shel Silverstein, Chet Atkins and I recorded *The First Nashville Guitar Quartet,* combining our talents with two studio guitarists, John Knowles and John Pell, whose steel and acoustic guitars enhanced our melodic lines. What a ball to be laying down tracks with three of Nashville's finest "pickers"! Arrangements of the "Washington Post" march and movements from the *Aranjuez* and *Brandenburg* concertos had a distinctly country flavour. Chet was as meticulous as any classical producer I have known; I marvelled at his performance and engineering skills. A year later, he offered to edit *Spanish Fantasy,* my new CBS solo album, which contained "Gran Jota de Concierto," "Guajira," and Sor's "Variations on a Theme by Mozart."

In 1981 Eric Robertson produced the next international release, *A Guitar for Christmas,* a reference to the gift I received as a teenager. The addition of harp, strings, oboes, and drums expanded my solo guitar tracks; as a challenge, I played "What Child Is This?" on the instrument of my childhood, the treble recorder. "Silent Night," "The Little Drummer Boy," and Bach's "Sheep May Safely Graze" adapted perfectly to the guitar, yet CBS Masterworks was sceptical that a classical guitar Christmas album would sell. However, after becoming the first classical recording to reach platinum status in Canada, it racked up impressive sales around the world. For the cover shot, I was flown to New York to have my image captured by the renowned photographer Deborah de Turberville. The gold-lamé pantsuit and silver fox coat her stylist picked out for me struck me as more appropriate for Diana Ross. A diaphanous white curtain with frosty patterns that I unhooked from the studio windows saved the day. Draped and pinned, it made a perfect outfit — if Scarlett O'Hara could, why not I?

In contrast to the high sales of *A Guitar for Christmas*, my first digital recording, *Virtuoso*, recorded in 1983 and containing more substantial selections — works by Berkeley, Torroba, and Villa-Lobos — had the weakest sales of all and was far outstripped by *The Best of Liona Boyd*, a 1982 release that fast achieved gold-record status. It was obvious, and not surprising, that most people preferred accessible melodic pieces to more complex contemporary works, but despite *Virtuoso*'s meagre sales, I was happy to have recorded the more demanding repertoire. As expected, the classical reviewers embraced *Virtuoso*. In my career, rave reviews have always occurred in inverse proportion to the number of records sold. I can please either the public or the critics, but seldom both. I have always believed, however, that the most important thing for an artist is to please oneself.

Although I do play music of many contemporary classical composers, my audiences will attest to the fact that my tendency is towards repertoire of an emotional nature. If a piece is merely a technical or intellectual exercise, it usually gathers dust on my shelves. I was amused to read a comment by Jascha Heifetz, one of the great violin virtuosi of all time, who wrote: "I occasionally play works by contemporary composers, and for two reasons: First to discourage the composer from writing any more, and second to remind myself how much I appreciate Beethoven." I like to think my listeners leave the concert hall uplifted, having touched some of the purity and ephemeral beauty conveyed by the guitar notes as they resonate in tune with their inner spirits. Whether music speaks of despair, loneliness, anger, and frustration, or of happiness and love, it is the language that is most able to probe our very souls — be it through a Beethoven symphony or a simple Carcassi étude. Like all forms of art, the effects of music are universal, without boundaries, timeless, and almost impossible to define.

When David Haber retired, Uriel Luft took over his company, hoping to make it stronger internationally. I met up with the elusive Quebecker in Brussels during the final concert of a solo tour I was playing around Western Europe. For a while, I harboured high hopes for a turnaround at Haber Artists, but a few months later Uriel abruptly abandoned the agency, his wife, and their children for an "alternate lifestyle" in Marrakesh. Such is the unpredictable music business!

At this point, my former agent, Ed Oscapella, resurfaced, hoping he and Sandy Castonguay could keep Haber Artists afloat, but this proved unsuccessful. When Ed offered to be my personal manager again, it felt like a step backwards. Fate was good to me at this moment of uncertainty. Bernie Fiedler, who had co-managed the careers of Dan Hill, Murray McLauchlan, and Bruce Cockburn, had just split up with his partner, Bernie Finkelstein. Through his long-time friendship with Gordon Lightfoot, he had become intrigued with my career. At first, I was apprehensive about entrusting a manager from the "pop" world with my classical business, even though he had once been a boy soprano with the Berliner Boys Choir. Would Bernie know how to deal with symphony directors and the characters who inhabited the rarefied air at CBS Masterworks? We had several meetings, during which he impressed me with his wide-reaching understanding of the "music business." Finally, here was someone who possessed the *chutzpah* and savvy I had been looking for. He would make a great manager.

Bernie's bright, good-natured personality and charm made him an excellent concert negotiator who represented my career in a more professional manner. I became very fond of him, tolerating his idio-syncracies as he did mine. He met with CBS staff, who were reluctant at first to use the whimsical photo Robert Vavra had taken of me on a white horse in Sevilla, Spain, for the cover of my *Best of . . .* album. "Horses are sexual animals. You should have worn riding-habit and not bared your leg," they objected. Even Bernie could not persuade CBS England, whose prudish attitude prevented its release, but back home the album went platinum. My manager accompanied me to

Japan for ten concerts at the Honda Theater in 1984, three of which Sony recorded for a *Live in Tokyo* album, released that year. We used the second concert with a few inserts taken from the first and third if a buzz or a really bad squeak intruded. The minimal editing, done at night after I left the theatre, made it the simplest record I ever made. Recording "live to tape" had been nerve-racking enough, but tensions were compounded when a strong earthquake sent me scurrying down thirty flights of fire escape.

Bernie's other artist, the singer-songwriter Dan Hill, who wrote the international hit "Sometimes When We Touch," came backstage after one of my concerts in New Orleans. We decided to take a walk as the southern night was invitingly balmy. As we returned to the hotel to drop off my guitar case, he asked, "Do you mind if I leave some money in your room? I'll pick it up later." My eyes bulged as he nonchalantly pulled thousands of dollars from his back pocket and stashed it under my pillow. "They're always loading me down with cash instead of cheques," he mumbled. Apparently in the pop music world there were certain promoters whose cheques evaporated with the morning sun — another lesson to be absorbed.

By the early eighties, my name was becoming well known all over North America. Requests for concerts and television shows flowed into Bernie's office. His expertise was propelling my career to new heights, and CAMI kept me zigzagging across the continent in their Community Concert Series. In those days of non-stop travel, I rarely had more than four hours sleep each night. *The San Francisco Chronicle* hailed me as "the guitar world's new superstar," the *Denver Post* wrote, ". . . nothing short of fantastic. . . . Liona takes one's breath away," and the *Ottawa Journal* said, "some of the finest classical guitar playing anywhere, and likely the best in North America." The Toronto music critic Wilder Penfield III wrote that I might be "the messiah to bring classical music to the masses!" *Chatelaine* magazine put me on their cover; three times Johnny Carson bantered with me on the "Tonight" show. My playing was featured by Tom Snyder on his "Tomorrow" show and my performance with the Boston Pops Orchestra, under the baton of John Williams, was broadcast by PBS. I did my best to answer personally the piles of fan-mail that arrived, frantically writing in airports and on planes. How gratifying it felt to read that for so many, my playing had introduced them not only to classical guitar, but also to classical music in general. I read how couples had used my recordings during their weddings and honeymoons, doctors had delivered babies to my guitar, and proud parents had named their daughters after me. People occasionally ask me why all this recognition did not "go to my head" as I suppose it does with some performers, but I could not imagine a change in my basic personality.

This lifestyle left no room for any close girlfriend, so for years my mother filled this role. She helped by co-ordinating the endless petty details that accompany a touring career, acting as liaison with travel agents, record companies, performing-rights societies, and publishers. In addition, she tackled my concert gowns, whose special features could not be found in the stores: no buttons to clang or rhinestones to scrape; no tight sleeves to bind, or bulky ones to deaden the strings. With only her imagination to guide her, she cut pieces of panne velvet, silk, or brocade, then painstakingly draped and pinned them onto my body. The gowns were created to withstand the abuses of travel and designed to catch the stage lights, falling to the floor in folds of light and shadow as in a Gainsborough painting. The lessons learned from the pink-taffeta dress she had improvised for me when I was a five-year-old "lady-in-waiting" in a school play had returned to haunt her.

My record sales, outstanding for a classical musician, garnered four Juno Awards from 1979 to 1988, and attracted the attention of Silver Eagle Records, a TV marketing company based in California, who entered into a joint venture with CBS for *The Romantic Guitar of Liona Boyd*. Besides standards such as "Tara's Theme" and "Maria Elena," I added my own "Shadows of the Wind," dedicated to the memory of the jazz guitarist Lenny Breau, whom I had met with Chet Atkins, and "If Only Love," which was chosen to be the single and video. Several months later, in *Billboard* magazine's chart, "If Only Love" placed number three, while Julio Iglesias's new single had to settle for number four! How fleeting are these positions of fame and fortune; in a few weeks, both of our songs vanished from the charts.

A few years earlier, in 1978, Jury Krytiuk of Boot Records, believing that my career could benefit from stronger connections in the U.S., had invited me to meet Seymour Heller, the personal manager of superstar entertainer Liberace. Seymour struck me as the stereotypical Hollywood manager — extroverted, gravel-voiced, toupéed, with a flair for risqué jokes and music-industry anecdotes. "Listen, honey, I can help you get ahead in the entertainment world, but ya just gotta move to L.A. I'll introduce you to all the guys in the business. Whaddya doin' livin' up here in Tranta, Canada?"

I agreed to consider his offer, but a week later, believing I was not ready to exchange the familiarity of Toronto for "the big time," I wrote explaining that I would keep in touch about my career. Over the years, Seymour jokingly referred to himself as my "manager without portfolio." In retrospect, I probably should have jumped at the opportunity to have his representation early on in my career, but I did not believe that my path was "showbiz," and I decided to pursue the more challenging, yet ultimately more satisfying, route of "classical artist." Seymour, however, was responsible for my appearances on twenty television shows and a gala evening where I shared the stage with Bob Hope, Henny Youngman, and Milton Berle. Seymour and his vivacious wife, Billie, became good friends of mine, inviting me to Liberace's glitzy shows, where "Mr. Showmanship" always arranged for a spotlight so I could be introduced to his audience. In January 1980, Liberace launched a classical series at the University of Nevada, Las Vegas, and opened with my recital. He gave me a flowery introduction from the stage and clapped heartily after each piece, then drove me around town in one of his Model-T Fords and invited me for drinks in his rococo house, which was furnished with gilded antiques gleaned from French châteaux and English castles. Liberace had created a fantasy world in which eight little white dogs scampered around a piano-shaped pool and leaped on ermine bedspreads.

I became privy to Liberace's backstage routine: two warm tea-bags placed on the eyes to reduce puffiness. I felt the weight of his rhinestone-studded costumes; witnessed his high-energy entrances from the wings; met the various boyfriends, protégés, and legions of adoring fans; felt the spray from his "dancing water" fountains; and saw how graciously he treated his staff. Although Liberace was more showman than great concert pianist, he introduced thousands of people around the world to light classical music, from Chopin and Liszt to Cole Porter and Gershwin. This phenomenal entertainer certainly deserved his superstar status.

Although I had decided to remain based in Toronto, spending January in the Beverly Hills Hotel to test the waters seemed like a good idea. Laurindo Almeida, the famous Brazilian jazz and bossa nova guitarist, and his wife, Didi, befriended me. After we exchanged musical and technical tips, he remarked, "Liona, you have such a natural feeling for Latin music, and the best tremolo in the business." Coming from someone with six hundred movie-score credits and strings of records, this was indeed a compliment. Seymour Heller and his assistant, Bette Rosenthal, took me around to entertainment events, flew me to Las Vegas for television shows, and introduced me at Hollywood parties. In between these showbiz activities and practising new repertoire, I kept an eye open for any interesting characters in the hotel, determined to make new contacts.

A silver-haired French film director struck up a conversation in the hotel lobby and claimed to know Alexandre Lagoya. "Would you join me for breakfast tomorrow, so we can discuss using your music for one of my films?" he inquired. Always enjoying the chance to speak French, and ever hopeful for this type of opportunity, I agreed to meet him in the coffee shop. The next morning, he phoned to ask if I would come over to his hotel bungalow instead. "I have already ordered breakfast from room service," he insisted. As soon as I entered I realized I had made a mistake. A heavily perfumed *monsieur*, making what he had calculated to be a dramatic and irresistible impression in a black-silk robe, lunged towards me in greeting while his lecherous hands slid below my waist. Angrily extricating myself, I told him I was expecting a business meeting; he laughed sardonically. "*Chérie*, you look so sexy when you are angry. Come and let me tame you, my gorgeous lioness." After a few barbed exchanges, I stormed out, leaving the bewildered Frenchman to his double order of *café au lait* and chocolate croissants. Brewing a pot of tea in the privacy of my small room, I reprimanded myself for being so naïve in regard to men.

Bette introduced me to a friend of hers in the entertainment business, hoping that he might help me with television contacts. "He has a bad reputation as a womanizer, but he's a dear man and I've told him not to try anything, so you needn't worry. He's invited you over to his house at four o'clock." Wearing a pantsuit to convey a businesslike manner, I purposefully made several references to his friendship with Bette. After an hour of exchanges about music and the media, he walked me over to his bookcase and proceeded to pull out prints of Japanese erotic art — an obvious ploy to gauge my reaction. "Here we go again!" I thought, glancing off-handedly at the gigantic samurai penises and spread-eagled geishas. "I've just been given some rather unusual films you might like to view with me later on," he persisted. I could guess full well the nature of his movies, and made excuses to leave before we had a confrontation.

Dismayed, Bette suggested another friend, the legendary manager of Merv Griffin and Jackie Gleason, George "Bullets" Durgeom, who might be able to help me. Offers of a musical cameo on "Love Boat" and a guest spot with Frank Sinatra at the White House were dangled provocatively before me, but once again the price became too apparent. No way was I going to oblige this opportunist, whose bald head came up to my shoulders. Couldn't these men find enough willing action in the starlet-packed studios they frequented?

A few days later, a well-known screenwriter approached me in the hotel corridor with a line all too familiar to aspiring actresses. I had the perfect face for a character in his new film. Would I like to come to his suite to audition and perhaps land a role starring opposite Nastassja Kinski? Slightly flattered, but definitely on my guard, I turned down his offer when it became obvious from his innuendos and body language that he had more on his mind than casting. My acting potential, which had such a rocky start with *The Mish-Mosh Bird* in Grade Eight, was again aborted before takeoff. Years later, running into him in Hollywood, I suggested he might score my guitar music for one of his films. "In order to use your playing, I have to have sex with you. It is nothing personal — just the way I always work with women," he stated. This man and I apparently had vastly different concepts of "scoring"! This, however, seemed to be what was expected of women by the men I encountered in the Golden State that spring. Los Angeles, with all its seductive sunshine, violet jacaranda trees, and swaying palms, seemed to attract a disproportionate number of raptors. I wished I could act tougher, like some of the American women I chanced to meet, but it was not in my nature. After a series of unsatisfying encounters, I left the Polo Lounge, the pool, and the red carpet of the Beverly Hills Hotel and headed home to the comfort of Toronto.

14

Fidel Castro

♪

*I*n April 1982, I was asked to perform the opening concert at the International Guitar Festival in Havana, Cuba. At my request, Pierre Trudeau sent a note of introduction to Fidel Castro, along with a *Spanish Fantasy* album. It was rather presumptuous to expect the leader of a country to rearrange his schedule just to hear me pluck a few strings, but my "nothing ventured, nothing won" philosophy prevailed.

The night before departing for Havana, I won my second Juno Award for Instrumental Artist of the Year. Wearing an exquisite, white sequined gown, which the CBC had had specially designed for the occasion, I performed a medley of solo pieces in a dreamlike sequence on a circular rotating set enveloped in clouds of dry ice — a complete contrast to the preceding rock act, Rough Trade. Afterwards, CBS personnel insisted that I visit their hospitality suite to rub shoulders with the media people. Fading fast and against my better judgment I choked my way through two hours shouting at the top of my voice to be heard above the ear-splitting rock music. Journalists thrust their microphones at me for comments, while CBS brass crowded in for photos and future album suggestions. Exhausted, I sank into the sheets around three in the morning, after hanging up the lovely white gown in my closet and thinking, "One day this will make a perfect wedding dress."

The next morning, my throat was so sore that I could hardly swallow. Flying over the Caribbean, I cursed myself for lacking the willpower to decline CBS's hospitality. On our arrival at Havana's Hotel Nacional, Mother and I were assigned a small, humid room, where I dosed myself with erythromycin and collapsed into bed. How wretched I felt — certainly in no state to rehearse for my upcoming performance, which was to be televised live all over Cuba. It was imperative that I recover, as a Canadian film company was planning to shoot a documentary film of my visit. My solicitous mother ran around the hotel trying to find fresh fruit juice and a better room, but nobody showed any concern in the pandemonium generated by the festival. A feverish night ensued as I tossed around in a lumpy bed thinking evil thoughts about the Junos, CBS, rock music, and smoke, and vowed never to jeopardize my health in this way again.

"Would you please agree to play for Fidel Castro at the Canadian embassy tonight?" a crackly voice shouted the next morning over the static on the telephone. I knew I could not refuse, even though in my stupor I was unable to sit up without feeling dizzy. This could be the opportunity of a lifetime! Pierre had kept his promise to send my album; now it was up to me to deliver. Restringing my guitar and struggling to wash my hair, I tried to ignore the swollen throat and fever while my mother desperately massaged my sore shoulders and fed me cups of honeyed tea in the overwhelming heat. At around five in the afternoon, an embassy car drove us to the elegant residence of the Canadian ambassador — "Our man in Havana." There was seating for about sixty people in a reception hall, where a low stage decorated with flowers had been constructed. As I checked the chair and footstool position, it became apparent that armed guards were taking up positions around the house. "This is a sure sign Fidel is planning to attend," the ambassador told me excitedly. "But we won't know until the last minute whether he will actually show up."

Five minutes before my recital was to begin, the legendary leader came striding into the embassy, accompanied by his small entourage. Lowering himself into one of the front-row seats, he listened attentively as I played a selection of pieces including "Guajira," "Campanas del Alba," and "Gran Jota de Concierto." Whenever I am unwell during performances, an amazing thing occurs — I become oblivious to any debilitating symptoms; cramps, sore throats, and fever miraculously vanish during my playing. When I surrendered to the music, my nose stopped running and my voice rang clear as I made the Spanish introductions. Fidel clapped enthusiastically and I noticed his foot marking time to the rhythms of the *jota*. I had seen him so often on television newscasts, but now his dark bushy beard, green khaki army fatigues, rimmed glasses, and commanding presence were just a few feet away. I played with as much expression and feeling as I could muster, enjoying the sensual sounds that my fingers were sending out into the sultry Havana evening.

After the recital, my mother and I were ushered into a private room, where the ambassador and his wife were talking to Fidel and his compatriots. He was charming. Suddenly, he was a real person to me — a Latino man with twinkling brown eyes and a big smile.

"*Venga. Siéntate aquí junta a mi*," he said, motioning to the empty space on the couch beside him. "I loved your playing," he enthused, examining my Ramírez guitar, and spinning a globe of the world as I indicated the places where I had played. "White . . . horse," he articulated carefully, as my fingers traced a line up to the Yukon. He held my hands, scrutinizing the fingernails while I explained their importance in classical guitar playing. Fidel nodded with interest. "Ah, but you must have Spanish blood in you, to interpret the Latin composers with such emotion," he insisted. My mother sat across from us, amused that her daughter was subjecting the renowned leader to a Spanish culled from the streets of Mexico.

Fidel expressed interest in my family. "Damien is studying genetic engineering at the university," I explained; he nodded in approval, asserting that this was one of the most exciting sciences of the future. "Here in Cuba, we believe in supporting medical research as much as we can, given our limited resources." Fidel, as the Cubans call him, broke into guffaws of laughter as he entertained us with amusing anecdotes, jumping out of his seat and gesticulating to his stories. This character, so full of levity, was a complete contrast to the stern dictator I had imagined meeting. "Britain has always had the best educational system in the world — just look at these Caribbean Islands; everywhere the British settled, they set up a marvellous school system, which has lasted until now. Britain treated her colonies much better than did France or Spain, don't you think?" I was surprised by his diplomatic appreciation of my native land. Fidel and his companions ate and drank only from special platters brought into the embassy by his own staff. Too many attempts on his life had made him fear the poisoned food and exploding cigars attributed to the CIA.

Two hours slipped by as a haze of smoke filled the room. Feeling relaxed and free of concert adrenalin, I found my "Juno cold" returning with a vengeance; my nose began to run and both eyes started to redden and water. "*Estas enferma, pobrecita?* (Poor dear, are you sick?)" he inquired, putting his arm around my shoulder. Now, telling Fidel Castro to butt out his Monte Cristo would have been tantamount to asking Winston Churchill to do likewise. It just wasn't done! "Oh, it's just a bit of a cold I caught in Canada," I sniffed, blinking rapidly to try to wash the smoke from my eyes. "You must take lots of fruit and Vitamin C," he advised. "I eat royal jelly, the food made by the queen bee for her workers. We've done research here into its health benefits," he continued. Smiling at him through his cloud of aromatic smoke, I agreed to try his remedies. Most of the guests had drifted out of the residence by the time we emerged from our enclave, but the TV cameras were patiently waiting for their leader's departure. An affectionate farewell kiss on both cheeks from El Jefe was caught by the national television news and inspired people to rush up the following day to greet "the girl Fidel had kissed"! The Cubans we met seemed to worship their charismatic leader.

The next morning, a miracle occurred: two smiling porters came to help us change rooms, and a car and driver were put at our disposal. My mother and I were transferred to a palatial suite whose enormous curved balcony overlooked the water. I could not help wondering how many distinguished guests had paced those stone floors both before and after the Revolution. Sea breezes cooled us, the beds felt wonderful, and the spacious rooms, the chandeliers, and antiques were a welcome change from our previous quarters. "Fruit for *la señorita*," the *compañero* said as a trolley bearing enough fruit for a small grocery store arrived at our door: pineapples, coconuts, papayas, crates of oranges, mangoes, and mammee — more than we could possibly eat. I recalled how Fidel had said that fruit could cure my cold. But having so much lavished on me while ordinary Cubans were rationed made me feel guilty. When I remembered Margaret Trudeau's experience of wishing out loud for a glass of orange juice and having it appear five minutes later at the doorway, my mother and I made a point of directing loud conversations at the walls, presuming our regal accommodations must surely be bugged. I was highly impressed with Cuba and the warmth of her people. At that time, prostitution and drugs had been eradicated; before the Revolution, Batista's Cuba had been sinking in a morass of decadence. It is well known that most of the Cubans in the U.S. would like to see the end of Fidel, but in 1982 I was left with a favourable impression of both the man and his accomplishments.

I played, in spite of my persistently high temperature, to a capacity audience crammed into the Teatro Nacional. Fifteen minutes before the concert, I realized that I had forgotten the elastic "bobbles" necessary to hold my hair in place, and I had to send my panic-stricken mother rushing by taxi back through Havana at breakneck speed to retrieve them from our hotel room. She returned breathless, only seconds before curtain time. The oppressive humidity in our dressing-room had rendered hot curlers useless and the bass strings of my guitar soggy. Later, viewing the footage, I was amazed at how together everything sounded and looked, in spite of my bedraggled state and the backstage adrenalin attack prior to the concert. The program included Sor's "Magic Flute" variations, Alonso de Mudarra's "Fantasía," and "Guajira" by Pujol, which I dedicated to Cuba's famous old poet of the revolution, Nicolás Guillén, whom I visited the following day. The concert was broadcast into thousands of Cuban homes and parts of it incorporated into a documentary "Liona in Havana," shown by the CBC.

Like "mad dogs and Englishmen," we filmed the documentary "in the noonday sun." Why had I not brought along a second, cheaper guitar on which to afflict such abuse, instead of my best Ramírez? The Canadian-Cuban production was hopelessly disorganized: no assistance for make-up, hair, or wardrobe, the script presented two minutes before action, and no help as my mother and I dragged the heavy guitar case along Havana's streets of decaying colonial architecture. My favourite scene involved a choir of smiling children singing "Guantanamera" as they sat in a circle around me on the lawn of the Teatro Nacional.

The minister of culture hosted a farewell evening at the Tropicana nightclub, where, under a full moon, we watched sensuous mulatto dancers pulsate like spangled birds of paradise to salsa rhythms along swaying catwalks encircled by tall trees. An honorarium given to me by the Cubans was spent at one of the artists' workshops on a selection of etchings that still hang in my house today. The Cubans are such a vibrant and resourceful people, with a passion for the arts. If only politics did not divide the peoples of the world, we would all be so much richer.

The cultural attaché to the Canadian High Commission in Hong Kong booked me a tour of the Far East in October 1984. Anticipating an unusual and exciting itinerary, I invited my mother and two girl-friends from Vancouver, Dale and Susan, to tag along. Our first stop was Beijing — imperial city of temples and ancient dynasties —

whose population of ten million filled the streets with seamless rivers of bicycles. The presence of several blonde western women did nothing to arouse their curiosity, since neither smiles nor frowns greeted us. We were met with only indifferent glances as we dodged precariously between bicycle wheels in an effort to cross the road. My lungs grumbled from the air, which was severely polluted from burning coal fires and factory emissions.

After fording the main thoroughfare, we were enticed to the back streets, where dusty pear-apples and bundles of bok choy were for sale. No music was being played in the little store fronts or living rooms into which we peeked. Everyone seemed diligently at work, but why wasn't there at least a song on the radio to accompany their chores? Perhaps music did not play a significant role in the daily life of the Chinese.

We were accommodated in the week-old Hotel Toronto, where, walking from the marbled lobby to the refuge of our rooms, we were greeted by "Goo mornings" from beaming staff, all proud of their new positions, starched uniforms, and curled hair. This courteous routine, amusing at first, almost drove us up the mirrored walls by the end of our stay!

Fortunately, I had been forewarned that audiences in China had a fondness for shuffling around and talking during concerts. This cultural tradition can be disconcerting for a guitar recital, where the sound is so delicate. Perhaps because of these distractions, I did not give them my best performance, but after the last encore a crowd of guitar students greeted me, insisting I critique their playing, and suddenly I was conducting an impromptu master-class in the green room. The students could not have had many such opportunities, as their level of playing was quite rudimentary, but it was only a matter of time before China's energetic, determined population would be producing concert guitarists.

Some audience members asked me to autograph copies of my records, which had been obtained through Hong Kong. It was disappointing to learn that CBS had turned down an offer by China's largest record company to sell my albums to their vast market, due to concerns over copyright infringement. A few years later, I was contacted by a Chinese doctor from Zhejiang who had started a fan-club with more than two thousand guitar aficionados. The members of the Union for Madame Liona Boyd sent photos of their meetings that displayed a huge silk banner with my name on it. I parcelled off posters and new releases, receiving in return effusive letters, packets of green tea, and powdered pearl-dust. Such is their passion for the classical guitar.

The day after the concert, China's ministry of culture held a lavish banquet in my honour. I was told that the gelatinous stringy material that comprised one of the portions on my plate was "shredded duck webs." During the long toasts and formal speeches that followed, I raised my glass and prattled on, expressing my pleasure in representing Canada and my hope that our two countries would increase artistic exchanges — all the usual diplomatic niceties expected of any self-appointed "cultural ambassador."

The next day was the obligatory drive to the Great Wall. After motoring us past hordes of peasants cycling to work and countless horse-drawn carts driven by men in straw coolie hats, our chauffeur waited in the parking lot while we explored a small portion of that amazing construction. Thoughts of Kublai Khan and the Mongolian hordes filled my mind as I scanned the wall that was snaking its way into the distant hills. "No worry, ladies, I remember you by leather handbags," the driver assured us. How amusing to realize that, to him, our bags were our only distinguishing features.

After so much experience with international travel, I should never have set the alarm clock incorrectly for a critical morning flight to Hong Kong. We were calmly munching breakfast when the terrible truth dawned: our plane departed in one hour's time! Packing up at breakneck speed, we made a mad dash for the hotel lobby, dragging and kicking our heavy suitcases without waiting for a bellboy. Trying to ask the smiling hotel doorman to locate the Canadian embassy car proved an exercise in futility, so I fled around the parking lot looking in vain for the maple-leaf flag. There was not even a taxi to be commandeered. After ten minutes of sheer panic, I realized it was pointless; the drive to the airport alone would take more than forty minutes. We growled "Goo morning" to all the smiling elevator girls, and I made an embarrassed call to the cultural attaché. The news of our blunder threw the embassy into a tailspin, as flights from Beijing had been sold out for the next three weeks. I started to have visions of us stuffed into a boxcar on the railway to Shanghai. Of all places in the world to miss a flight! China was opening up to the West, and the businessmen rushing in and out with briefcases full of deals caused planes to be routinely over-booked. However, through much persistence and elbow-shoving at the airport terminal, we miraculously secured tickets for the next day to Hong Kong via TienTien, connecting to Singapore and finally to Jakarta. My brazen bribes of guitar brooches and tapes had worked their magic on the wait-list official.

While we passed from northern hemisphere to southern, I thought of the title *Persona* for the planned new album. Ideas for musical themes or lyrics to songs often come to me while airborne; maybe the sensation of disconnection from the world below helps stimulate the creative process. After flying over the equator, we finally descended to the steamy island of Java, one of the world's most densely populated areas. Jakarta sweated like a sumo wrestler in mid-bout, the street markets colourfully alluring after the drabness of China. Our luxurious Hilton Hotel rooms were perfumed by exotic flowers, strange fruits, and a foot-long guitar of sculpted chocolate, decorated with creamy truffles and marzipan rosette! This exquisite culinary masterpiece, created for me by the hotel's Swiss chef, guaranteed that we would not suffer any weight-loss in Indonesia! After the hard single beds of Beijing, Jakarta's soft and pillowy mattresses were much appreciated by our travel-weary bodies. We awoke revivified, ready to indulge in a deliciously decadent breakfast of sweet papayas and chocolate finger-board.

I played to a packed concert hall, attended two Canadian embassy receptions, and conducted a master-class at the Arts Institute. Sixty eager students were crammed into a stuffy corridor where, holding court like an elder statesman, I answered questions about the guitar. The levels of playing were amazingly high. How pleasantly surprising to hear the "Chaconne" and "Nocturnal" coming from the competent fingers of young pupils. Several students presented *The Best of Liona Boyd* cassettes for autographs, but on closer examination, I noticed many of the titles listed were pieces I had never recorded! The cover appeared normal, but what were titles like "Bridge over Troubled Water" doing there? "All our tapes are 'pirated,' so the contents aren't very accurate," the students chuckled. I was horrified to discover that my playing had been combined with that of some unknown guitarist and packaged under my name. There and then I decided not to let my published music book, entitled *First Lady of the Guitar*, fall into the hands of a pushy guitar teacher who kept trying to grab it for "photocopies." I could already see thousands of duplicate copies filtering around the guitar libraries of the Far East. These pirated books and tapes invariably find their way back to the North American and European markets, where each year artists, composers, and publishers lose millions in unpaid royalties.

Our next stop took us northward one degree from the equator to the sparkling city of Singapore, so well laid out and so neatly "British." We were given a spacious apartment and sprawled the humid contents of our suitcases around. Feeling once again like a political pundit, I conducted a press conference while a dozen newspaper reporters and various TV interviewers fired questions. How amazing that a classical guitarist would generate such media attention. My recital in the convention centre was sold out and the promoters delighted by the rave reviews. During a master-class with some local players, I tried to impart technical and musical advice as I remembered Lagoya and Bream doing during my student days.

In my free time, I padded barefoot with my mother around an Indian temple, where gaudily painted gods glared at us from cobra-heads; bargained for silk on Arab Street; and sipped Singapore slings at the bar of Raffles Hotel, where Somerset Maugham penned his novels of the British Empire. Venturing into the Bugis Street night market, we sampled fried rice and spicy vegetables at steamy stalls where, to my dismay, caged reptiles awaited their destiny on the dinner plate. Fruit vendors shared the pavement with pirated-tape hawkers; fortunately, my titles were not in evidence. After midnight, Bugis Street transforms into a colourful transvestite hangout, but unfortunately, it is impossible to experience everything on a concert tour!

Precipitously descending between thunder peaks bruised with dark shades of violet, we landed in Bangkok and made our way to the hotel through the muddy, flooded streets. Once again, our rooms were laden with flowers and fruit baskets overflowing with melons, papayas, raputans, passion-fruit, and pineapples. My concert was staged in the Hilton Hotel ballroom, and the cream of Bangkok society had been invited by the Canadian embassy. Bejewelled women in gorgeous silk gowns glided gracefully along the corridors, trailing gossamer wraps and oriental perfumes, while suave Thai businessmen and politicians sipped sherry with their Canadian hosts. I winced as, for a few unnerving moments before the performance, my mother plunged everyone into darkness, fusing the lights by plugging my hot-pot into a non-compatible electrical socket.

Bangkok enthralled me. Fragile bamboo homes supported by high wooden stilts lined the Chao Phraya River and the narrow canals that drained into it. A noisy confusion of barges, tugs, fishing craft, ferries, and speedboats plied the waterways for pleasure and commerce. Shopping in the bazaars and floating markets, we admired the exquisite temples that appeared around each bend of the majestic brown river, where laughing young boys dived naked from the bridges. At the Temple of Dawn, decorated by hundreds of carvings of Buddha, we eavesdropped on saffron-robed monks chanting their prayers. And at the Palace of the Emerald Buddha, we marvelled at mosaics of pure gold. This was one wonderful concert tour!

As evening fell, we investigated the infamous Pat Pong, where my Vancouver friends were swept up in a shopping frenzy for fake Rolex watches. Jostling kids tried to flog marble Buddhas, bronze temple dancers, Fendi wallets, and their sisters, while from the doorways ladies of the night solicited customers. What a cauldron of humanity! The colour and vitality of the scene caused me to suspend my judgment momentarily, and I almost forgot that this thrall of desperate enterprise cloaked so much human degradation.

After Bangkok, my girlfriends departed for emerald-bartering adventures in the Golden Triangle, but for me another concert hall awaited in Kuala Lumpur, capital of Malaysia. One recital at the city hall was a fund-raiser for an organization that assisted abandoned women, and a second took place at the Petaling Jaya Hilton. After each show, I was loaded down with so many bouquets of flowers that there was no alternative but to float them in the bathtub.

The streets of Kuala Lumpur displayed a fascinating mixture of racial origins and dress: veiled Muslims, saried Indians, and saronged Malays. My mother and I respectfully wrapped scarves around our heads before entering a huge mosque where devout followers of Islam were performing their ablutions, but an old doorman thrust black robes into our hands, pointing disdainfully at our bare shoulders. Before we left, we visited weaving factories, coconut plantations extracting palm oil, and a workshop where brightly coloured butterflies, beetles, and scorpions caught by the hill tribes were being entombed in Plexiglas. Damien would have been in seventh heaven.

In Hong Kong, we stayed at the home of Randy Stansfield, the Canadian diplomat who had helped orchestrate this tour. Forfeiting our luxurious Hilton suites for his children's bedroom, which was stuffed with our suitcases and his kids' toys, was an adjustment, but Randy proved a charming host. At the exclusive Aberdeen Country Club, we enjoyed the spectacular Hong Kong skyline by night: twinkling lights flashing coloured neon onto the sampans and scintillating harbour waters like one of those gaudy paintings on black velvet. My concert, which was broadcast by the major classical station, started a little late, as one of my fingernails broke off a minute before show-time; only hastily applied Krazy Glue and a "Player's Nail" saved the day!

After a 5:00 a.m. wake-up call to appear on "Good Morning, Hong Kong," I squeezed in a couple of radio shows and newspaper interviews and then was whisked off by hydrofoil to the Portuguese island colony across the Pearl River delta. Macau's cobbled streets, winding sleepily up the hillside to a colonial fortress, were reminiscent of a lethargic Portuguese fishing village. My concert was held in the Don Pedro V Theatre, where their usual evening fare was the raunchy "Crazy Paris" show. Randy later recounted how a group of Chinese businessmen had come creeping into the theatre, only to shuffle out moments later, muttering that I was taking too long to disrobe. A Bach bourrée–playing blonde must have seemed too tame an act compared with the striptease they had anticipated. The following day, we hovercrafted back through the island-dotted bay for another television show, where my playing was sandwiched between a parade of pink poodles and a panel on venereal diseases. Then we were swept back into the vortex of Hong Kong, one of the most congested and frenzied cities on the planet. This crossroads of the world is an international shopper's paradise, where electronic gadgetry, jewellery, and fashion tantalize bargain-seekers. Two days of intense damage to the credit cards seemed a pretty good reward for my concert efforts.

My mother flew home to Toronto with bulging bags while I winged my way to Tokyo for a return tour of Japan. Aki, the road manager from the Kyodo Tokyo agency, dragged my suitcases and guitar around railway stations and airports. The Japanese promoters allowed minimal free time, cramming every minute with television shows or press interviews. Nagoya, Nagano, Sapporo, Yokohama, Osaka, and Fukuoka laid out the red carpet, and smiling and bowing guitar enthusiasts flocked to my performances. After I played a standing-room only matinée at Sendai's Bach Hall, we found the road to the train station so grid-locked by the vehicles of my departing audience that Aki became panic-stricken, realizing that the last train to Tokyo was about to leave. What a terrible loss of face for him if I missed my plane to Vancouver later that night!

As soon as our driver approached the station, Aki and I raced at breakneck speed up three flights of steep stairs, hurling ourselves through the train doors seconds before they slammed shut. In Japan, land of efficiency, trains are never late. I cannot imagine how we made it after pulling in at only 4:28 for a 4:30 departure. For a few minutes, we lay sprawled on the benches of the compartment, completely winded by our superhuman exertion, while curious passengers peered from behind their magazines at the strange spectacle of a sweaty, red-faced Japanese man with two suitcases and a dishevelled blonde with red roses and a guitar. I panted and choked, trying to catch my breath as we sped along the tracks. Never had my heart pounded so rapidly as during that frenetic finale to my tour of the Far East.

15

A Normal Existence

𝒟uring the fall of '82, in the middle of a thirty-city North American tour, an exciting idea started to form in my mind. Each night after my concerts, while soaking in various hotel bathtubs, I became more determined to carry out my plan to treat myself to an entire year off. Why not relinquish this fast-paced performance lifestyle for a more normal existence in Vancouver, where I had a circle of friends? My career had made me financially independent, yet I had allowed myself little free time and had not even learned to drive a car. Bernie would have to stop booking engagements for the following year — hardly the sort of instruction a manager wants to hear. When I recalled how burned out and travel-weary some of my colleagues had become from years of non-stop touring, I regarded the break as preventative medicine, needed before I too lost my zest for the concert lifestyle.

The sabbatical had a hidden agenda that I only half admitted to myself. Tiring of always playing the role of girlfriend, I wanted to find someone with whom I could share a larger part of life. The years with Pierre had been full of interest and excitement, but he had never been the passionate soul-mate of my dreams. When Pierre and I spent time together at Harrington Lake discussing our futures, he sensed my restlessness. "I know you'll fall in love with some young fellow out west," he mumbled sadly, on learning of my sabbatical plan. I tried to assuage his concerns with heartfelt hugs, assuring him chances were slim that I would be swept off my feet, but Pierre intuitively knew this was my hope. "You keep me feeling young, Liona," he said, gently stroking my hair and nuzzling my neck. I felt a flood of affection for this exceptional man, with whom I had shared so many intimate times. Occasionally he had suggested that we live together, but I had not jumped at the idea. Although I felt immense respect for Pierre, and cared deeply about him, I knew that neither of us was really prepared to offer unconditional love. Our age difference had never been a factor, as I was usually attracted to older men, and he had always kept himself young in spirit and body. Of greater concern was the fact that we were in such different phases of our lives. My career was in full swing, whereas he was winding his down so the three boys could become the focus of his days.

When I visited Pierre a few years later at his art-deco mansion on Pine Avenue in Montreal, he seemed somewhat lonely and pensive, but appeared to have achieved a state of domestic happiness with his children. How could I ever have become attached to this Ernest Cormier–designed house? The cold marble floors and stone steps were described in *Architectural Digest* as "mausoleum-like" — the writer obviously experienced the same chilly vibrations as I did. Perhaps it lacked a woman's softer touch. Somehow, Pierre's residence accurately mirrored his personality: so classy and distinguished, yet in a sense rather cool, imposing, and austere. Those indefinable qualities of human warmth that I longed for in a man and in my home were absent from both his personality and his choice of dwelling.

In the spring of 1983, it was time to begin my sabbatical. I rented a pretty two-bedroom condominium on West 7th Avenue, with a spectacular view of the Vancouver skyline silhouetted against the magnificent snow-capped mountains! A delicious feeling of freedom swept over me like a warm wave as I unpacked suitcases and arranged my clothes, guitars, and music. I had not lived on my own since Paris, and the knowledge that no concerts had been booked for almost a year filled me with euphoria. In barefoot abandon, I danced on the soft, white broadloom singing along to one of my favourite Julio Iglesias records.

My friend Dale Mearns, a beautiful, energetic, and intelligent woman with a kinetic personality, was soon busy organizing my social schedule — bicycle trips with her friends, dances at Vancouver's favourite watering holes, exercise classes at her gym, swimming at the tennis club, charity balls, and cocktail parties. Never had I indulged in such a plethora of social activities, and I frequently had to excuse myself to spend time with the guitar. Although there were no imminent concerts, I had packed an assortment of new pieces to arrange and learn. It takes a fellow-performer to understand the constant commitment artists feel towards their instruments. Neglecting the guitar was like neglecting a part of myself. Three new transcriptions — a prelude, a nocturne, and a waltz by Chopin — began to fill my manuscript notebook. Although composed for the piano, these selections lent themselves to guitar arrangement.

A decade later, I was to visit the monastery of Valldemosa in the hills of Majorca and touch the very piano on which Frédéric Chopin had written his famous Prelude, op. 28, no. 20, in C Minor. In the company of the flamboyant French writer George Sand, this genius of the Romantic era had spent the winter of 1838 battling chronic consumption, while composing some of the most beautiful piano music the world has known. Chopin never wrote for the classical guitar, but I like to think he would have enjoyed savouring my transcriptions. With a cup of freshly brewed tea beside me, I used the pre-breakfast hours for music study; the Vancouver skyline provided a kaleidoscopic panorama of morning clouds and pastel light.

A young Quebec composer, Richard Fortin, sent me several

arrangements. "Why don't you compose some original music, perhaps a tremolo piece?" I encouraged. A few weeks later, the first draft
of "L'Oiseau Triste" arrived. His melody so appealed to me that I
asked him to extend it by adding an introduction, central second
theme, and some descriptive bird-like effects. By phone and mail, we
worked together on ideas for several pieces, including "Classical
Nash" and "L'Oiseau Capricieux." After returning from dinner outings
with new-found friends, I often worked late into the night, tentatively
starting to compose original music. Slowly, "Concerto Baroquissimo"
began to take form. I had already sketched out a theme for the first
movement at the urging of the film director Lewis Gilbert, but now I
found time to expand the fragment into a Vivaldi-style concerto for
guitar and strings, which Fortin later orchestrated. We also collabo-
rated on "Songs of My Childhood," a work based on the familiar
folk-songs I had played on the recorder during my infancy, including the SS Columbia's talent-show duet, "The Bluebells of Scotland."
Without this year's break from touring, I would never have developed my composing skills. Creativity cannot be rushed; it requires
time to unfold and nurture itself.

Numerous concerts and theatrical productions filled my weekends
— the Vancouver Symphony Orchestra, theatre at the Vancouver East
Cultural Centre, David Bowie at the new Coliseum. What a welcome
change to be part of an audience instead of always facing one. I hardly
seemed to miss the limelight at all; it was rather refreshing that most
people did not recognize me while I was cycling around the colourful
lanes of the Granville Island market or shopping in the stores along
Robson Street. For ten years, my face had been beamed over so many
TV channels and featured in so many magazines and newspapers that
I had become used to recognition, but in Vancouver it was a relief to
be treated as a normal person. There is great freedom in anonymity.
The burdens of a public persona were minimal, and I blended in
easily with the sporting West-Coast lifestyle of summer in "lotus land."

Stanley Park became my favourite retreat — dewy woods, lily-
padded lagoons, and bicycle trails that wound along the beaches

and sea wall. Taking deep breaths of the salty air, I marvelled at this paradise of a city. My arm was even twisted to attend a few soccer games — a first for me — and I was invited to judge the Miss Grey Cup competition! This relaxed and pleasurable pace was certainly a new way of living. No urgent deadlines, flight schedules, or managers intruded on those self-indulgent days.

Through Dale, I met Lois Milson, a developer and socialite who loved the arts. We exchanged Lawrence Durrell books, hiked around the city swapping gossip, and spent an amusing weekend at the Galiano Island cottage of the broadcaster Laurier LaPierre and his guest, the future president of the CBC, Patrick Watson. The Gulf Islands off the coast of British Columbia are glorious during the summer, and I revelled in their rustic charms: loons, blue heron, and families of sea otters floating playfully on their backs or sunning themselves on the rocks. Dale and Lois introduced me to a series of West-Coast bachelors who extended invitations to dinners, on yacht trips, and to parties, but after several months I had not been "swept off my feet." "Liona, you are just too darn fussy," my girlfriends concluded. There had never been any problem attracting men's attention, but nobody had caused my pulse to quicken. "*Que sera, sera*," I figured, enjoying my celibate life. Pierre's prediction was proving to be wrong.

For a change of scenery, I made a couple of trips to California. One day in a Venice restaurant, I struck up a conversation with Dudley Moore, who impressed me with his vast knowledge of classical composers — he had two degrees in music from Oxford, no less! He invited me to dinner, after which, sitting in his car, we listened to tapes of his amazing jazz piano performances. The bouncy English actor's devilish sense of humour was even better in real life than on screen.

The only interruption in my sabbatical was a Merv Griffin taping in Los Angeles. *Virtuoso*, my first digital record, was released by CBS around August, but any media promotion would have to wait until I resumed touring. Nothing could persuade me to disturb this luxury of a year's hiatus from the music business. When I realized that a bicycle was not the most practical mode of transportation around rainy Vancouver, I signed up for driving lessons. After a few weeks of faltering lane passes and parallel-parking practice, I had at last caught up with the rest of the world. It was a few years, however, before I got around to buying a car.

Lois introduced me to a dynamic man eight years my junior. In the past, I had never shown interest in younger dates, but Sam Houston, with his thick mop of dark hair and mischievous green eyes that interlocked with mine, was about to temporarily change my habits. Along with his sharp intelligence and British private-school education, Sam possessed a playful childlike quality that endeared him to me instantly.

As we explored each other's personalities over beach walks and picnics, Stanley Park bicycle rides, and dinners that stretched late into the evening hours, I learned about his unorthodox childhood in Baffin Island with his parents, Alma and James Houston — the first people to teach printmaking to the Inuit — his wild escapades at boarding-school near his uncle's castle in Scotland, and his career as a dealer in both Native and contemporary art. Instead of the usual movie and dinner dates, Sam gambled on more adventurous experiences: a totem-pole-turning party and salmon-bake at the Haida artist Robert Davidson's country house; a sketching expedition to Pender Island in the artist Toni Onley's flimsy private plane; and a forbidden rendezvous in the University of British Columbia's Japanese Nitobe Memorial Garden, which involved scaling high walls and barbed wire at 1:00 a.m. How dangerously romantic it felt to lie together beside the moonlit lily ponds on a stone shrine, sharing the cedar-scented night air. Sam was an eager puppy dog, bursting with exuberant passion for life, full of fantastic daydreams and grand plans for his future. After a week, he was already plotting out our life together, and I was swept away by amorous emotions, intensified by our pact not to consummate the relationship for some time. He slipped poems under my pillow, read me art-history books, and kissed me like no previous lover of mine. Although completely

smitten by this gorgeous, sensual twenty-six-year-old, a part of me
always felt uncomfortable with our age difference; this was akin to
dating one of my brother's friends! We travelled to Los Angeles,
where I felt uneasy at a luncheon with Arthur Erickson, Geneviève
Bujold, and Shirley MacLaine's daughter, Sachi. Much as I adored
Sam's youthful energy, I wished he would control it a little in the
presence of people we did not know too well. Disquieting moments
of doubt started to cloud my feelings.

Back in Canada, we hiked Mount Seymour, ran around the Pacific
National Exhibition like two high-school kids, and attended a
Simon and Garfunkel concert, to which I had invited my brother,
who was temporarily living in Vancouver. Observing Sam and
Damien's animated conversation and knowing they were born the
same year, I despaired that Sam lacked another ten years. I hated the
feeling of being an "older woman" in his eyes, realizing that he, just
like Damien, could be easily attracted to twenty-year-olds! Had I
not always enjoyed looking up to older men whose life experience
surpassed my own? In spite of its refreshing buoyancy, this love affair
was starting to feel all wrong.

Pierre had called me from time to time, wanting to come to stay
with me in Vancouver, but I made excuses. At summer's end, however, I played a convention in Ottawa and agreed to spend a few
days with him at Harrington. Canoeing the waters of our familiar
lake, wearing his old straw hat, I told Pierre that I had been dating
someone. He smiled wistfully, nodded his head, and said, "See,
Liona, I told you you would."

Allan MacEachen, the deputy prime minister, came to discuss the
downing of Korea's flight 007 with Pierre, and while the two men
sat on the patio debating Canada's position on this international
incident, I serenaded them through the upstairs window with the
Chopin transcriptions. Over a candlelit dinner, the conversation again
turned to the future of our relationship. "If you ever decide to marry,
you must give me first choice," he whispered, but I knew that in
many ways, with his independent spirit, he would be happier living

alone. Back at 24 Sussex, I gazed for a while at a Toni Onley painting on Pierre's bedroom wall. Sam, who represented Onley, had
confided that he had concealed a personal message behind the
frame, as he knew it was destined for the prime minister, whom he
greatly admired. How strange it felt knowing that, unbeknownst to
Pierre, Sam's secret words were only a few feet away from us. During
our few days together, Pierre struck me as so inflexibly set in his
ways and seemed older than ever; yet when my thoughts returned to
Sam, I realized how naïve and unseasoned he was in comparison.
Was I never going to find the right balance of *joie de vivre* and
intellectual sophistication in my relationships? Back in Vancouver,
I reluctantly started to cool my fledgling romance, and after a few
weeks, we saw less and less of each other.

One Sunday, I consented to a spur-of-the-moment invitation from
a group of friends: bicycle riding along sea dykes to the fishing town
of Steveston. I was busy reworking some of the chords on the first
movement of Baroquissimo, so initially I declined, but I was finally
persuaded to come and enjoy the glorious August afternoon. One
member of the cycling party was a slim, athletic man named Joel
Bell. As we pedalled along the trail, he asked what I did. "Oh, I
play the guitar," I replied casually. "Really! So does my sister," he
volunteered. I later learned that she could strum three chords! I
preferred to be introduced without my career persona prejudicing an
impression, so I welcomed his unfamiliarity with my name. A woman
who rode alongside me for a while sounded surprised that I, in turn,
had never heard of Joel Bell. "He's the brilliant lawyer who was
Pierre Trudeau's top economic advisor, a founder of Petro-Canada,
and is now CEO of the Canada Development Investment Corporation," she puffed. Enjoying the scenic coastline, I was blissfully
unaware of the role that Mr. Bell would soon be playing in my life.

The internationally acclaimed architect Arthur Erickson and his
partner, Francisco Kripacz, had become my good friends. We spent
time at Robert Altman's Malibu beach-house, had tea with Timothy
Hutton, and partied with Donald Sutherland. My date book was

beginning to fill with names from the glossy international set that
Arthur cultivated like Mikimoto pearls.

On impulse Arthur, Francisco, Lois, and I flew to Italy for a couple of weeks. What a blast to be in Europe without the pressure of
concerts. Arthur had been adopted by the aristocratic social circles of
Rome, and for several evenings we dined in the glamorous company
of Italian countesses, barons, tycoons, fashion designers, and film
directors — *La Dolce Vita* had come to life before my eyes. Roloff
Beny, the renowned photographer, invited us to stay in his apartment
where, after sipping Cointreaus on the balcony, he approached me
with his camera. The resulting portrait appeared on the cover of an
Italian publication. Years later, it hung in the Canadian embassy in
Washington, D.C., on loan from the National Archives in Ottawa.

After a few hedonistic days in Rome, our foursome headed off to
soak up some Mediterranean sunshine in Capri, staying in a quaint
hillside hotel where the luggage was transported along narrow streets
in wheelbarrows. Riding in a cable car one afternoon, we glided
in dreamlike slow motion over sweet-smelling orchards and autumn
vineyards burgeoning with grapes. In the evenings, dinner parties with
jewelled countesses and playboy industrialists kept us entertained.
Sometimes bored with the name-dropping jet set, I excused myself
around midnight to have some guitar time back at the hotel. How
calming it felt to finger out my new Massenet transcriptions. Partying
was fine in small doses, but I tired easily of the one-upmanship and
the clouds of smoke from strong European cigarettes and cigars.

While sunbathing on one of Capri's rocky beaches, I noticed
Adnan Khassoghi's yacht had pulled into the cove and weighed
anchor. "I played a concert on the *Nabila* the day she was christened.
Why don't we go over so I can introduce you?" I suggested, trying a
little name-dropping myself, as Arthur had never met the infamous
Arab arms dealer. A handful of *lire* persuaded a boy to ferry us across
the water. As our small fishing boat pulled alongside *Nabila*'s
dazzling whiteness, two uniformed patrols peered down into our
humble craft, which was bobbing up and down beside the flanks of

their enormous yacht. I felt as though we were entering an exotic James Bond location. At any minute, the *Nabila*'s secret steel panels would slide open to draw us into the bowels of the villain's world-controlling headquarters. "*Momento, signorina,*" one of the "bad guys" shouted from above, as he whispered suspiciously into his black walkie-talkie. There was a delay while our presence was conveyed to their boss. A few moments later, the notorious "sheik" himself appeared on deck, dressed in white from head to foot. A ladder was lowered over the railing, and we were helped on board by two handsome crewmen. Khassoghi greeted me warmly and welcomed us to his floating extravagance. "Please make yourselves at home. I have to go to shore for a meeting, but I'll return within the hour. Please use the pool if you'd like to," he said with a magnanimous gesture, then slipped out of sight.

The ship seemed to be deserted apart from the two tanned officers. Arthur and I sipped tall glasses of iced juice and stretched ourselves out on the deck, while the music of Mozart's Piano Concerto no. 21 floated down from hidden speakers. Yes, I remembered from Bond's *The Spy Who Loved Me* that there was always Mozart playing as the villain greeted his guests. I inspected the pool, half expecting to see a pet shark lurking in the turquoise shallows. A silver platter of sweet Mediterranean fruits and chocolate truffles appeared as we lay back on plush cushions, enjoying the gentle sound of waves lapping against the *Nabila*'s hull. This is how Jackie must have felt on Onassis's yacht, the *Christina*, I daydreamed. After an hour, an attendant informed us that his boss had been delayed on shore, but he offered a tour of the boat. What a different experience from my previous visit, when hundreds of "beautiful people" were boogieing the night away in prodigal splendour, their designer-clad bodies spilling into every stateroom and deck! That afternoon in Capri, the *Nabila* was ours alone.

We walked down the curved staircase past the chamois leather walls to explore the bird's-eye maple staterooms, the tortoiseshell ceiling and onyx fixtures in Khassoghi's suite, and the movie theatre where I had played on the evening of *Nabila's* first big bash. The yacht had its own operating theatre, helicopter landing pad, satellite communications system, desalination unit, 150 telephones, a laser-equipped disco with bronze dance floor, and a crew of fifty! No expense had been spared in her rich furnishings, which included paintings by Picasso. *Nabila* had cost thirty-five million dollars to build, and another fifty million had been lavished on the interior. On one of the private sundecks, there was a telephone platform that raised itself up at the touch of a button. James Bond would have been "frightfully impressed." The sheer extravagance of this floating palace was overwhelming. In this sybaritic world one probably never had to contemplate poverty and unemployment — problems that only exist in the real world. The *Nabila* was pure fantasy. We tried to absorb as much as possible. Few were privileged to have the *Nabila* to themselves for an entire afternoon, yet a mixture of awe and revulsion filled me as I tiptoed over thick broadloom and stroked the ocelot bedspread in Mrs. Khassoghi's suite.

"I'm afraid we have to leave now," Arthur apologized. Two uniformed sailors were summoned to transport us to shore in the sleek aerodynamic *lancha* whose design was featured in one of the 007 movies. Perhaps on reaching the shore, it would sprout wheels and drive us back to the hotel, *Spy Who Loved Me*–style. The sunset had begun to spread washes of crimson and orange across the sky as we skimmed across the incandescent water, leaving a wake of white spray. When we were halfway to the Capri harbour, Khassoghi passed us in his returning *lancha*. The two boats signalled to each other with flashing lights and everyone waved. What further adventures might possibly have befallen us had we lingered aboard ten minutes longer?

Lois and I had been offered a villa on the island of Hydra, so we left the men and headed for Greece, loaded down with one of Roloff's photographic tomes for Melina Mercouri. What a treat to have a sumptuous hillside estate on this isle of white-washed walls and narrow stone streets. Donkey rides up mountain pathways gave us saddle-sores and aching backs — a small price to pay for the splendid vistas and warm reception we received in a remote nunnery at the end of our ascent. The hospitable inhabitants, moussaka, souvlaki, and retsina of outdoor *tavernas* lulled us into the lazy pace of island life. One evening, we invited to our villa a dozen bronzed businessmen who had sailed into port on a private yacht; one turned out to be the president of CBS Sweden! He was equally amazed to encounter one of his recording artists, and serenaded us on the piano while I coaxed some Villa-Lobos from my strings and Lois kept the wine glasses filled. Sadly packing to leave next morning, I vowed to return one day to those enchanted islands.

16

Conflicts of
the Heart

𝄞

As I staggered through the front door of my apartment, dragging my heavy suitcase and guitar, I heard the jarring sound of a ringing telephone. Forty sleepless hours of flying to Vancouver from Athens via Amsterdam had not put me in a talkative mood. Joel Bell was on the line, asking jovially if I would like to accompany him that evening to a tennis tournament. I knew my weary legs would have trouble heaving my body onto the bed, never mind downtown, so I declined, explaining the need for at least three days to recuperate from jet-lag. After yanking the phone cord from its socket, and still dressed in travel-wrinkled clothes, I sank into a sound sleep, to awaken ten hours later feeling full of energy. I dialled several friends but, finding no one at home, regretted having rebuffed Joel. It might be fun to spend a few hours with the interesting man from last month's bicycle trip who had sounded so eager to see me again. These thoughts had no sooner formulated than, with telepathic precision, the phone rang again. Joel was trying his luck on the off chance I had changed my mind and fancied dinner at the home of Hanne and Maurice Strong. "Faint heart never won fair lady."

The refrigerator was bare, my travel fatigue vanquished, and I had always wanted to meet the charismatic Strong, whom I knew was greatly admired by Pierre Trudeau. A few hours later, Joel arrived at my doorstep to drive me to Tsawassen, forty-five minutes south of Vancouver. How easy this man was to talk with, and what a pleasant change from some of those pretentious tobacco-puffing Europeans I had endured in Italy and Greece. We soon discovered we had acquaintances in common, even though our worlds of music and government were far apart. Joel had served as Trudeau's personal economic advisor for several years, and it was clear the man had no deficiencies in grey matter. I rarely read the business pages of the newspapers, and Joel, it seemed, rarely read the arts section, which accounted for our failure to recognize each other's names. Nevertheless, over animated dinner conversation at the beachfront home of the Strongs, I started to feel intrigued by my new companion, so versed in international affairs and possessed of the same political savvy I admired in Pierre. Joel and Maurice had been friends and business associates at Petro-Canada, with the respective positions of executive vice-president and chair; now Maurice was working with the United Nations, while Joel headed a government holding company, Canada Development Investment Corporation, which ran such diverse operations as Canadair, De Havilland Aircraft, Teleglobe Canada, Massey-Ferguson, and Eldorado Nuclear. Men with exceptionally bright minds had always impressed me, and I was starting to feel impressed!

The following day, Joel invited me to an afternoon tea that stretched into dinner at one of the Granville Island restaurants, and for the next two days, we found excuses to see each other before he was obliged to fly back to Ottawa. In Joel I discovered someone who totally understood the devotion I had to my career, as he himself gave 100 per cent to his demanding position. Admiring the way I had pursued my musical goals, he seemed fascinated by every aspect of my profession. We shared anecdotes from our extensive travels, which had almost overlapped several times thanks to our common denominator, Pierre Trudeau. In contrast to some of the playboy characters who had crossed my path in Vancouver and Europe, this forty-two-year-old bachelor seemed sensitive and serious. Joel's gentler nature revealed itself in thoughtful and considerate gestures.

Telephone calls started to come in from Toronto, Halifax, London, or Paris. During his intermittent visits to Vancouver, sensing his appreciation of my music, I played him my new digital release, *Virtuoso*; in turn, "W5" kept me glued to the television screen watching him represent Canadair at an international trade fair in Dallas. This man appeared to lead a rather interesting life.

Joel Bell had been brought up in Montreal, where he had graduated in law from McGill before receiving both business and law degrees from Harvard. Raised in a Jewish family but not overly religious, he had enjoyed such adventurous travel as a six-week mountain trek up K2 on the China-Pakistan border. Needing only a few hours' sleep a night, he was constantly reading through briefs or dictating memos on corporate files. All this was familiar territory for me after my years with Pierre; perhaps that connection initially played an unconscious role in our relationship.

One day, my manager Bernie called to tell me he had been contacted by a representative from the Canadian military wanting me to perform at a "top secret" event. Mysteriously, he was unable to reveal any details, but we were assured that it was to be a prestigious affair. The function had to remain hidden from media attention, so I was asked to be discreet with any of my associates, which of course included my new boyfriend. Coincidentally, Joel was required to fly to Ottawa for a few days and seemed rather vague about his assignment. "It's confidential government business, which I'm not free to discuss with you, Liona," was all I was told.

When I arrived in the capital, I was informed by an RCMP officer that I was going to play for all the NATO ministers of defence. He conveyed the distinct impression that this was a rather clandestine military affair. In contrast to my previous government functions, Pierre Trudeau had had nothing to do with my involvement. As I walked through the National Arts Centre lobby after my half-hour recital, I was amazed to run smack into Joel, who hugged me and laughed at the realization that neither of us had been at liberty to divulge our participation. Of course, I should have surmised that his aircraft companies would have military connections. We had both been invited to a reception at which the ministers of defence were being served drinks and hors d'oeuvres. Joel introduced me to several guests, while others came to offer their congratulations on my playing. The German and Greek ministers had already discovered my albums on sale in the NAC boutique and asked for autographs. The wife of Turkey's defence minister apparently played the guitar, and to this day Joel credits me with facilitating the Turkish government's interest in buying Buffalo planes from De Havilland. One of the Europeans remarked how relaxing it had been for him to listen to classical music at the conclusion of two intense days of planning nuclear-war scenarios. So that was the reason all the ministers had been convened! What a sobering thought to realize that these refined and civilized gentlemen had actually been contemplating the doomsday buttons. No wonder they had not wanted the media to get wind of their apocalyptic games. I shuddered as my mind flashed to the Wannsee Conference, where a group of Nazi leaders, probably equally "refined and civilized," met to plan the annihilation of the Jews. Perhaps they also had found time to savour some classical music.

Joel asked if I would like to accompany him to an airline convention in the Bahamas; I initially declined, but after three weeks of persuasive phone calls, I capitulated. It had been a long time since I had shared a trip with a boyfriend, yet suddenly this man had jettisoned himself into my life. Flushed with the excitement of a new romance, we flew down by private plane to Lyford Cay, outside Nassau. Convention obligations aside, we were able to spend many peaceful hours luxuriating in each other's company in a beach cabin beside the azure waters of the Caribbean. The salubrious break did us both a world of good. Our relationship picked up tempo during the autumn months, and for the Christmas holidays, we rented Mick Jagger's house on the island of Mustique.

In January 1984, Joel and I flew to New York for a reception in the Vanderbilts' home and the National Arts Centre Orchestra's performance of Handel's *Rinaldo*. Pierre Trudeau, looking as dapper as ever, was in attendance. At the post-performance party, my new boyfriend selflessly granted me a dance with my former amour. It felt rather unsettling to be held by those familiar arms, which had embraced me so often yet were no longer part of my life. Pierre and I had maintained occasional telephone contact, so he knew that Joel and I were together. "You certainly made an excellent choice out there in Vancouver," he remarked, with a twinkle in his eye. The two men, who shared many similar interests and held each other in great esteem, now had a girlfriend in common.

My self-indulgent sabbatical was about to be rudely broken by a thirty-city tour of Canada and the U.S., starting in the Maritimes in March of that year. Bidding a reluctant farewell to my West Coast friends, I packed up the contents of La Mariposa, the condominium where I had spent the past year. Gary McGroarty, my road manager, and I flew to Nova Scotia for the first concert in Pictou, where I was premiering many new pieces learned or written during the year off: Chopin's prelude, waltz, and nocturne; Fortin's "Classical Nash" and "L'Oiseau Capricieux"; and my own "Songs of My Childhood" for solo guitar. All of a sudden, I found myself sitting onstage with a few hundred hushed people hanging on to every note. Adrenalin started to pump through my body, playing havoc with my normally calm nervous system. Pieces that I had plucked to myself a hundred times before suddenly seemed to consist of unfamiliar chords that propelled me from one section to the next while I tried to cover up the memory lapses that plagued my performance. Why had I not anticipated the effect that an audience would have on me after spending an entire year away from the concert stage? Why had I chosen such new and difficult music? I could feel the muscles of my arms and shoulders tense up, while my hands strained to reach their correct positions. As I concluded the concert, for which my dear, loyal audience gave a standing ovation, I despaired at the thought that I had let them down. How would I ever manage to play well in some of the major cities that loomed ahead if my nerves were this frayed for a small town?

I collapsed into a hot bath, trying to soak out the cramps from the trauma of that evening's concert and wondering if a life away from the concert scene might not be an easier choice. Perhaps I could teach and make records instead of putting myself through this touring ordeal. My new relationship with Joel had been demanding a lot of time: time that should have been used more diligently in preparation for these concerts. Classical guitar, considered the most difficult of instruments, requires tremendous dedication and self-sacrifice; even Segovia practised for hours each day. In every concert, there are thousands upon thousands of notes that have to be formed and then plucked on the strings in order for the music to flow. Accuracy is essential. For a performer, having one's nerves go to pieces on centre stage is the stuff of nightmares. That night, I thrashed around on my bed consumed by guilt and anguish. As the tour progressed, however, the quality of my playing improved; by the second week, my fingers felt so secure that any doubts about performing had completely evaporated.

Shuffling flight schedules, Bernie and I were somehow able to accommodate a sudden booking, in the middle of the tour, to play at a Toronto luncheon for King Juan Carlos and Queen Sophia of Spain. In Nashville, my next stop, after a concert with George Jones and Tammy Wynette, Chet Atkins arranged for me to serenade the governor of Tennessee and appear along with a rambunctious Boxcar Willie on "Nashville Now," a television show with an audience of thirteen million. A few days later in New York, I was seated at the head table, a few feet away from Michael Jackson, at a CBS Records charity event, and Liberace gave me tickets to the première of his

After the *Merv Griffin Show.*

At NBC's *Today Show,* with Gene Shalit.

The great Brazilian guitarist Laurindo Almeida, after my concert at UCLA.

Radio City Music Hall, with Liberace. *(CINDY CHARKOW)*

My favourite cellist, Yo-Yo Ma.

David Gilmour
and I relax at
Hook End
Manor after
recording
Persona.

My *Persona* persona.

Frank Mills and I after performing my piece "Kitty on the Keys."

With President Ronald Reagan at the Montebello Summit Conference.

Peter Ustinov and I after our concerts in Lethbridge, Alberta.

In New York with Neil Diamond.

Backstage at the Met with my favourite tenor, Placido Domingo.

With Queen Sophia and King Juan Carlos of Spain.

Royal Command Performance in Edinburgh, with Linda Evans. (*BERNIE FIEDLER*)

In Costa Rica with "Commandante Zero," Edén Pastora. (*JOEL BELL*)

My Malibu neighbour and friend, Olivia Newton-John. *(JOHN B. SIMON)*

The easy life: aboard the Molina yacht, Acapulco. *(LINDA MORTIMER)*

At "Arabesque" in Acapulco, with Joan Collins. *(JOHN B. SIMON)*

My favourite trophy photo! At Windsor Castle with Queen Elizabeth and HRH Prince Philip.

My first dinner with Prince Philip, at the Toronto World Wildlife Foundation event. (*GRAEME ROGERS*)

extravagant show at Radio City Music Hall. The following day, Mr. Showmanship took me in his limo to watch the filming of NBC's daytime drama "Another World"; my Albinoni "Adagio" had provided the soundtrack for one of their melodramatic episodes. I found out just how addicting the "soaps" can be as, to my horror, I became hooked for the next six months!

After several concerts in American colleges, I veered north to Canada, playing with the McGill Chamber Orchestra in Montreal, participating in Quebec City's music festival, and strumming a few pieces for the inauguration of Jeanne Sauvé, Canada's new governor general. Once again I was back on track in the exciting world of music and show business, my carefree sabbatical days but a memory.

Joel and I tried to see as much of each other as possible, not an easy task given our two crowded schedules, but he made heroic efforts to be at my side, sacrificing sleep and juggling bi-coastal meetings. In spite of my occasional misgivings about a long-term relationship, the concept of living together started to creep into our conversations. Although I had not been swept off my feet by unbridled passion, Joel's company made me happy and I was starting to realize that there would be a certain level of comfort in sharing our lives. Since we both loved the scenic beauty of the West Coast, Vancouver became the focal point of our attention. Maurice Strong knew of a house for sale down the beach from his, and in no time Joel and I were discussing its purchase. How cozy it would be to enjoy log fires, beach walks, and our two interesting careers.

Any lingering feelings I might still have harboured for my young love of the past summer, Sam Houston, faded as the months slipped by. Joel seemed so much more mature, well grounded, and suitable for my social milieu. I did occasionally think back to the joyful sparks that Sam and I had ignited, and wished that I could instill some of that creative zest into Joel's more cerebral and pragmatic approach to life. Perhaps with time, I rationalized, I would learn to appreciate our differences of character, and besides, a stable personality might balance my artistic temperament. Pierre stepped down from the leadership in June and called to see whether my relationship with Joel was still ongoing. "I'm finally free of politics!" he exclaimed, hoping I might be available to see him; but times had changed, and my life was now revolving around his former advisor. I thanked him for keeping in touch and teased him about all the attractive women who would be only too willing to keep him company.

Just as Joel and I were fine-tuning the Tsawassen real-estate contracts, an event that was to alter our destinies occurred. In September 1984 the Liberal party was defeated by the Conservatives; Prime Minister John Turner, who had taken over from Trudeau, was replaced by Brian Mulroney. "I have a hunch I may be out of a job soon" was Joel's wry prediction. He knew that in the minds of many, his position was too closely linked to the Liberal party. It was Joel who had helped draft Canada's National Energy Program and who championed protectionism with the Foreign Investment Review Agency. How the Conservatives would relish removing Trudeau's golden boy. Sure enough, in October, Sinclair Stevens, the minister of Regional Industrial Expansion, fired Joel from his position at CDIC, which led him to file a lawsuit over the terms of his termination. No one could have imagined how long the litigation would drag on in the Ontario courts, finally leading, ten years later, to the CDIC's settling with him. Having lost his Vancouver office, Joel suggested living in Toronto, which seemed to make more sense as my brother, Damien, had been experiencing some serious health problems and I felt my family needed me there for support. It was also more practical to be close to my manager and record company, although I knew I would miss Vancouver's backdrop of mountains and ocean.

In spite of having to record *The Romantic Guitar* album and make appearances on several U.S. and British television shows, I found time to spend a relaxing week with Joel in Martha's Vineyard; my punishment was a severe case of poison ivy for the following month. Arlo Guthrie and I shared the billing in Cohasset, Massachusetts, but playing concerts with blistered hands and legs was agony! Although

Joel and I enjoyed each other's company, I started to notice how little gestures of consideration were neglected; when my birthday passed by unacknowledged I began to feel taken for granted.

Sam Houston resurfaced in Toronto, fresh-faced with his youthful enthusiasm and pledges of devoted love. He had just ended a relationship and was eager to pick up ours from where we had abandoned it the previous summer. Suddenly, Joel seemed old and tired compared with my green-eyed romantic; cautiously, I began to resume that friendship. Sam had charmed the New York art world with his knowledge and business acumen while representing the famed contemporary artist Philip Rauschenberg. He was spending most of his time in Manhattan, but rented a second house in Toronto, where his art deals were flourishing. One evening I would sit in Sam's Yorkville *pied-à-terre* sipping mint tea by candlelight as he read poems and fantasized about living in a farm house in Connecticut with the children he hoped we would have; the next evening I would dine with Joel and his political friends. My terrible inner conflicts over these two contrasting suitors continued for several months, culminating in a break-up with Joel, who sent bouquets of roses and desperately followed me to L.A. where I had flown to tape the "Merv Griffin" and "Tonight" shows. Somehow, my concerts were being wedged in between this crisis of the heart.

Career bookings took me on a tour of the Far East; to the Juno Awards, where I was again voted Instrumental Artist of the Year; and to Germany for a promotional tour. Each time, I was consumed by the same dilemma on returning to Canada. One man offered passion, romance, and total insecurity, the other stability and loyalty. If only I could have combined the two! The writer from *Vancouver* magazine who referred to me that autumn as "Miss Goody Two-shoes" would have blushed had she been privy to all the clandestine shenanigans involved with carrying on two simultaneous love affairs in the same city! In the midst of all these frenetic days and nights, Pierre Trudeau tried his chances once again, phoning to invite me on a skiing holiday with his boys. But I already had plenty on my plate trying to sort out my feelings for Joel and Sam, so there was no option but to decline.

As I had done once before, after abandoning Cal in San Francisco, I fled to the comfort of my family, who were holidaying in San Miguel de Allende, where I promptly succumbed to the flu. Music has always provided me with solace in times of despair, and out of troubled emotions was born the Adagio movement of my *Concerto Baroquissimo* for guitar and orchestra. I have found that the composing process is such that certain mental states trigger inspiration. The euphoria of a new love affair or the anguish of a failing one have, throughout the ages, stimulated the composer's muse, which inhabits life's peaks and crevasses rather than the stable plateaux. In the evenings, alone in a small apartment down the street from my family's crowded house, I pencilled the notes as the shadows from the flickering fireplace danced across my manuscript. Only two months into the New Year did I make the decision that put an end to the months of sleepless nights.

Despite nagging doubts that Joel would ever be able to fully understand my artistic nature, I concluded that I could build a good life based on our love and respect. Sam, with all his promises and daydreams, was proving too volatile and undependable, leading me to realize that our relationship would be fraught with pitfalls. He was like a competitive child; I needed a grown man to share my life. Perhaps, in retrospect, I should have listened more carefully to my cautioning inner voices, but Joel and I were to spend eight reasonably happy years in each other's company. I felt greatly relieved that Sam was out of my life, and that Joel and I could get on with the challenge of establishing a home base.

As winter turned into spring, we began to house-hunt among the Rosedale ravines and the lakefront of Toronto. We both relished the idea of finding somewhere with a view of the water, because of our West Coast experience; but until the right house came along, I lived with my parents and Joel rented a harbourfront apartment. After searching as far as Oakville and the Credit River, we happened to spot a tiny area just beyond the neighbourhood known as The Beaches. A steep hill led to Fallingbrook Drive, with its expansive view of the lake. "Oh, Joel, if only one of these houses were for sale. This is perfect!" I exclaimed. "Let's knock on the door of this contemporary one and see if the owners know of anything for sale. Look, it's even my lucky number, seven!"

"Who told you we were planning to sell the place?" the man answering the doorbell queried. Our eyes could scarcely conceal our excitement on learning that we had stumbled across the one house on that street that was about to be put on the market! A few months of negotiation ensued, until eventually number seven became ours. I could not have imagined a more ideal spot in Toronto. The house was built on five half-levels, with large picture windows that looked over a sloping lawn leading to a cliff where stairs descended to a sandy beach. Before us, like a Tom Thomson painting, stretched the blue waters of Lake Ontario, which were often sprinkled with sailing boats, kayaks, and canoes. For both of us, playing homemaker, exploring the cheerful Beaches neighbourhood, and frequenting auctions for *objets d'art* were novel and exciting. Joel bought me an antique ruby-and-diamond ring in September 1986, and we threw a combination engagement and house-warming party for two hundred people, hiring a yacht to offer excursions on the lake and even carpeting part of the beach for the convenience of our high-heeled guests! A touch of finesse was added by John Duncan, who performed Debussy on his gift to me: a golden Dalveau harp.

In many ways, Joel and I were a good partnership — our contrasting interests and specialties tended to expand both our horizons. I had little in common with many of the wives of his corporate associates; but because Joel showed such tolerance for some of the offbeat characters from my world of music, I did my best to assimilate into his gregarious circle of friends. Together we attended business and social functions, at which our two symbiotic worlds often overlapped. At fund-raising, musical, or theatrical events, I knew the artists, whereas Joel knew the sponsoring corporations. We were each proud of the other's level of accomplishment, and gave total support to the other's career. When Joel spoke eloquently and spontaneously at the Air Show, my admiration was evident; when he sat in my audience during the Guitar Festival, I was told he exuded pride. We found ourselves swept into the Toronto social scene: dinners at the home of friends Conrad Black, the press baron, and Mario Bernardi, the conductor; cocktail parties with impresario Gino Empry; invitations to the Royal Winter Fair, Tennis Canada tournaments, political fund-raisers, and Rosedale soirées.

In spite of my previous experience with "luxury" ships, Gurtman and Murtha, my New York concert agency, persuaded me to accept a cruise booking for September 1985. As Joel was tied up with business, I availed myself of my mother's company and flew to Athens to board the Royal Viking *Sky*. Trailing through the ruins of Ephesus on the coast of Turkey, we paused in the ancient marketplace and brazenly bargained for leather goods in the bustling Grand Bazaar of Istanbul. On the island of Mykonos, which stood stark and white against a cerulean blue sky like a huge Constructivist painting, we wandered through narrow alleys in the claustrophobic heat of the afternoon and scaled breezy hillsides to reach the famous windmills. History books came alive in the ancient ruins of Knossos on the island of Crete, where I recalled the Minotaur of Greek mythology while negotiating dark, labyrinthine passages. Our friendly Norwegian crew joined the passengers in listening to my concerts, the first of which took place on the one evening of rough waters, as we sailed past the Blue Mosque through the Bosporus and into the Black Sea. My poor mother was hit by *mal de mer*, but luckily the only things that came rushing back to me were my memories of performing on the *Massalia*. Why do these ships always decide to pitch around in perfect synchronization with my concerts? Tárrega's music had enough slurs and slides without help from the ocean.

Under a starlit Aegean night, dancing with the ship's handsome Norwegian doctor, I understood why so many romantic liaisons develop during cruises. There is something magical about sailing into unknown waters — a sense of suspended time, of being at one with the oceans and history — that is nourishing to the soul. My mother, who was experienced at roughing it on the campsite and had been disparaging of people pampering themselves on cruises, readily succumbed to the luxuries of life aboard the *Sky*.

Stopping over in the Soviet cities of Yalta and Odessa, we shuffled in coarse woolen slippers like obedient children through the white summer palace of the czars, where Churchill, Roosevelt, and Stalin had held the Yalta Conference.

After a day lazing on deck watching the mountains and inlets of the spectacular Dalmatian coastline, we glided dreamlike into the celestial city of Venice. Out of the morning mists appeared the shapes of Renaissance architecture as we cut our pathway through the rippling green waters. Having spent a week in the "City of Canals" with Nadine ten years earlier, Venice felt familiar to me, so I eagerly guided my mother to the Piazza San Marco and the Bridge of Sighs. Reluctantly leaving behind the security of our floating home, we dragged our suitcases to a sparsely furnished room in the Rialto Hotel, overlooking the famous bridge that spans the picturesque Grand Canal. From our high, open windows, we listened to the strains of "Santa Lucia" as striped-shirted gondoliers skimmed the waters of the canals singing in full-throated abandon.

Wandering through the maze of streets and bridges, I stumbled across the home of Albinoni and the music school where Vivaldi had once taught his orphan girls. Looking at the Renaissance *palazzos* and their reflections dancing in the viridian canals, I understood why such exquisite music flowed from the pens of those eighteenth-century Venetians. In this ephemeral city, they were surrounded at every turn by harmony and beauty.

We sat in outdoor cafés savouring frothy cappuccinos and jumped on and off the *vaporetto* like two schoolgirls on a merry-go-round. I insisted we take an evening ride in a gondola through the narrow backwaters that flow off the main arteries of the city. Here the lights were dim and the faded pastel walls of old houses reminded us of façades from stage productions of *Rigoletto* and *Don Giovanni*. Gliding through these waterways with an Italian gondolier singing operatic arias was surely one of the most seductive experiences imaginable. My mother and I sat facing each other on velvet cushions, commiserating that we did not have more romantic company!

I hoped one day to play in Venice's famous theatres, and to perform the music born in this remarkable city created by man, hundreds of years ago, from the swamps of the Mediterranean. We had come from the bouzoukis of Greece through the balalaikas of Russia to the tenors of Venice. I mused to myself about the universality of music, this sound-making that is such an integral part of our psyches, and with my six simple strings, I felt happy to be one of its humble creators.

To raise money for African famine relief in 1985, a group of well-known Canadian musicians, including me, came together to sing "Tears Are Not Enough" by Bryan Adams and David Foster. Hearing all those great voices made me wish my vocal skills could equal a fraction of my talents on the guitar. Teaming up with Chet Atkins, I played "Sunrise" at the National Hockey League awards, which were hosted by Rich Little; staged a benefit concert for tornado victims in Orangeville, Ontario; played at the Kennedy Center in Washington, D.C., for the American Cancer Society; was honoured with the keys to the city in South Bend, Indiana; and survived a rainy outdoor concert in New York City. After I performed in Montreal, Pierre Trudeau invited me over to his house the next day for breakfast. "The Russian ambassador was here last night and left this box of chocolates. Here, Liona, take them," he said magnanimously. I thanked him, smiling at the recollections of Pierre's generosity with unwanted edibles.

Although I had vowed never again to climb aboard a Concorde after my last supersonic experience, it was the only mode of travel available to connect between two Michigan concerts and a Royal Command Performance in Edinburgh, Scotland, where I had been given star billing along with Robert Goulet, Juliet Prowse, Kirk

Douglas, George Segal, Linda Evans, and Andrew Lloyd Webber. Linda Evans and I were asked to share a dressing-room in the basement of the Playhouse Theatre, but Scotland Yard's security forbade us to leave after our 9:00 a.m. rehearsal. Being locked up for thirteen hours in a small room with a scantily clad Linda Evans would have been most men's fantasy! Indeed, Bernie, who had flown in from Toronto, ran around checking his face in every mirror and trying to get photos of himself with the buxom star of "Dynasty", who sat meditating to the accompaniment of my guitar.

The show was to be televised throughout Britain; I prayed that the lights and sound system in the three-thousand-seat hall would prove adequate, and that the toupée tape holding the shoulders of my diaphanous Wayne Clark gown would not dissolve under the lights. "Recuerdos" and "Granada" went off without a hitch, and I smiled up at the Queen, Prince Philip, and Princess Anne in their royal box. Later, one of the producers told me that the only time Prince Philip put on his glasses was during my playing. At the conclusion of this Royal Gala, we were presented in a line-up and I curtsied to Her Majesty. Prince Philip lingered momentarily to talk, remembering my private concert in Ottawa with Pierre Trudeau. "How ever do you get all those sounds with just two hands? It sounded exactly like two instruments were playing at once," he commented, smiling at me. The prince obviously liked tremolo. "Do you pluck the lute like Julian Bream?" he inquired. The following day, the *Evening Standard* ran a photo of me standing beside the Queen and the celebrity interviewer Terry Wogan. After I chatted with Andrew Lloyd Webber at the post-concert reception, he handed me his private phone number in London, which I entrusted to Bernie. Who knows what beautiful guitar themes might have been composed had my dear manager not lost the number from his tuxedo pocket!

I flew to Jamaica for a few days, in the company of Bernie and my mother, to perform two concerts at Jamfest in April 1985. The celebrations for the musical festival commenced when President Edward Seaga hosted a cocktail party on the lawns of his Kingston residence, where I strolled through the motley crowd of politicians, journalists, dancers, and musicians from many nations. Gregory Alliston, my Jamaican duet partner from my University of Toronto days, drove my mother and me around Kingston, steering us through the dangerous streets of Trench Town and accompanying us to Bellevue, the mental institution. I had heard through the grapevine that Anthony, my Jamaican friend from Acapulco, had been committed years ago when psychedelic drugs had driven him into psychosis. My mother, Gregory, and I sat in the hot wooden shed that served as a waiting room while a demented young man screaming obscenities was restrained by his relatives. The heavy-set black custodian finally capitulated to our pleas, granting our request to search through the wards in hope of locating my friend. I was transported back to the Middle Ages as we passed men and women confined to huts with barred windows. "'Ey man, we hose 'em down some days for de heat," the cheery male nurse assured us as we walked timidly past rows of caged humanity.

Once inside the main complex, we were allowed to enter the communal courtyards where groups of men were idling away their days under the supervision of one staunch, seated, Buddha-like nurse. Some of the men were mumbling or wailing unintelligibly to the walls, fighting their own private demons, but others appeared quite normal. Defusing the tension, Gregory asserted in the vernacular, "'Ey man, ever'ting cool — no problem 'ere, man." He repeated the phrase mantra-like as he passed through the inmates, who trailed us with curiosity. Noting the wild, crazed eyes that betrayed abnormal mental states, I only relaxed when a set of keys turned in the heavy metal doors and returned us to the safety of the admitting shed. Anthony was not to be found among Bellevue's population — leading me to breathe a sigh of relief. Still, wanting to pursue the rumours of his committal, I asked to be shown a thick, tattered book of hospital admissions. There, on a smudged page, I finally came across the faded name of my friend. Although he had once been detained at Bellevue, he had apparently been transferred to a hospital in England.

A year later, I tracked him down and discovered that he had made a good recovery. I don't know what compelled me to trace the life of an acquaintance from twenty years past — perhaps a mixture of curiosity and compassion. Or was it a lingering memory of a summer night in Mexico, when my fertile imagination listened to him talk of family feuds, suspected poisonings, fierce inheritance battles, sibling rivalries, and predictions that "they'll probably lock me up to get rid of me"? Those images of the caged inmates at Bellevue were the most poignant memories of my visit to the island of dreadlocks and reggae. Easter Sunday in Kingston had been a window on the world of wounded humanity.

A few years later, my guitar-playing friend Gregory was killed in Kingston by a head-on collision with a drunken driver, just as his new album was soaring to the top of the Jamaican music charts. "Farewell My Friends," from my record *Dancing on the Edge*, was dedicated in part to his memory. Whenever I think of Gregory, I hear that boyish voice with the soft Carribean lilt saying gently, "'Ey man, ever'ting cool — no problem 'ere, man."

Back in Toronto, Joel offered me legal assistance in my contractual dealings with CBS Records and helped untangle the web of the haphazard investments I had been making over the years. How wonderfully secure it felt, after having been on my own for so long, to have the benefit of Joel's adroit thinking to analyse and solve these various financial and career problems. I admired his logical thinking and *savoir faire*, and enjoyed observing the complex strategic negotiations of his own business dealings.

On the dance floor, Joel was an exceptional partner; whenever the opportunity arose, he would fling me around the ballroom deftly executing waltzes, two-step, tango, or jive. Exercise had assumed great importance, and he insisted upon running several miles a day along lakeside trails while I often accompanied him on my bicycle. When spring returned, we bought two canoes, which Joel hauled on his back down the steps to the beach so we could paddle along the rocky shoreline in the company of ducks and seagulls. September was our favourite month — the serene lake waters turned blue as lapis lazuli and the air smelled sweet with drying autumn leaves from the golden and russet maple trees. I knew of no other Torontonians fortunate enough to canoe out of their back gardens.

Occasional trips to Florida, Washington, Montreal, and New York often combined social visits with meetings for either Joel's business deals or my career. Paul Desmarais lent us his New York apartment, invited us to dine with Governor-General Jeanne Sauvé at his Palm Beach home, and flew us by Challenger jet to his forty-thousand-acre Murray Bay estate for tennis, trout fishing, and skeet shooting. A dinner party with my former heartthrob Rudolf Nureyev, a ballet gala with Lord Thomson of Fleet, slow dancing with Placido Domingo, who amused me with his imitation of Julio Iglesias's Castilian accent, and a brunch with Neil Diamond were some unusual highlights of a home life that was settling me into a routine of quiescent days and peaceful evenings. My parents were happy that I had decided to fold my wings and settle down in Toronto. Liona Boyd, the intrepid world traveller, had finally flown home to nest beside the familiar shores of Lake Ontario.

17

Boyd —
Not Floyd!

𝄞

During the mid-eighties, CBS Masterworks suggested I do a pop record. Gleefully noting the impressive sales figures racked up by Andreas Vollenweider's electric-harp albums, the executives decided I should jump aboard the New Age bandwagon. Always ready for a challenge, I agreed to the experiment. Bernie, whose background had been in the popular side of music, was also keen to get my fingers around "something more hip and contemporary." In 1985, he introduced me to Bob Ezrin, producer of hit records for Alice Cooper and Peter Gabriel, who in turn arranged my introduction to Michael Kamen, with whom he had worked on Pink Floyd's *The Wall*.

Meanwhile, several variety-style television programs had been booked for me in Germany, and Bernie, with his impeccable German, accompanied me. While I was taping the popular "Paul Kuhn Show," fellow guest Gilbert Bécaud showered me with his repertoire of Gallic charm. Afterwards, Peter Hofmann, the towering Wagnerian tenor, engaged me in a playful snowball fight in the studio parking lot until I capitulated, afraid of broken nails. With the holiday season in full swing, Bernie and I took time off to sip hot mulled wine and join the festivities of the colourful Christmas market. After savouring steaming pies and Bavarian sausages, Bernie steered me to the shops to buy himself a felt hat, which provided him an excellent excuse to check his reflection in the mirrors of Munich. "Any hat looks just wonderful on you, Bernie!" I repeatedly assured my good-humoured, irrepressibly narcissistic manager.

Michael Kamen, a bearded man with a quick sense of humour, flew to Munich to meet us and discuss plans. "I'd love to work on a record with you. Do you have any pieces in mind?" he questioned. I volunteered three of my recent compositions: "Sunchild," "Destiny," and "Persona." Michael suggested a haunting Venezuelan folk-song, which he transformed into "Sorceress." He also proposed a Greek melody by Manos Hadjidakis, "Mother and Sister," which would feature the soulful cello of Yo-Yo Ma, and Bernie cleverly recommended "L'Enfant" by Vangelis, the theme from *The Year of Living Dangerously*. Back in New York, pleased that Michael would undertake the production, CBS immediately authorized a budget of $100,000. This high number concerned me, as I knew it would all be deducted from my royalties, but everyone insisted the figure was low compared with an average pop budget.

Subsequent meetings with Michael took place in Toronto and New York, and my suggestion to include "Recuerdos de la Alhambra" with string accompaniment met with approval. Michael decided to include Fortin's "L'Oiseau Triste," divided into two sections and retitled "Flight of the Phoenix" and "Phoenix Reborn." My pieces "Destiny," "Sunchild," and "Persona" were added to the list, as well as one of his own compositions. The search for New Age repertoire was over. My artist mother set about painting a colourful canvas with images from the titles, which CBS used as a backdrop for the album cover.

"When can I start to learn your piece, Michael?" I asked. "Oh, I haven't written a note yet," he said, shrugging off-handedly. "Don't worry, Liona, I'll compose it when we're in the studio." Michael's piece, "Labyrinth," took as much time to record as all of mine put together. He wrote and rewrote the composition, having me stay up late into the night to learn the score only to be told the next morning that he had changed his ideas. It was a frustrating experience for me because I was accustomed to knowing my music well ahead of entering the studio. "Just relax and get into the groove of the music," Michael repeated. "Liona, you really should smoke some grass. It will help you improvise." Improvisation has never been a classical artist's forte, and I wished he had done his homework more efficiently outside the pricey studio. I watched the expensive hours mounting up on my account, but this producer was used to working with Pink Floyd, for whom time and money were irrelevant.

Michael possessed an exceptional faculty for combining unusual sounds, and would go on to write many brilliant movie scores. For this album, to be called *Persona*, several of his musical buddies were hired as session players — Andy Newark, who had played drums for John Lennon; Dean Garcia, bass player for the Eurythmics; and Roy Emerson, who filled the studio with weird and wonderful gongs, chimes, and rattles. Some of *Persona*'s percussion was achieved through shaking a jam jar filled with soybeans! David Gilmour, the innovative guitarist from Pink Floyd, agreed to lend his name and talents to our project in the private studio of his fourteenth-century country estate, Hook End Manor. Accommodating and relaxed, a barefooted Gilmour noodled around with strings and guitar-knobs for a couple of hours, listening attentively when Michael or I gave him directions. At first his solo seemed to have no connection with the melody, so I persuaded him to echo my theme and improvise around the three-note phrase of "Persona." The resultant solo was guaranteed to shock my classical listeners. David also added electric guitar lines to "L'Enfant," all but drowning out my playing. For that number, I strummed a bass chord that the engineer sampled and sequenced for the duration of the piece — a novel way to exploit classical guitar sounds.

Trying to convince Michael that "L'Enfant" was too long, and needed editing to become the single for radio play, was useless. My producer intended his own piece to be chosen — as of course it was, since his friend Eric Clapton was persuaded to contribute some "licks." The bass lines were created by stuffing Kleenex underneath my guitar strings to give them a dampened, double-bass effect, but some of my intricate "riffs" were barely detectable. Michael erased most of our London recording, insisting I re-record some arbitrary changes he had made to my guitar part in New York. "Labyrinth" was my least favourite piece; even Richard Fortin, whom I had flown in to help with arrangements, muttered that it sounded "like a jam session." At such times, I needed a strong, forceful manager to insist on limits and exercise some control. Bernie made an effort, but was somewhat in awe of "such a genius" and did not dare to offend. Meanwhile, Michael, accustomed to calling the shots, resented my questioning his extravagant style. It made for some strained discussions.

Rather than book hotel rooms, I had rented a small apartment in Kensington, inviting Bernie and Richard to use the extra bedrooms. If I had taken my producer's hotel suggestions, we could have easily blown another ten thousand dollars. As it was, we ran twenty thousand dollars over budget, which gave CBS an excuse not to pay my normal contracted fee. If only Michael had realized I was Boyd — not Floyd!

Annie Lennox of the Eurythmics, who had agreed to play the flute on "Mother and Sister," developed throat problems that caused her to be hospitalized for a minor operation at the time of our sessions. Zamfir promised to contribute his pan-flute to the album, but after we flew our producer and engineer to New York, a cold sore prevented him from playing. Those were two minor disappointments, but why did we need more competing sounds and guest artists? Was not this album supposed to feature my guitar? Any real classical guitar presence was limited to the music Richard and I had written. All in all, however, the resulting project created an interesting fusion of sounds and styles. *Persona* was going to raise eyebrows and send shock waves around my classical career.

Inside the studio control room, I found it painful to breathe as a toxic cocktail of various kinds of smoke clawed at my throat and stung my eyes. Never had I witnessed so much drug use — hashish, marijuana, and cocaine all laid out routinely on the sound console for anyone to partake of — chemically induced highs in the name of art. This album was certainly being produced in a very different manner from all my previous recordings!

Joel and our friend Sheldon, who came to England towards the end of the sessions, were dispatched to buy a thousand dollars worth of French wine for David Gilmour. It had been hinted that cocaine would make a better token of gratitude, but the only white lines I had ever seen in my life were in our control room, and I certainly was not about to start hustling for illegal substances in the back streets of London!

When the editing and mixing drew to a close, I headed off with Joel and Sheldon for a much-needed holiday. How wonderful to breathe the rain-rinsed air of the English countryside after being imprisoned in that blue studio haze. We stayed with Mary O'Hara, my Irish friend who sang and played the harp. Having been a nun for ten years, she was now engaged to a former priest. The delightful couple possessed an infectious Irish sense of humour, and we collapsed into fits of laughter as we shared such backstage trials and tribulations as our resourceful use of milk cartons and Evian bottles in certain theatres where performers have no bathroom access during intermission! They inhabited a quaint thatched-roof cottage in Watership Down, nestled in the verdant hills of Berkshire. Wandering along pebbly country lanes, I remembered some names from the books of pressed wildflowers I had made during my English childhood: wood sorrel, harebell, foxglove, and scarlet pimpernel.

Two country inns, Sharrow Bay and Miller Howe, in northern England's Lake District, welcomed us with quilted eiderdowns, cosy fireplaces, and British cuisine at its best. Under drizzling skies we walked the dewy, green hills to the home of Wordsworth.

Remembering "far from our home by Grasmere's quiet lake," we sloshed through farmers' fields, climbed over wooden stiles, and sampled juicy blackberries from the hedgerows. Here was the England I remembered from my youth. It still had a special place in my heart, yet I was pleased that my parents' vision had led them to a life in North America.

After I had suffered weeks of sedentary studio life and cramped accommodation, motoring around Britain provided a welcome change. Across the sweeping Yorkshire moors, the "rough mixes" of *Persona* played over and over on the rental car's tape deck and looped relentlessly inside my head. Suddenly, the pastoral strains of "Greensleeves" had been replaced by the hard-driving rhythms of "Destiny." Where would this unusual new project take me and my guitar? What would be the repercussions of this radical change of style? I had chosen the cards for one of my career's strangest episodes.

As 1986 progressed, I began to wonder if I had made the right decision to leave CAMI and sign with Gurtman and Murtha, the New York agency I had expected would advance my U.S. career. Their three solo bookings — Toledo, Tulsa, and Oklahoma City — could hardly be considered a U.S. tour! Scanning the empty pages of my once-crammed calendar, I realized that many of my U.S. and European engagements had resulted from personal contacts, without any agent's involvement. Where were those international orchestras they had promised? Apparently it was time to begin another search south of the border.

"If anyone can find you a good U.S. agent, Bruce Allen can," assured my friend Sam "the Record Man" Sniderman. I had briefly met Bruce in connection with David Foster's African famine-relief project. He was the strong, no-nonsense manager who had launched the careers of BTO, Loverboy, and Bryan Adams. With a reputation for being brash and short-tempered, he was considered one of the most powerful managers in North America. At first I hesitated to phone, presuming he would not be in touch with classical or "cross-over" agents, as his speciality was the world of rock music. But with few other leads, I eventually decided to consult him about U.S. representation. "Isn't Fiedler handling you?" he questioned. "Yes, but mostly in Canada, and I need help finding someone in the U.S.," I explained. There was a long silence. "How would you like me to manage your career?" he asked. This was not what I had in mind. I reiterated my need for a new U.S. agent, not a personal manager. "I bet I could make you a huge international star," he continued. "There are no other guitarists with your marketability and potential to capture large audiences, especially with this new pop record of yours. Without strong management, *Persona* will be lost among the flood of New Age albums."

I asked Bruce how, with the rocker Bryan Adams as an artist, he would even entertain the idea of managing a classical guitarist. While I played for audiences averaging five hundred a night, Bryan was selling out stadiums around the world. It seemed that Bruce, encouraged by his wife, viewed me as a unique challenge to add a new facet to his career. "Honey, I'll call in all the favours," he assured me, "We'll have you playing in every major city in the U.S.A. You'll be on the covers of dozens of magazines in no time." I was dumbfounded by this vision of instant fame. "I'll think about it and call you back," I said, stunned, and hung up, wondering what Pandora's box I might be opening.

Joel and Sniderman were astonished by Bruce's suggestion, but concluded that I could not refuse this "offer of a lifetime." What to tell poor Bernie? He had been the one responsible for the planning and recording of *Persona*, and now Bruce was coming along to steal his act. I spent a couple of troubled nights wondering if entrusting my career to Bruce was really a wise move. If I had harboured concerns about Bernie's ability to deal with the classical department at CBS, how would Bruce Allen, rock-star creator, go over?

I called Bruce back to say I was interested in his proposal. Suddenly, my career had assumed unimaginable new dimensions. Here was one of the music business's moguls about to mastermind my rise to international superstardom! CBS would be amazed that I had bagged a manager of Bruce's calibre. Bernie's efforts paled in comparison with what I dreamed my new manager could accomplish. *Persona* would have the benefit of pop marketing, a promotional video, and international tour support. Bruce even promised he could arrange to have me share the billing with a superstar act such as Paul Simon. Suddenly, everything seemed within my grasp, and he set my hopes soaring with rashly stated promises. Of course, I believed him: the man had so many associates in the music business and knew promoters across the continent.

A week later, Bruce Allen, in the company of Bryan Adams, invited me to tea at the Four Seasons Hotel in Toronto, where he proposed taking over my career immediately. "I'll keep fifteen per cent of fees and you'll cover office expenses. I'll have my staff contact you this week so you can get to know them. Sort out the stuff with Fiedler and let's get your act on the road." His forceful personality gave me the feeling that from then on, I would not be involved in the day-to-day business affairs of management, as I had been with Bernie. Perhaps this would free up more time to concentrate on playing and writing. Confident that I was making the right decision, I resolved to break the news to Bernie as gently as possible.

A few days after my Toronto meeting with Bruce, I received a succinct letter from him. "I have decided to take a pass on your career," he stated bluntly. I was flabbergasted. What had made him change his mind just when I had accustomed myself to the idea? No explanation was given. How could he have seemed so enthusiastic one moment, yet so off-handedly negative the next? In my mind, his beguiling promises had almost become reality, and the thought of returning to a situation where I had poor international management and the distinct chance to lose momentum around *Persona*'s release was too disappointing to contemplate. "Perhaps I should go to Vancouver to talk with Bruce and find out what happened," I told an equally dumbfounded Sniderman. "Yes, that's a good idea," he agreed, embarrassed by this turn of events.

The following day I flew to Vancouver and showed up at Bruce's office. "Liona Boyd for you," his secretary called over the intercom. "Tell her I'll ring her back later," was Bruce's reply, thinking I was merely at the end of a phone line, not sitting a few feet away from him in the lobby. "Jesus f—— Christ! You came two thousand miles to see me?" he exclaimed. Bruce informed me that he had decided to write the letter after talking to a couple of his buddies in the record companies who alleged I had a reputation for being difficult to manage. "What do they mean by that exactly?" I queried. Bernie had always told me that of all the artists he knew, I was the most co-operative. "They say your mother runs your career, and I hate having to deal with mothers," he retorted. Bruce, I later discovered, had a mother complex. I assured him he would never have to utter two words to my mother if he so wished. I explained that she managed my business affairs and advised me personally, but was not involved directly in concert or record company decisions. "Well, if that's true, I guess I'll manage you, Liona," he stated, doing another about-turn. "I like women with the balls to go after something they want. If you want me as your manager, you've got it. Now get your ass outta here and go home!"

I would have liked to take advantage of being in his office to meet his staff and familiarize them with my career, but Bruce refused. Like a chastised child, I thought I had better follow his peremptory orders. Why was I not centred enough to realize this was not my style or way of doing things? Until then, had I not always protected my freedom to make my own decisions? But I had been led towards the mountain top, and was sorely tempted by the shimmering possibilities that lay ahead.

My immediate challenge was to form a band to realize the *Persona* album onstage. Richard Fortin agreed to be my assistant for musical arrangements, and his classical, electric, and steel-string guitar abilities were invaluable. I required a minimum of two synthesizer players and extensive sequencing in order to replicate the multilayered effect Michael Kamen had achieved in the studio. After chasing leads through studio references, and consulting Graham Shaw at

Bernie's suggestion, I hired two keyboard players, Rick Tait and Anthony Pannaci, and for drums and percussion, Steve Mitchell, the jester of the group, who kept us amused when the trials of the road began to wear us down.

Rehearsals commenced in the spacious lower level of Fallingbrook in August 1986. Learning how to hold an electric classical guitar presented a major challenge for someone who up until then had used only the Segovia position. It required considerable adjustment for me to play standing upright, with a leather strap around my neck and a new angle for the left-hand wrist. I learned by trial and error; Richard coached me on how to communicate with the band by pointing the guitar neck down while twisting at the hips. With this signal, hopefully, we would all land in unison on the last chord! I pranced around Fallingbrook at night doing my best to get the hang of moving like a rocker while watching my reflection in the large glass windowpanes. Was I really going to be able to pull off this pop persona? Joan Jett I certainly was not!

"Samba-Chôro for Liona," dedicated to me by Laurindo Almeida, worked well as a duet; Richard Fortin arranged a Beatles medley for an encore, transformed "Carnival" into a duet, and added keyboard parts to our joint composition, "Fugato" (later renamed "A Canon for Christmas"), which several reviewers subsequently mistook for J. S. Bach — quite a compliment! For the rest of the repertoire, our challenge was to sound like the *Persona* album. To duplicate the complex recording engineering, in which Kamen had layered and mixed sounds, my small group's capabilities were stretched, but we eventually achieved a sound close to the original. Richard did his best imitation of Eric Clapton and David Gilmour during the electric-guitar solos, while Steve handled drums, gueros, wind-chimes, and cymbals.

It was fun to be making music with four young guys instead of all alone, as I had done for many years. We enjoyed pooling our musical talents and shared expectations of being on the brink of an exciting career breakthrough. Bruce Allen flew into town at the end of August to introduce himself to the band. "Yesterday I booked you four dates within five minutes," he bragged. Boy, had I been lucky to find such a manager! He took me to hear the electric harpist Andreas Vollenweider at the O'Keefe Centre and expressed confidence that *Persona* would soon help me sell out similar venues around the world. He also promised Richard a new custom-built guitar from Vancouver, which put my trusting guitarist on cloud nine for weeks, but the guitar never arrived.

Overnight, my relatively calm days were replaced by the frantic whirlwinds of fashion shoots. Bruce had decided to remake my image, and claimed I would become "the sex symbol of the eighties." How would I like to wear a crew-cut or shave my head for a new look? When I refused point-blank, I was whisked downtown to Toronto's "hairdresser to the stars," who needed twenty minutes of meditation before trimming, layering, and screwing mousse into my long tresses. What a ridiculous fuss everyone was making over three inches of hair, I thought, shaking my head in front of the bathroom mirror.

In Montreal, after recording with the Quebec superstar André Gagnon a piece he had dedicated to me called "Chanson pour Liona," I was taken to the Montreal *Gazette* for the most insulting fashion shoot of my life. No more delicate draped clothes for Liona Boyd. The *Gazette* was out to destroy the romantic image that had been mine, and replace it with the heavy leathers and unfeminine punk designs of the eighties. The fashion editor, Iona Monahan, dressed me in black leather jodhpurs. "Sit on that stool and spread your legs farther apart. We're after an open-crotch shot," she instructed. I couldn't believe the type of clothes and poses I was being asked to go along with, but kept remembering Bruce's emphatic admonitions that I must co-operate and not challenge their expertise in the area of fashion. For one shot, my hair was scraped back into a ridiculous chignon, so that it looked as though I was wearing a bell-hop cap; in another, it was crimped so tightly with curling irons that I could have been mistaken for a show poodle rather than a classical guitarist. "We'll use beige foundation to disguise those awful veins in your hands, and what about some nail polish?" the make-up girl suggested. "Your hair is too golden, your lipstick too pink, and that antique gold jewellery you're wearing doesn't make a strong enough statement." It seemed that everything about me offended the fatuous world of fashion. Sunken brown cheeks and exaggerated eyebrows completed the total destruction of what I had naturally been for the previous twenty years. Even Bruce Allen was horrified when he saw the shots. "Holy shit, Liona, why did you let them do that to you?" he exploded.

I rushed back to my hotel, grateful that Joel had flown in to meet me. Once my hair had been repaired and layers of make-up scraped off, we taxied to Pine Avenue to have drinks with Pierre Trudeau. I told him how shabbily the *Gazette* had treated me. "It doesn't surprise me, Liona. Just look what they've written about me this week!" he said with a wry smile and commiserative shrug. "I've always loved your hair and clothes. Why do they want to change you?" It was all far too complicated to explain, so I sat back in his art-deco living room nursing a glass of wine and listened while my past and present lovers discussed international politics.

Bruce had made me hire an "image consultant," who happily ran around the Toronto clothing stores with my credit card, grabbing expensive "hip" outfits to match my new persona. Bruce's assistants offered hair and wardrobe advice. The rock-band photographer Dimo Safarian was dispatched to shoot images of the new look while I posed in leather pants and dark sunglasses. Before I knew it, my peaceful lakeside home had been invaded by the world of rock music.

For *Vancouver* magazine's cover, the hair and make-up took four and a half hours. In a black leather miniskirt, red leather jacket, and stiletto high heels, I felt ready to strike a pose on Hollywood Boulevard. "Everyone at the office thinks this new image is working great!" Bruce reported. "*Toronto Life* magazine also wants you on its cover." I groaned at the thought of more fashion shoots, and wondered how my poor hair would ever recover from the constant abuse. I was spending more time perched on make-up stools than behind my guitar. Would all this image stuff really propel my career to new heights? I wondered. Yet who was I to question proven star-builder Bruce Allen? It was not easy for me, but since I had agreed to venture down this path, I determined to make every effort to co-operate.

"The new Liona Boyd" had her debut at the televised Toronto Arts Awards, where my band and I played the title cut from the *Persona* album. Metallic tights and a gold-sequined jacket with exaggerated shoulder pads made me feel like a cross between Liberace and a goalie for the Maple Leafs. The Toronto arts establishment must have done a double-take on seeing their classical darling transformed into a pop rocker. My parents were horrified; Andrés Segovia would have rolled over in his grave.

Bernie, who had reluctantly accepted my decision to go with Bruce Allen, kept in touch, as he had already started to book some of the dates for my *Persona* tour. Bruce was busy rescheduling and delaying the concerts by six weeks. "Don't forget about Thunder Bay," Bernie cautioned me, "you're due to play there in three weeks, and the promoter tells me you're almost sold out. There's no question of rescheduling." Bernie had booked this engagement months before and forgotten to tell me. I anxiously called Bruce and finally got him on the line. He assured me that the tour had been delayed and everything booked by Bernie had been cancelled. "Don't worry, Liona, we've taken care of Thunder Bay. You definitely don't play there until later in the season. Just relax." This identical conversation was repeated three subsequent times, as a nervous Bernie insisted the promoter was still counting on my concert. I was at my wit's end. The date was only two weeks away and Bruce was furious at me for believing Bernie, whom he continually denigrated. With so many new pieces to learn, the band desperately needed another month of rehearsal before stepping out onstage.

Finally, Bernie called a week before the supposed concert date to warn me for the last time about the situation. The only thing to do was to phone the promoter myself. He confirmed my worst fears. The concert was on, the house sold out, and as two artists had already cancelled from his '86 series he was not about to let me off the hook. "But it will be a disaster!" I warned. "Please let me reschedule." "Liona, I'm begging you not to cancel," he pleaded. How furious it made me to remember the number of times Bruce had assured me not to worry; now I had it straight from the horse's mouth. The concert was most definitely on.

"Don't worry, kiddo, just fly up and do a solo concert," he said comfortingly. Small comfort! I had neglected my solo repertoire for several months in order to concentrate on the pop material. Summoning the band, I told them we were beginning full-time rehearsals as we had a sold-out show the next week. Feeling panicked, I hired a road manager, Bruce Anderson, to make the arrangements. There was so much equipment to take — five thousand pounds of gear! My lighting and sound crew drove up in a truck, while the band flew Air Canada along with several guitars and a stack of emulator keyboards. I joined them in Thunder Bay after three exhausting days of wall-to-wall press interviews in Vancouver, Calgary, and Edmonton, which Bruce's office had insisted on.

Before curtain time, our nerves were like frayed guitar strings about to snap. We flung ourselves into "Destiny," trying to pull confidence from each other and ignore the palpitations in our hearts. The lighting cues were perplexing; one minute my hands were dazzling purple, the next crisscrossed by blue and green shadows. During "Baroquissimo" we found ourselves out of sync. Richard and I were trying to keep together, Rick and Anthony had lost each other totally, and for ten unbearable seconds, a red-faced Anthony was left playing an unscheduled solo! Our sound engineer had mixed up the monitor cues, so none of us could hear the others. In a band, you are at the mercy of the sound man, and without certain instruments in the monitor, keeping together is a nightmare. Instead of a cohesive "Concerto Baroquissimo," it deteriorated into an avant-garde cacophony. I quickly launched into "Sea of Tranquility," hoping the audience would think the previous piece a contemporary take-off on the baroque style! "Morning Sundance," a Villa-Lobos prelude,

"Chinatown," "Samsara," "Aranjuez," "Conquistadores," and "Sunchild" came across well. Most effective of all was the addition of dry-ice clouds and bird sounds to "Danza Inca," which I played on a hand-made small guitar, or *requinto*.

During "Persona," waiting for Richard's electric-guitar solo, I noticed a glazed, catatonic expression on his face. "Pssst," I frantically signalled to snap him from his trance. After the show, he admitted that he had been sitting there wishing he had become a doctor instead of a musician! I empathized with his feelings but implored him to please choose a better time to contemplate his destiny.

Finally, it was time for my debut on the electric guitar. As Steve hit the first beats of "L'Enfant," I confidently started to play the melody. No sound came out of the speakers. I saw horrified looks on the faces of Anthony and Steve, probably reflecting my own expression of panic. Bruce Anderson bounded onstage with connecting cables and, for what seemed an eternity, proceeded to rewire monitors, guitars, and amplifiers. It was the Denver Coliseum all over again! Trying to make light of the situation, I explained to the audience that as this was my first concert with a band, these technical malfunctions were to be expected. At that moment, I would have preferred to be a beggar on the streets of Calcutta than a guitarist standing helplessly at centre stage. Incredibly, the concert was warmly received by my appreciative, generous audience. Even the reviews, which I expected to tear me to shreds, were moderately favourable. Personally, how-ever, I felt sick about the entire experience. Our *Persona* performance had been unprofessional; I had let down my public.

A few months later, a circular that was being sent to all the concert halls and colleges across North America came to my atten-tion. A report by the Thunder Bay presenter claimed I had been "uncooperative and unprepared." The latter was indisputable, but after risking my name and reputation to save his series, I felt betrayed and angry that my good turn had been used against me. This bad critique sabotaged several concert bookings for the next season.

The real *Persona* tour began with a "warm-up date" on October

12, 1986, in Labrador City, a remote, icy town where I had never before performed. After we arrived, I spent the afternoon trying to borrow some hip clothing, as my suitcase and my disorganized tour manager had parted company in Newfoundland. In spite of some minor technical hitches, we pulled off a passable performance cheered on by an enthusiastic audience. St. John's, Halifax, Moncton, Ottawa, Kingston, Winnipeg, Saskatoon, Edmonton, Calgary, Kamloops, Victoria, Vancouver, London, Montreal, Quebec, Toronto, and Hamilton were just some of the thirty cities strung across Canada where our *Persona* caravan plugged in for performances.

Bruce, who caught a couple of the concerts, seemed wowed by the crowd's response. My band combined flights and bus trips, while the road manager and I flew between cities until blizzard conditions forced us all to endure the bus. I yelled repeatedly at the sound and lights men for choking up the air with marijuana smoke, furious that they chose to ignore the requests of the person who was footing all their bills. As I listened from my bunk bed to the sounds of the bus's grinding gears and my inebriated snoring musicians, who made the most each night of our Molson Breweries' sponsorship, I thought how smart Segovia had been to remain a soloist. Compounding my stress, Bernie had decided to demand his percentage of the tour profits up-front and was threatening a lawsuit. After the long drive from Fort McMurray to Calgary, where a sold-out Jack Singer Auditorium awaited us, I collapsed on the green-room carpet for two hours and had dreams of losing my way on icy roads. Thank goodness for adrenalin — that amazing natural energizer enabled me to prance onstage with panache.

We became accustomed to standing ovations and complimentary reviews. *Billboard* magazine praised the *Persona* album and *People* magazine also gave it a favourable write-up. The Montreal *Gazette*, however, had been handed on a platter the perfect excuse to attack my entire career. Their classical music critic, Arthur Kaptainis, relishing the opportunity, devoted a full page to his mission of destroying my reputation. This confirmed member of the "Boydbusters organization," was out to prove that "Liona Boyd cannot play the guitar to save her life." He reported that an unnamed concert promoter called me "a blot on the good name of Canadian musicianship," and quoted an invidious comment that my albums were "a criminal waste of vinyl!" Referring gratuitously to "my conga line of boyfriends," he reprinted the ghastly *Gazette* fashion shoot to add fuel to his argument that my career had become the laughing-stock of Canada.

Oh, the "slings and arrows" one has to endure at the hands of music writers! How frustrated they must be to see a woman succeed in a field where they themselves never stood a chance. To misquote George Bernard Shaw, "He who can, plays. He who cannot becomes a critic." One of my favourites was, "She has a dreadful mid-Atlantic accent that sounds like an airline stewardess demonstrating an oxygen mask." The Canadian writer then proceeded to criticize my hair, the onstage plant, and the colour of the chair upon which I sat! Had I taken to heart some of these vituperative personal attacks, I would probably have abandoned my career years ago. But even the greatest performers and composers have come under fire since the time of Beethoven. That all-time musical genius suffered such reviews as: "Beethoven produces music so impenetrably obscure in design and so full of unaccountable and often repulsive harmonies that he puzzles the critic as much as he perplexes the performer. . . ." "The effect which the writings of Beethoven have had on the art must, I fear, be considered as 'injurious'. . . ." "Beethoven is deficient in esthetic imagery and lacking a sense of beauty." When one realizes that every major artist has, at one time or another, been lambasted by vitriolic criticism, one learns to accept the detractions along with the praise. Having had my fair share of both, I like to remember the old Arabic quote used by Truman Capote that we printed on the *Persona* cover: "Dogs bark but the caravan moves on." In between concerts, I squeezed in television and radio shows, in-store album promotions, newspaper interviews, a telethon, and more tedious fashion shoots for magazines.

After a much-needed Christmas holiday in North Africa, I decided to upgrade my band, hiring a new keyboard player and new percussionist. Bruce Allen had promised that the U.S. tour would begin in February, so I wanted to be fully prepared for all the major cities he was lining up. Each day we rehearsed, fine-tuning the arrangements and polishing our performance. We were really going to impress those American audiences.

Joining forces with Rik Emmett, the rock guitarist from Triumph, Alex Lifeson, the guitarist from Rush, and the jazz player Ed Bickert, I recorded "Beyond Borders" for *Guitar Player* magazine, which featured "The Canadian Guitar Summit" on their cover and included a CD of the piece in each copy. Once again the new image demanded tight leather pants and frizzed hair. My new band teamed up with rockers Steve Howe and Rik Emmett at the Diamond Club fund-raiser "Night of a Thousand Guitars," whose footage was later used in the documentary *Guitar Festival.* At last I was starting to feel in control of the band, the body language, and the new electric-classical guitar Yamaha had made for me. Everything seemed in place for the tour ahead.

Apart from our own dates, Bruce was apparently negotiating for us to open for Supertramp and Bruce Hornsby and the Range. The dates had been postponed until March, which soon dissolved into April and then into May. These delays were becoming very costly, and Bruce seemed to be avoiding my calls. The people at CBS New York, informing me that Bruce never returned their calls, repeatedly asked when and where the U.S. tour was starting. "Will you just get off my damn back about the tour dates, Liona!" he barked, "I've already told you we have Philadelphia, Boston, New York, Chicago, and Cincinnati in place. You'll know the minute we're set to go."

In late May, I flew to New York to meet with Terry Rhodes, the ICM agent who was supposedly putting the tour together. "Oh, Liona," he admonished, "Bruce is too preoccupied these days with Bryan Adams. All we are discussing for you are some bookings with a New Age violinist next October." I was speechless. Bruce had not been giving me the attention I needed. I had even agreed to turn down a fourth appearance on the "Tonight" show; Bruce had suggested I wait until his tour itinerary was finalized. In doing so, I forfeited a wonderful promotional opportunity, as by then *Persona* was no longer considered a new release. It was clear to me that Bruce was absorbed with Bryan Adams, but no excuses could justify the havoc he had wreaked on my career. In despair and anger, I told him it was all over. I had had enough of the "bullshit" — to use his language.

In July, with no management, I flew to Vancouver for CBS's international convention, at which president Al Teller surprised me by having a ballroom full of music-industry heavyweights sing me "Happy Birthday." Was I still part of their family of recording stars, or was this their vocal version of a golden handshake? As I watched Cindy Lauper prance around onstage to her hit, "Girls Just Wanna Have Fun," I wondered if I could ever rescue my classical career. The future of *Persona* looked pretty dismal without good management. At my suggestion, Bernie Fiedler had become heavily involved with the Canadian Brass and was no longer an option. In talking to Irwin Katz, the A and R (artist and repertoire) man for CBS Masterworks, I was given the distinct impression that even my record company had a perfunctory attitude. With no manager, no U.S. dates, no international bookings, and no clear direction, why should I expect their support? "All I can suggest, Liona, is that we send you down to Mexico to make a low-budget mariachi album there." He looked uninterested, avoiding eye contact. To no avail, I tried to convince him that I had been composing some good original music. I began to think perhaps he would prefer to be rid of me altogether, and my senses eventually proved correct. In October, Irwin indicated that I could walk away from CBS and my five-record contract if I so wished. The company that had helped build me up was now ready to dump me, so foolishly I signed a release, confident that a new and more supportive record company would soon snap me up.

Desperate to revive my evanescent career, I initiated talks with other possible managers in New York, including my Carnegie Hall impresario, Joseph Pastore. No one seemed to understand my music. I was too classical for the pop scene and too pop for the classical. After doing the rounds of managers in L.A., I finally decided to work with Rick Hansen, José Feliciano's sanguine former manager. He claimed to know my guitar market, but after several months we called it quits. Apart from a role on Fox TV's sitcom, "Throb," where I had to switch from classical to electric guitar sporting a feather earring and pink boa, nothing was achieved.

Back in Canada in 1987, I made a couple of inane appearances on the "Super Dave" show and joined the Mendelssohn Choir to record a piece I had composed for the Calgary Olympics called "Hands of Man," which was released by a small label that soon faded into oblivion like yesterday's news. "My brilliant career" seemed to be following suit. For many years, I had taken its future for granted, never realizing there would be a price for straying off the traditional classical path and swimming against the mainstream. My mother, who had been negative from the start about my "pop" experiment, repeated with irritating regularity, "I knew all along this was a mistake."

Frustrating trips to Los Angeles and New York continued, as I met with more record companies and agents. "Don't call us, we'll call you" started to have a hollow ring. *Persona* had contaminated my classical reputation and now my pop career had been aborted — so much for CBS's ingenious idea of making me the latest, greatest "crossover artist"! In the company of my good friend Dale, in March and September 1988, I flew twice to Seoul, Korea, for TV shows and Olympic Arts Festival concerts, then took off for Mardi Gras in New Orleans, staying with two African-American women friends. We stuffed ourselves with sugary *beignets*, danced to jazz bands, and hung out with the Neville Brothers at Tipitino's. A few days of decadence in "the city that time forgot" were a welcome distraction from the vicissitudes of the music business. As my favourite writer, Lawrence Durrell, once wrote, "Life is too short not to be taken lightly."

Finally, after discussions in New York, Dick Asher of PolyGram, whom I had known from his former position as deputy president of

CBS, offered me a two-album contract for Canada and the U.S. Relieved, I returned to New York to shake hands and seal the deal, anxious to re-enter the womb-like security of a recording studio. Unfortunately, the legal paperwork would take at least a month. "Are you guaranteeing my Christmas album will be released by PolyGram next December?" I persisted. "Liona, you have my word," he replied, his hand firmly in mine. He was amazed that I had flown back the same day just to shake his hand. More fool I for not insisting on a written contract.

A month later, on the verge of recording, an apologetic Dick Asher told me he was "taking a pass," as PolyGram lacked the promotional staff. Realistically, I knew that even a written deal would have been worthless. Musicians have little chance of enforcing a contract with a major recording company without enormous negative repercussions, and without support and publicity a recording is doomed to failure. The bad feelings that would inevitably be engendered by any confrontation could contaminate a career and blacklist a name. There was nothing to do but accept Asher's apology. I kicked myself for having walked away from my five-album CBS deal, which most classical guitarists could only dream of. In many ways, it was one of the biggest blunders of my career.

Eventually, Joe Summers, the president of A&M Records, offered a distribution contract and initiated a good, long-term relationship. I nevertheless continued the rounds of agents, most of whom insisted, "You jus' gotta learn to sing, babe," and discouraged me from moving back in a classical direction. "You wanna play guitar societies and church basements or have a hit like Kenny G? By the way, are you free for dinner? How about coming to Connecticut with me for the weekend? My wife's out of town, and we can discuss your musical ideas." These career frustrations were compounded by Joel's aggravating lawsuit with the CDIC. He moped around his office despondently shuffling old files or flicking aimlessly through television channels. The drive and enthusiasm that had attracted me had evaporated, and our two careers seemed to be fizzling out with each passing day.

Within a short time, CBS Records was acquired by the Japanese giant Sony, and their classical division transferred to Europe. In the process, most of the people I had been dealing with were fired; there would be no going back. Not surprisingly, this takeover had played a role in Masterworks' indifference; when jobs are in jeopardy, commitments become difficult. After soaring to gold, *Persona*'s sales plummeted due to lack of promotion. The royalty statements, however, showed that my old catalogue of classical music continued to sell steadily.

Realizing that my uniqueness as a guitarist was in part due to an original and varied repertoire, I decided to record a new album, to include some of my own compositions and transcriptions: "Latin Suite"; "Shadows of the Wind"; "Fallingbrook Suite"; a prelude, nocturne, and waltz by Chopin; and Puccini's "O Mio Bambino Caro," recorded in the fine natural acoustics of Toronto's Church of Saint Timothy. Solo guitar was my real strength. The past frustrations with Bruce Allen and resulting negativity from record companies would be pushed aside by the resurgent demiurge I reharnessed for *Encore*, the first of several albums I produced under my own label, Moston Records. In another inspired moment, I composed a frolicking flotilla of notes — "Kitty on the Keys," which the nimble fingers of the pianist Frank Mills promptly recorded. Mila Mulroney, the wife of the Canadian prime minister, asked me to perform at a dinner for the spouses of the G7 representatives at the McMichael Canadian Art Collection in Kleinburg, Ontario. After the last encore she blew me kisses, thanked me for speaking out for the Non-Smokers' Rights Association, and invited me to join her, Nancy Reagan, and Mrs. Helmut Kohl for a Lake Ontario cruise on the *Oriole*. The days when Pierre booked me to play for their husbands had long since passed.

Feeling the urge to "hit the road" again, I hired Sally Heit, a bouncy blonde soprano, as my special guest on a tour whose program included Villa-Lobos's "Bachianas Brasileiras" and "Ave Maria," then shared a Christmas show with Jim Nabors and a TV special with Chet Atkins. Once again, I was back on track as a classical guitarist. On hearing that tickets to my concerts were being scalped outside the theatres, I felt a rush of gratitude towards my loyal followers, who had tolerated the *Persona* experiment and must have breathed a sigh of relief that their ears would no longer be assaulted by drums and electric guitar. However, my forays into the jungle of pop music had won hundreds of new aficionados for the classical guitar; from Los Angeles to Fredericton, kids who idolized Metallica and Van Halen were now coming to hear Bach, Albéniz, and Schubert.

The following season, in October 1988, I decided to do a series of concerts using a private tour bus. If Waylon Jennings and Loretta Lynn could bus across the continent, why not a classical guitarist? My bus came equipped with beds, a TV, a kitchen, and a shiny green bathtub — quite a contrast to the vehicle I had used on my *Persona* tour! The road manager and driver, who had expected a prima donna, were apparently taken aback by my down-to-earth attitude. It felt more like a camping trip with two young friends than a concert tour! Every night after performances, while burning up the asphalt miles, my good-natured road manager and I sprawled on the couches gobbling junk food while watching old James Bond movies or laughing ourselves silly over *This Is Spinal Tap*. No more schlepping suitcases into hotel rooms — classical artistes have no idea what fun they are missing.

Finally, I recorded my second album of familiar carols. For the pieces "Christmas Dreams" and "Song of Peace," for which I had composed both lyrics and music, my producer, Eric Robertson, enlisted the Orpheus Choir of Toronto and the Toronto Children's Chorus. Through countless phone calls, I persuaded Georges Zamfir, with whom I had played "Concerto Baroquissimo" at a number of symphony concerts, to lend his haunting pan flute to three cuts, including "Ave Maria," and the charming balladeer Roger Whittaker to add his voice to my guitar tracks. After taking the odd singing lesson, on the advice of those New York agents, I decided to test my vocal chords on "Christmas Dreams" on the condition that Whittaker did most of the work! As it turned out, we took three hours in Reno, Nevada, to record his voice and were left only fifteen minutes to record mine. Having been thrown out of a nursery-class choir for "growling," I felt vindicated by this modest accomplishment, although my voice still sounded like that of an English schoolgirl. "Christmas Dreams" became the single that propelled the album to gold.

In the middle of my thirty-two-city cross-Canada tour, I was invited to play at the new Paris Opera House at La Bastille, and fought off jet-lag to give the very first performance in the still-unfinished hall. A New York WQXR concert of flute and guitar duets with Doriot Anthony Dwyer was followed by performances in Athens, Ankara, and Istanbul. Perusing a program for the Istanbul International Music Festival, I was highly amused by the bizarre notes that some imaginative writer had composed for the Atatürk Centre concert. "Miss Boyd will be playing "Parranda," one of her original works inspired by a dance performed while hunting alligators!" In spite of the hundred-degree temperature in the concert hall, the Turkish audience was effervescent, particularly applauding my arrangement of a Turkish folk-dance. The next day was spent filming an hour's TV special; a video copy of the show was offered in lieu of fee. To this day, it has not arrived.

The festival organizers informed me that, as a great honour, I had been selected to perform a private concert at the home of Nejat, "the Rockefeller of Turkey." Counting on that last free day to lose myself among the perfumes and bric-a-brac of the Grand Bazaar, I was not overly thrilled by this unexpected "honour." "Don't worry, Miss Boyd, he will give you a wonderful present," I was assured by "Typhoon," my highly strung Turkish assistant. After sacrificing the better part of the day to prepare for the concert, then playing my heart out to a gathering of cigar-smoking, sherry-toting, upper-crust Turks, I was ceremoniously handed a small box. Visions of filigreed gems swam before my eyes as I profusely thanked the old tycoon, bidding him goodnight. When I opened the "treasure" back in my hotel room, I could hardly believe my eyes. How readily the wealthy presume that artists should be happy to perform "for the honour." There, in all their sugary, solitary splendour lay a few paltry pieces of Turkish delight!

18

Adventures in Housekeeping

𝄞

𝒟uring the six years Joel and I lived at Fallingbrook, we shared our home and routines with a colourful assortment of house staff, as neither of us had a proclivity for house management. Although our gastronomic needs were simple, we required a multitalented housekeeper who could tackle vegetarian cooking, house-cleaning, laundry, chauffeuring, the idiosyncrasies of the intercom system, infrared alarms, double-coded garage doors, and secret "panic buttons." Ours was not an easy house to run.

On the morning that Anje, my diminutive Polish houseman, started his year at Fallingbrook, a threatening man came pounding on the door demanding money. "Is no problem," asserted my little Pole, brandishing a bread knife. "I vill kill bad man if please you, madam!" I assured him that the knife would not be necessary, and that this was not an everyday occurrence. Anje proved to be an excellent driver, housekeeper, and cook. Tea and fruit salads were delivered on bedside trays at seven-thirty each morning; delicious recipes were presented with smiles of accomplishment. When my Olympic song, "Hands of Man," required a group of accompanying singers on a national telethon, Anje eagerly volunteered his fine tenor voice. I watched as he slowly swallowed a raw egg before our performance. "Good Polish recipe for throat, Miss Boyd. You like to try for nice voice?" I would have done a lot of things for "nice voice," but swallowing raw eggs was not one of them.

Lenny was our next attempt at a housekeeper, after Anje left to work together with his wife. He was a soft-spoken young Canadian from a domestic agency that had checked his references — or so they said. Joel was frequently away in Paris, which left me alone in the house with Lenny. He seemed well suited to the job and excelled at making delectable desserts; Joel and I congratulated ourselves on having made a good choice. At my request, Lenny installed a hidden safe in the kitchen, and a "Beware of the Dog" sign on our gate to the beach. "If Fallingbrook is ever targeted for a robbery, this sign might act as a deterrent," I confided.

The first thing to disappear was my mink coat. This was in the days before my animal-rights consciousness had been raised, leading me to realize how wrong it is to use the skins of animals for our sartorial satisfaction. Although I had always opposed the trapping of animals, even lobbying Trudeau against seal hunting, I had naïvely believed that ranch-raised minks did not suffer. I have since learned otherwise and would never buy fur again, as man-made fabrics are a more ethically acceptable alternative. After hours of searching for my coat, I concluded that a delivery man must have "lifted" it from the front closet. The next items to vanish were my headsets and some cash. It just did not seem possible that Lenny could be behind these unexplained disappearances, but when Joel flew out of town on business I was left with a slightly uneasy feeling. "Would you run a check on my new houseman?" I asked an acquaintance in the police force. The report that came back was enough to put me into cardiac arrest. Lenny had just been released from the Denver penitentiary after serving several years behind bars for armed robbery, drug pushing, forgery, and car theft. An inspection of his room turned up the ownership papers of Joel's car, practised forgeries of both our names, correspondence from his jail buddies, stolen merchandise, and a large butcher's knife. "Oh, don't worry, Liona. He's not really dangerous," the police assured me as I anxiously eyed the sharp edges of the knife. "He studied butchery and pastry-making in the Colorado penitentiary." Suddenly, I understood his talents for creating desserts, but visions of Sweeney Todd and his meat pies swam before my eyes.

In a panic, I emptied the safe he had installed and begged my parents to come over in a hurry. When Lenny showed up, confrontation seemed the only solution. Under scrutiny, he confessed to the thefts, handing back the stolen cash and even disclosing the furrier to whom he had hocked the mink. Shaking like a nervous needle on a Richter scale, he ran out of the house, and for days did not resurface, leaving the police frustrated in their attempts to arrest him for a previous car theft. I felt as though I had been dragged into an episode of "Miami Vice" when the officers started camping out in my basement.

After many false leads, our escapee finally showed up. As I handed over his suitcase in the dark driveway, three policemen with handcuffs sprang from behind my cedar bushes. Our security key was discovered tucked into his socks, and the car he had been driving was stolen. Lenny was sentenced to one year in jail, from where he repeatedly called collect, begging me to sponsor his rehabilitation. Several neighbours had experienced petty thefts while our houseman worked at number seven. Joel and I thought we might know the reason.

Determined to find someone more trustworthy, we interviewed two dozen hopeful housekeepers, eventually hiring a respectable-looking man in his late fifties with impeccable references and perfect manners. Humphrey set about tidying with a vengeance, neatly folding my pantihose and classifying Joel's unruly socks. Regular cups of tea were served with deference and downcast eyes; it was obvious that he was not a very happy soul — smiles never brightened his face — but he worked diligently, putting in long hours without complaint.

The lies started innocently enough with nutmeg. "Oh, Humphrey, what a delicious carrot cake," I exclaimed. "What spices did you use?" "Nutmeg, ma'am," he replied. I knew we had no nutmeg in the cupboards, and for that matter, no carrots. "Did you use a cake mix?" "Oh, ma'am, how could you even think such a dreadful thing! I only ever bake cakes using fresh ingredients." It seemed such a minor issue that I let it pass, believing that somewhere hidden away in the dark recesses of my cabinets, Humphrey had stumbled on a jar of nutmeg and a couple of long-forgotten carrots. That evening, rummaging in a kitchen drawer, I was startled to come across five flattened cake-mix boxes. There was the shortbread he had made "from scratch" the previous week, and the raisin scones I had served with tea to my guests. The same sickening feeling of betrayal I had experienced with Lenny came flooding back. I returned the incriminating evidence to its drawer, pondering my next move.

When Humphrey returned, I sat in the kitchen and cut myself a slice of nutmeg-carrot cake. "Humphrey, I really have to know if this was made from a mix. I won't hold it against you, as I am hopeless at making cakes," I laughed, casually nibbling the dubious cake. Humphrey indignantly swore that he would never resort to mixes and showed no signs of contrition during my interrogation. Perhaps it would be best to await Joel's return so he could advise me on whether I was making too much of a trivial matter; in the meantime, why not take a peek in Humphrey's room? Normally, I would never have dreamed of going into my houseman's private quarters. But the revelations of his room made me glad I had become a snoop. On the night-table was a bundle of hateful letters filled with obscenities, and behind it a collection of leather whips and child pornography. We had presumed Humphrey was gay and held no prejudice, but his writings, which focused on child abuse and self-degradation, made me realize that behind the perfect manners lived a very distrustful and disturbed individual. How could we once again have misjudged character so badly? In this case, nutmeg was the least of my worries.

After the distasteful task of dismissing Humphrey, I took off for a month's tour, leaving Joel to fend for himself. When I returned, the interview routine resumed, until finally we hired Sav, a young Kenyan wild-life artist who ran our household for more than a year. I slyly negotiated back massages at seven in the evening when his favourite show, "Wild World of Animals," was on television and delighted him with my purchase of a little biscuit-coloured rabbit. Joel, adamantly opposed at first, soon also became quite entranced. He had never been close to an animal; the experience brought out some gentle qualities not revealed before in him. Unfortunately, after several months, we both developed allergies to our adorable pet and were obliged to give him away. One far-fetched headline in the local newspapers said, "Liona Boyd Gives Away Her Baby!"

A Portuguese couple took over the housekeeping duties when Sav departed to work at the zoo. Apart from the plump wife's daily mantra — "I want kill this man. I hate 'usband!" — and nightly sobbing sessions on the telephone to her family in Lisbon, life at Fallingbrook was relatively peaceful.

19

Pilots, Planes, and Pachyderms

♪

During the eight years that Joel and I shared the same roof, we always invited our friend Sheldon Chumir to join us on holidays. A former Rhodes scholar, he was a Liberal member of Parliament from Alberta who used his legal expertise to champion human-rights issues *pro bono.* Sheldon's educated perspective on the world complemented his good-natured eccentricities and offbeat sense of humour. Before my arrival on the scene, the two bachelors had shared adventures from the Arctic to the Amazon. Having Sheldon along was ideal, as it provided Joel with an extra companion while I practised, and what woman would not appreciate the company of two attentive men? Sheldon was always in search of his perfect soul mate, but apart from the North African trip, when he brought along a girl-friend, he seemed content to play second fiddle. Our *ménage à trois* shared holidays in England, Costa Rica, Burma, Thailand, Mexico, Morocco, Martha's Vineyard, and Mustique.

In December 1983, we rented Mick Jagger's beach house on the

Caribbean island of Mustique. Only Jerry Hall's beach clothes in the closet, Mick's friendly dog, and a gigantic trampoline hinted that this was the hideaway of one of rock's megastars. A canopy of netting draped over the bed offered some protection from the mosquitoes, but we had to resort to lighting repellent coils when the wing-borne wildlife became fierce at dusk. Serenading the fiery sunset cost me an irritable few days of scratching. I should have realized how closely the name Mustique resembles the French word for mosquito, *moustique*!

Nevertheless, the tiny island was an idyllic playground. We snorkelled in the balmy reefs, sailed around the Tobago Keys in a private yacht, dined in Mustique's Sugar House, danced to tropical steel bands at Basil's Bar on Christmas Day, and became acquainted with some of the community's colourful characters. Sir Rodney and Lady Touche, friends from Canada who lived along the beach from Jagger, introduced us to Colin Tennant (Lord Glenconnor), the flamboyant British aristocrat who had bought the island in the late fifties and threw scandalously wild parties in his colonial mansion. We dined at the resplendent home of Arne Hassalquist, who had designed many of Mustique's exotic mansions, and sipped cocktails with Diego Arias, former governor of Caracas; and George Lang, owner of Café des Artistes. Princess Margaret, who maintained an estate on a rocky promontory, had chosen this secluded jewel of the Caribbean for her retreat. With its bumpy dirt roads and white sand beaches, it provided an ideal getaway for the "beautiful people," yet after two weeks, I started to tire of the claustrophobic cocktail scene and titillating society gossip.

For several hours each day, while Joel pored over CDIC files or ruminated with Sheldon on political ethics, I laboured away editing music and guitar-fingerings. Even though our holidays were mostly recreational, the passion for our careers was always evident. When we flew back to Toronto, thanks to an indiscreet secretary, one headline read "Liona Boyd Sleeps in Mick Jagger's Bed." Well, yes, and in Gordon Lightfoot's bed, too, several years before, but not in quite the way people might have concluded.

The beds in Morocco were less comfortable than on Mustique, but there were no bugs to disrupt our sleep — at least not the flying kind. During Christmas of 1986, we had somehow steered ourselves into Tafraout, Ouarzazate, Taroudant, and Tagounit — the remote villages and towns of central Morocco; Agadir, Casablanca, and Marrakesh seemed too commercialized for our tastes, so we had headed off along the desiccated desert highways of the vast Drâa Valley, where the barren fields seemed to be growing nothing but stones, and goatherds by the roadside watched their scraggy animals climb spiny-branched trees in search of new shoots. Never had I seen cloven-hoofed creatures manoeuvring themselves precariously high into the branches of trees whose parched leaves seemed to be their only food source. The sight of trees filled with agile, hungry goats in Chagall-like phantasms was both amusing and distressing, as it brought to mind how harsh life was for both humans and animals in this inhospitable terrain.

We were invited to partake of pigeon pie and *tagine* (a vegetable and couscous dish), in the hillside home of a handsome "blueman" and his family — with sign language and smiles the only method of communication. Kneeling on thick carpets, we scooped up steaming food with our fingers and swilled it down with fresh goat's milk. Their cuisine tasted even better than a similar meal I had shared in Washington, D.C., in 1981 with the two Saudi Arabian princes Saud al Faisal and Bandar Faisal at the home of Abdeslam Jaidi, the Moroccan ambassador to the U.S. and good friend of Pierre Trudeau. Our gifts of my black MuchMusic T-shirt and Sheldon's Pink Floyd one delighted our hosts: symbols of a world so foreign to theirs, in which videos and rock music played no role. After shopping in the *farouks* amid silversmiths' wares and leathergoods, we playfully decked ourselves out in djellabas, the long Moroccan robes worn by both men and women, and rode camels in the sand dunes. The red desert dust aggravated Joel's allergies, causing us sleepless nights, but if we were determined to experience "the real Morocco," some discomforts were to be expected. If one always adheres to well-trodden tourist routes, frequenting recommended hotels and eating in safe Michelin Guide restaurants, one can count on an enjoyable, but rather predictable, holiday. By contrast, I have always had a predilection for those spontaneous adventures whose memories and surprises will remain long after momentary hardships have been erased by time.

Our trip to Costa Rica had moments of discomfort, moments of sublime tranquillity, and one moment of pure terror. The three intrepid Canadians, Joel, Sheldon, and I, and a Japanese "beach guitar" set off in December 1988 for Tortuguero National Park on the shores of Costa Rica. Basing ourselves at the main lodge, we explored the fascinating jungles and wildlife, introducing ourselves to exotic toucans, iguanas, and howler monkeys. Navigating through tropical waterways after nightfall, we spotted caymans and tree-hanging sloths amid the sultry and eerie chorus of the rainforest. Only the day before, Joel and I had been battling freezing rain and snow in Toronto, so the lush vegetation and sweet, aromatic air of the rainforest filled us with contentment.

Joel's acquaintance, Maurice Strong, had invited us to stay in his beach house in Puerto Viejo, where his colourful friends Julio Garcia, a former witch-doctor, and Carlos Echeverría, the minister of culture, were fellow houseguests. As my fingers plucked out the notes to "Mallorca," I could tell the minister was intrigued. "Liona, how would you like to play with our symphony orchestra?" he inquired. I was thrilled, as I needed an orchestra to première *Concerto of the Andes*, which Richard Fortin and I had been working on for the past two years. You can never tell when a spontaneous practice session might result in career opportunities.

While practising in the first-class lounge of the Dallas–Fort Worth airport three years earlier, I had caught the attention of a Latino man and his blond companion who, like me, were passing time before a flight departure. The Latino seemed mesmerized by my playing, smiling appreciatively, then disappeared momentarily. "Ma'am, do you know who you've just been playing for?" the blond fellow asked as he came over to shake my hand. "That was the great Edén Pastora, or Comandante Zero, Nicaragua's national hero, who led the fight against the corrupt Somoza regime. We sure like the way you play guitar!" At this point *el comandante* returned and, seeing his friend in conversation with me, came striding over. Realizing I understood Spanish, he spoke in his own language. "Our plane is leaving soon, but I want to invite you to come to play in Nicaragua once we have won the war and my country is at peace. We love the guitar and I have never heard it played so expressively. My home is in the high Sierras where we are training our guerillas, but when the time is right we will meet again." Then he penned the following note in Spanish: "Liona, I saw your beauty and heard your music which left me fascinated. I will remember you all my life. With the heart of a guerilla and the soul of a patriot, and with much affection — Edén Pastora." Latinos do not waste a minute when it comes to impressing a woman!

Several months later, Edén Pastora's name was flashed across our television screen during the nightly news. He had held an international press conference at La Penca, a jungle hideout accessible only by river. His purpose was to inform the world's press of Nicaragua's plight: the corruption of the government and the CIA's involvement in his country's civil war. A terrorist's bomb planted there had exploded, killing an American journalist and injuring many; Pastora escaped with only superficial burns and a broken leg. They never determined for certain who was responsible, but many clues pointed towards the CIA. Pastora blamed them for ten attempts on his life, and later recounted to us how they had tried to bribe him with a briefcase containing half a million dollars in cash. Idealists such as Pastora cannot be bought. It was rumoured that the blond companion whom I had met in Dallas was a CIA agent whose assignment had been to kill the courageous *comandante*. Pastora had been in a helicopter that had exploded, and the blond was a prime suspect. Thank God no bomb had been planted in the airport lounge.

The Costa Ricans had welcomed Nicaragua's charismatic visionary to their peace-loving country. Miraculously, Edén Pastora materialized at the Cariari Hotel, where Joel and I were staying after Sheldon returned to Canada. We greeted each other like long-lost friends, and he invited us to spend a couple of days with his wife and children in the remote fishing village of San Juanillo. Getting there involved a one-hour flight in a small one-engine passenger plane and my memory was still raw. Only three days earlier, I had experienced the worst flight of my life. Joel and I, travelling alone with a pilot from Puerto Limón to San José, had been caught in a thunderstorm over the mountain range of central Costa Rica. The hands of our panic-stricken pilot had flown off the controls as he yelled unintelligible words into his headset, punctuated by an expression I understood only too well: "Ay, Dios socorranos! (Oh God help us!)" Our aircraft was careering through the clouds and plunging out of control as wind currents tossed us around like a paper plane; screaming with fright and clutching onto Joel, I was convinced that we were about to meet our Maker. My stomach contracted into knots and my heart pounded with adrenalin while Joel remained stoically calm, gripping my shoulders and yelling that we would be all right. When we finally emerged from the black storm clouds and landed on terra firma, I kissed the earth in gratitude. We never should have taken off in such dangerous skies, and I swore it was the last time I would risk my life in one of those flimsy one-engine planes. Now Comandante Zero was offering us a unique experience that required another mountainous flight. Being an incorrigible adventurer, I rationalized away my recent terror and accepted. Pastora flew with us from Pavas airport assuring me that after ten failed assassination attempts, he surely led a charmed life, so I felt more relaxed as he directed the pilot to a tiny landing strip by the Gulf of Nicoya. Joel nudged me, pointing to a gun inside Pastora's jacket. His son Panfilo greeted us at the airport and drove us for an hour over rugged terrain in his sturdy jeep. As we forded muddy streams and strained up steep inclines, I pictured myself in an Indiana Jones movie. My guitar certainly led me to some unusual places.

Pastora's charming wife (number four), Yolanda, greeted us, introducing five of the twenty-one children he had fathered. The house was humble, yet perfectly situated on the shores of an exquisite cove. A group of Pastora's disciples, who had followed him to this northwest corner of Costa Rica, gathered at the house. What better way to tame the heart of a Latin guerilla than with music? My "beach guitar" resonated off the walls of Pastora's home, playing songs by Falú and Ponce as Yolanda and her daughter prepared a feast of *ceviche*, pineapple chicken, rice, and beans. Our accommodations were minimal — a couple of the children's beds in a room half open to the sky. At 2:00 a.m., peeking onto the beach, I was met by the phenomenal sight of thousands of spider-like hermit crabs all marching across the sand in the same direction. As far as my eyes could see stretched an army of shells and moving claws.

At the *comandante*'s suggestion, we decided to rise at 4:00 a.m. to go tuna fishing. Everything was dark and cold to the touch, our jeans and socks damp from the salty air. Revived by hot coffee, we clambered into one of the motor boats being prepared by several fishermen who were compatriots of Pastora. I was frozen once we started across the barely lit ocean; the bumping of my body against the boat as we hit the waves every few seconds made me feel as though my spine was being jolted out of place, but since nobody else complained, I suppressed those unpleasant sensations, trying to enjoy the aquarelle sunrise and exhilarating speed of the boat.

After an hour, such a spectacular sight greeted us that it made all my corporeal complaints disappear. Hundreds of dolphins danced around us, leaping high into the air, arching and frolicking in the boat's wake, splashing me with salty water. Dolphins indicate the presence of tuna, but they were in no danger from this type of fishing, I was relieved to learn, though they are from the large commercial drift nets that ensnare them. The indigo seas were calmer, and I was elated by the resplendent vision we had observed.

How wonderful to be on the sparkling tropical waters of the Pacific with a coral sunrise, a legendary *comandante*, my stalwart fiancé, and hundreds of nature's friendliest creatures performing playful acrobatics before my eyes. That magical moment has remained strong and clear in my mind's eye.

My lifestyle has necessitated a great amount of flying, with thousands of hours logged in airports and planes. These supraterrestrial imprisonments provided welcome stretches of time in which to listen to music, attend to correspondence, and keep up with my diary. Although hardly a white-knuckle flyer, I must confess to a sensation of relief each time I re-establish contact with terra firma. The bigger the plane and the bluer the skies, the better I feel about installing myself inside whatever flying contraption the schedule provides, be it helicopter, 747, Concorde, or Cessna.

When I was flying out of Thailand on Canadian Airlines, three DC-10 pilots invited me to sit up front with them for the trip from Bangkok to Hong Kong. In retrospect, I would have been much wiser to refuse such kind offers, as by the time we touched down in Asia's most congested capital, I had been reduced to a mound of jelly.

Taxiing to our takeoff position, the pilots requested permission to select an alternative route, as a dangerous typhoon was lurking in the normal flight corridor. The control tower had plotted our course right through it moments before takeoff. "We must be careful not to stray into Kampuchean air space, or we risk being shot down," the friendly captain chuckled to me over his shoulder. "Here's your oxygen mask, but if anything should happen, just follow us," they joked. The hundreds of knobs and dials were reminiscent of mixing consoles in recording studios, and I hoped these men knew, better than some studio engineers, what every switch represented. The pilots ran through their routine checklist, which gave me some reassurance because all answers appeared to be affirmative. If the lightest feather falls to earth, how do these steel monsters conquer gravity with only thin air for support, I pondered. Obviously my understanding of aerodynamic thrust was abysmal.

From a cockpit perspective, the miraculous act of takeoff is suffused with a sensation of unreality: a slow-motion release from the ties of earth. Once airborne, the pilots had dozens of dials to fine-tune and buttons to press. A continuous dialogue between the pilots and the control tower kept everyone alert. Quiet as a mouse, I listened as mysterious numbers were read aloud and dials corrected to keep our flying machine on course.

The mosaic of muddy canals and green, watery fields surrounding the city of Bangkok shrank smaller and smaller as we climbed heavenward. The pilots seemed to breathe easier now, and we questioned each other about our contrasting careers. "Seventeen thousand hours, my dear," the senior pilot informed me, which I presumed was the time he had spent behind the controls of various planes. I wondered how that compared with my thousands of hours behind the guitar strings.

Soon we were flying over the brown rivers of Laos, avoiding the typhoon that was stirring up some nasty business in the South China Sea. Layers of black clouds were visible to our left, and I was thankful the pilots had insisted on their detour. Finally, we made contact with the Hong Kong tower, and an air-traffic controller with a Chinese accent instructed us to take "the checkerboard approach." "Oh, Liona, wait until you see this particular route to the runway. It's the trickiest one and requires a sharp turn banking low over a heavily built-up area." My memories of Hong Kong were that the entire city was heavily built up and visions of an oriental version of the opening scenes from *West Side Story* flashed through my mind.

"I sure hope they're not going to make us circle around," the second-in-command muttered. His words were no sooner spoken than new instructions came over the headset asking us to assume a circling pattern over the city, which was obscured by a woolly layer of grey clouds. We had resigned ourselves to fifteen minutes of cruising above the cumulus, when the captain suddenly yelled, "Jesus Christ!" A large jet zoomed straight at us from out of nowhere. "Where the hell did he come from?" The co-pilot and reserve pilot looked at each other anxiously, then scanned the skies to make sure no other projectile was heading our way. The plane had come so close that we were able to read the Northwest Airlines sign on its side. "Don't worry, honey, there was lots of space between us," the captain reassured me, but he continued to peer around through the windshield, alarming his guest. I checked my side, preparing to yell, "Duck!" if I saw another plane hurtling in our direction. Was this any way to steer a jumbo? "What happens when you can't see at night?" I queried, but a nod in the direction of the instrument panel was their answer. Didn't the radar screen warn of nearby flying objects? Apparently not; it is used only for plane-to-ground contact.

"They'd better not keep us circling 'cause we'll soon be out of fuel and will be forced to land in Canton" was the next tense announcement, as we took off on our third loop around Hong Kong. "Geez, does the air-traffic control guy down there own shares in the fuel company?" This was the pilot's effort at humour. "We're already an hour late due to that damn typhoon." Intermittently, they read the fuel-level numbers to each other; they seemed to be going down at an amazing rate.

In the nick of time, we were cleared for landing and banked steeply into dense clouds as the windows streaked with rivulets of water. Alarming red lights and loud buzzers caused me to grip my seat a little tighter. In the movies, red lights and noisy buzzers signify "failure," "loss of power," "abort landing," or "fire," hardly anodyne to one's nervous system. Suddenly, in our headsets we heard the air-traffic controller yelling, "The rain, the rain!" which seemed a strange comment for someone surely accustomed to landing planes in any weather. "What does he mean?" I anxiously asked the assistant pilot, as I sensed a sudden lift in altitude, then noticed a rocky hillside not far from my side of the plane. "He's warning us we're too damn close to that mountain," the co-pilot grumbled. The controller had apparently been yelling, "Terrain, terrain!" I thought of the other lucky passengers calmly sipping their cocktails back in the cabin.

"Are you up to this landing now, Bill?" was the next comment that jangled my nerves. The pilot flipped through his map madly searching for what I feared was the correct approach, but later realized was the terminal layout. Surely, in all those seventeen thousand hours, he had performed this "checkerboard approach" a few times, I prayed. "Here we go," he told me and made an announcement over the PA. "Many passengers become nervous when they see the plane coming in so close to the buildings," he confided. "Yup," I gulped, noticing that by now my knuckles were as white as the tops of Mount Kilimanjaro. As with the takeoff, the landing seemed to happen as if in slow motion, but I conceded that the pilots scored an A-plus for a smooth touchdown.

It surprised me to hear them admit that their adrenalin had been pumping away, that they expected to feel "wired" for the next few hours. Performers often suffer adrenalin rushes, but I had no idea that experienced pilots succumbed to nervous tensions akin to my own. After all, nerves have been known to wreak havoc on my surest pieces! "Yeah, sometimes we have real trouble getting to sleep after a tricky night landing," they admitted. So much for my theory that pilots have nerves of steel and underactive adrenals. I looked thankfully at the wet tarmac beneath us.

For the flight from Hong Kong to Vancouver, a different crew again offered me their jump-seat, but I politely declined and knocked myself out with sleeping pills. If the next leg involved a midair rendezvous with an unannounced airliner, fuel shortages, typhoons, enemy airspace, checkerboard landings, or warning calls of "terrain, terrain," I would rather sleep away in ignorant bliss.

Flying through the clear night sky above the Arabian Desert, I gazed down at the lights of Bahrain on the Persian Gulf twinkling like so many stars in an inverted sky. In February 1987, my mother and I were at last on our way to India. After a long flight, while drowsily imagining what countries and oceans were passing beneath us, we finally landed in Bombay at three in the morning. Still sleepy from being propelled halfway round the world, we were greeted at the airport with bouquets of roses and cameras demanding publicity shots for the morning papers.

The silent night streets looked empty as we sped along in the stifling heat towards the Queen's Necklace, a semicircle of lights that blinked on the coastline of the Arabian Sea. Once our eyes adjusted to the dark, we realized that the earth-coloured bundles along the sidewalks were bodies of people sleeping in family heaps, like clustered sandbags. Guiltily we glided through the night to our opulent Oberoi Hotel, with its luxurious beds and air-conditioned rooms. The next morning, an opalescent sky emerged while we stared from the high window of our room to the brown-sailed fishing boats below. The opposite coast of the bay came into view when curtains of pastel mist rolled away, revealing huge black birds whose wings, like spiky, broken umbrellas, flapped through the air. Our first morning in India rang out like an epiphany — a homecoming to a land unseen.

Later, leaving the cooled air of the hotel, we ventured into a steamy cauldron of sights and smells that titillated our senses and seduced us to explore. I could understand the powerful allure that this continent must have had on the empire-building, colonial British of the last century. Wide-eyed children with beautiful smiles — denizens of the dusty sidewalks — played in the humid heat, while women draped in rainbow-coloured silk saris glided past like exotic birds of paradise. Street hawkers, holy men, snake charmers, beggars, and businessmen all blended into a fascinating tapestry of humanity that proved a challenge to drivers and pedestrians alike; so much colour, so much variety. I was grateful that Air Canada, the sponsor of the tour, had allowed me two free days to play tourist and recover from any jet-lag. After ferry-hopping to see the temples of Elephanta Island, I reflected on the contrasts and similarities of their enormous elephant god, which was carved into the walls of a dark, mysterious cave that once enshrined supernatural power and dread, to the towering nuclear-power station dominating the bay — a monument to twentieth-century omnipotence.

We paid obeisance to Gandhi's spinning wheel, absorbing the silence of his simple room, then walked to the Bombay harbour, where so many thousands of colonials had first set foot on Indian soil. The usual round of receptions ensued, and expatriate Canadians expressed pleasure in greeting visitors from back home. An Indian friend of my mother's, whom she had not seen since her student days in London, told us, with a glint in his eyes, how much his friend Indira Gandhi had enjoyed Margaret Trudeau's tell-all book *Beyond Reason*. How far the written word travels, and into such unlikely hands! My concert in the Tata Theatre was well received in spite of the audience's annoying habit of whispering to each other during the performance; apparently, it is acceptable Indian etiquette to exchange remarks and wander in and out of concerts. A garland of headily fragrant gardenias was placed around my neck, almost intoxicating me during the encores.

The following day, thinking that some of the raggedy street urchins could earn a few rupees by selling my lovely bouquets of roses, which I would otherwise be leaving in the hotel room, my mother and I handed them to a couple of little girls; as we walked away, they started to hungrily eat the petals. Equally perturbing was the action of a deformed leper to whom we gave some hard-boiled eggs left over from our room-service breakfast. He grinned with appreciation and, balancing the eggs on his two stumps, started to munch away — shells and all! There was no such thing as waste among India's poor.

In New Delhi, many Canadian diplomats, including former prime minister Joe Clark, were in evidence at my two concerts in the Kaman Auditorium, part of a Canada Week celebration. The *Hindustani Times* wrote, "Boyd's playing with such precision, grace and supremely elegant phrasing ranks her amongst the finest exponents of classical guitar today." One evening, which stretched into the early-morning hours, I found myself jamming with several of India's leading virtuoso tabla and sitar players. My attempts to fake a raga amused the guests. I was fascinated by the plectrum that sitar players wear on their index finger and the huge callouses that build up as a result. This instrument was even harder on the hands than classical guitar. The tabla player explained that he had been studying since he was three years old, practising ten hours every day. Enjoying the incredible Indian rhythms and harmonies, far more complex than those of our western musical language, I marvelled at how his entire life had been devoted to music.

Since the long, hypnotic concerts in India traditionally last for several hours, one flustered reviewer came backstage demanding to know why I had played for only two. "Here, we expect at least a four-hour performance, madam," he asserted rather piquantly while several others nodded, leaving me feeling guilty for having cheated everyone out of another two hours.

Visits to the ethereal Taj Mahal, the bustling Crawford market, and the sloshing waters of the dhobi ghats (where cartloads of clothes were washed, then trundled off to dry along the railway lines) filled our free days before we had to fly off to Calcutta, near the Bay of Bengal. Hiring an old wooden boat, we drifted down the steamy river Hooghly and watched timeless Hindu washing rituals being performed along the muddy shores amid rafts of orange flowers floating on the murky waters. Whiffs of burning incense reminded us that we were witnessing a spirituality expressed through symbolic ceremony. My mother and I were guests at the White House, the home of Hugh Faulkner, a former Canadian secretary of state, and his wife, Jane. They kindly put their home and driver at our disposal, and invited us to dine with their amusing friend Princess Roma of Nepal. My concert, organized as a benefit for the Calcutta Music School, took place in the Birla Auditorium beneath a Hindu temple. Several Canadian students fought their way through the backstage curtains to talk with me afterwards, and one young man suggested I bring my guitar over to Mother Teresa's hospice, where he was a volunteer worker.

The poignancy of that visit to Calcutta's most renowned eleemosynary institution will remain with me forever. There, in the sweltering heat, with only a few tropical ceiling fans for relief, rows

of terminally ill people lay on narrow cots: some, on hearing my
guitar, raised their heads to see where the strange music was coming from. I played in both the men's and the women's wards,
perching on the edge of vacant beds whose previous occupants had,
no doubt, recently departed this world. Being surrounded by a
strong smell of disinfectant, intrusive noises from the busy street outside, and the debilitating heat was hardly my concept of "dying in
dignity." As I looked into the soulful brown eyes of those skeletal
remains of mankind, I was overcome by a mixture of compassion
and anger. India could not continue to increase her population without thousands of people such as these paying a tragic price. Having
to scratch out an existence in the gutters of Calcutta was no life at
all for nature's most godlike creation. Here were people whose
limbs had been eaten by leprosy, people with open sores, malarial
fevers, and wasted bodies. Much as I had to admire Mother Teresa
for her self-sacrifice and dedication to the world's poor, I felt that
travelling around the world preaching vehemently against abortion
and calling on women to have more babies was wrong. In that
humble hospital, the pitiful and miserable results of overpopulation
were clinging to their lives by threads that were rapidly unravelling
like broken guitar strings. Smiles illuminated some faces, but others
were obviously too feeble, or in too much pain, to open their
eyes. Their hours were numbered. I hoped all their religious beliefs
came to their aid, and prayed that karma would deal them a better
life next time around.

After I was driven to the sanctuary of the Mother House, where
Mother Teresa and her staff of nuns resided, I gave a twenty-minute
recital in the courtyard under the dark velvet canopy of night sky.
Classical guitar and western music are not too familiar to the general
population of India — I was somewhat of a novelty — but the
silent blue-and-white robed sisters sat on the ground in a semicircle
enthralled by this unusual diversion from their daily routines of
mercy. I wondered if they could feel Bach's passion for life as I
played "Jesu, Joy of Man's Desiring" in the midst of so much death.

Later that evening, my foolhardy mother and I hired a bicycle rickshaw, risking our precious lives while careering through chaotic traffic to experience Calcutta by night. The red-light district, always one of the most colourful and lively parts of any city, was a seething sea of commerce where everything and everyone seemed to be for sale. Pungent smells of spicy curries from street stalls mingled with cheap tobacco and saccharine perfumes. Jewelled baubles, cobra-skin wallets, and multicoloured yards of sari silk were all traded alongside girls with lustrous brown eyes who displayed themselves in doorways and windows. In spite of all the poverty, we were struck by the astonishing vibrancy and energy of the populace. Was I already being seduced by these exotic superficialities? Although life was cheap and apparently disposable, it possessed such an intense vitality that was fuelled by the wealth of constant human contact. I felt more thankful than ever, however, for my privileged life in North America.

Joel flew in from Toronto on Valentine's Day, journeying on with us to Kathmandu on Royal Nepal Airlines through explosive thunderstorms. We gripped our seats through the buffeting roller-coaster ride, and while lightning ricocheted from cloud to cloud and skated across our wings, we descended into the mountain kingdom. The town seemed much more orderly, quieter, and cooler than India. Colourfully clad men in Sherpa hats wandered around the centre square selling their trinkets; alongside them was the odd American remnant from the psychedelic era, still drifting around with head-band, long hair, sandals, and beads. We had entered the legendary land of the gurus, where one came to seek spiritual enlightenment.

Another excursion took us up the mountain roads that wove and whorled around hairpin bends with spectacular Himalayan vistas of the rooftops of the world. A towering Mount Everest shimmered powder-white against a hyacinth sky. In the town of Bhaktapur, I was transported back to medieval times, watching craftsmen and potters squatting on the streets practising their primitive skills. Attracted by eerie-sounding wind instruments, we trailed a small street procession until, to our horror, we realized that a bleating lamb was about to be sacrificed. As we were the only uninvited strangers in this assembly of weird-looking men, whose music had become more and more frenzied and off key, it felt time to beat a hasty retreat. Pashupatinath, another town where we lingered, is one of the holiest shrines of the Hindu world. Weathered-looking pilgrims and barefoot holy men with otherworldly eyes were descending on the town from remote corners of India. While we sat watching this motley crowd, the wild unfriendly monkeys in the park eyed us suspiciously, spitefully grabbing at our legs as if sensing we were outsiders.

My concert to benefit the United Church Mission was somehow fitted in during these days of new excitements. Joel was unfortunately summoned to Paris on urgent business and missed a memorable safari to Tiger Tops Lodge. After we arrived by bush-plane, Mother and I headed into the falling dusk atop a mammoth-sized elephant in search of wild animals, with the fervent hope that we not encounter a sleeping tiger. Our majestic beast, driven by a tiny guide perched on the elephant's neck, swayed through tall dry grasses and waded across rocky river beds, stopping whenever a rhino, hippo, or warthog came into view. Several people had apparently been mauled and killed by startled tigers or charging rhinos, but what good is any wildlife safari without an element of risk?

Exhausted from the elephant ride, we ascended into our tree-top accommodations, where cosy hot-water bottles had been tucked into our camp beds. At two in the morning, alarm bells interrupted my dreams of swaying pachyderms. We had been told there was a possibility of observing a "tiger kill" in the wild. In haste, we pulled on our clothes, grabbed flashlights, and piled into an open Land Rover that steered several miles along bumpy jungle roads through the Stygian night. Two guides led us single file along a narrow path, signalling us to remove our shoes. As we silently padded barefoot along the barely visible sandy trail, I felt like a character from the books of Rudyard Kipling. Strange bird calls and distant animal sounds resonated through the moonless forest, filling us with eerie sensations of unreality. Where was this tiger, and what could our guides do to protect us if he were suddenly disturbed and angered? This was the real thing, not a *National Geographic* documentary! Crouching in silence in the "blind," a flimsy tent-like structure, we observed a large, female tiger tearing apart the carcass of a hapless young gazelle. Since we were downwind of her, we apparently attracted no attention, but as I watched those massive fangs dismembering her poor victim, I hoped the wind did not decide to change direction. Back at our tree-top encampment, with my jungle-dusty feet on the hot-water bottle, I pondered the strange surprises that my tours as a classical guitarist were continually providing.

20

On the
Road Again

The fallout from the mismanagement of my career had resulted in scarcely any concert bookings. How depressing to flip through all those blank pages in my 1987 calendar. Soaking in my bathtub, trying to dispel the winter blues, I could not help daydreaming; I had travelled solo around Europe, why not try this continent? It would be fun to challenge my new driving skills without a concert at the end of the road, and what more spectacular route than the Pacific Coast Highway between San Francisco and Los Angeles? Joel, brooding over various business deals, put up no opposition to my impulsive decision, so in November, beckoned by memories of family holidays and my days with Cal, I escaped the gun-metal grey skies of Toronto to land in the sparkling City by the Bay.

Half Moon Bay was the starting point of my week-long odyssey. At a beach-side café, my eyes feasted on the nacrous blue ocean and sculpted cliffs. Inhaling the salt air, which was seasoned by heaps of kelp drying in the sunshine, I gingerly dipped my toes into the edges of the spreading waves. How wonderful to be twenty-five hundred miles from those grey waters of Lake Ontario. I steered past the primeval majesty of the giant redwoods and the flat fields of artichokes, into the college town of Santa Cruz to sit, feeling wonderfully anonymous, listening to folk music in a student coffee house. Frequent roadside stops let me explore the sandy coves, tidal pools, and rocky promontories, browse through gift shops, and refuel myself and the car. Carmel, with its sand as soft as wholewheat flour, quaint boutiques, cafés, and art galleries, glowed picture-perfect in that dazzling Californian light; vivid greens, golds, sapphires, pinks, and turquoises blended into a tapestry of iridescent colour.

I began to approach the landscapes so beloved by Henry Miller and Robert Louis Stevenson — Big Sur's wild romantic coastline, where honeysuckle and eucalyptus scents blend with tangy ocean air to caress the most rugged and glorious countryside of the continent. Passing the mecca of "Me generation" therapies, Esalen, I stopped at Nepenthe, where, as I had done twelve years earlier with Cal, I sipped *café au lait* to the peaceful sounds of wind-chimes. At the Ventana Inn, log fires warmed the night and hot tubs bubbled and frothed under a canopy of stars. In the dining room, I struck up a conversation with a screenwriter, Chris Beaumont, who took me for a late-night stroll around the hotel grounds while we discussed films, music, and the pros and cons of Californian life. A week later, looking him up in Los Angeles, I introduced him to my actress friend Gloria Loring, the former wife of Alan Thicke, whom he married soon after.

Alone behind the wheel, I turned up the volume on Jennifer Warnes's tribute to Leonard Cohen, *The Famous Blue Raincoat*, and continued southward around vertiginous cliffs. While the road snaked and switch-backed along precipices dropping thousands of feet to pounding surf below, I fell once again under the spell of the Pacific coast. Here fog banks often sweep in from the sea, but I was lucky: a perfect Californian sun guided me towards the legendary San Simeon, built by publishing tycoon William Randolph Hearst. As I climbed the imposing staircases, I wondered what it must have been like during its glory days, when Winston Churchill, George Bernard Shaw, Charlie Chaplin, and Cary Grant were wined and dined by the man who supposedly inspired *Citizen Kane*.

The curves of Route 1 became more elongated as it swept me past Morro Bay and San Luis Obispo to the pastel pinks of Santa Barbara, where two Paraguayan harpists enchanted me at the Biltmore Hotel's Sunday brunch. Resuming a southerly course, I passed Montecito, in the foothills of the gentle St. Ynez Mountains. Who would have thought that six years later I would be honeymooning in this flower-festooned paradise, or that eight years into my future I would be living in Malibu, my final rest stop along the highway? Six days and three hundred miles of asphalt later, all that remained was to wind along Sunset Boulevard into Beverly Hills, where I had arranged to stay. The hours behind the wheel had given me ample time for reflection on both my personal life and my career. Although both appeared to have ebbed to low tide, my inner creative life was coming to the rescue; plans for a new record were formulating, and I had been jotting down thematic ideas for future compositions. A love affair with Nature had nourished my spirit.

The very sound of the names Rangoon, Pagan, and Mandalay conjured up images from the yellowed pages of my grandfather's Rudyard Kipling and Somerset Maugham books. They evoked a bygone era when the British Raj was in its heyday: a starchy gathering of British colonels with waxed moustaches sipping sherry at the Rangoon country club while ladies in flowery Edwardian gowns balanced tea and shortbread.

"I strongly advise you not to go into Burma at this time," exhorted Canada's ambassador to Thailand. In October 1989, the political situation was highly unstable due to recent student uprisings; the repressive military government had imposed a nightly curfew to control the restless population after a series of violent demonstrations.

With Joel and Sheldon tagging along, I had just played a concert at the Thai-Canadian Association's Thanksgiving banquet and a children's concert at the International School. Now that the performances were behind me, Burma was going to provide the backdrop for an unusual holiday. After surviving the flight on one of Burma Airways' decrepit Second World War Fokker planes, we landed in Rangoon, where entering the once-elegant Strand Hotel felt like stepping back into the last century; a musty aroma hung in the air and oozed from long, dingy corridors; teak ceiling fans creaked as they circled at the pull of a string. In the bare-walled dining room, with its strong smell of disinfectant and its harsh lighting, grim-faced waiters served chicken-bone curry and strong tea with diluted Carnation milk in a tiny, well-worn cup that had been made in my mother's home town in the Midlands. How many thousands of cups of tea must it have served over the years? There dwelt such an appealing sense of history in that old tea cup, with its faded green design that read Strand Hotel Rangoon. A clandestine deal ensued, with the waiter surreptitiously secreting the prized cup into my handbag in exchange for three green bills slipped into his dollar-hungry hand. "Very, very dangerous, madame," he whispered, his eyes furtively skimming the length of the room, checking that nobody noticed our hasty transaction. On the black market, he would be guaranteed a generous supply of local *kyats* for his illicit sale of hotel property.

Going through Burmese customs a week later, I tucked the nostalgic trophy for my mother into a well-used sock and hid it inside my running shoe; luckily, the official passed right over my contraband. A few nights in a Burmese jail for grand larceny was definitely not on my agenda! Everywhere in Burma, street hawkers and tour guides produced secret stashes of grubby American bills concealed in bamboo cases, frayed tapestry bags, and lacquered owl-shaped jewellery boxes. In the Bangkok airport, as I was about to board our flight to Rangoon, I had been approached by a travel guide who asked if I would take his wad of twenty-seven hundred dollars in hundred-dollar bills into the country for him. It was legal for foreigners to have large sums of currency, but to be safe I concealed the money inside my bra, which expanded from a C to a D cup in a matter of seconds. Too afraid of watchful eyes in the airport, our contact waited until nightfall to show up at the Strand. Even there, he insisted that Sheldon take the money from me and rendezvous with him later, when the coast was clear, in the men's toilet!

When we returned from Burma, a woman we had befriended asked if I would transport a package of rubies in my purse and hand them over to an uncle of hers. Smuggling jewels and money had never been my practice, and only after considering the oppressive regime did I reluctantly agree. She assured me that Burmese officials never searched tourists. As a precaution, I unwrapped her small parcel to check its contents. A tea cup was one thing, but an unexamined package could have spelled trouble! It was the closest I ever felt to being an international smuggler. For the Burmese people, trusting their savings to total strangers seemed to be the only way to get funds in and out of the country to overseas relatives. On both occasions, my willingness to co-operate brought forth a torrent of gratitude.

Rangoon must have been a truly grand city in her glory days in the late nineteenth century, when ornate colonial buildings and spacious avenues reflected the skillful civil planning of the British; but now peeling paint, cracked wooden balconies, and rotting doorways revealed neglect. The gritty streets were teeming with vendors selling their wares from rickety stalls: freshly cut pineapples and papayas, rice sweetmeats, spicy fried vegetable patties, framed photos of Buddha, cotton and silk sarongs, and displays of imported cosmetics. Almost on a par with the Burmese desire for U.S. dollars was their craving for imported make-up. Swarms of little girls trailed behind me making finger gestures to their lips and uttered squeals of delight when I allowed them to paint their eyelids. They smeared my cheeks with a concoction of powdered wood paste and giggled as they handed me some wildflowers. "Beautiful yellow hair," a five-year-old whispered, then scampered off to hide behind her sister's skirts. Their smattering of English words and V for Victory hand signs astonished us: a legacy from the Second World War still being handed down to future generations.

From Pagan to Mandalay, the country seemed devoid of tourists. To prevent a terrorist hijacking, two armed guards accompanied us on one flight, even though we were the only passengers. Pagan, once the capital of Burma, is still revered for its thousands of temples and *stupas*, which are monuments containing relics of Lord Buddha; its religious architecture is unequalled anywhere in Asia. Pierre Trudeau, who had spent time there with his sons, had urged us to do likewise. Under the hot sun, we struggled up and down eroded stone steps to view countless images of the Buddha. (Being a tourist can be exhausting; one temple alone contained fourteen thousand statues!) Pilgrims who had travelled from other regions of the country to pay homage lit candles, burned incense, and knelt in supplication before the immense holy carvings while saffron-robed monks chanted ancient incantations. In the main gold-domed temple of Rangoon, Shwedagon, an elderly monk with a toothless grin, offered me a pinch of orange herbal powder to sample and invited us to join a throng of chanting worshipers kneeling on prayer mats. Our devout hosts, excited that we came from Canada, insisted we partake of their spicy soup; my prayers that evening were that our reckless dinner would not lead to a bout of "Burmese revenge"! These amazing shrines dated to the time of Buddha and even outshone those in Bangkok. Precious jewels were encrusted in solid-gold statues that were housed inside gilded temples of unbelievable proportions and intricate design.

It was distressing to see so many flea-bitten stray dogs and puppies hungrily roaming the streets, and the hundreds of little girls who patiently threaded coloured silk onto huge looms. They worked in silence, sitting on long wooden benches, nimble fingers dancing along the length of the weft. Their innocent faces offered shy smiles as we passed by admiring the complex patterns. What daydreams filled their minds during the long and tedious shifts? What would happen, I wondered, if those agile fingers were trained to pluck the strings of a guitar?

My travel companions were highly amused to learn what was causing such a flurry of excitement among the hotel staff. Word had raced around the corridors that the North American blonde with the guitar was none other than Madonna! Later that evening, a lobby full of teenagers had to settle for "La Gitane" and "Carnival." In exchange, we were offered a ride into the village before curfew. Swaying along deserted lanes in a horse-drawn carriage with only the horses' plodding to break the silence, we passed tenth-century pagodas brushed by the rays of a full moon. Time had spun me back to ancient Burma, before the invention of cars, planes, and tourists. That magical night lies embalmed in a special repository of memories that holds those peak experiences I hope will never fade.

Back from Burma for only three days, I luxuriated in being able to spend some quiet time at home. Finally, I could catch up with the mail, the laundry, telephone messages, and new repertoire. The lake waters lapped peacefully against my beach as two mallard ducks paddled along the shoreline enjoying the fading warmth of Indian summer. A sharp telephone ring disturbed my happy reverie. Elliot Roberts, Tracy Chapman's manager, was on the phone from Los Angeles. "Liona, can you come to Europe this weekend for a three-week tour? Every concert is sold out and we're playing all the major cities. Sorry it's such short notice."

In a daze, I sat down to digest this unexpected offer, my weary body still somewhere on the road to Mandalay. Tracy Chapman was one of the hottest American singers, with "Fast Car" moving into the number-one position on the international charts. The opportunity to perform for new audiences in all the opera houses and symphony halls of Europe was tempting, as it might lead to future solo tours. Elliot faxed me the itinerary. It looked a killer. The last time I had participated in a pop tour was with Gordon Lightfoot ten years earlier, and I wondered if Tracy's audiences would be as receptive to my classical style. Did she have a hip young following that would delight in booing me offstage? My mind flashed back to a similar decision made in San Francisco regarding Lightfoot's Minneapolis offer. "Nothing ventured, nothing gained" had always been my *modus operandi*. A few hours later I called back to accept, then began throwing various items of clothing and music into my suitcase, which was still impregnated with the dust of Rangoon. When she learned that I was leaving so soon, my mother thought I was out of my mind. "But darling, you've only just arrived home!" she cried in disbelief. Joel, thankfully, supported my rash decision, content to spend some undisturbed weeks with the house to himself preparing for his upcoming CDIC trial.

Two days later, I was on a plane to Amsterdam with John Telfer, a new manager whom A&M had suggested. The tour kicked off with a concert in the Muziektheater, where, to my relief, the Dutch audience was generous with its applause, even calling me back for an encore. Scarlet Rivera, the red-maned electric violinist, and the percussionist Bobbye Hall played subtle accompaniments to Tracy's songs about loneliness, racism, and class struggle. Hers were not the lyrics of a happy woman. She refused to have anything to do with anyone in her entourage, and my attempts at conversation ended in stony silence. Her only remarks to the band were ones of criticism, and I heard them vowing it would be the last time they worked with her. Our prima donna took an inordinate amount of time doing her own sound check, barely leaving me five minutes to test my microphones. In contrast, I remembered how considerate Gordon Lightfoot had been to his fellow musicians. Life on the road held enough stress without added tensions.

We played venues that included the Theatre Brancaccio in Rome, Teatro Monumental in Madrid, Austria Centre in Vienna, and Royal Albert Hall in London. Walking onstage in the Coliseum of Lisbon, I received such a tumultuous welcome from ten thousand fans that I suddenly knew the "rush" rock stars must experience. The crowd, berserk with enthusiasm, insisted on clapping in time to my Spanish pieces. Lightfoot's audiences had been great, but this one was wild! The Parisians, on the other hand, were in a foul mood due to a two-hour delay; the noisy French audience was inattentive and rude to both of us. My former manager, Bernie Fiedler, surfaced in Hamburg, amazed at the response my playing drew from his native country. Frankfurt's Alte Oper and Munich's Deutsches Museum welcomed us during the electrifying week the Berlin Wall came down. When Boris Becker slipped backstage to say hello, Bernie made sure we were photographed together for the press. I was beginning to realize that, much as I liked him as a person, Telfer was not the ideal manager. His understated British personality lacked the *chutzpah* my career required, and his defeatist approach was summed up in the downbeat name of his company, Basement Music! A few months later, I was relieved when Fiedler offered to direct my career again. Finding the right manager can be as difficult as choosing the right husband.

21

The Ultimate Canadian Experience

♪

I frequently heard friends' accounts of wilderness white-water canoeing trips. Their tales of heavy portages, treacherous rapids, and clouds of mosquitoes had always been enough to dissuade me. Gordon Lightfoot, who organized annual canoe expeditions to the Northwest Territories, had regaled me with macho stories of survival in Canada's north-lands, and my writer-friend Tom York had spun many a yarn about his perilous adventures with his Native buddies in the bush. Pierre Trudeau had challenged several great northern rivers and returned inspired by the spectacular beauty of his native country. "Travel a thousand miles by train," he wrote, "and you are a brute; pedal five hundred miles on a bicycle and you remain basically a bourgeois; paddle one hundred miles in a canoe and already you are a child of nature."

My own concept of canoeing had evolved while I lazed on a foam cushion watching Pierre's agile arms dip polished wood into water as he ferried me around Harrington Lake and discussed the political and social events of the day. Having to actually paddle for hours on end, doing battle with swirling rapids and bugs, sounded far too strenuous, so it came as a surprise to my friends when, in the summer of 1989, I agreed to venture on a two-week white-water canoe trip up the Missinaibi River to James Bay. Shaftesbury Films wanted to produce a documentary about a well-known Canadian navigating a northern river, and for some reason they chose me — a city slicker. All these years, I had called Canada home but avoided "the ultimate Canadian experience." I was about to find out firsthand what I had been missing.

Our party of ten intrepid adventurers included Vlad the director, his "strong-like-a-bull" Polish assistant, inveterate canoeists David and Linda Silcox, the producer Christina Jennings and her boyfriend, a writer, and an aide to help portage five canoes and tents. As Joel and I packed inflatable mattresses, life jackets, long underwear, a waterproofed guitar case, and a neatly folded outfit for my concert in Moose Factory, I wondered what I was getting myself into, especially knowing that once on the river, we would have no radio contact with the outside world.

Air Ontario flew us to Timmins, where the Ministry of Natural Resources had scheduled a twin-Otter float plane to airlift us to Missinaibi Lake. As we circled over expanses of Precambrian rock and forests sprinkled with lakes, I remembered Longfellow's epic poem, which I had loved so much as an eleven-year-old English schoolgirl — the poem that had somehow started to forge my Canadian identity. Now, almost three decades later, I was heading for Gitche Gumee, about to become part of the legendary land of Hiawatha. When I emerged from the bush plane, a deer-fly welcomed me with a sting on my thigh; I hastily donned long pants and shirt despite the heat, but the blackflies, no-see-ums, and mosquitoes beset us in droves. Silvery lacy-winged dragonflies swooped around catching bugs in mid-flight as Joel showed me how to assemble our tent: a tangle of poles, ropes, and pins. Everything from our socks to our sleeping bags felt clean and new; thank goodness we could not envision how different they would be in two weeks.

Vlad suggested some shots of me honing my skills with a paddle, and cajoled me to nearby Whitefish Falls, where I did my utmost to look experienced for his camera. "Just manoeuvre your canoe a little closer to the falls. This shot is great," he yelled over the roar of churning water as I worried about getting swept into the eddy. Thoughts of my frequent "wave" nightmares and fear of moving water gave me pause. Had not the great Spanish composer Enrique Granados suffered a similar lifetime phobia, only to be drowned the first time he dared take a ship across the Atlantic?

After surviving the falls, I paddled around Fairy Point, whose ancient bear-oil pictographs of caribou, bear, fish, and war-canoes were a quiet reminder of the spiritual beliefs of the Native people inhabiting this wilderness. "Figures strange and brightly colored; / And each figure had its meaning, / Each some magic song suggested. / The Great Spirit, the Creator." Contemplating the tranquil beauty of these mysterious paintings, I felt overwhelmed and humbled.

Rocky outcrops delighted our eyes with splashes of colour: orange and yellow lichen, red berries, and dark green moss like plush velvet from a Renaissance gown. Twisted pines, tamarack, spruce, and silver-birch trees leaned precariously from the ledges, evoking the paintings of the Group of Seven. We made it back to camp, "And the evening sun descending / Set the clouds on fire with redness, / Burned the broad sky like a prairie." I was already feeling the forces of Nature rekindling my childhood love affair with Hiawatha and making me a part of this great Canadian landscape.

After a campfire guitar serenade, I turned in early, trying to resist scratching my bothersome bug bites. Suddenly, I was awakened by heavy footsteps padding around our tent. I roused Joel, as we had been warned that prowling bears posed a real danger. My irritable tent-mate ordered me to go back to sleep and stop imagining things, but my mind kept focusing on the bag of candies tucked into my pack and the warnings never to keep food in the tents. I lay awake wondering what to do if a large furry paw ripped through our mosquito netting. Should I bash him over the head with my guitar case or, grabbing Joel as a protective shield, throw him the licorice allsorts as a peace offering? I heard a loud grunting and banging and again shook Joel to consciousness. Why didn't any of the other tents respond? "For God's sake, Liona, go to sleep and quit fantasizing about bears! It's probably one of our group knocking something over on their way to take a leak in the woods." I slept uneasily, dreaming that Grandma's brown-bear rug — one of my early childhood fears — was chasing me around her house. The next morning, I was vindicated. During the night, two bears had entered our campsite, destroyed the fish-cleaning table, and torn apart our supply tents! My ursine fears had been well founded. Guiltily, I wolfed down the licorice all-sorts for breakfast!

The mosquitoes and blackflies were unremitting; bug hats were essential when emerging from the tents, as thousands of bloodthirsty creatures surrounded the netting anticipating a meal. As I crouched in the steamy canvas, trying to reorganize my waterproofed guitar case, I felt trapped in a David Cronenberg horror movie. Our Deet repellants, lemon oils, and rituals of vitamin B and garlic seemed like a cruel joke; the relentless bugs loved it all.

As we loaded our five canoes, I could not believe the quantity of gear we were taking. The "wanigan" was filled with so many gourmet provisions and so much dry ice as to render it almost unliftable. With daiquiri cocktails, Waldorf salads, and shish kebabs, our meals would have amazed the *voyageurs*. It was time to push away from terra firma and trust our lives to the river. Becoming familiar with the art of navigating rapids, I learned how to calculate the fickle pull of current on paddle and to recognize the first tell-tale signs — an ominous sound of rushing water and acceleration in river drift. We had to rely on our director's superior knowledge about which channels and currents to select, but each couple had to fend for themselves once the canoes became caught in the capricious rapids. One wrong decision could mean a sudden capsize into swirling water. Several accidents did ensue, but a guardian angel was helping steer my craft. I learned how to head into the V, manoeuvre deftly around boulders, spot concealed rocks, and back-paddle as though my life depended upon it. My heart raced as we occasionally broadsided a wave and the canoe filled with foaming water. We were heading down what had been one of Canada's legendary water routes at the height of the Hudson Bay fur trade in the eighteenth century.

Retreating into my clothes, I sought protection from the swarms of blackflies and mosquitoes, preferring sweating beneath a Gortex jacket to being slowly eaten alive bite by bite. The bug hats were designed to prevent the pests from attacking our faces, but the bloody bites on my neck and ears were a testament to either their inefficiency or my own lack of expertise. I became proficient at drinking tea through the netting, but eating pasta proved a greater challenge! Dive-bombed in my sleep, I awoke to discover that one eye was swollen shut, rendering me half-blind all day. Feeling wretched from the painful bites, I was in no mood to face cameras and felt renewed respect for those courageous pioneers who once inhabited these remote outposts.

At times, as we made our way past Swamp Rapids, Peterbell Marsh, Deadwood Rapids, and Thunderhouse Falls, we experienced interludes of supreme tranquillity, exalting in feeling at one with our natural surroundings. A huge bull moose paused to savour the unfamiliar strains of classical guitar. "Recuerdos" was obviously not quite his musical taste, and he nonchalantly waded into the brush that fringed the river. At noon the bugs abated, allowing us to drift downstream drying laundry in the sun. In the quiet reaches of the river, alongside beavers, families of ducks, and great blue herons, we caught pickerel and pike. How satisfying to sit around a jack-pine campfire reliving our trials and triumphs as our catch of the day sizzled on the embers and scintillating showers of fireflies surrounded us. "Wah-wah-taysee, little fire-fly, / Little, flitting, white-fire insect, / Little, dancing, white-fire creature, / Light me with your little candle, / Ere upon my bed I lay me, / Ere in sleep I close my eyelids!"

I started to compose the film's soundtrack: a simple melody evoking the imagery of Native paddlers and constant river motion. Another theme that I scribbled onto my crumpled manuscript paper was inspired by the raindrops falling like silver pearls into the still, reedy waters that we traversed. For a couple of days, we had to paddle through driving rain and portage our canoes through deep mud. "Portage," I learned, is a euphemism for carrying a heavy object that is supposed to carry us! My hands, constantly wet inside rubber gloves, were in poor condition to play the upcoming concert.

July 11, my fortieth birthday, was to be a hard one; ahead lay the worst portage of the voyage. Pulling on cold, soggy jeans and wet socks in the dark, I wondered what madness could possibly have possessed me. Why, at a time of my life when I could have been soaking up rays on the Riviera, had I consented to such a gruelling ordeal? Liona Boyd must have taken leave of her senses! If this was the ultimate Canadian experience, then I would happily leave it to real Canadians. Every muscle was aching, and my complexion was a blotchy mess from all the repellant oil and insect bites. We paddled on in grim silence, through drizzling rain and along the monotonous river bends of the Missinaibi, until eventually a ribboned fir tree, the marker to our portage, was spotted and we began the muddy chore of unloading and dragging canoes up the slippery bank.

Suddenly, to our jubilation, a float plane circled and landed on the river. Perhaps the ministry had decided to mount a rescue and fly us amateurs back to civilization. But there was no such luck. A friendly couple on a fishing trip who owned the only lodge in the region had spotted our canoes from the air and come to investigate. They offered to fly our heaviest equipment over the portage to the lake on the other side and guide us to their lodge. We nevertheless had to spend the next three hours struggling over the land portage with the rest of our gear — an onerous task I hope never to repeat! Sinking waist deep in squelchy, black mud, we frequently lost our footing on moss, slippery logs, and rocks. The swarms of implacable bugs droning their incessant chorus would have driven me mad were it not for the protective hat. Finally, our spirits soared. We emerged from the dense tangle of undergrowth to a breathtaking lagoon of bulrushes and pale yellow water lilies — "To a pond of quiet water, / Where knee-deep the trees were standing, / Where the water-lilies floated, / Where the rushes waved and whispered."

After a two-hour speedboat tow, a welcome sight of human civilization came into view: a couple of wooden structures built on the rocky shore. Never had cold beer tasted so delicious or a hot shower felt so euphoric! We had been transported to another world. The couple greeted us like family, preparing a birthday feast of smoked fish while I premiered my Missinaibi theme in the living room. The contrast between the day's sodden struggles with the evening's unexpected festivities was overwhelming. Our timely rescue had been my ultimate birthday gift: one whose memory I would treasure forever. But all good things have to end; the next morning, it was back to the trenches, where we and our freshly laundered clothes soon succumbed to the Missinaibi's muddy embrace.

Our director suggested Joel and I climb a rocky canyon — spectacular scenery for the film, but one slip and we would plummet a thousand feet into the boiling waters of the gorge. Climbing up the precipice, I already saw the headlines: "Classical Guitarist Meets Sudden Death in White-Water Canoe Accident — Body Unrecovered." By the time we had inched back down the rock face, it became clear that we would never make it back to camp before sunset with just the one canoe. Navigating rapids in the dark scared me as much as the many bear footprints we had been noticing in the sand. But our ingenious director organized the hasty construction of a raft, lashing together seven long driftwood poles. It floated perfectly, carrying us down river like Huckleberry Finn as the last orange streaks were fading on the horizon.

A guiding spirit was with me when my guitar and I struggled over the portage alone rather than shoot rapids at Allan Island with the others. Joel and "Strong-like-a-bull" smashed our canoe head first into a protruding rock. Like a red arrow it flew into the air, its riders and all our gear swept downstream in churning water. Everyone rushed their canoes into the river in a fast rescue operation, while on the bank I gave a silent prayer of thanks to have been spared.

After a few more days of arduous paddling, we reached the estuary where the Moose River empties into James Bay. In the town of Moose Factory, the sons and daughters of Hiawatha now ride around in motorboats and on dirt bikes and live in wooden government-built houses. They cooked us bannock scones in a smoky teepee carpeted with cedar branches and showed us an old museum housing remnants from the days when this town was at the centre of the fur trade. Countless mink, beaver, fox, and muskrat pelts had crossed the Atlantic to satisfy Europe's craving for felt hats and fur collars.

In the evening, I played a concert in the Anglican church, where stained-glass windows depicted gigantic trading canoes, missionary churches, and Native pow-wows. There was standing room only; every pew was crammed. The band's chieftain introduced me in his sing-song language, a wonderful dissonant choir sang Cree hymns, and then the audience gave rapt attention and a standing ovation to my performance. Bach had been composing in Europe the piece I played at the same time as Moose Factory was being established in Canada — such contrasting worlds, yet both somehow present during my concert. I spoke a few words of greeting in Cree: "*Watchee ne mililten uta ministiguk.*" Never in my life, I told the audience, had I worked so hard to come to a concert. The ladies' auxiliary held a reception in their common hall, and I was swarmed by autograph-seekers from three years to ninety. One young Cree had been making tenacious efforts to teach himself classical guitar. How ironic that he had been doing battle with a Paganini study in Moose Factory while I had been struggling with the Native art of canoemanship.

The concert had been my parting gift to the proud people of the

Missinaibi. In the eyes and furrowed faces of the town's elders, I read that theirs had not been an easy life. The white man had brought both blessings and curses — electricity and television, welfare, drugs, and liquor. Our lumber and mining companies had clear cut Hiawatha's forests and polluted his lakes with mercury. The land that our indigenous peoples had cared for so conscientiously over the centuries was paying the price for our daily newspapers and paper bags.

As we prepared to leave the land of "Minnehaha, laughing water," the medicine man sang a farewell song, beating out its timeless rhythm on a hand-held drum. "Get up, morning is coming, the birds are singing, and our land is beautiful." Within his reedy voice, I felt the Spirit of the Wind passing stealthily through the rushes and heard the heartbeat of our great northern rivers. In some inexplicable way I had grown and changed. Hiawatha, you had brought me here to share your world, and yes, my little friend, I had passed your initiations and survived "the ultimate Canadian experience"!

22

Birth Pangs in Costa Rica

The minister of culture, Carlos Echeverría, invited me to perform eight concerts with the National Symphony Orchestra of Costa Rica in February 1990. Richard Fortin had just finished orchestrating *Concerto of the Andes*, which we had been working on together for the past year, meeting frequently to improve and tighten melodies, shape structure, and refine instrumentation. This would be the perfect opportunity to première our new opus, and Jim Hanley, of Sleeping Giant Productions, jumped at the chance to film it for a documentary.

Richard and I flew to San José expecting to be met at the airport by a representative from the cultural ministry, as arranged. After an hour of battling crowds to retrieve our luggage, and having realized we were on our own, we dived onto the protruding seat springs of a taxi, where prerequisite white-noise radio and a dangling plastic Virgin Mary bewildered Richard; it was his first visit to Latin America. Our home for three weeks, the Irazu Hotel, was swarming with pasty

Canadian tourists who made a beeline for the pool-side *chaises longues* to fry themselves with coconut oil in the equatorial sun, to the synthesizer serenades of "Spanish Eyes." Not to be left out of this ritual, we too baked ourselves medium rare and suffered from our folly for days.

Because the regular conductor was away on leave, Benjamin Gutiérrez had been assigned the task of directing the seventy-five youthful members of the Costa Rican symphony orchestra. During rehearsals in a warehouse, Richard and I adjusted dynamic markings on the score while trying to teach Maestro Gutiérrez our intended tempos. As both orchestra and conductor kept dragging the rhythms, it became a challenge to keep them in time. Neither I nor the musicians could follow Gutiérrez's elliptical arm movements — he flailed around like a discombobulated windmill. It came as no surprise when he admitted he was really a composer, not a conductor. Completely ignoring my suggestions, he looked only to Richard for directions. My astonished composer was advised by Gutiérrez that he "never take instructions from a woman. Females are pretty to look at, but know nothing." During breaks, the orchestra implored Richard to take control of the baton himself, but having no experience in conducting, he declined.

The concerto, which Richard and I had decided needed much heavier orchestration than Rodrigo's *Aranjuez*, was proving a challenge for the musicians, but they persisted. Gutiérrez's role became increasingly redundant, and eventually the four movements started to take shape. Richard and I taped the rehearsals in order to listen back at the hotel for ways to improve or correct. The work itself thrilled me. The haunting spirit of the Andes Mountains had begun to permeate our concrete warehouse in the suburbs of San José. Members of the orchestra, impressed by Fortin's writing skills, came individually to congratulate him, convinced that he must have spent time in South America to write so persuasively in the Latin American idiom.

Our first performance was to be held in the main church of Sarchi, a town one and a half hours from San José up grinding mountain roads. The film team arrived early with us in order to do a sound check, but mass was still in progress. Richard attempted to help the film crew hook up their mixing board, mikes, and monitors, which were incompatible with the church's electrical outlets. As I sat tuning in the priest's tiny bedroom, he dashed back and forth with desperate reports of his lack of success. "No worry, *señorita*," one of the clergy reassured me. "All be very good by time you playing guitar." Little did I know that as we proceeded across the country, we would be leaving a trail of blown fuses and distraught priests in our wake.

When I made my entrance, I saw with horror that my small podium and microphone had been placed several yards in front of the conductor, eliminating any eye contact between us. My chair had been positioned practically on top of Richard, who sat behind the mixing board with a terrified expression as I tapped the microphone and no sound came forth. During what seemed like an eternity, as men scrambled around on the dusty floor testing and reconnecting cables, a hand-wringing Gutiérrez repeatedly apologized to the public while trying unsuccessfully to stop the orchestra from whispering and fidgeting with their instruments like unruly schoolchildren.

Finally, from the sibilant speakers, a guitar-like sound could be detected. I threw myself into the concerto like a poorly armed foot-soldier heading valiantly into battle, while Gutiérrez gave indeterminate entries to the various sections. His dragged tempos and lack of precision in the third movement resulted in the winds and guitar playing one entire measure ahead of the strings. Richard and I exchanged looks of disbelief as the conductor raced into the fourth movement at double tempo. Craning my neck backwards, I yelled desperately, "*Más despacio* — slow down!" over the orchestral din, which was amplified by the church's resonant acoustics. When my entry came, I seized the opportunity to halve the tempo, playing with exaggerated rhythmic precision so everyone would get the message, but the inattentive percussionists raced onward at twice the intended speed and the trumpets and trombones panicked, blowing wrong notes, which added to the cacophony. Only during the last two pages did everyone come together. Gutiérrez, in his three-piece velvet suit, was dripping with sweat as though he had just finished a marathon. What an excruciating performance! I had done my part, memorizing my score perfectly; there was no excuse for all these errors. Following the orchestral debacle, I was thankfully called back for a solo encore by the appreciative audience, which consisted of local farmers, craftsmen, merchants, and their families. The film company had been crawling around with cameras, catching "interesting angles," but I prayed that none of this traumatic world première would ever make it to the final cut. Richard and I commiserated that just as Thunder Bay had been our disastrous first concert of the *Persona* tour, Sarchi was its Costa Rican equivalent. We groaned in unison.

On the drive back to San José, our seasoned film director, Jim Hanley, and his assistant ended up in a ditch beside the road, throwing up and succumbing to a terrible bout of Montezuma's revenge. Until Richard and I learned that they had consumed contaminated ice, we feared it was their gut reaction to the ignominious debut of our concerto! How were we ever going to whip the poor Andes into shape for a film to be shown to thousands of people? I lay awake that night, despondent; how could this wonderful piece of music be so mutilated by professional musicians? "Why did you take the fourth movement at double speed?" I asked Gutiérrez the next day. "Oh, I was angry with those women flute players and wanted to see if I could trip their fingers" was his astonishing justification. It was evident that the orchestra members had been disgruntled, talking during the concert and radiating more frowns than smiles; their manager was approached and soon the reason became apparent. The musicians were not being paid extra for the television rights, and felt inconvenienced by a film crew clambering around their stage with cameras and extension cords. The minister of culture decided to raise their wages and Hanley offered to throw a salsa party in their honour. The temperamental players were thus placated into making greater musical efforts during subsequent performances. It must be difficult playing in an orchestra for minimal remuneration under strenuous conditions while a soloist gets most of the accolades, but despondent musicians with an eccentric conductor can really get a new concerto off to a rocky start. At Hanley's party, as I flung myself around to lively salsa music with one of the clarinetists and Richard shared rum punches with a pretty violinist, I sensed a shift in mood in the National Symphony Orchestra of Costa Rica.

We presented our symphonic road show in the picturesque hill-side towns of Pacayas and San Pedro de Poás, built on the slopes of the great Poás volcano. Some of our audience members had obviously walked for miles; farmers sputtered up on tractors and leathery-skinned men came in carrying sugar-cane machetes. Dozens of children attended the free concerts, looking with wide-eyed wonder at the musicians and their instruments. In the steamy Caribbean port of Limón, stray dogs greeted us as we pulled up at the ornate cathedral just in time to hear an evening mass that included ten guitar-strumming nuns singing Spanish hymns. I tuned my soggy guitar strings in the rear courtyard, where a darkened window improvised as my mirror. A winsome young priest with a golden smile swung his incense burner, billowing clouds of scented smoke into the humid air. These "backstages" were certainly more colourful that those predictable dressing-rooms in North American theatres! When we arrived at the banana port of Siquirres, I was ushered into a locker-room already occupied by ten tae-kwon-do students practising kicks and leaps. There was no option but to dress inside a dark closet and try to tune as best I could behind a crate that had been discovered by a few choice cockroaches. Ah, the glamorous life of a guest soloist!

While the crew filmed me playing my guitar on the beach the following day, I befriended two young boys searching for fish in the warm tidal pools and scampering along the sand like frisky puppies. Later, that footage was used in the music video for my composition "Fallingbrook Samba." Jim Hanley interviewed me on camera as we careered along torturous mountain roads, and I tried to answer his questions on Central American politics and the role of music in society as we inhaled clouds of black fumes from the diesel trucks sharing our route. One shot required Richard and me to perform "Carnival" in the ornate lobby of the National Theatre, and another had us play it in the town square, where a large crowd of curious onlookers encircled us. The people of Costa Rica love guitar music, and wherever we played their enthusiasm was palpable. The locals taught me a popular song in La Esmeralda, a gathering place for San José's *mariachi* bands, and I was suddenly back with our Mexican *novios* and the romantic *mariachi* serenades of my youth in San Miguel de Allende.

Five a.m. wake-up calls became routine, as Hanley sought to capture Costa Rica's exquisite scenery during the hours of translucent morning light. After a three-hour drive from the capital, we spent the day floating downstream on a rubber raft, dangling our legs into the tepid water of Guanacaste as our cameraman shot footage of cheeky howler monkeys and iguanas basking along the tropical shores. The minivan made it back to the Irazu Hotel as dusk was descending on San José. At the last minute, I had been asked to play at the home of President Oscar Arias. In a state of panic, I jumped into the shower to scrub the river grit and sun-tan lotion off my skin. Itchy blisters from dyshidrosis, a skin allergy that always afflicts my hands in the tropics, had been adding distress to my fingers.

Two hundred animated guests were balancing cocktails and conversation in the courtyard. This was Arias's farewell dinner for his party faithful, since *La Libertad* had recently conceded defeat. I had seen his face on the evening news so often: accepting the Nobel Peace Prize for his Central American peace initiative or crusading for co-operation among the unstable neighbouring countries that were torn apart by civil war and military coups. When we came face to face, I felt he had none of the charisma of Fidel Castro or Pierre Trudeau. His velvety brown eyes seemed soft and submissive, his weak, welcoming handshake gave no hint of the passion I expected from such a renowned political statesman. Margarita, his attractive wife, on the other hand, was full of pep, skilfully working the tables and embracing her guests. She introduced me to the gathering by asking everyone to welcome their special *invitada* from Canada who had agreed to play at such a short notice — "Elizabeth Boyd"!

I played a few pieces while the film crew struggled to shoot me from the shadows. The president and his wife led the clapping and requested a couple of encores. Arias agreed to an interview with Jim Hanley in his private study, but first we were invited to partake of a buffet dinner. Plate in hand, I wandered around the Arias home, inspecting the various photographs that all world leaders seem to display on their walls — photos of themselves posing with other world leaders.

Jim was hoping *el presidente* would expostulate on his statement that "If humankind is to write its history with culture instead of blood, then I predict Costa Rica will play an invaluable role in the future of humanity." The president stared blankly at the sentence, looking ill at ease; there followed an interminable silence as we waited for his words of wisdom on the subject of peace, the arts, and democracy. Arias shifted uncomfortably in his chair, explaining that he would prefer to talk about his government's achievements — a subject I had heard him cover earlier in the evening during his farewell speech. He seemed tired and unfocused, perhaps from a too-busy schedule or too many cocktails. Finally, as though in slow motion, he made a few desultory attempts at political philosophy, but soon lost his train of thought. I last saw Arias with his head down, backing out of the door and mumbling, *"Lo siento mucho* — I am very sorry. Goodnight." It was a disappointment for our film, but even Nobel Prize winners have "off nights."

After concerts in the churches of Turrialba and Tibas, we were ready for the National Theatre and the many government officials who would be in attendance. Costa Ricans are immensely proud of their Viennese-style hall, with its draped boxes, gilded pillars, and velvet curtains. There the excellent acoustics helped my guitar sounds blend in with the rich sonorities from the symphony.

The orchestra starts the first movement with whole-tone harmonics, evoking the grandeur and mysterious majesty of the Andes Mountains. The guitar enters with a series of strummed D-major chords that seem to introduce a human element into the natural setting. The characteristic Peruvian rhythms and harmonic progressions lend themselves so perfectly to the guitar, the instrument of their creation. The second movement combines a haunting melody with contemporary and impressionistic harmonies. At times, the guitar and oboe answer each other in lyrical dialogue, concluding with an exuberant melodic passage in which the entire orchestra participates. The romantic third movement features a solo cadenza, and lush strings support the guitar's melody. Finally, in the last movement, Richard introduces dissonant harmonies and syncopated rhythms, leading to a playful percussion interlude where I contribute rhythm by tapping on the body of the guitar.

The orchestra, conductor, and I were drenched in perspiration by the end of the performance. Fortin's compelling showpiece received a thunderous ovation from the full house. Edén Pastora, Nicaragua's "Comandante Zero," and his family came to offer congratulations, as did various guitarists, embassy staff, and delegates from the ministry of culture. How elating to realize that, in spite of its agonizing birth pangs, our "Concerto of the Andes," composed by a French Canadian and performed by an English Canadian, had been so passionately appreciated by the people of Costa Rica.

23

The
Golden State

𝄞

*J*oel and I had been coexisting, but the romance had disintegrated into a friendship and I had retreated to the downstairs bedroom. Why was I spending some of the best years of my life with someone with whom I was no longer in love? We had been performing in rallentandos for too long; I craved some accelerandos and allegros. Perhaps Joel would actually be relieved if I made a move, but it was hard to predict, as his emotional side had always played second fiddle to his brilliant intellect. During a dinner on March 22, 1990, to launch Pierre's new book, *Towards a Just Society*, to which Joel had contributed a chapter, I observed the two cerebral men who had both played significant roles in my life as they charmed the gathering of Toronto literati. Yes, there were definite parallels between Joel Bell and Pierre Trudeau.

Although my loyalty to Joel prevented me from seriously looking for someone else, I started to harbour fantasies about a new encounter. An aristocratic Englishman wooed me until I realized our lifestyles were incompatible. How could champagne lunches with the polo crowd and weekends on his Saint-Tropez yacht accommodate a concert career? Conflicts would be inevitable. However, it did feel good to be appreciated again; the doldrums at Fallingbrook had been draining my energy. A relationship with more emotional depth and intimacy would require a new partner. Joel, preoccupied with his government lawsuit, did not seem to notice my extended absences.

That year, in addition to a string of solo performances, and the release of my children's album *Paddle to the Sea*, for which I had narrated the story and composed the music, I gave a number of benefit concerts — including one for underprivileged children at Toronto's Dixon Hall and another in support of Nelson Mandela — and received an honorary law degree from Brock University. Backing up Kimberly Richards, who recorded two country songs I had written, provided a welcome return to the familiar recording studios. I visited a Toronto girlfriend, Trish Cullen, who had relocated to Santa Monica, where she was studying composition and conducting. We bicycled along the Venice boardwalk, discussed musical ideas, accidentally exploded her VW convertible in the middle of the Santa Monica Freeway, and picnicked at the Hollywood Bowl. If Trish, already an established film composer in Toronto, could uproot to California to start a new life, why not I? After several stimulating forays to Los Angeles, where I stayed in Moses Znaimer's house in the Hollywood Hills, I became more resolved than ever to investigate the possibility of a fresh life on the West Coast.

Christmas 1990 was approaching, and I suggested to Joel a vacation in San Miguel de Allende. I sensed it would probably be our last trip together, but I had not had the heart to confront him with these inner thoughts. The fundamental differences between us could never be resolved, and I was convinced we both needed new beginnings. Sheldon, whom we were to lose a year later to cancer, met us in Chihuahua, and then a dusty, smoke-filled train swung us along the scenic bends of the Copper Canyon.

San Miguel had changed little except for some new housing developments on its outskirts and the annoying presence of more cars ill-suited to the narrow streets. As I retraced the familiar paths of my youth, mulling over my new resolve to leave the man with whom I had shared the past eight years, my mind wandered back to another life-altering decision I had pondered while treading on the same cobblestones. Twenty-two years earlier, at one of life's junctions, I had chosen music over my intended path of studying English literature. Now I was at another crossroads, with a difficult decision troubling my mind.

Joel flew back home and I went to California where, despite my ambivalence about leaving Canada, I had persuaded Dale, my Vancouver girlfriend, to help me establish a base. With no immediate concert bookings, why rush back to the sub-zero temperatures, grey skies, and icy driveways of Toronto? We window-shopped on Rodeo Drive, attended movie premières in Westwood, and tried on funky clothes on Hollywood Boulevard. Although we were both in our forties, we felt like carefree kids again. One night, while eating corn tortillas in downtown L.A.'s Olivera Street, I imagined I was back in Mexico with my beloved *mariachi* music; the next evening, I was dressed to the nines at the American Music Awards. I spent a day of recording on an album with John Lennon's son Julian, and had brunch with the expatriate balladeer Leonard Cohen. All these contrasting experiences were waiting to be savoured in this complex metropolis — this city of dreams. For the rich, Los Angeles provides a paradise of trendy restaurants, exclusive clubs, and stretch limousines, but struggling actors and writers survive in a competitive jungle where agents and managers manipulate fortunes like cards on a Las Vegas gaming table. For those power brokers of the entertainment industry, life revolves around Studio City, Burbank, and Hollywood, where deals are hammered out over power lunches. Movies and television shows for global consumption are conceptualized, produced, packaged, and sold in legendary Tinsel Town. It is a place built on fantasy, to which people pursuing their dreams have been flocking for decades — a place of year-round sunshine, palm trees,

Pacific surf, and smoggy air. The droves of Mexican gardeners, San Salvadorean maids, Iranian taxi drivers, and Korean merchants that contribute to the ethnic patchwork of L.A., all gravitated to this melting-pot intent on establishing lives better than the ones they left behind. I too had come here in search of a different life. I had already rejected Los Angeles once before, in 1982, but I wanted to give it a second chance. Toronto still provided the security of family and friends, and a man to whom I was still engaged.

A two-bedroom bungalow came vacant next door to Bette, and in no time Dale and I were playing house at 1310 San Ysidro Drive. In the fifties, Marilyn Monroe had apparently been a frequent visitor, as it was the residence of her drama teacher. Tastefully furnished, the place came with everything necessary to run an intermittent life in Beverly Hills: fax machine, filing cabinets, reference library, and photocopier. My flowery pink bedroom and marble Jacuzzi overlooked a hillside of gardenias and camellias. In addition to finding this temporary home in winding Benedict Canyon, another more important occurrence fuelled my feelings of exhilaration. A year before, while travelling in Thailand, Dale had met an American named John Simon. Over the Christmas holidays, while Joel and I were in San Miguel, Dale again ran into John, or Jack, as he was known to his friends, on the Crystal *Harmony* cruise ship. Impressed by his gentle nature and distinguished looks, Dale, my "Celestina," told him that her close friend was planning to move from Toronto to California.

Shortly after my arrival in Los Angeles, Dale made the introduction. A few days later, he asked me out to dinner. In the flickering candlelight of a French restaurant, we offered random fragments from our lives — his days in the U.S. navy and studies at Duke University, my years of touring and recording; the tragic loss of his wife eight years earlier to leukemia; his sons, my albums; his love of classical music, my love of the Pacific coast. His voice was one of the first things to impress me: the strong voice of a man proud of his achievements, yet with a sensitive nature. We eyed each other with curiosity, and I took note of his chiselled features and shock of silver hair. This man was so different from the characters I had expected to meet in L.A.: those jaded and brazen entertainment-industry sharks with the grating telephone voices and leathery "lunch by the pool" complexions.

That night, I hardly slept — my emotions had suddenly been thrown into a mad spin. "Oh, Liona, don't be ridiculous," Dale reprimanded. "Jack is the first single man you've met here. He could be one of these L.A. phonies." But something about his demeanour suggested sincerity, and my better instincts told me he was special. Zsa Zsa Gabor later confided to me, "Dahling, every woman in Beverly Hills tried to catch Mr. Simon, but he was far too elusive."

Almost a week passed before our second date. Perhaps I had not made as much of an impression on him as he had on me — those uncontrollable female insecurities plagued me with self-doubt. Finally, the phone rang and a deep resonant voice spoke my name, asking if I would like to join him for dinner and bring along my guitar — ah music, my favourite way to a man's heart! After "Plaisir d'Amour," Chopin's "Nocturne," and "Recuerdos de la Alhambra," I knew that a tentative romantic note had been struck between us. He reciprocated, playing Mendelssohn and Schubert on the piano. One solitary Julian Bream album comprised his entire guitar collection, but I already sensed that this man was going to learn more about classical guitar than he had ever dreamed possible!

Back in Toronto, storm clouds were gathering. The awful task of explaining to Joel my desire to separate lay ahead. How sad and dejected he would feel when he learned that I wanted to abandon our life together. If only he had been unfaithful, things would be so much easier. There was no need to mention Jack, as my determination for a new life had preceded this recent introduction. Still, Joel was devastated. The pained look in his eyes as he attempted to convince me how right we were for each other was so sad that my stomach twisted into cramps. For nights, I lay awake agonizing, as I knew he must also have done. He wrote loving letters, hoping he could express his emotions better with the written word. If I had believed that marriage counselling would reconcile our basic differences, I would have given it a chance, but during the previous two years, I had become convinced that Joel and I were not suited to be husband and wife, and I had resolved on countless occasions to leave. Although we had shared some glorious times together and had enriched each other's lives, our paths had to diverge.

For the next several months, I flew across the continent burning up frequent flyer points at a mad rate. The awful news that Trish Cullen had died left me in a state of shock for days. In the midst of this emotional turmoil, my mother accompanied me to Canada Week in Bermuda, where in addition to the evening concert, I treated the attentive white-clad crew of our Canadian icebreaker *Skeena* to an informal performance on deck.

In February, the fiercest month in Toronto, I took my family to the Caribbean. Regent Holidays' "First Lady of the Guitar Cruise" featured eight islands in seven days, as well as a home-grown Canadian star. It was to be the MS *Pegasus*'s first and last classical booking. Standing on deck during life-boat drill in the port of Santo Domingo, I flashed back thirty-four years to a similar scene aboard the *Columbia* when we were about to embark from Liverpool on our first transatlantic crossing in 1957. The Boyd Gang was once again on a Greek liner full of Greek waiters and cabin-boys, both ship and men looking slightly the worse for wear. Our cruise director mischievously admitted that *Pegasus* had already sunk once off the Alaskan coast, only to be dredged up by an enterprising tour company — such a comforting thought during a night of turbulent seas.

The island stops were enchanting: snorkelling with my brother and sister in the aquamarine reefs off Bequia, market-hopping with Mother in Antigua, and retracing our footsteps in old San Juan. As I sat in my cabin contemplating a future with Jack in Los Angeles, I fingered out "Lullaby for My Love," a composition I had just written for him. Stan Klees, the organizer of Canada's Juno Awards, danced salsas and lambadas with me during steel-drum deck parties, and

ignoring the rock and rolling of old lady *Pegasus*, I gave a concert of
Fortin, Falú, and Lauro.

The Caribbean "gig" provided our family with the chance to be
together for a week, something we had not experienced since San
Miguel. What a salutary way to combine my work with a family
reunion! Three months after we bid farewell to *Pegasus*, she caught
fire and sank back to the salt-water cradle of Davy Jones's locker. I
imagined sea creatures gliding silently along the corridors towards
my barnacle-encrusted suite, and the stage where my concerts were
held draped in seaweed and shells.

My romance with Jack began to intensify, yet I felt obliged to
host a Passover Seder at Fallingbrook. Joel could not believe I was
serious about leaving him; California must be a temporary whim I
would get over once I came to my senses. By May, however, I felt
it was time to tell Joel about Jack. As I stood beside him in the
provincial legislature building and accepted the Order of Ontario, I
was overcome with guilt. Here was the man who had loyally supported me in countless situations, battled the record companies on
my behalf, and sorted out my business and legal affairs. I flashed
back to our adventures on the Missinaibi, our travels around the
world, his attentiveness whenever I or my family had been ill, and
his tolerance of the *Persona* rehearsals at Fallingbrook. Yet now I
had to tell him that I was involved with another man. In a four-page
letter, the most difficult letter I have ever had to compose, I tried
to console him and take the blame for the final disintegration of
our relationship.

Jack and I were sharing the magical feelings of being in love.
For years, I had harboured fantasies of meeting such a refined,
intelligent, and sensitive man. No one had ever captivated my heart
this way, and I felt my defences and reservations about marriage
dissolving in the euphoria of our days and nights together. Jack was
my perfect lover, my prince charming — the ultimate romantic,
who seduced me with handwritten poems and bouquets of flowers,
candlelight dinners, and a Van Cleef & Arpels diamond engagement

ring. There was a difference of more than twenty years between us, but his youthful spirit and zest for life belied the gap between our birthdates. My parents were overjoyed and his four sons embraced me with obvious affection, pleased that their father had finally found happiness. I was fascinated to hear about his adventures as a young naval officer during the Second World War, his brief acting career in Hollywood, his struggles to start a small glass company that eventually expanded into the largest chain in the western United States, and his trips around the globe with the Young Presidents' Organization. I was dazzled by his photographic memory and his vast store of knowledge, while he marvelled at my ability to compose and my dexterity on the finger-board. Love had cast its spell over both of us, making even the mundane enchanting.

There were times, however, when I could not help questioning how my whole life had suddenly been transformed. Was Liona Boyd really about to trade in her single status and independence for a new role as Mrs. Simon? Were we rushing into marriage, each projecting our preconceived ideas of an ideal partner on the other? Could my career survive a more domestic lifestyle than I had chosen in the past? Surely these occasional misgivings and pre-nuptial nerves were to be expected. Finding such a husband seemed a miracle; I was going to make this relationship the focus of my life.

Simon Fraser University in British Columbia bestowed on me an honorary doctorate of law on June 6, 1991, and I could see the glow in Jack's eyes as he watched me play guitar in blue velvet cap and gown. Weekend getaways to Newport Beach and Santa Barbara gave us long hours to explore the intricate subtleties of our two personalities. Yes, there were differences to be reconciled; I had been bathed in liberal ideologies and philosophy during my years with Pierre and Joel, and here I was with a Republican! We listened to each other's views on important issues and found that, in spite of labels, there was a remarkable confluence in our thoughts. Rejoicing in our similar tastes and preferences, we felt that some kind of divine destiny had brought us together. All those times I had stayed in

Beverly Hills our paths had been drawing close, yet the timing had not been right until then.

When my lease expired, I moved into Jack's house on Doheny Road, where our neighbours were Frank Sinatra and Merv Griffin. The house backed on to Dean Martin's former estate and Rachmaninoff, in the thirties, had chosen to live in a house a few blocks south of us. My family was curious to meet the man who had swept me off my feet, so we flew to Toronto and he was introduced to the Boyd Gang. My parents were impressed by my fiancé's obvious devotion and showed him the city where their daughter had spent most of her life. We danced with the colourful crowds at Caribana, and I introduced him to the world of recording when I had to re-mix the drum levels on "Renaissance Fair" from a jazzy new age album I had just completed called *Dancing on the Edge*. After I performed at Baddeck's music festival, we took advantage of a trip to Nova Scotia to explore the rugged coast of the Cabot Trail and retrace the steps of pirates and rum-runners on the old French colony of Saint-Pierre and Miquelon.

In the fall, after the tension of the Los Angeles riots, we travelled to a World Presidents' Organization conference in Brussels, where, with Jack's international assortment of friends and business associates, we attended lectures by Margaret Thatcher, Henry Mancini, and Deepak Chopra, among others. Having flown back from Paris for two days to play at a Montreal convention, I lunched with Pierre Trudeau. We walked through the city streets together — two old friends nostalgically reminiscing about times past. Cautiously, I told him about my decision to leave Joel and my joy at having become engaged. By phone a few weeks later, Pierre jokingly reprimanded my future husband for stealing "one of Canada's national treasures"! Jack and I resumed our European holiday by visiting Bernard Maillot's Savarez guitar-string factory in Montpellier, where we watched in fascination as copper and silver strings were spun, polished, measured, and packaged for guitarists' fingers around the world. Then we sojourned at several private châteaux in the rustic hamlets of Provence.

Later that year, Gavriil Popov, the mayor of Moscow, invited us to a New Year's Eve extravaganza. It was my first visit to the legendary city of the czars, which in the fall of 1991 was struggling with the incipient birth pangs of democracy. Mikhail Gorbachev and Boris Yeltsin were vying for power, promising major reforms in Soviet government and society. Anticipating inedible pork stews and salty salami, we packed a supply of health food to snack on when the Russian cuisine proved inedible. At week's end, we braved the icy winds and sub-zero temperatures to distribute our left-over bounty on Arbat Street, where Muscovites were discovering the challenges of capitalism in a proliferation of stalls hawking wooden handicrafts, western cosmetics, and clothing. We donated our food to destitute old ladies in moth-eaten woolen coats who kissed our hands in gratitude. The long queues of people patiently waiting to purchase their meagre rations of meat and vegetables made us realize how fortunate we were to live in the West.

During a private tour of the fabled Kremlin, I mischievously played the first chords of "O Canada" on Lenin's piano and, when no one was looking, irreverently lay on Catherine the Great's bed for a quick photo. On New Year's Eve, we joined the elite throng in the ballroom of the Kremlin, where Mayor Popov's gala was under way. The cream of Moscow society — politicians, scientists, and writers — were gorging on caviar and vodka. We sensed such a feeling of excitement in the air: a palpable hope for a more progressive system of government and a brighter future for the Russian people. At eleven o'clock, the gala performance in which I was taking part began, as guests sat beneath balloons at long tables overflowing with cabbage pies, sausage, caviar, and pâtés. When the Soviet Army Chorus belted out a hearty rendition of "God Bless America," I was struck by the irony. Here we were in the former centre of Communist policy-making, cheering "America, land of the free"! I was the only non-Russian to perform, and I realized what a great privilege it was to be able to communicate through music to our appreciative hosts. The warm audience response was gratifying, and my elegant tuxedoed fiancé looked as proud as a peacock escorting me back to our table. The concert, featuring a cellist, a tenor, a symphony orchestra, and soloists from the Bolshoi, concluded as the Moscow skies erupted with explosions of fireworks. The Soviet Union was now officially over. In its place had emerged the Commonwealth of Independent States. But although the hammer and sickle had been replaced, bitter rivalries persisted among the higher government echelons. Nevertheless, my guitar and I had been present in the Kremlin at a historic moment — the emergence of a new era in Russia's long and troubled evolution.

Back in the sunnier climes of Los Angeles, after a concert in Washington, D.C., Jack and I busied ourselves with wedding preparations. I decided to wear the gown the CBC had designed for me for the 1982 Juno Awards. With its layers of white sequins and embroidered lace petals, it was perfect for my wedding, and I had been storing it in my closet over the years with such a purpose vaguely in mind. The Canadian Maple Leaf and the Stars and Stripes flapped together in the breeze as guests pulled up to the Regent Beverly Wilshire Hotel, where a classical trio and bouquets of butterfly orchids greeted their arrival. My mother and sister fussed around with my hair and dress, enjoying every moment.

As I walked down the aisle on February 2, 1992, on the arm of my father, I could hardly believe that this was really happening. There was my tall brother, Damien, looking handsome in his tuxedo; a pink-sequined Dale, my maid of honour; and Mother, sitting in the front row smiling at us all. The moment was extra poignant for those familiar with the loss in Jack's previous life, and for those who never thought the day would come when I would put a wedding band on my guitar-playing fingers. Vivien's nine-year-old son, Colin, acted as ring-bearer, carrying the gold bands in a velvet-lined miniature guitar case that my inventive brother had sewn onto a cream satin cushion.

Once the ceremony was over, we led the dancing to "If I Fall in Love," knowing that everyone in the room shared our happiness. Later, I took to the stage for a few pieces, including "Lullaby for My

Love," and this was followed by a whirl of toasts and speeches. Jack swept me up to our suite, along with mountains of ribboned gift boxes and a guitar that pleaded not to be left behind in the excitement. A few days at the San Ysidro Ranch offered us rest, relaxation, and horseback riding in the scenic foothills of Montecito, where John and Jacqueline Kennedy had honeymooned. We looked into each other's eyes, ecstatic in the knowledge that we had found each other at last.

Three weeks later, to assuage my muse, I hit the road again for a fourteen-city tour, but this time in the company of a brand-new road manager — my husband! Our life together became an exciting mix of international travel, private times with Jack's family, mountain hikes, theatre, and concerts. There were invitations to Zsa Zsa's horse ranch, dinner at the Playboy mansion, the inauguration of Jack's cousin as mayor of Beverly Hills, picnics under the stars at the Hollywood Bowl, charity events, and private parties. We often had to beg off just to preserve our quiet times together. In our garden of palms, olive trees, oleander bushes, and birds of paradise, I composed "Habanera" and "Preludio Poetico" on a blanket spread for me by Ofelia, our Mexican maid.

We decided that we needed a new house with better office and entertainment space. While house-hunting, we saw many homes, including a few belonging to celebrities. Jacqueline Smith's was too old-fashioned, Sylvester Stallone's ranch too far away, Cher's villa lacked good views, Burt Bacharach and Carole Bayer Sager's place was overly quaint, and Goldie Hawn's former house was too "country" for our taste. Eventually, we concluded that nothing we viewed pleased us entirely, so we decided to build. In the spring of '93, the old house was demolished and one of L.A.'s renowned architects designed us a "contemporary Mediterranean." The new house featured spacious offices, walk-in closets twice the size of my Parisian accommodations, a domed-ceiling music conservatory, a guest wing, a gym, a library, a huge sunny kitchen, wraparound balconies, and magnificent views of the city to the south and

Greystone Park's eucalyptus trees to the north. Jack and I were involved with every decision along the way, from structural engineering to tiling, and interior decorators shuttled us around showrooms to choose plumbing fixtures, fabrics, appliances, and marble.

During the year of construction, we opted for beach-side living on the stretch of the Pacific Coast Highway known as Malibu. Here surfers' rusty jeeps and beat-up convertibles shared the road with Rolls-Royces and Ferraris. The rolling foothills and winding canyons concealed hideaways belonging to Barbra Streisand and Nick Nolte, while perched on the ocean cliffs sat the estates of Johnny Carson, Julie Andrews, and Bob Dylan. We leased a house in Paradise Cove which had sweeping ocean vistas and 150 steps to a sandy, kelp-strewn beach that expanded or diminished with the changing tides. White-washed walls blanketed in crimson bougainvillea delineated a grassy back lawn that was, to my delight, the playground of two wild rabbits and their progeny. Our guest apartment and pool attracted a stream of house guests, who found the sunny, blue skies and lullabies of breaking Pacific surf hard to resist.

Tina Turner had rented the place before us, and on the other side of our wall of crimson bougainvillea, Olivia Newton-John had built her dream house. The charming Australian who had risen to superstardom in the seventies suggested that her subterranean bomb shelter might be a good place to record my new CD, *Classically Yours*. After testing it, we realized that although faint rumblings of breaking surf might have enhanced a New Age album, my classical recording required absolute silence. Jack and I were frequent guests at the home of our lovely neighbour, who used my guitar to compose new songs. It was there that I was introduced to Robert Redford, who mentioned that he had been collecting my records for years. The handsome "Sundance Kid" invited me to attend the orchestral scoring of his movie *Quiz Show*, and revealed that he had always dreamed of playing classical guitar. I realized, as I sat in the darkened control room at the MGM studio while he held my hands in order to check my nails and my fingertip callouses, that I would have been the envy of millions of women. With those charismatic eyes and tousled blond hair, he proved even more irresistible than on the big screen.

Jack and I alternated brisk morning walks up in the hills with runs along the ocean's edge, filling our lungs with air scented by orange and eucalyptus trees. My previous life in Toronto seemed like another world, and when I returned to those familiar Canadian theatres and airports, I experienced a strange dislocated feeling, realizing that I now had a separate existence in California. I set about composing a three-movement musical tribute to Canada, entitled "My Land of Hiawatha (Spirit of the Moving Waters, Spirit of the Forest, and Spirit of the West Wind)," most of which was completed while staying at Baja California's Rosarito Beach. Perhaps the distance from Canada fuelled my inspiration. One of our Malibu neighbours, David Foster, introduced me to Barbra Streisand, who looked puzzled when I whispered we once had a boyfriend in common. "You came before Margaret and I came after" caused her to smile at the memory of Pierre.

In November, tragedy struck. The Malibu hills, which had been carpeted in yellow daisies, Californian poppies, and sweet-smelling chaparral, were left charred naked by the worst firestorm in years. Whipped by scorching desert winds, the Santa Anas, uncontrollable fires had raced up and down the canyons, burning all the way to the ocean front. Not realizing the severity of the Malibu fire, Jack and I set off for meetings in Beverly Hills, presuming that it would be contained within a matter of hours. But radio reports became more frenzied and a sky-high plume of smoke could be seen for miles. Fire-fighting reinforcements were being flown in from neighbouring states, but houses and ranches were already being devoured by the monstrous conflagration. A full-scale emergency evacuation started, as people frantically rescued their pets and valuables. Horrific live pictures from helicopter cameras revealed the magnitude of the disaster. The Pacific Coast Highway had been closed down to allow the passage of fire-fighting equipment and thousands of fleeing residents, leaving us no choice but to return to Beverly Hills, where we sat anxiously glued to the TV watching fire-fighters and water bombers trying valiantly to contain the blaze. We phoned our neighbours, who assured us that our little stretch of paradise was still safe, but said that people were hosing their roofs as a precaution. I began to worry about my guitars and stalwart bears, Mosey and Tonka, left alone in the house. When I was five years old and my family was holidaying in England, the sea wall near our campsite had caught fire, throwing me into a panic as I tried to persuade my parents to run back and rescue Mosey from our tent. Some things in life never change.

When night fell, the images of Malibu ablaze became more hellish on screen as the full extent of the fires became apparent. When we called our neighbours again for an update, we detected panic in their voices. "The fire just jumped around Pepperdine University and is heading towards us. You'd better try to get here, as we're all evacuating." Realizing it would be expedient to return, we looked at each other in silence, slipped on running shoes, and in separate cars started the devious drive through the San Fernando Valley and the twisting canyons of Kanan Dume.

As we neared the ocean, we were met by a stream of loaded cars and horse trailers heading in the opposite direction. Police at road blocks demanded proof of residency, then warned us to exercise extreme caution. Against the night skies, an eerie, orange glow silhouetted the burning ridges; smoke masked the hills and white ash sifted down on us like snowflakes. Our neighbourhood was still two miles away from the fire line, but with the fickle "devil winds," it was no time to take chances. We frantically loaded up guitars, bears, photos, musical scores, and Jack's Picasso, Renoir, and Chagall paintings. The noises from wailing police sirens, helicopters, and water bombers were followed by eerie silences punctuated by the beating of our hearts. When our cars were piled to capacity, we bade farewell to the house, praying that it would survive.

The Spirit of the West Wind was kind to us and the fire abated by daybreak, but 350 houses had been burned to the foundations and thousands of acres of wilderness destroyed. Our beautiful hillsides were strewn with blackened palm trees, baked cacti, fried bougain-villeas, and the smouldering remains of people's dream homes — such a terrible toll in terms of both human suffering and ecological waste. I wept at the thought of the countless innocent creatures that had been burned at the hands of arsonists, and of the British film director who had perished trying to save his pet cat. Our life was unaffected by the tragedy, but I shuddered to think how different things might have been had we rented farther down the Pacific Coast Highway. Even with her resilient residents, poor Malibu would take a long time to heal. The Canadian media interviewed me for eyewitness accounts of the disaster, and I joined local artists for two concerts to benefit the fire victims, whose cheerful spirits and bravery filled me with admiration.

In December, I agreed to do a concert in an old fortress over-looking the Gulf of Acapulco, to benefit a children's charity, Para Los Niños. "Señor Jack, we promise to your wife berry berry good sound system of Germany, and berry good pink colour lights," the techni-cal man insisted. My husband, a novice in dealing with sound men, felt confident that all would be in place as promised by four o'clock the following day, but I knew Latinos and felt a little sceptical. The next afternoon their "berry good system" had been replaced by ten apologetic Mexicans positioning five hundred chairs. "Sorry, Mrs., all good speakers used for especial Christmas shows. In one hour will arrive for you different speakers. Please no worry." My promoter was nowhere to be found when the crew began to bathe me in jaundiced light, which alternately blinded me or left me in darkness. The "berry good pink colour lights" were obviously being used in their "especial Christmas shows" along with the speakers.

The monitors were completely broken, and no unplugging or rewiring of cables could make them functional. One speaker made a brave effort at amplifying my guitar, but the other emitted a deaf-ening roar resembling Niagara Falls. "*Muy bien tenemos sonido!*" the triumphant technician yelled to his compadres, ecstatic to hear any sound at all. I despaired, knowing that three television stations planned to cover the show. I am often amazed how insensitive the average person's ears are to musical sound. After the concert, congratulatory crowds assured me that the sound had been great! Maybe their hearing had become so impaired by the loud music levels polluting our world that they could no longer distinguish subtleties of sound and judged on volume alone. Nevertheless, the concert received a standing ovation, and enthusiastic locals offered to show us the sights. Our itinerary had already been arranged, however. The patrons of Para Los Niños, the Baron and Baroness di Portanova, had invited us to stay with them.

As we entered Arabesque, the most spectacular home in Acapulco, I could almost hear Robin Leach's awe-filled voice speaking to me as I gazed in amazement at the huge Moorish arches, stone minaret, and life-size sculptured camels on a terrace large enough to accommodate helicopter landings. A funicular railway, which glided up and down the hillside to Arabesque's six levels, transported us to the guest suite, La Mariposa, with its private turquoise pool. Our rooms were decorated with gold and pink *mariposas*: butterfly bathroom fixtures, butterfly headboard, butterfly silk curtains, butterfly sheets, rugs and mirrors; even the tables and chairs were carved in the shape of *mariposas*. Bizarre surrealist sculptures of female heads sprouting butterfly wings, and human hands and feet emerging from ceramic eggs recalled the works of Bosch or Dali. The James Bond movie *License to Kill* had featured Arabesque, but neither film nor photograph could do it justice. The enormous open-air living room and its wraparound pool gave the illusion of stretching far out into the Bay of Acapulco. A heady aroma from agapanthus, frangipanis, and tuberose blossoms wafted from large vases, while operatic music played like a movie soundtrack underscoring the splendid opulence. Our bags were whisked away to be unpacked while iced hibiscus juice was offered for refreshment.

At cocktail hour, Sandra, the beautiful, buxom baroness, draped in orange and purple Arabian silks and accompanied by the debonair Italian baron, emerged to welcome us. The Portanovas were munificent hosts, and were in their element entertaining friends from around the globe: on the bar signed photos of Henry Kissinger, Placido Domingo, and Julio Iglesias shared space with those of Jackie Onassis and Frank Sinatra. We were introduced to the other guests: curvaceous Joan Collins, poured into a Ferragamo catsuit, and her blond British lover, Robin; Marianna Nicolescu, the corpulent Romanian diva, resplendent in turquoise velours and a gold-plated headpiece straight out of *Aida*; Kathleen Hearst and her Greek shipping tycoon, Spiros Milonis; Lucky Roosevelt, Reagan's former chief of White House protocol; Abe Rosenthal, editor of *The New York Times*; and lovely Anastasia Kostoff, with her British novelist husband, Roderick Mann. I felt as though I had been transported into a Fellini movie as I tiptoed down the stone staircase in a white-and-gold Grecian robe with my elegant husband at my side.

The Portanovas were consummate raconteurs whose dinner conversation, which flowed from politics and religion to society gossip, was always witty and urbane. Sandra and Rick shared a great appreciation for the performing arts, and their largesse extended to many charities, including an orphanage for Acapulco's poorest.

Joan Collins and Robin fried themselves in sun-tan oil before lunch, Marianna trilled soprano exercises in preparation for La Scala, and I began to work on two new guitar compositions: "Danza de las Mariposas de Mexico" and "Aria de Portanova." On New Year's Eve, I chatted with a giggly Melanie Griffith and Don Johnson, several Mexican tycoons, a Kuwaiti prince, and a number of titled Europeans. The table centrepiece was a sixty-foot miniature railroad with trains transporting tiny tequila glasses to the guests. As I fingered my dainty mother-of-pearl spoon, scooping caviar from its delicate jewel-encrusted silver eggshell, I realized that my guitar had let me participate in a lifestyle that few are privileged to experience. I played in Arabesque's disco, where mauve and turquoise lights shone from sculptured alcoves. Marianna sang excerpts from *La Traviata* atop the marble staircase, the dance floor throbbed with Brazilian *lambadas*, *mariachis* strummed, and fireworks lit up the bay to welcome in 1993.

On our final evening, as we sat aboard the billionaire Enrique Molina's yacht watching crimson washes of sunset, my mind wandered back to 1967, to the innocent days I had spent with my family camping on the Acapulco beach at the Old Gringo's Trailer Park. Who was that girl playing guitar scales and university-entrance repertoire under a palm tree? Could she ever have dreamed up Arabesque and the Baron and Baroness di Portanova?

24

Noblesse
Oblige

♪

In 1993, the World Presidents' Organization was holding a seminar in Egypt, where I was able to arrange a simultaneous concert booking. The Cairo Opera House was packed, and I received one of the most effusive reviews of my life, with a headline that read "Beyond Virtuosity!" After some of the caustic criticisms my concerts had generated in Canada, it was gratifying to be so enthusiastically received in the Land of the Pharaohs. A private jet belonging to the Aga Khan flew us to Abu Simbel, near the Sudanese border, where a choir of beaming Nubian children in orange robes clapped their hands and chanted welcoming songs. Gigantic stone statues of King Ramses II and his Queen Nefertari had been relocated there after the building of the Aswan High Dam. The unbelievable proportions of these sun-struck symbols of antiquity, the enigmatic structure of the pyramids, the silent Sphinx, and the hieroglyphics in the Valley of the Kings left me with a profound sense of connection with the past. Who were these industrious and creative people who lived four thousand years ago, believed in an afterlife, and even embalmed their pet cats to accompany them to the world beyond?

The Aswan Dam and the great Temple of Karnak in Luxor were no longer merely names from my history book. One evening, dressed in djellabas, we rode camels through the desert darkness led only by stars, a crescent moon, and our guide's flaming torches. Giza's great pyramids rose against the obsidian desert sky. Balanced precariously between the two humps of my swaying camel, I listened to the music from *Lawrence of Arabia* playing in my head and was transported to a distant era, long since eroded by the shifting sands of the great Sahara. The magic of that night will always stay with me.

In January 1994, we moved into our new Beverly Hills home, the Peach House, named for its colour and its peach trees. On January 17, at 4:31 a.m., the vertical shaking of a 6.8 earthquake hurtled our sleeping bodies from the bed. Afraid that our new house would tumble down on us, we clung to each other in the doorway, deafened by the quake's stultifying roar, and everyone's burglar alarms, which had been triggered by the earth's gyrations. We could see, from our curtainless windows, explosions lighting up the night sky as if an aerial battle was being fought between Beverly Hills and Century City. Later, we learned that the electrical arcing of transformers created those dramatic fireworks. The city of Los Angeles was not blowing up, as I had first believed.

"God, this is 'the Big One'!" Jack yelled, stumbling around in the dark in search of his flashlight and portable radio. Aftershocks kept our adrenalin flowing, as police, fire, and ambulance sirens wailed in the pre-dawn darkness. We gave a prayer of thanks to have survived with our house intact, especially as reports of mass destruction in the valley, fires, and collapsed freeways reached us via the battery-operated radio. All we had suffered was cracked plaster and shattered nerves.

Somehow, the news media succeeded in contacting me for a live hook-up with CBC's Newsworld. As we were about to start filming in the studio, a 4.8 aftershock hit and tiles from the ceiling began to fall. We raced down to the safety of the street, where the interview proceeded. Having now covered fires and earthquakes, I joked that I had become Canada's L.A. disaster correspondent. As a precaution, Jack and I spent the next week sleeping at ground level with flashlights, shoes, and bicycle helmets at the ready. Aftershocks were to continue into May, and each time we felt one, we made a mad scramble into the garden. Jack, who had previously made light of my "Canadian earthquake phobia," now shared it. Amazingly, only sixty-one people died, but nine thousand were injured, twenty-billion dollars of property was lost, and countless lives were changed forever.

The next disaster to strike was a series of mud slides. Torrential rains had caused the fire-denuded hillsides to smother houses along the Pacific coast. Jack and I left for a cruise concert in Australia before the CBC could reach me, but Mother Nature's rages still dogged us: a cyclone sent mountainous fifty-foot waves crashing up to the eighth deck for two days. My life in Toronto might have seemed pretty uneventful during the previous few years, but riots, fires, earthquakes, and cyclones I could happily have done without.

After innumerable housekeeper interviews, we hired a middle-aged Sri Lankan who added to our happy life. Having worked for twenty years for the ruling political family of Sri Lanka, Dervin had plenty of experience running a busy household, and he fast became an expert with my Canon computer. To my delight, I discovered that he had been trained as a masseur by his former boss and was able to oblige me with back rubs when I felt stiff from guitar practice. Our new houseman had a wife and daughter in Colombo and another daughter at school in California, and took pride in supporting them while adding order to our complicated lives.

There was only one small detail missing from my fairy-tale existence with the man and the house of my dreams. "There are two means of refuge from the miseries of life . . ." wrote Albert Schweitzer. "Music and cats"! All my life I had longed for a feline friend, but with my mother's and Joel's allergies and my busy travel schedule, it had never been feasible. Whenever I visited homes where one of those delightful creatures lived, I fussed over them, promising myself that when the time was right, I would have my own furry companion. Jack gradually began to share my enthusiasm, even attending cat shows to become familiar with the different breeds. One beautiful and affectionate Shaded Silver American Shorthair impressed us with her soft, silky coat, enormous emerald eyes, and trustful disposition. Six months later, after an extensive search for this rare combination, we located one who had just produced kittens. All three were little males, but my preference for a female was forgotten the minute I felt my lovely Muffin jump into my lap and start to purr. He was still only two months old and needed another few weeks of his mother's nurturing, so photos were all we could take home that day.

In May, after returning from Cuba, where I performed in the Matanzas Opera House and the Teatro Nacional of Havana, we headed fifty miles south to collect our little charge. He meowed disconsolately all the way back to Beverly Hills, but settled down after much stroking and some tasty tuna. Muffin became at ease in his palatial surroundings, scampering up and down the stairs and performing acrobatics with his toy mice. Each night, the gentle little creature crept onto the bed with us and slept curled up between our pillows. When the morning birds started to sing in the oleander bushes, he gingerly tiptoed around the covers nuzzling our necks or sneaking sips of water from the bedside glasses. In my music room, he amused himself playing with balls of discarded guitar strings, chewing them and chasing them around the floor. Together we spent the afternoons playing with the strings each in our own fashion. Jack and I became more and more besotted with Muffin; from the moment he entered our lives, we turned into confirmed "cat people." There was now absolutely nothing that could possibly be added to my complete life in the Peach House, and I realized that these times would surely be among my happiest memories.

The Toronto World Wildlife Fund organizers invited me perform at their fund-raising gala on October 13, 1993, and asked me to sit next to their honorary president, Prince Philip, who greeted me with a twinkle in his pale blue eyes. When he noticed that the fork was missing from my place setting, he scurried around the buffet tables of the crowded Trillium Restaurant, returning triumphantly to my side, fork in hand, a few moments later. What fun to be waited on by royalty! *Noblesse oblige.*

The prince proved a delightful dinner companion, sharing anecdotes of his extensive travels. Was this really the Queen's husband chuckling mischievously as he told me how, one night in Labrador while balancing on a hastily constructed wooden "loo" outside his tent in the pouring rain, he was bitten by mosquitoes and blackflies on certain unmentionable body parts that he had neglected to spray? I sympathized, recounting my bug experiences from forays behind the bushes on the Missinaibi River — such a refined topic for royal dinner conversation! Prince Philip had been president of the WWF for many years and I was impressed by how he willingly lent his name to countless functions on behalf of this fine organization.

I had to excuse myself to perform "My Land of Hiawatha," but he insisted I return to the same chair when I was through. Lucky me to have the best seat in the house! I sat enjoying the Nylons' lively numbers, while the prince hummed along to "All I Have to Do Is Dream" and "The Lion Sleeps Tonight (Wimoweh)" or chuckled, whispering humorous commentary in my ear. I should have guessed this man was born under the sign of Gemini. A week later, in a registered letter from Windsor Castle, he wrote: "Fund-raising events are seldom unmitigated pleasure!! but your company at Ontario Place made it a very happy evening for me."

Soon afterwards, on December 10, I was invited to perform at a black-tie tribute to Martin Scorsese. Six hundred of Hollywood's heavyweights turned out to honour the director of such films as *Raging Bull* and *The Age of Innocence*. Scorsese was presented with the Britannia Award by Prince Philip's youngest son, Prince Edward, to whom I was introduced. Charles Bronson whispered that *The Best of Liona Boyd* was in his collection, Shirley MacLaine raved about the guitar tone and the draping of my skirt, Michelle Pfeiffer explained how she had once played classical guitar but lost patience, Sid Caesar gave me a wink and a thumbs-up, Scorsese pumped my hand, and Monty Hall hugged me in appreciation. I was spinning from all the celebrity encounters when an English voice addressed me. "Would you be available to perform for the Duke of Edinburgh Awards?" My ears pricked up at the mention of my royal acquaintance. "I am here with Prince Edward, but would like to invite you to Scotland to play for Prince Philip." Never one to miss an opportunity to serenade my favourite member of the Royal Family, I agreed to take my guitar to Glasgow.

The gala event was to benefit an organization that rewards enterprising students who have demonstrated excellence in a wide variety of fields. Once again, I was given the seat of honour beside Prince Philip. As the bagpipers piped him in, I could see looks of curiosity on the patrician faces of the ladies seated close by. "I would like to introduce you to Lady Butter," one of the guests chimed with an upper-crust accent. I suppressed a giggle as the titillating thought of introducing her to my film producer acquaintance Cubby Broccoli fleetingly came to mind. The prince offered compliments on my playing and concert gown, but complained about the green footstool, which was looking slightly the worse for wear. Like an admiral surveying his fleet, he did not miss a thing. When I returned home, it was promptly given a spray of gold paint. Royal commands must be heeded!

In the company of Dale, who had joined me in Scotland, I drove to Loch Lomond for a lunch of salty kippers. We then spent a day exploring Edinburgh, reminiscing about our adventures around the world, our romances, and our plans for the future. I hugged her goodbye in the Chicago airport, unaware it was to be our last time together. A month later, the vivacious woman who had been my best friend was killed when her boyfriend's car plunged over the Vancouver sea wall into the waters of False Creek. The senseless death of someone so full of life was incomprehensible. Instead of playing guitar at her wedding, as I had always promised I would, I was asked to play at her funeral. "Recuerdos de la Alhambra" was all my fingers could manage. Friends and family had flown in from all over the world; even Prince Philip sent his condolences. I will always feel the loss of her generous spirit, which touched my life in so many ways. "Serenades for the Seasons," from *Classically Yours*, was dedicated to the memory of my dear friend, at whose Vancouver Island summer home much of the music had been composed.

The success of my Glasgow concert led to an invitation to perform at Harewood House, in November 1995, for the Outward Bound Trust, which is supported by the Duke of Edinburgh Awards Foundation. Two orchestral engagements with the Greensboro Symphony the day before forced me to "red-eye" it from North Carolina via Chicago to Manchester, where I was picked up and driven to the grand country estate of Lord and Lady Harewood. In the Gallery, where I was to play, paintings by Titian, Bellini, and Tintoretto hung in opulent gold frames between Chippendale mirrors, carved pelmets, and candelabras.

At the dining table, with Prince Philip on my right and the white-bearded Earl of Harewood on my left, any symptoms of jet-lag vanished. The duke amused me with accounts of his recent trip to Australia and his summer cruise aboard the royal yacht *Britannia*. When I performed Panin's "Eskimo Dance," my own "Spirit of the West Wind," and "Asturiana," two Bach selections, and a couple of lively Latin numbers, the microphone was unnecessary. The wooden floors and high carved ceilings provided excellent acoustics and, to Prince Philip's approval, I played "*au naturel.*" A firework finale with uniformed guards "beating the retreat" concluded the gala. During dinner, my favourite prince had generously invited me to fly to London in his private jet the following day.

At the Leeds Hilton, I sank exhausted into the pillows only to be rudely awakened at 3:00 a.m. by fire alarms. Stumbling around in the dark, unable to locate light switches or shoes, I opened the door to see guests in various states of undress heading towards the fire escape. Wrapped in only my flimsy silk robe, I joined in the descent to the street level, where firemen ushered us out into the freezing night air. Trembling with cold, we picked our way through icy puddles and into a tunnel a hundred yards from the hotel, where fire trucks were beginning to line up. A chivalrous man covered me with his jacket, then, following the example of Sir Walter Raleigh, who placed his cloak over puddles for Queen Elizabeth I, let me balance my bare frozen toes on his leather shoes. Only a few hours before, I had been toasty warm beside my royal dinner companion, and now I was about to catch my death of cold from the icy pavement. After what seemed like an eternity, the hotel was declared safe, and I raced upstairs to thaw my feet in a hot tub. "It was very kind and generous of you to make the long trip to Leeds and to give that marvellous performance," Prince Philip later wrote. "I hope you realize how much pleasure it gave everyone that evening. I am only dreadfully sorry that your night was disturbed by the fire alarm. Jet lag is bad enough without any further interruptions to a night's sleep!"

A few hours later, the prince's valet and I were driven to the airport. Awaiting us was a shining Hawker Siddeley 146 with the British Union Jack painted on its tail. While His Royal Highness was visiting a local bakery, I chatted with the crew, sat in the Queen's chair, tested out her "loo," and nibbled on crustless cucumber sandwiches, experiencing a sensation of unreality. The valet, security officers, and pilot playfully drew lots for the last copy of my *Christmas Dreams* CD as we awaited Prince Philip's arrival. To my surprise, he took the controls and flew the plane himself! Bumping through woolly layers of grey cumulus, I was relieved to learn he had thousands of hours of experience in the cockpit. After landing us at an American base in Norfolk, H.R.H consented to a cabin photo with "Lunch," his furry hedgehog mascot. A quick kiss on the cheek and my charming prince had vanished into the morning rain.

The telephone rang six months later. "Buckingham Palace calling for a Miss Boyd," pealed a high-pitched British voice. "Hang on for Sir Guy Acland." Perhaps Prince Philip wanted me to perform at another fund-raiser? The offer was even better — the *ne plus ultra* of bookings — a recital on June 20, 1996, in Windsor Castle for the

Queen, the Duke of Edinburgh, and some of their friends. Thrilled by the honour, I composed a piece inspired by a documentary I had seen of Elizabeth and Philip's early romantic years at Windsor.

Jack and I flew to London early, to allow a few days of recuperation from jet-lag. We lunched with fellow Torontonian Conrad Black, publisher of the London *Daily Telegraph*; caught up with our friend Charles Fawcett, the former French resistance hero who rescued Marc Chagall and hundreds more from the Nazis; braved the crowds at Wimbledon; sipped cocktails at the House of Lords with Lord and Lady Wedgewood; rubbed shoulders with Ivana Trump; and dined with Gordon Getty (the only classical composer billionaire I know).

On the afternoon of my "Windsor gig," one of the Queen's Mews cars chauffeured us to the castle. After tea and shortbread in our "Casson" suite, we were led across the courtyard to inspect the Queen's Guard Chamber, where I would play. Not one detail had been missed by the courteous staff, who had assembled a gold-trimmed, red-carpeted stage and positioned spotlights to illuminate my hands and pink-brocade gown, which was designed by Gilles Savard.

Over cocktails, Prince Philip introduced us to the charming Queen Mother and Princess Margaret. The Queen, a regal vision in orange silk, emeralds, and diamonds, seemed in good spirits after her day at Ascot. Joining us for dinner in the White Hall were a few members of the Court, along with the Duke and Duchess of Argyll. During the meal, Her Majesty conversed with the person to her right, and we guests did likewise, until the "sweet" was served, signalling a shift to the left, a royal tradition. Meanwhile, her seven corgi dogs, one of which had earlier come perilously close to biting off my nose, roamed at our feet. The menu was printed in French — Queue de Lotte Murat, Couronne de Cailles Pompadour, Glâcé au Caramel — and the meal served by gloved waiters.

After dinner, we joined the small group of the Queen and Prince Philip's friends from Ascot who had been invited to the recital. My Vasquez Rubio guitar, a sonorous instrument made for me by a Mexican luthier living in Los Angeles, resonated with the première performance of "Serenade for a Summer's Evening," which I had composed for and dedicated to the royal couple, whom I knew were seated in the first row. Blinded by the lights, I squinted to locate their faces. "Here we are, Liona!" Prince Philip called out, waving his hand.

Later, he showed us the armour of Henry VIII, some pistols and swords from the vaults of history, and an insidious door lock that could fire bullets at any unwelcome visitor. Touching on the topic of the day, mad-cow disease, the Queen commiserated with the farmers and expressed concern for her Highland cattle. She explained that all her corgis are descended from ones she had as a child, "but that one belongs to my mamá." Encouraged by her affable demeanour, I produced a small photo of my Muffin for a murmur of royal approval. He too had come to London to see the Queen. Generally, no photographs were allowed, but I ventured to ask a favour, which the Queen graciously granted. Jack extracted my small camera from his tuxedo pocket and, with Prince Philip on one side and the Queen on the other, the resultant photo was a perfect trophy.

After a few hours tucked beneath a satin eiderdown, a tea tray and "Ma'am, shall I run your bath now?" roused me from sleep. We descended past rows of potted purple fuchsia to the breakfast room, where Prince Philip was already munching his toast and marmalade. The drone of bagpipes from the castle grounds signalled Her Majesty's wake-up call, and a few of her corgis came to sniff around, wagging their tails. Their mistress would be taking breakfast in bed, so her husband bade us farewell as we sailed through the gates into the world of commoners again. When I was a child visiting Windsor with my parents, I never could have imagined being a guest of the Royal Family, following in the footsteps of Bach, Mozart, and Liszt, who often performed their compositions for the monarchs of Europe. It had been one of my life's triumphs.

Coda

An Andalucian sun splashes the stone walls of Calle Romea and bathes in palpitating light the balconies and window boxes dripping with blood-red geraniums. I am in the southern Spanish town of Linares, where my grandmother and the legendary guitarist, Andrés Segovia, were born nine years apart. It is to these well-worn streets and houses that I have come with my husband to trace one of the sources of my passion for the guitar.

Last night we sat with my Spanish relatives discussing the twists of fate that brought my great-grandparents from Scotland and Northern England to settle towards the end of the nineteenth century in Linares, where most of their descendants married Spaniards and established themselves in Bilbao, Sevilla, and Madrid. My father's diverse family runs the gamut from an aunt who ran off to join the circus, an English teacher, doctor, and Baptist minister, to the president of one of the largest banks in Spain, who earlier on this trip had taken us to lunch in Madrid accompanied by armed bodyguards.

I had been welcomed into the home of an aging friend of Andrés Segovia who showed me the maestro's guitar manuscripts and scrapbooks of the more than 4,500 concerts he had given during his lifetime. As a parting gift I was handed some of the strings he had used for one of his last concerts. Later in Paseo de Linajos I placed a bouquet of flowers at the feet of a huge statue of Segovia commemorating his birth there in 1893 — another connecting thread in the tapestry of my life.

After motoring past hilly olive groves and the red poppy-stained fields of Andalucia, Jack and I had met up with my Cuban composer friend, Leo Brouwer, who invited us to hear the symphony orchestra of Córdoba, which he conducts, and later we sat sharing sherry and guitar- world gossip. Within the historic city of Granada we lunched with Laura, the niece of the poet and playwright Federico García Lorca, who took us on a tour of her uncle's former house. In 1936 the Fascists had executed, by firing squad, Spain's most famous and vibrantly creative poet. After showing us his faded manuscripts, Laura bid my fingers bring life to the sweet and delicate guitar her uncle had immortalized in his drawings and poetry — "Oh guitar, heart deeply wounded by five swords." The mayor of Granada, Gabriel Berbel, shared his box with us in the Manuel de Falla Theatre for an evening with the Orchestra of the City of Granada, then tempted me with the idea of performing in his city next summer. Inhaling air scented with cypress, myrtle, and rosemary, Jack and I wandered through the ornate rooms and gardens of the Moorish palace — the Alhambra — which had inspired Manuel de Falla's "Nights in the Gardens of Spain" and Franciso Tárrega's "Recuerdos de la Alhambra." Ten days earlier in a Madrid café we had nibbled tapas with Amalia Ramírez and reminisced about my pilgrimage to her father's workshop thirty years ago, and about her family to whom I had dedicated my composition "Madrileña."

As a moonchild with my sun in Cancer, born during the Chinese year of the Ox, it seems I had no choice but to be drawn to a career in the arts. Maybe, in the words of Hamlet, "There's a divinity that shapes our ends, rough-hew them how we will." The classical guitar has provided me with a passport to the world and embroidered my life with richly contrasting experiences. As if flicking through television channels, I sometimes tune in to the varied images my mind has stored away: on tour with Bernie, the view from the engine room of a CN train spray-ploughing through the pristine snow-quilted forests of British Columbia; a master-class I gave one humid Havana afternoon, in which young Cubans smouldered with passion for the guitar; a candlelit recital in Tuscany at the sumptuous villa of friends, the Count and Countess Pesci-Blunt.

Only a month ago, in April 1998, before flying down to El Salvador for performances to benefit a theatre restoration, arranged by the composer Carlos Payet, who resurfaced, after twenty years, at my Guatemala concert, I was dancing to the rhythms of a samba band in the Brazilian jungle village of Parintíns. A few days earlier we had listened to Mozart in the fabled Opera House in Manaus, played with baby crocodiles on a late night canoe ride up the steamy Amazon River, and explored the windswept former penal colony on French Guiana's Devil's Island. Last year we had picked our way through the market-places of Hanoi and Saigon, sipped Metaxa in smoky Greek tavernas after my concerts in Athens and Thessaloniki, and luxuriated for two weeks in the Palazzo Cini on Venice's Grand Canal. Earlier that year I had orchestrated a Boyd family reunion in San Miguel de Allende in the rented home of skater and painter Toller Cranston. My concert there, at the Angela Peralta Theatre, arranged by Jaime Fernández, my teenage boyfriend who was now the town's mayor, had woven another circular pattern into the colourful tapestry.

Ahead await recording sessions where I will blend my guitar with the poetry of Lorca and Neruda for a new album, *Whispers of Love*, then a few recitals in Ontario, an interview for a CBC TV *Life and Times* documentary, and a quick trip to perform in Hong Kong's City Hall concert series. Bernie Fiedler, whom I consider a personal friend, continues to manage my career, which has now spanned three decades, while his resourceful former associate, Elisa

Amsterdam, carries on assisting with international bookings. Music and travel interweave throughout my days.

New designs are formed in the fabric as old relationships emerge in different configurations: not so long ago Pierre Trudeau visited our house for lunch and attended my concert with the McGill Chamber Orchestra at l'Église Notre-Dame in Montreal; Costa Pilavachi, my former agent at Haber Artists, has become president of the international division of Philips Music Group and is discussing new projects with my producer and U.S. manager, David Thomas. Last year Edgar Kaiser played me some of the new songs he has composed, and Prince Philip continues to delight me with his letters from Buckingham Palace and Balmoral. I still wait for more doors to open so that I might record Richard Fortin's orchestration of *My Land of Hiawatha* and *Concerto of the Andes*, which I recently performed with the symphony orchestra in Bogotá, Colombia.

I am no longer on tour for weeks on end, and believe I have struck a perfect balance between my home and professional life. My relationship with Jack grows closer each year, and although it took some adjustments at first, he has become accustomed to my itinerant ways and the time demands imposed by my career. Sometimes he chooses to accompany me on tours, enjoying the Saltspring Island home of my artist friend Robert Bateman; getting to know my dear elderly "cat ladies" in Medicine Hat, Alberta; and meeting the eccentric little Quebecker Jean-Jacques, who makes paper mobiles and pedals hundreds of miles on his bicycle to surprise me at concerts.

Jack is the most generous and loving of husbands, kind-hearted, philanthropic, and filled with a sense of appreciation for each day we share. Although our seven years together have mostly been filled with contentment, there have been times when shadows obscured even California's golden sun. Some family health problems and the loss of a number of friends including guitarist Laurindo Almeida have caused darkened clouds and grey skies.

A constant source of happiness for Jack, Dervin (our houseman), and me is our playful, jewel-eyed cat, Muffin. One of my life's most intense moments of pure joy occurred when he bashfully returned to my tear-stained pillow in the early morning hours after creeping through an unlocked screen door and venturing into the coyote-threatened world beyond our garden. The three of us have grown to love our furry little companion who hides his toy mice in our suitcases to guarantee we feel pangs of guilt when travelling.

Life in LA has spawned many new relationships with creative people from the worlds of music, art, science, and film. Working with Maurice Jarre, the French composer who wrote the music for *Lawrence of Arabia* and *Dr. Zhivago*, to record *A Walk in the Clouds*, which took the Golden Globe for best film score, was a thrill. The city has on occasion coughed up some singular experiences: Judge Lance Ito's invitation to serenade, in his courtroom, the sequestered O. J. Simpson jury who rose in a standing ovation, then a few months later stunned the world with their controversial verdict; a request from a dynamic couple who are fond of my music, Charlton and Lydia Heston, to play for their family and friends. How could I possibly turn down "Moses"? When I find myself chatting with "Rocky" — Sylvester Stallone — at the frozen yogurt counter, or dancing with a kilted Rod Stewart at a Malibu Christmas costume party, I am just as star-struck as some of my guitar fans seem to be with me.

My world is often filled with amusing diversions, but my days are always punctuated by the constant discipline imposed by my relentless taskmaster, the guitar. Andrés Segovia religiously practised five hours a day into his nineties, proof that even for a master such as he, "If you miss a day you know it, if you miss two days your instrument knows it, and if you miss three days your audience knows it!" There are still times when after a substandard concert I feel a wretched inadequate failure, but after an exceptional performance I am filled with pride at my accomplishments — the agony and ecstasy of a concert performer. Chopin once said, "There is no more beautiful sound in the world than a classical guitar, save perhaps two guitars!" For all its charms, however, it is an exasperatingly difficult instrument to play on the concert stage. I was delighted to be given a place in

Guitar Player magazine's "Gallery of Greats" after winning their "best classical guitarist" international poll for five years, and I am very grateful for the five Juno awards I have received in Canada. It is particularly gratifying to know that some of my fellow guitarists are now including in their own repertoire selections from *Classically Yours*, the album for which I composed all the music. It is pleasing to think that one day my pieces might outlive me in the hands of future guitar players.

Learning to play my role as a Beverly Hills hostess, I enjoy organizing dinner parties for our international group of friends, such as author Nathaniel Branden, actor Michael York, former prime minister Kim Campbell, solar energy pioneer Ishaq Shahryar, film directors Barry Spikings and Ken Annakin, fitness mavens Gilda Marx and Jack LaLanne, and producer Loreen Arbus. Oil painting, overseeing my Website, and participating in various family and charity events enrich my home life with Jack.

We have become involved with many different animal organizations and have tremendous respect for the dedicated people who work to help educate the public about the atrocities inflicted upon animals by the chemical and cosmetic industries, and the military and science research laboratories. I respect Mahatma Gandhi, who repeatedly spoke out against vivisection and said it was one of the blackest crimes committed by man. Of course everywhere in the world there has always been cruelty to animals; the meat industry, fur trapping, bullfighting, and the slaughter of marine mammals. I am repulsed by it all, yet none seems so abhorrent to me as the systematic, widespread abuse of living creatures in the labs. The numbers of animals killed (100 million each year in the U.S. alone) and the barbaric experiments are so shocking that most people would never believe what goes on behind locked doors. Several large charities have finally stopped supporting animal research and in Britain medical schools have banned vivisection with no apparent lowering of surgical skills. Not so very long ago child labour and slavery were acceptable to our society; it is my hope that as we become more enlightened towards our fellow human beings so might we also towards other species. I am grateful to the many groups, both in Canada and the U.S., that have through their books, pamphlets, lectures, and videos taught me more than I ever wanted to know about the rapacious vivisection industry, and the existence of criminal rings that routinely sell stolen pets to laboratories. In recent years I have tried to lend my voice and talent to help the selfless people who little by little are making progress towards changing some of the laws and teaching people that more clinical human studies are what we should focus on. An enormous number of chemicals tested on animals have been approved for human consumption but years later are found to be toxic to us as we are biologically and biochemically different from animals. These mistakes inevitably take their toll on human health and our planet's environment. The world will be a much more humane place when we learn to live in harmony with each other and with nature.

My father pursues his ongoing interests in eco-villages and sustainable ecology, while my mother manages my company and is breathing a sigh of relief that this book is finally finished, as she has been offering editorial advice and typing and retyping my manuscript into a word-processor for the past eight years — an invaluable contribution as my fingering skills have never been applied to a keyboard. My brother, Damien, is the manager of a bio-technical pharmaceutical company, and my sister, Vivien, who has just built a new dental office in Cambridge, Ontario, spends time with her partner Jim, her teenage son from a previous marriage, and their latest golden retriever.

I suppose that I have been the adventurer of the family pursuing a performing career that demands so much concentration and travel. It is a career that continues to challenge, punish, frustrate, and delight me. I would not trade it for any other. To those of you who have been tangled in the web of my destiny, I wish you well; to all of you around the world who have attended my concerts, and enjoyed my recordings, I offer my heartfelt gratitude. Over the years

I have enjoyed sharing my music with you, and now this has been my attempt to tie together the warps and wefts of my personal tapestry — the threads that constitute my "Flax of Dream."

But, of course, this chapter is not really a coda at all. Its final chords are already starting to play the prelude to the rest of my life.

APPENDIX

Liona Boyd Discography and Music Publications

DISCOGRAPHY

Whispers of Love (Moston/PolyGram)
Classically Yours (Moston/PolyGram)
Dancing on the Edge (Moston/PolyGram)
Paddle to the Sea (Oak Street/Sony)
Encore (Moston/PolyGram)
Highlights (Moston/PolyGram)
Christmas Dreams (Moston/PolyGram)
Persona (CBS/Sony)
The Romantic Guitar of Liona Boyd (CBS/Sony)
Liona Live in Tokyo (CBS/Sony)
Virtuoso (CBS/Sony)
The Best of Liona Boyd (CBS/Sony)
A Guitar for Christmas (CBS/Sony)
Spanish Fantasy (CBS)
Liona Boyd with Andrew Davis and the English Chamber
   Orchestra (CBS)

The First Nashville Guitar Quartet (RCA)

The First Lady of the Guitar (CBS)

Miniatures for Guitar (Moston/PolyGram)

The Guitar Artistry of Liona Boyd (Boot/London)

The Guitar (Boot/London)

MUSIC BOOKS

Favourite Solos (Hal Leonard Publishing)

The First Lady of the Guitar (Hansen House)

Folksongs for Classical Guitar (Hal Leonard Publishing)

A Guitar for Christmas (Hal Leonard Publishing)

Meet Liona at the Classical Guitar (Gordon V. Thompson/Warner
   Chappell Music)

Miniatures for Guitar (Hal Leonard Publishing)

Index